Lessons from the Northern Ireland
Peace Process

Lessons from the Northern Ireland Peace Process

Edited by

TIMOTHY J. WHITE

The University of Wisconsin Press

Publication of this volume has been made possible, in part, through generous support from the Anonymous Fund of the College of Letters and Science at the University of Wisconsin–Madison and from Xavier University.

The University of Wisconsin Press
1930 Monroe Street, 3rd Floor
Madison, Wisconsin 53711-2059
uwpress.wisc.edu

3 Henrietta Street
London WC2E 8LU, England
eurospanbookstore.com

Printed in the United States of America

Library of Congress Cataloging-in-Publication Data

Lessons from the Northern Ireland peace process / edited by Timothy J. White.
   p.   cm.
   Includes bibliographical references and index.
   ISBN 978-0-299-29704-6 (pbk.: alk. paper)
   ISBN 978-0-299-29703-9 (e-book)
  1. Peace-building—Northern Ireland.   2. Northern Ireland—Politics and
    government—1994–   I. White, Timothy Jerome, editor.
JZ5584.N75L47   2013
941.60824—dc23
2013010431

Contents

Foreword

MARTIN MANSERGH

This valuable collection of studies edited by Timothy J. White seeks to distill from the experience of the Irish peace process many of the aspects of its relative success that may be of potential interest, relevance, or inspiration in other unresolved conflict situations. Close study helps to clear up misconceptions and facile oversimplifications but may also enlarge the scope for achieving not identical but equivalent progress elsewhere.

The last few years have seen a gradual consolidation of the Northern Ireland peace process. Most of the major strategic steps on foot of the Good Friday Agreement and follow-on agreements have been fulfilled, but, as a number of contributors point out, much remains to be done in advancing reconciliation between communities and removal of the barriers that in so many places still segregate them.

The political settlement has done more than establish peace in Northern Ireland. It has also closed the final chapter in the conflict between Britain and Ireland, never continuous but stretching back over centuries. Recent encounters with Queen Elizabeth have, at a symbolic level, marked the end of the Irish republican boycott of British royalty, dating back at least to the Boer War and Queen Victoria's last visit to Ireland in 1900. The sense of détente and the confidence that forced or imposed solutions have led to a marked relaxation in relations and a willingness to cooperate could not have been envisaged twenty years ago. On the other hand, there remains an accumulation of legacy issues, only a limited number of which have been adequately addressed.

The important decade of centenaries, marking the anniversaries of the historic events between 1912 and 1922/23 that saw the formation of the Irish Free State and Northern Ireland, an end not foreseen at the beginning with the introduction of the Third Home Rule Bill, will afford an opportunity for commemoration and reflection as well as mutual respect. To a degree, thanks to the peace process, the more virulent oppositions of the past can be transcended.

There are foreseeably other important factors, which, depending on how they turn out, may have a considerable impact on the context for Northern Ireland and indeed the Republic. The economic crisis affecting the Eurozone has put great strain on many of the peripheral European Union (EU) countries, forcing them to avail of an EU/IMF (International Monetary Fund) bailout with onerous conditionality attached. The vulnerability of a small country like Ireland in an era of globalization has been highlighted. It has to recover control of its destiny. If the Eurozone crisis settles down, closer integration may emphasize the divergent paths of the two parts of Ireland and of Britain and Ireland. Were the Eurozone to break up, any restored independent Irish currency would very likely move to a closer alignment with Britain both politically and economically.

A second factor is the looming independence referendum in Scotland in 2014. While independence as opposed to enhanced devolution still looks a less likely outcome, the Ulster-Scots tradition, cultivated in recent times as an alternative to Irish nationalism as well as a basis of unionist identity, would be seriously challenged as a guide to political belonging in the event of a surprise result.

This volume primarily focuses on the issues thrown up by the peace process so far. Whatever the difficulties and frustrations felt by all the participants from time to time, viewed from further afield the peace process is regarded as an exemplary success, showing that a transition from intractable conflict can be made. Few of those now engaged round the table of the Northern Ireland Executive, particularly from the two main parties, Sinn Féin and the Democratic Unionist Party (DUP), were known in the past for their moderation. Notwithstanding this, and even if late in the day, the political leadership of communities in conflict, including where closely associated with a major paramilitary organization, have given a rare lesson in statesmanship and capacity to live with compromise that might benefit or have benefited people in other situations.

At the outset, inclusivity began to displace exclusivity. Opening up dialogue was never unconditional and would have had grave potential dangers if it were. Some conditions were laid down at different times by all sides, with usually at least a temporary stalling effect. A certain constructive ambiguity not only is inherent to most negotiated agreements but also lies behind much political discourse. Sincerity was not always practiced, and this created distrust. If there was to be any peace, it had to be based on the reality of the community divide. The thin centrist strand made a valuable contribution but was not nearly strong enough to support a settlement on its own.

The American role was immense in terms of confidence building and problem solving, when the process was stalling, not just during the Clinton era but also under the presidency of George W. Bush. Most of the leaders would not have been too familiar with political science concepts such as consociationalism or been too worried about neoconservative or revolutionary nationalist ideologies. Nevertheless, the collapse of the Soviet bloc in 1989 removed a center of support for national liberation movements and the principal model for a socialist republic, in principle irreversible and inconsistent with the potential for power rotation inherent to democracy. A combination of the Colombia Three adventure, with the type of technology transfer that assisted the African National Congress (ANC) in the 1980s, and the horror of 9/11 ensured that there would be no congressional tolerance for further prevarication about the definitive ending of terrorism by any group wishing to participate in government, or about the withholding of weapons decommissioning or of support for a reformed police service. The price of full democratic participation meant permanently foregoing other options and coming to a conclusion on points outstanding. Of course, one of the biggest challenges on all sides was to bring one's respective constituency with one.

Professor Timothy White has been bringing his students to Ireland for many years. It has been my privilege and that of many contributors to this book to meet them for briefing and discussion in the congenial surroundings of Bansha Castle, enjoying the hospitality of its owners John and Teresa Russell. The castle was once owned by a famous general from the locality, General Sir William Butler, who reacted against the excesses of imperialism and became sympathetic to Home Rule. I also had the pleasure of visiting Xavier University and other North American universities to speak about the peace process and also the significance of major historic anniversaries. It is good when at some point the substance of oral teaching, lectures, and seminars is put down in writing for the benefit and critical attention of a wider audience. Ireland benefits enormously from the interest and support it has received from the United States, including its political institutions, corporations, and academies, and above all its people. The conclusions drawn here have an interest not just for the foreign policy community but for anyone with an interest in contemporary world developments and in Ireland.

Acknowledgments

I first want to thank the contributors to this volume. Their work has inspired me to rethink many assumptions regarding the peace process in Northern Ireland as well as the process of making peace more generally. I would also like to thank those who helped fund the seminar in the summer of 2010 that served as the foundation of the research contained in this book. These include grants from Janice Walker, Dean of the College of Arts and Sciences, and James Buchanan, Director of the Brueggeman Center for Dialogue, at Xavier University. This seminar was also made possible by generous gifts from John Murphy, Reta Rupich, Dave Manthus, Kate Eich, and Patrick Liddy. This seminar was cosponsored by Peace Studies, the Office of Peace and Justice, and the Department of Political Science and Sociology at Xavier University. The participants in the seminar greatly appreciated the hospitality provided by John and Teresa Russell at Bansha Castle in the summer of 2010. The contributors to this volume benefited from all who participated in the seminar, especially our guests Martin Mansergh and Eamonn Wall. Additional funding for this edited volume came from Dean Janice Walker of the College of Arts and Sciences at Xavier University. I would especially like to thank David Mengel, the associate dean, for assistance in securing this funding.

The preparation of this volume was facilitated by a research sabbatical provided by Xavier University for the fall of 2011. I would like to note my appreciation of the members of the University Faculty Development Committee who recommended me for this research leave, during which I served as Visiting Research Fellow at the Moore Institute of the National University of Ireland, Galway (NUI Galway). Nicholas Allen, then the director of the Moore Institute, as well as the staff of the institute, Maria Shaughnessy and Kate Thornhill, offered me a wonderful venue to prepare this volume. I am also indebted to Pat Woeste for her facilitation of the funding of this grant at Xavier University. I would also like to thank the staffs of the library at NUI Galway and Xavier University, who were helpful in preparing this volume. My research position at NUI Galway funded my participation in the Conflict Research Society's Annual Meeting at the University of Lancaster in September 2011 as well as the Annual Meeting of the Political Studies Association of Ireland in Dublin in October 2011. I would like to thank Maria Power and Sandra Buchanan, who were on my panel at the Lancaster meeting, where I presented an initial version of my introductory chapter for their feedback and support. My mentor at NUI Galway, Niall Ó Dochartaigh, provided valuable support as I prepared this volume, especially when I presented its major findings on November 28, 2011, at the Moore Institute. During October and November of 2011 I gave a series of lectures at University College Cork, and I want to thank Fiona Buckley and Theresa Reidy, who made these lectures possible. On November 30, 2011, I lectured on the role of civil society in the Northern Ireland peace process (much of what I contributed to chapter 9 in this volume) at University College Utrecht, and I appreciated the feedback from Jos Sondaal, Katherine Kirk, and Professor Kirk's students and colleagues.

In preparing this book, many provided useful suggestions and assistance. I would like to especially recognize the support of my colleagues at Xavier University, Graley Herren and Mack Mariani. Their comments and criticisms were especially helpful. Additional suggestions, comments, and insight came from Jon Tonge, Peter McDonough, Jonathan Powell, Theresa Reidy, Mark Haas, Timothy Lynch, Neal Jesse, Mitchell Reiss, Deborah Pearce, Brian Walker, William (Bill) Williams, Shannon Sweeney, Irvine (Dusty) Anderson, Suda M. Perera, Michael Bressler, Ruiséil Gray, Denis (Des) Marnane, Jim Leahy, Josemaría Mantero, Tiest Sondaal, Kelley Boldt, Matthew Evangelista, Andrew J. Riley, Albadr Abubaker Al-Shatari, Kate Morris, and two anonymous reviewers for the University of Wisconsin Press. My leave in Ireland was facilitated by the generous support of Michael Long, Frances O'Shea, Jane O'Shea, and Phil and John Waldron as well as many friends. These include John and Teresa Russell, John and Martina Magner, Jim and Nancy Leahy, James and Melanie Russell, Michael and Anne White, Brian and Nell Roche, Jane Russell, Neil Delamere, Michael and Joan Ferris, Jim and Ann Gallagher, Mary Graham, Gerry Joyce, Jim Russell, Joe Ward, and Margaret and Siobhan Magner. Kameryn Jones also served as a research assistant in the latter stages of preparing this volume and was most helpful. Finally, and most importantly, I need to acknowledge the patience and support my wife, Mary Visconti, provided as I worked long hours "on the book." I hope that the final product is worthy of her sacrifice. There are others whom I am not thanking by name but know how much they contributed to my stay in Ireland and the preparation of this volume. Of course, all errors and omissions are my responsibility.

Lessons from the Northern Ireland
Peace Process

1   Lessons from the Northern Ireland Peace Process

An Introduction

Timothy J. White

Amid continuing ethnic and communal strife in much of the world, there is a need to draw the appropriate conclusions from the much applauded peace process in Northern Ireland. While the peace process has had many challenges and problems, Northern Ireland has clearly moved beyond the period of the "Troubles," characterized by paramilitary groups in both the nationalist and unionist communities carrying out acts of violence against members of the other community. The period of the Troubles, from 1968 to 1998, also featured republicans in Northern Ireland attacking the British army, who were seen as foreign occupiers and defenders of the unionists. The peace process that resulted in the signing of the Good Friday or Belfast Agreement (hereafter identified as the Agreement) in 1998 began a decade earlier with negotiations between many of the parties to the conflict. Ultimately, after ceasefires in the 1990s, negotiations intensified between representatives of the British and Irish governments as well as unionist and nationalist politicians. While not all took part in these negotiations, most of the major parties in Northern Ireland and the British and Irish governments were part of an inclusive series of talks that culminated in April 1998. After the Agreement was reached, referenda in Ireland and Northern Ireland ratified it and provided it legitimacy, but it was not until 2007 that the institutions of the Agreement became fully operational and accepted by all of the major parties in Northern Ireland.

Scholars have employed a variety of theoretical approaches to explain this process, but there have been far fewer attempts to identify lessons that emerged that could be helpful in other contexts.[1] Most of the published work thus far regarding Northern Ireland analyzes the nature of the peace process. One of the continuing strands of debate is whether the peace agreed to in 1998 and since modified by the St. Andrews Agreement has been consociational or is explained more accurately by other theoretical constructs.[2] While this debate may be of interest to some, especially those who have placed their academic reputation on the merit of consociational approaches to peacemaking, the literature has begun to move on and focus more on the means of implementing the Agreement now that it has been in place for more than a decade.[3] Though John Doyle uses consociationalism to explain policing and security in chapter 6, most of the chapters in this volume go beyond the debate regarding the proper theoretical name for institution building in the Northern Ireland peace process. The authors in this volume employ a variety of theoretical approaches from international relations, foreign policy analysis, peace studies, peacebuilding, and conflict resolution to explain both the successes as well as the difficulties in making peace in Northern Ireland. Several of the authors emphasize recent or introduce new theoretical approaches to explain the lessons of the peace process, including theories of social identity formation and change, neoconservatism, revolutionary analysis, and civil society and grassroots peacebuilding.

Many of the studies published to date on Northern Ireland focus on one aspect of the peace process or come from a particular perspective and, therefore, do not concentrate on lessons learned by the various actors or from the multitude of issues involved with making peace in Northern Ireland. Recognizing the dangers of drawing broad-based conclusions from a discrete context,[4] the contributors to this volume nonetheless carefully explore what has been learned by participants and scholars and critically applied to other conflicts. These lessons are in some instances unique to this case, but some are clearly applicable to other ethnic conflicts.

Different Actors Learned Different Lessons

Various groups involved in the Northern Ireland peace process learned very different lessons. When scholars identify lessons, they are often quite different from ones learned by those directly involved in the peace process. As William A. Hazleton cogently explicates in chapter 2, the lessons that were learned in Northern Ireland were numerous, varied based on the participants' parochial environment, and developed as the peace process evolved. Landon E. Hancock in chapter 3 demonstrates that, despite its delays and difficulties, the peace process gained support from people on both sides of the communal divide. The 1994 cease-fires and 1998 Agreement expanded the role choices available to both Protestants and Catholics, allowing them to redefine their identities in a way that altered their attitudes and behaviors toward those in the other religiously defined community.[5] This allowed the beginnings of a more civil and less sectarian society to develop long after the initial Agreement was signed.[6] Thus, the peace process built momentum and trust among the different actors, helping to surmount a history of suspicion and failed efforts to break the continuing pattern of violence.[7]

By the early 1980s many nationalists and republicans had concluded that defeating the British militarily to achieve a united Ireland was highly unlikely. Once they reached this assessment, the prospect of a negotiated settlement became conceivable. These counterstate nationalists, as they are identified by Ó Dochartaigh, may be able to draw inspiration from locally based nationalism, but they suffer from lacking the resources of the state to build and reinforce their nationalist aspirations.[8] In the peace process, nationalists had to learn to trust that the British government was interested in a political settlement and did not seek a complete victory and elimination of the republican threat of violence nor a return to a pre-Troubles political arrangement for Northern Ireland. For the nationalists and republicans, the peace process was a way of advancing as much as they could their ultimate goal of an Irish Republic, while in the near term negotiating better terms of representation and guarantees of rights for the Catholic community.[9] As Hazleton explains in chapter 2, Gerry Adams perceived the need of republican support for his concessions as critical to success.[10] In the end, nationalists and republicans have been able to redefine their interests so that Sinn Féin now supports power sharing with unionists in a Northern Ireland Assembly rather than holding out for a thirty-two-county republic.

Unionists were also more flexible in their political positions than many had presumed and learned to modify their own identity, which had historically been formed in opposition to the empowerment of Irish Catholics or as a reaction to a sense of betrayal by the British government.[11] Those unionists who agreed to participate in the peace negotiations, the Ulster Unionist Party (UUP) and its leader, David Trimble, in particular, learned that the goal of keeping Northern Ireland part of the United Kingdom need not be sacrificed by sharing power with nationalists and developing relations with the Republic of Ireland. In fact, a negotiated settlement would provide further guarantees of the continued status of Northern Ireland within the United Kingdom. If successful, peace would mean an end to the violence that had terrorized their lives.[12] Unionists' identity has proven to be more constructive than oppositional or reactionary. As Wendy Ann Wiedenhoft Murphy and Mindy Peden explain in chapter 4, the recent turn to the Ulster-Scots diaspora in the United States by unionists indicates their attempt to navigate the uncertainty of the peace process and a desire to construct an identity that is constituted by a dynamic history and culture instead of an entrenched sectarianism.

The British government and especially Tony Blair learned that he could persuade the Unionist politicians, David Trimble in particular, and the Protestant community to make the concessions necessary for an agreement. In the process, as explained by Hazleton in chapter 2, Blair might take grief from unionists and others, but he could take the abuse that came his way. Blair also learned that he was able to work effectively with the Irish government and even build enough of a rapport with republican leaders to negotiate with them in good faith. Blair learned other lessons, like not letting small problems become big problems, and he refused to be sidetracked by what he perceived as small problems that need not interfere with the larger goal of a peace agreement. He was more than happy to accept what some have identified as constructive ambiguity to keep the peace process moving forward.[13] This allowed the different parties to interpret or emphasize different elements of the Agreement to satisfy themselves and their constituents. When difficulties emerged, Blair believed that creativity was required, or what Paul Dixon calls "honorable deception."[14] This may be criticized in hindsight for making the implementation of the Agreement difficult, but perhaps it was necessary in order to reach an agreement at all.[15]

The Irish government also learned to trust the British, republican, and unionist politicians and thus came to believe that its interest in peace in Northern Ireland needed to be pursued vigorously. The long-term aspiration for a united Ireland need not be forsaken but could be achieved at some indefinite date in the future on the basis of the principle of majority consent.[16] Peace would provide stability and guarantees for the Catholic minority in Northern Ireland with which the Irish government identified and that was under attack from its perspective during the Troubles. In addition to the different lessons learned by different actors, more general lessons can be identified and perhaps applied to other conflicts.

Be Inclusive in Negotiations and in Settlement

One of the chief lessons of the Northern Ireland peace process is that it is important to be as inclusive as possible in organizing negotiations for peace. Those whom Dixon identifies as "orthodox" in chapter 5 argue that the Northern Irish case demonstrates that it is always, or nearly always, a good idea to talk to the enemy, even if they are or have historically been seen as terrorists.[17] After all, if those who are engaging in violence are not included in a peace process, is there any hope for peace? Dixon exposes the problems with the neoconservative challenge to this orthodox lesson taken from the peace process. Neoconservatives argue, counterintuitively, that it is almost never right to "talk to terrorists" or "negotiate with evil." They falsely conclude that this only encourages terrorism and is a dead end in terms of bringing about peace.[18] Dixon demonstrates that neoconservatives produce a confused and unconvincing account of the Northern Ireland peace process because their analysis is ideologically driven and biased toward the lessons that they want to draw from the case rather than an accurate account of the complexities, contingencies, nuances, and moral compromises that were present in Northern Ireland.

Before the Agreement was reached in Northern Ireland, previous efforts at negotiating a peace settlement had failed. They failed for a variety of reasons at different points in time, but a common criticism was that they were not open to, or inclusive of, all the parties to the conflict. Efforts by the British government to impose power sharing on those unwilling to support it in Northern Ireland ended in failure in the 1970s.[19] In the 1980s, the Anglo-Irish Agreement was negotiated by the British and Irish governments, with no role for the local parties to the conflict. For many, especially unionists in Northern Ireland, it was inconceivable to have a peace to which they would have to subscribe but to which they had not been a party or a negotiation partner.[20] Hence, unlike earlier failed efforts, the Northern Ireland peace process of the 1990s ultimately succeeded in part because it was able to find agreement among the two governments, the British and Irish, as well as the leaders of most of Northern Ireland's political parties.[21]

Not only were the negotiations inclusive of all parties who sought to participate, but the Agreement provided for an inclusive power-sharing arrangement.[22] In addition, the Agreement sought to satisfy issues of concern for the various parties. For example, the Agreement called for the decommissioning of weapons, which had been a key demand of the unionists. The Agreement also created a governing system, which guaranteed nationalists and republicans a share of power in the local assembly as well as a reform of policing, demilitarization by the British armed forces, and release of political prisoners.[23] These arrangements, in turn, led to a drastic reduction of violence. This success has led to various actors with competing political agendas claiming to have discovered the lessons of Northern Ireland for other conflicts.

As Few Preconditions as Possible for Negotiations

Highly related to, but conceptually distinct from, the need for inclusivity is the necessity for minimal preconditions for negotiating and entering peace processes. This encourages all to participate and minimizes the possibility that any of the parties can contend that negotiations are not open or fair. Historically, preconditions have often been used as a pretext to prevent negotiations from beginning and to attempt to "defeat" the other side by exposing the rival's greater willingness to make an initial concession. In Northern Ireland, the British government under John Major had insisted on decommissioning to demonstrate the commitment of the Irish Republican Army (IRA) to the peace process. Major feared that the IRA might use the ceasefire and negotiations as a means of delay before a future return to violence. Once the British government had demanded decommissioning by the IRA, unionists quickly came to agree with this precondition. Looking back we can see that decommissioning proved to be a roadblock preventing meaningful negotiations among the parties.[24] George Mitchell, who presided over the negotiations that led to the Agreement, insisted that the only precondition for entering the talks was that parties had to forego using violence during the negotiations.[25] This allowed Sinn Féin to be included in the negotiations after the IRA had agreed to their second cease-fire. The lack of additional preconditions meant that all parties who chose to participate were also able to do so. The lack of preconditions also allowed representatives of the different parties in the negotiations maximum flexibility while seeking to craft an agreement in their interests. Without the minimal conditions for entering negotiations, it would have been easy for those involved in talks leading to the Agreement to grandstand and highlight how they would never yield their principles instead of search to find common ground.[26]

Providing Security

The provision of security for all the parties to a conflict is critical in peace processes and is usually a major source of conflict as different groups are armed in many ethnic conflicts. Peace theorists have asserted the importance of just policing as an alternative to war and conflict.[27] Increasingly, scholars have recognized the need for security sector reform to be part of the peace process.[28] In the case of Northern Ireland, the transformation of policing was pivotal to a peace agreement, since it was necessary to link legitimacy to security in Northern Ireland.[29] This was especially true in nationalist areas, where Protestant police had lost legitimacy in the community.[30] Given the recent finding that negotiated settlements tend not to be the most effective means of ending civil conflicts,[31] the Northern Irish case would appear to defy this trend or tendency. Toft contends that negotiated settlements typically fail because of the lack of attention to security sector reform in the negotiations.[32] While the Agreement did not settle the need for security reform, its call for an independent commission that ultimately brought about meaningful police and security reform defied the tendency Toft cites for negotiated settlements to end in failure.[33] The second reason Toft cites for the failure of negotiated settlements is that they neglect to threaten groups who defy the settlement.[34] While the implementation of the Agreement proved to be lengthy and arduous, the desire not to return to the violence of the past provided a major incentive for all the political elites to implement the Agreement. The centrality of policing to the conflict and the peace process was made evident by the fact that it was not until 2007 that the parties in Northern Ireland agreed to the reforms of policing and the operations of a justice ministry. The issue of policing in Northern Ireland was thus both highly contested and of utmost importance in the peace process.

Prior to the Good Friday Agreement, policing was one of the central issues that divided the two communities. Historically, the police and British forces were used to maintain the status quo or protect people with power, namely the Protestant community. This perception meant that policing and the provision of security in Ireland needed major reform. Many have portrayed the peace process as being built on the premise that nationalists agreed to local power sharing in the context of a constitutionally reformed United Kingdom. In return, nationalists were given reforms in the areas of civil and human rights, including policing. This perspective reduces the transformation of policing in Northern Ireland to the status of a concession to nationalists that was forcefully resisted by unionists but finally agreed upon once they believed that they had secured their constitutional preferences. Contrary to this view of policing as a concession in negotiations leading up to and after the Agreement, Doyle convincingly demonstrates in chapter 6 that the negotiations on policing were not removed from the core dispute regarding sovereignty. Through a review of the prior positions of various actors, the long negotiations, and the ultimate agreement on policing, Doyle argues that the transformation of policing reflected the consociational character of the 1998 Agreement and its institutionalized linkages between Northern Ireland and the Republic of Ireland.

The reform of policing via an independent and international commission whose views ultimately prevailed despite British government unease is also significant and provides a model that is potentially transferrable to other conflicts. By attempting to depoliticize the policing issue and assigning it to a technical and professional review via the Patten Commission, policing and the provision of security in Northern Ireland was reformed in a way that allowed all the parties to ultimately accept the reforms that were made and endorse the means of enforcing law and order in Northern Ireland. Those reforms were difficult for unionists to accept, since symbolically the police became less explicitly linked to the crown and the British government. The historic lack of trust by the nationalist community of the police in Northern Ireland made them extremely suspect of these reforms and doubtful about whether justice could be found in a reformed police service. The police reforms were critically necessary in order to marginalize those who continued to advocate or use violence by convincing many (especially in the republican movement, who were historically hostile to the police) to accept the new police service of Northern Ireland as legitimate. As Doyle contends in chapter 6, the conceptual basis of agreement and the process by which it was achieved makes the transformation of policing in Northern Ireland instructive for other peace processes.

The Role of Third Parties in Peace Processes

Third parties, external actors, and international organizations have often been seen as necessary or facilitative of promoting peace in states suffering from ethnic conflict and civil war.[35] Given the diversity of roles and functions that third parties play as mediators of conflict, it is difficult to come to a simple, general conclusion regarding the role of mediators.[36] Some research indicates that they may help in the short run to forge an agreement between parties, but this does not necessarily lead to enduring solutions to conflict.[37] It is increasingly recognized that foreign military intervention may not be critical to facilitating peace and stability: "There are no purely military solutions to insurgencies."[38] Instead, third parties can play a more significant role in terms of diplomacy and in providing economic aid that may support a fledgling peace. After all, if the parties could have solved their differences themselves, they would have already done so.[39] While the diplomatic role of third parties should not be exaggerated, they can play a positive role if they are perceived to be fair mediators of the conflict.[40] This does not mean that mediators or third parties need to be unbiased, just not too biased.[41] If third parties are biased, this can be used as leverage to influence the party to which they are allied.[42] This can be especially beneficial when the external actor can support the weaker ethnic group in the context of the negotiations.[43] Unfortunately, third parties typically intervene at the height of the conflict, when the parties to the conflict are not ready to negotiate or come to an agreement to end the conflict.[44] Thus, mediation is historically not seen as successful in solving enduring rivalries.[45] Nevertheless, if the local parties to the conflict are ready to negotiate and are relatively small and weak compared to the mediating actor, the mediating power can play a productive role in promoting peace.[46] The critical third party in the Northern Ireland peace process was the United States. While there is no agreement in the literature on the overall significance of the US role (some scholars and actors emphasize this role and others minimize it), it is clear that George Mitchell, Bill Clinton, Richard Haass, Mitchell Reiss, and others were heavily involved in the efforts to achieve an agreement and implement it afterward.[47] The tendency for the United States to intervene and play the role of a mediator or third party to the Northern Ireland conflict conforms to the general trend that those with ethnic ties are more likely to intervene in ethnic-based conflicts.[48]

Mary-Alice C. Clancy in chapter 7 reveals that the Clinton administration's role in the peace process was neither as benign nor negligible as some have assumed. Careful analysis of the Bush administration similarly confounds scholars' expectations. While Bush was less personally vested in Northern Ireland, the autonomy granted to his special envoys meant that his administration was indeed heavily involved in the peace process.[49] While the United States may have made claims to being honest brokers under Clinton and Bush, it more often than not sided with the Irish government rather than the British government when there was a dispute between these two states.[50] US mediation and intervention often had the effect of promoting the peace process and implementing the Agreement even though policies were often built on faulty assumptions and were often perceived to be uncoordinated with the British and Irish governments. The apparent differing policies of the United States and other governments allowed each to play a constructive if different role in promoting different actors to make the necessary concessions to reach the Agreement and then implement it.

Economic Aid and Peacebuilding

One of the incentives that third parties can offer combatants or parties in civil conflict is foreign aid. Foreign aid can provide assistance that helps yield stable democracy after civil conflict.[51] This foreign aid can assist states in providing social welfare, which has been found to undermine civil conflict.[52] In the post-accord peacebuilding phase, economic aid may ensure equality and justice for all citizens. Economic aid is thus integral to peacebuilding and is part of a multitrack peace process in Northern Ireland. Aid is meant to yield economic development and intercommunal cooperation in bringing about peaceful coexistence and reconciliation. External third-party aid aims to take into consideration grassroots perspectives and be tailored to local communities' needs, thereby supporting the creation of civil society and building trust, goodwill, and a culture of peace. In the context of Northern Ireland, few immediate results have come from external assistance given in the aftermath of the Agreement, but there is hope that there will be long-term payoffs in terms of improved community relations in Northern Ireland.[53]

Chapter 8 explores how foreign or external economic aid arrived in Northern Ireland through the International Fund for Ireland and the European Union Peace Funds. This aid was provided to address the legacy of the conflict by empowering local communities, promoting socioeconomic development and peacebuilding, and reducing sectarianism and violence in Northern Ireland and the border area.[54] This aid was premised on the belief that it would support the implementation of the Agreement. Challenges still exist in bringing about a sustainable peace, as evidenced by the increase in unemployment as well as continuing violence by rogue breakaway loyalist and republican paramilitaries. Chapter 8 also explores the links between economic development and intercommunal cooperation in bringing about peaceful coexistence and reconciliation. It also explores the necessity of external third parties to include grassroots people's perspectives in tailoring economic aid to local communities' needs in order to support civil society projects working to sustain cross-community relations. In reality, international aid can often meet resistance or does not work as intended. Roger Mac Ginty contends that hybridity best explains the result of liberal efforts to employ aid in the peacebuilding process, as this aid and the values that often accompany it interact with the local or indigenous.[55] Whether aid works in building peace thus greatly depends on the local context and whether aid is successful in bringing about the economic and social change that is desired.

Civil Society and Reconciliation

The exclusion of ordinary people from the peace process in Northern Ireland made it easier for political representatives to craft an agreement, but it also meant that the mass public was demobilized from the political process until it was needed for ratification of the Agreement.[56] Since the early efforts to implement the Agreement, many have recognized the need for grassroots reconciliation so that the groups in the conflict can begin to develop trust and a civil society. This would create the social capital necessary for the differing groups to begin to interact with each other in a much more positive framework. The importance of trust has been widely cited as important in economics, sociology, and political science.[57] In international relations, scholars have assumed that trust allows states and decision makers to avoid the perils of anarchy and never-ending conflict.[58] Reconciliation is a critical aspect of building peace in highly divided societies that have a history of violent conflict. Many scholars agree that the truth must be told about those who held and perhaps abused power before a formal truce or peace agreement is signed. For people at the grassroots to forgive and forget past injustices requires that those guilty of past injustices admit to them or at least be identified as guilty. Many believe reconciliation is needed before peace can truly be achieved. Recent research indicates that reconciliation needs to restore a sense of power to the victims and restore the moral image of the perpetrators.[59] At the very least, this transitional justice needs to carry the promise of social change as part of the effort to both confront the grief of those who were victims and seek to offer some form of redemption to those who are seen as guilty of crimes.[60] In the Northern Ireland context, because of the need for the peace process to include those who were associated with, if not involved in, the organizations that perpetrated violence, the decision was made to not replicate an equivalent process to the South African Truth and Reconciliation Commission. This led to continued suspicion on the part of many that those who historically had been associated with violence would never truly rescind this option and they therefore were not to be trusted. Some believed that a truth commission would somehow benefit the other side in the conflict.[61] Hence, the lack of reconciliation in Northern Ireland has made the implementation of the Agreement difficult.[62]

In chapter 9 Timothy J. White, Andrew P. Owsiak, and Meghan E. Clarke explore the implications of the lack of reconciliation as part of the peace process in Northern Ireland. The continued suspicion each community has for the other prevents them from being able to acknowledge wrongdoing, forgive, and create a shared future. While there seems to be a general recognition of the need for those guilty of crimes during the Troubles to be identified and brought to justice, many remain skeptical that "all" of the truth will ever be gained.[63] Such a reconciliation between the communities would make the building of civil society a much easier task as we look to the future, but the fear remains that the truth might foment a sense of retribution as much as it might provide a sense of restorative justice.[64] Individuals and groups need to recognize their own pain and grief and also recognize the losses members of the other community have experienced before true reconciliation can occur. This process, if it is to happen, will take a long time and will need to be experienced as broadly as possible to have its desired effect of providing a mechanism for healing the rift between the communities in Northern Ireland.[65] Though clearly not enough, at least the Agreement recognized the rights of victims as well as the importance of the need for all to be included in the political process.

Negotiations Need Intense Engagement

Peace processes require intense engagement with the issues associated with the conflict by all the parties, and agents make a difference. Successful peace processes also require courageous leaders who are ready to take risks for peace.[66] There were many involved in the negotiations that led to the signing of the Agreement, not only leaders but also advisors who played critical roles. It is difficult to imagine how the peace process would have been successful without advisors who had the knowledge, wisdom, and commitment that allowed all the obstacles to an agreement to be overcome. For example, would the Irish government have been successful in pursuing the negotiations without the skill and capabilities of Martin Mansergh? He played a very important role in establishing relations with republicans in the North and in revising the Republic's conception of majority consent. This allowed Articles 2 and 3 of the constitution to be changed and provided some role for the Republic in Northern Ireland's politics. Similarly, Mo Mowlam played a critical role as secretary of state for Northern Ireland, successfully engaging republicans like no previous representative of the British government had.[67]

Those leaders and advisors to the peace process had to focus on preventing unnecessary delay and encouraging the necessary compromises to reach an agreement. The greater the intensity of the negotiations, the more likely parties will make the concessions necessary for peace. Blair has emphasized how the cramped and uncomfortable quarters in which he lived during the final week of negotiating the Agreement promoted an extra incentive to bring the negotiations to a successful close as soon as possible.[68] President Clinton stayed up much of the night during the final week of negotiations in order to elicit a final deal among all the parties. George Mitchell argues that without a deadline for the negotiations the parties would never have made an agreement in Northern Ireland.[69] The use of a deadline encouraged the parties to make concessions and created a climate that produced the ultimate deal. In such an intense negotiating environment, each party was willing to agree to the necessary concessions and find the common ground of an agreement.

The fact that most parties were perceived to have made all the concessions they possibly could meant that the Agreement was a take it or leave it proposition. No one wanted to go back to the period of the Troubles. While many were wary of aspects of the Agreement, it provided a historic opportunity to go beyond the violence of the past and bring peace to Northern Ireland. This assessment was especially important in gaining support from Protestants who were suspicious of the Agreement. Hancock, employing prospect theory, contends that by claiming there was no alternative, the Yes Campaign convinced at least a slight majority of Protestants and an overwhelming majority of the Northern Ireland electorate to support and ratify the Agreement.[70] As Hancock further explains in chapter 3, the Agreement broke the historic narrative of never-ending violence and allowed both nationalists and unionists to redefine their identities.

While the negotiations leading to the signing of the Agreement may be seen as heroic in and of themselves, caused by a determination of many in the negotiations to bring them to a fruitful conclusion, the peace process was by no means complete. Throughout the period from 1998 through 2007, many problems emerged, including decommissioning and reforming the police, that seemed to make the promise of the Agreement unlikely to be fulfilled. The determination of the British and Irish governments, led throughout this period by Blair and Ahern, as well as the parties in Northern Ireland ultimately proved able to overcome major difficulties. While we can look back now and see that the institutions created by the Agreement would finally become fully functional, this was not so obvious as the local assembly in Stormont was closed from 2002 through May of 2007. The continuing involvement and commitment of all the parties was necessary to reach the political accommodation that resulted in the successful implementation of the Agreement.

Support Moderates and Marginalize Spoilers

Those who support the peace process should support the moderates as they take risks for peace, so that they are not outflanked by critics of the peace process who see moderates as traitors to their cause. This means supporting not just the moderate parties and their leaders but also moderates within the more extreme parties or groups associated with violence. Clinton's granting of a visa linked to the first IRA cease-fire to Gerry Adams is an example of this kind of effort. Supporting moderates can also be achieved through the use of back-channel negotiators who bypass potential spoilers.[71] If those who refuse to negotiate (hard-liners) can be isolated, they will be weakened politically.

In addition, the peace process in Northern Ireland has in some ways changed who we perceive as moderates and extremists. Because of the electoral decline of the two moderate parties whose leaders won the Nobel Peace Prize for negotiating the Agreement, the two largest extreme parties during the peace process of the 1990s have become the two largest parties responsible for governing since the Stormont Assembly resumed functioning in 2007.[72] Tonge argues that there has been some moderation on the part of Sinn Féin, as they have had to learn to work together with the Democratic Unionist Party (DUP) and govern jointly in the Northern Ireland executive.[73] Similarly, we have witnessed a moderation in the position of Ian Paisley and the DUP, from refusing to participate in the negotiations that led to the Agreement to agreeing to jointly govern in the Northern Ireland Executive.[74] This moderation has continued as Peter Robinson succeeded Paisley as leader of the DUP and first minister of Northern Ireland. The moderation of these former extremist parties means they no longer benefit from their former strategy of ethnic outbidding, and their popular advantage over the historically more moderate parties has diminished as they themselves have moderated and are responsible for governing.[75]

After initially trying to include all in the negotiations, those who are recalcitrant and continue to oppose the peace process or agreement (spoilers) must be marginalized so that they do not undermine support for the process or agreement.[76] Often, the moderates in a community fear the extremists in their own group more than they trust the moderate representatives of the other community.[77] This makes compromise with leaders of the other community impossible. John Hume played a critical role in the Northern Ireland peace process, developing the relationships with leaders of Sinn Féin, Ulster unionists, and the British, Irish, and American governments that led the political elites to trust each other enough to negotiate the Agreement. The peace process in Northern Ireland strove to be inclusive so that representatives from both communities would feel that the new governing institutions represented their interests. This was intended to marginalize those who continued to use or advocate violence.[78] Ultimately, the public must refuse to sympathize with or protect those who would use violence to upend the peace process.

Despite the successful integration of many republicans and loyalists in the peaceful political process, some dissident republicans still threaten the peace.[79] The decommissioning process and political mainstreaming of Sinn Féin has left a political vacuum for fringe republicans to continue to identify with and advocate violence in the attempt to derail the peace process. Their marginalization and inability to disrupt the peace process is based on the fact that the mass public in both communities do not agree with the use of violence even if they may have lingering sympathies for the political cause of dissident republicans.

It is important to keep the peace process moving forward. The momentum of the peace process assisted those who made concessions for peace and marginalized those who opposed the process. Delay only serves to fuel the critics of the process and minimizes the prospect for success. This requires creativity on the part of leaders and negotiators to develop solutions to roadblocks in the peace process. This also helps to build trust among those who are negotiating and increases respect among negotiating partners. Negotiators in Northern Ireland learned to respect if not empathize with the concessions their partners had to make. This is best illustrated by what Paul Dixon calls "saving Dave," referring to efforts by nationalist, Irish, and British politicians to assist David Trimble in getting the necessary support in the Protestant community to accept and implement the Agreement.[80] The leaders negotiating during the peace process demonstrated enough flexibility in their own positions as well as sensitivity to the interests of their negotiating partners to reach an agreement.[81]

Since the signing of this Agreement, leaders from all the political parties have concluded that the devolved Northern Ireland Assembly is the only alternative to direct rule from Britain and is better than that option. This constrains politicians' behavior and seemingly compels them to operate within the framework devised by the Agreement.[82] This was most vividly illustrated in 2007 when the DUP and its leader Ian Paisley agreed to share power in the Northern Ireland Assembly with Sinn Féin and its parliamentary leader Martin McGuinness.

Changes in Structural Conditions May Make Peace More Likely

Changes to the domestic circumstances of the conflicting parties may help alter the conditions that make peace more likely. The most fundamental external pressure on Northern Ireland since the earliest stages of the Troubles was the growing relationship of trust and joint pressure on the North coming from the Irish and British governments.[83] This led to changed positions from the parties inside Northern Ireland. As Snyder stresses in chapter 10, the IRA's and Sinn Féin's renunciation of violence paved the way for the peace process in Northern Ireland. This move was brought about by structural shifts at the international level that undermined revolutionary nationalism in favor of cooperation and integration. Similar changes brought about changes in Egyptian foreign policy under Sadat and in the Palestinian Liberation Organization (PLO)'s renunciation of violence and the Oslo Accords.[84] Other changes in the actors were also important to the Northern Ireland peace process. For example, the modernization and secularization in the Republic of Ireland made the Irish government a more attractive negotiating partner for the British and the unionists.[85] It also made the Irish government able to alter Articles 2 and 3 of its constitution to rescind irredentist claims to Northern Ireland. Other changes like globalization and the growing regionalism within Europe challenged the inherited identities of the different groups in Northern Ireland.[86] This allowed unionists to realize that Catholics had to be assured of their rights and representation in order to secure peace. This concession was as important as that made by republicans that violence was not leading to a united Ireland. The international and especially US response to 9/11 also provided more pressure on the IRA to decommission their weapons and for Sinn Féin to accept a reformed police service in Northern Ireland,[87] and these had been important obstacles to implementing the Agreement.

The difficulty of ending violence and managing conflict like that in Northern Ireland is that individuals often choose to accept and build on inherited narratives that marginalize those who are identified with another group in society.[88] To escape discourses of the past that only continue violence and prevent breakthroughs in terms of a peace process, parties to the conflict must be willing to recalculate their interests. Powell argues that leaders who emerged in Northern Ireland, Britain, and Ireland in the 1990s represented a new generation of leadership that had learned that the policies of the past had to be abandoned in order to go beyond the Troubles.[89] Ripeness or readiness theory suggests that the parties must be at the point where they are willing to make the compromises necessary for a peace agreement and they no longer believe using military force or violence can provide a long-term advantage. Ripeness does not emerge on its own but only comes after the efforts of those who earlier began negotiations. Typically, intermediaries play a critical role in getting negotiations started.[90] Once the parties reach an agreement, they must view the return to violence as less likely to achieve their goals than continuing to operate under the terms of the agreement.[91] While many identified major elements of the Agreement long before the parties finally accepted them in 1998, the Agreement could only be finalized when those in the negotiations came to accept that old realities had changed and that new conditions warranted the concessions they were making. One of the key elements of the Agreement that allowed the parties to go beyond the historic impasse of sovereignty and territory was the cross-border institutions that allowed the relationships among the different parties to the conflict to develop.[92]

Conclusion

Peace processes are journeys, and it takes time for parties to forget enough of the past to envision a different future. Thus, peace is the destination that is sought while the process of politics continues. One needs to accept that conflict will continue after an agreement, but peace processes offer the hope that conflict can be managed and violence minimized. While politics and competition between the two communities in Northern Ireland continues, there has been a substantive reduction in violence and in the perception that violence is likely or appropriate.

The success of the peace process in Northern Ireland has led Americans and others to believe that they can play a positive role in mediating seemingly intractable conflicts in other parts of the world and that the success of Northern Ireland might provide a blueprint for conflict resolution or management in other contexts. It seems more than a coincidence that George Mitchell and Tony Blair have attempted to play critical roles in negotiations between the Palestinians and Israelis. Because of the different historic context of that conflict and the different actors involved, one must be careful of drawing too many parallels between Northern Ireland and other regional conflicts. As one of the principal negotiators for the Irish government has said, the Northern Ireland peace process was "sui generis."[93] Nevertheless, one should not ignore those factors that made the peace process in Northern Ireland successful when considering other seemingly intractable conflicts. The following chapters provide detailed and careful analyses of what we can learn from the Northern Ireland experience. Except for chapter 10, they do not attempt to specifically compare Northern Ireland to any other conflict. Rather, the lessons cited by the contributors to this volume are based on what we now know about the peace process as it developed and evolved in Northern Ireland.

NOTES

1. For one book that seeks to identify what we can learn from the Northern Ireland peace process, see Robin Wilson, *The Northern Ireland Experience of Conflict and Agreement: A Model for Export?* (Manchester: Manchester University Press, 2010). The limited number of comparative studies include: John Bew, Martyn Frampton, and Iñigo Gurruchaga, *Talking to Terrorists: Making Peace in Northern Ireland and the Basque Country* (New York: Columbia University Press, 2009); Guy Ben-Porat, *The Failure of the Middle East Peace Process? A Comparative Analysis of Peace Implementation in Israel/Palestine, Northern*

Ireland and South Africa (New York: Palgrave Macmillan, 2008); Stacie E. Goddard, *Indivisible Territory and the Politics of Legitimacy: Jerusalem and Northern Ireland* (New York: Cambridge University Press, 2010); Michael Kerr, *Imposed Power Sharing: Conflict and Coexistence in Northern Ireland and Lebanon* (Dublin: Irish Academic Press, 2006); Francesco Letamendia and John Loughlin, "Learning from Other Places: Northern Ireland, the Basque Country and Corsica," in *A Farewell to Arms? Beyond the Good Friday Agreement,* 2nd ed., ed. Michael Cox, Adrian Guelke, and Fiona Stephen (Manchester: Manchester University Press, 2006), 377–94; Gregory M. Maney, Ibtisam Ibrahim, Gareth I. Higgins, and Hanna Herzog, "The Past's Promise: Lessons from Peace Processes in Northern Ireland and the Middle East," *Journal of Peace Research* 43 (2) (2006): 181–200; and Charles A. Reilly, *Peace-building in Guatemala and Northern Ireland* (New York: Palgrave Macmillan, 2009).

2. See Paul Bew, "Myths of Consociationalism: From Good Friday to Political Impasse," in Cox, Guelke, and Stephen, *A Farewell to Arms?,* 57–68; John Coakley, "The Challenge of Consociation in Northern Ireland," *Parliamentary Affairs* 64 (3) (2011): 473–93; John Coakley, *Pathways from Ethnic Conflict: Institutional Redesign in Divided Societies* (New York: Routledge, 2010); Paul Dixon, "Why the Good Friday Agreement in Northern Ireland Is Not Consociational," *Political Quarterly* 76 (3) (2005): 357–67; Andrew Finlay, *Governing Ethnic Conflict: Consociation, Identity and the Price of Peace* (New York: Routledge, 2011); John McGarry and Brendan O'Leary, "Consociational Theory and Peace Agreements in Pluri-National Places: Northern Ireland and Other Cases," in Ben-Porat, *The Failure of the Middle East Peace Process?,* 70–96; John McGarry and Brendan O'Leary, *The Northern Ireland Conflict: Consociational Engagements* (New York: Oxford University Press, 2004); Ian O'Flynn, "Deliberative Democracy, the Public Interest and the Consociational Model," *Political Studies* 58 (3) (2010): 572–89; David Russell, "Power-Sharing and Civic Leadership in Lebanon and Northern Ireland," in *Global Change, Civil Society and the Northern Ireland Peace Process: Implementing the Political Settlement,* ed. Christopher Farrington (New York: Palgrave Macmillan, 2008), 214–33; and Rupert Taylor, *Consociational Theory: McGarry and O'Leary and the Northern Ireland Conflict* (New York: Routledge, 2011).

3. The focus on the transition from war to peace in this period is stressed in Feargal Cochrane, "From Transition to Transformation in Ethno-National Conflict: Some Lessons from Northern Ireland," *Ethnopolitics* 11 (2) (2012): 182–203, and Fionnuala Ní Aoláin and Colm Campbell, "The Paradox of Transition in Conflicted Democracies," *Human Rights Quarterly* 27 (1) (2005): 172–213.

4. The need for caution when drawing lessons from Northern Ireland is emphasized by Hazleton in chapter 2 of this volume and by James Anderson, "Partition, Consociation, Border-Crossing: Some Lessons from the National Conflict in Ireland/Northern Ireland," *Nations and Nationalism* 14 (1) (2008): 86; Paul Bew, *The Making and Remaking of the Good Friday Agreement* (Dublin: Liffey Press, 2007), 143; Adrian Guelke, "Lessons of Northern Ireland and the Relevance of the Regional Context," in *The Lessons of Northern Ireland,* ed. Michael Cox (London: LSE IDEAS Special Report 008, November 2011), 8–12; and Eamonn

O'Kane, "Learning from Northern Ireland? The Uses and Abuses of the Irish 'Model,'" *British Journal of Politics and International Relations* 12 (2) (2010): 239–56.

5. The reduction of the salience of ethnic or sectarian identities is critical to Hancock's analysis. For the general argument that the conflict in Northern Ireland is based on a struggle over identities, see Brian M. Walker, *A Political History of the Two Irelands: From Partition to Peace* (Basingstoke: Palgrave Macmillan, 2012). The importance of salience of ethnic identities as opposed to polarization to civil war and violence is highlighted in Ravi Bhavnani and Dan Miodownik, "Ethnic Polarization, Ethnic Salience, and Civil War," *Journal of Conflict Resolution* 53 (1) (2009): 30–49.

6. Jennifer Todd supports this argument in "National Identity in Transition? Moving Out of Conflict in (Northern) Ireland," *Nations and Nationalism* 13 (4) (2007): 565–71.

7. This perspective is supported by Jonathan Tonge, Peter Shirlow, and James McAuley, "So Why Did the Guns Fall Silent? How Interplay, not Stalemate, Explains the Northern Ireland Peace Process," *Irish Political Studies* 26 (1) (2011): 1–18.

8. Niall Ó Dochartaigh, "Nation and Neighbourhood: Nationalist Mobilisation and Local Solidarities in the North of Ireland," in *The Challenges of Ethno-Nationalism: Case Studies in Identity Politics*, ed. Adrian Guelke (New York: Palgrave Macmillan, 2010), 161–76.

9. For the evolution of nationalist politics, see Cillian McGrattan, "Modern Irish Nationalism—Ideology, Policymaking, and Path-Dependent Change," in Guelke, *The Challenges of Ethno-Nationalism*, 177–90; Niall Ó Dochartaigh, "Republicanism Domesticated? All-Ireland Politics in an Age of Austerity," *Political Quarterly* 83 (2) (2012): 256–64; and Jonathan Tonge "Nationalist Convergence? The Evolution of Sinn Féin and SDLP Politics," in *Transforming the Peace Process in Northern Ireland: From Terrorism to Democratic Politics*, ed. Aaron Edwards and Stephen Bloomer (Dublin: Irish Academic Press, 2008), 59–76. For the role of the Social Democratic and Labour Party in the peace process, see Seán Farren, *The SDLP: The Struggle for Agreement in Northern Ireland, 1970–2000* (Dublin: Four Courts, 2010), and Peter J. McLoughlin, *John Hume and the Revision of Irish Nationalism* (Manchester: Manchester University Press, 2010). For the evolution of Sinn Féin, see Kevin Bean, *The New Politics of Sinn Féin* (Liverpool: Liverpool University Press, 2007), and Martyn Frampton, *The Long March: The Political Strategy of Sinn Féin* (New York: Palgrave Macmillan, 2009). Tommy McKearney in a recent book, *The Provisional IRA: From Insurrection to Parliament* (London: Pluto Press, 2011), contends that the dynamic of the republican movement was built on an opposition to the old Northern Ireland state, not just the aspiration for an Irish republic.

10. This point is also emphasized by Jonathan Powell, *Great Hatred, Little Room: Making Peace in Northern Ireland* (London: Bodley Head, 2008), 15–16 and 24–25.

11. This siege mentality is best explained in Arthur Aughey's *Under Siege: Ulster Unionism and the Anglo-Irish Agreement* (New York: St. Martin's Press, 1989). The idea that the identities in Northern Ireland, including unionist identity, are constructed, fluid, and constantly being redefined is supported in Neal G. Jesse and Kristen P. Williams, *Ethnic Conflict: A Systemic Approach to Cases of Conflict* (Washington, DC: CQ Press, 2011), 132,

and Máiréad Nic Craith, *Plural Identities—Singular Narratives: The Case of Northern Ireland* (New York: Berghahn Books, 2002). For how this redefinition of unionist and loyalist identity has transpired, see James W. McAuley and Graham Spencer, *Ulster Loyalism after the Good Friday Agreement: History, Identity and Change* (Basingstroke: Palgrave Macmillan, 2011), and Lee A. Smithey, *Unionists, Loyalists, and Conflict Transformation in Northern Ireland* (Oxford: Oxford University Press, 2011). For how reconstructing identities can help build peace, see Maney, Ibrahim, Higgins, and Herzog, "The Past's Promise," 196.

12. For Trimble's critical role in the peace process, see Dean Godson, *Himself Alone: David Trimble and the Ordeal of Unionism* (London: HarperCollins, 2004); Henry McDonald, *Trimble* (London: Bloomsbury, 2000); and Frank Millar, *David Trimble: The Price of Peace* (Dublin: Liffey Press, 2004). For Ian Paisley's role in Northern Ireland, see Steve Bruce, *Paisley: Religion and Politics in Northern Ireland* (New York: Oxford University Press, 2007). David Gordon explores what happened to Paisley and the Democratic Unionist Party once they agreed to govern with Sinn Féin in *The Fall of the House of Paisley* (Dublin: Gill and Macmillan, 2009).

13. Tony Blair explains this in his autobiography, *A Journey: My Political Life* (London: Hutchinson, 2010), 184–85, and this process was also highlighted by Blair's assistant, Jonathan Powell, in *Great Hatred, Little Room*, 18, 108, and 314–15. Several scholars have identified the constructive ambiguity that was at the heart of the agreement. See John Coakley, "Has the Northern Ireland Problem Been Solved?," *Journal of Democracy* 19 (3) (2008): 107; David Mitchell, "Cooking the Fudge: Constructive Ambiguity and the Implementation of the Northern Ireland Agreement, 1998–2007," *Irish Political Studies* 24 (3) (2009): 321–26; Fionnuala Ní Aoláin, *The Politics of Force: Conflict Management and State Violence in Northern Ireland* (Belfast: Blackstaff Press, 2000), 11; and Eamonn O'Kane, *Britain, Ireland and Northern Ireland since 1980: The Totality of the Relationships* (New York: Routledge, 2007), 160–61.

14. Paul Dixon, *Northern Ireland: The Politics of War and Peace*, 2nd ed. (New York: Palgrave Macmillan, 2008), 271–74. For how the choreography of the peace process and the misleading of the public caused the failure to implement the Agreement, see G. K. Peatling, *The Failure of the Northern Ireland Peace Process* (Dublin: Irish Academic Press, 2004), 94–105. For the lessons learned by the British, see Tony Blair, *A Journey*, 185–88, and Powell, *Great Hatred, Little Room*. For background to the British policy in Northern Ireland, see Frank Millar, "Ireland: The Peace Process," in *Blair's Britain, 1997–2007*, ed. Anthony Seldon (Cambridge: Cambridge University Press, 2007), 509–28.

15. John J. Mearsheimer emphasizes how lying to one's public can undermine confidence in government and corrupt domestic politics in *Why Leaders Lie* (New York: Oxford University Press, 2011), 13 and 85–86. Eamonn O'Kane contends that the British tended to offer more inducements to republicans during the peace process and while trying to implement the Agreement. This had the effect of undermining unionist support. See Eamonn O'Kane, "To Cajole or Compel? The Use of Incentives and Penalties in Northern Ireland's Peace Process," *Dynamics of Asymmetric Conflict* 4 (3) (2011): 272–84.

16. For the Irish government's perspective, see Bertie Ahern, *Bertie Ahern: The Autobiography* (London: Arrow Books, 2009), and Albert Reynolds, *My Autobiography* (London: Transworld Ireland, 2009). For further background on the Irish government's perspective, see the writings of one of the key advisors to the Irish government, Martin Mansergh: "The Background to the Irish Peace Process," in Cox, Guelke, and Stephen, *A Farewell to Arms?*, 24–40; *The Legacy of History for Making Peace in Ireland* (Cork: Mercier Press, 2003); and "Mountain-Climbing Irish-Style: The Hidden Challenge of the Peace Process," in *The Long Road to Peace in Northern Ireland*, ed. Marianne Elliott (Liverpool: Liverpool University Press, 2002), 105–14. The process of how the Irish government came to rethink its territorial claim to Northern Ireland is explained in Markus Kornprobst, "Argumentation and Compromise: Ireland's Selection of the Territorial Status Quo Norm," *International Organization* 61 (1) (2007): 69–98.

17. This position is supported by Powell in *Great Hatred, Little Room*, 313.

18. Ironically, by claiming to not talk to terrorists and then secretly entering into negotiations with them, states weaken their bargaining position. See Julie Browne and Eric S. Dickson, "'We Don't Talk to Terrorists': On the Rhetoric and Practice of Secret Negotiations," *Journal of Conflict Resolution* 54 (3) (2010): 379–407.

19. Michael Kerr, *The Destructors: The Story of Northern Ireland's Lost Peace Process* (Dublin: Irish Academic Press, 2011).

20. Arthur Aughey and Cathy Gormley-Heenan, "The Anglo-Irish Agreement: 25 Years On," *Political Quarterly* 82 (3) (2011): 392. While the Anglo-Irish Agreement is typically seen as failing in terms of its inclusiveness, recent analysis suggests it may have helped to bring about institutional change that promoted later developments in the peace process. See Jennifer Todd, "Institutional Change and Conflict Regulation: The Anglo-Irish Agreement (1985) and the Mechanisms of Change in Northern Ireland," *West European Politics* 34 (4) (2011): 838–58.

21. The importance of including armed groups in negotiations that lead to political settlements is emphasized in Nuala O'Loan, "What Lessons Have We Learned from Our Troubled Past in Planning for a Peaceful Future?," Tipperary International Conference of Peace, July 6, 2012, at the Ballykisteen Conference Center in County Tipperary, and Chandra Lekha Sriram, *Peace as Governance: Power-Sharing, Armed Groups and Contemporary Peace Negotiations* (New York: Palgrave Macmillan, 2008). The argument that inclusive settlements are needed to prevent the recurrence of civil war is emphasized in Charles T. Call, *Why Peace Fails: The Causes and Prevention of Civil War Recurrence* (Washington, DC: Georgetown University Press, 2012). This argument is the flip side of the contention that excluding ethnic groups from access to power causes civil war. For this, see Lars-Erik Cederman, Andreas Wimmer, and Brian Min, "Why Do Ethnic Groups Rebel? New Data and Analysis," *World Politics* 62 (1) (2010): 87–119. The need to include Sinn Féin in the negotiations leading up to the Good Friday Agreement is emphasized by Powell, *Great Hatred, Little Room*, 8. States are more likely to be inclusive when those who have historically been excluded from negotiations (like Sinn Féin) are less threatening. See Devashree Gupta, "Selective Engagement and Its Consequences for Social Movement Organizations: Lessons from British Policy in Northern Ireland," *Comparative Politics* 39 (3) (2007): 346.

22. For a good overview of how devolution has worked in Northern Ireland, see Colin Knox, *Devolution and the Governance of Northern Ireland* (Manchester: Manchester University Press, 2010). For the general argument regarding the need for inclusiveness after civil wars to stabilize the peace, see Caroline Hartzell, Matthew Hoddie, and Donald Rothchild, "Stabilizing the Peace After Civil War: An Investigation of Some Key Variables," *International Organization* 55 (1) (2001): 185–86.

23. For an analysis of decommissioning and its linkage to these other issues, see Colin McInnes, "A Farewell to Arms? Decommissioning and the Peace Process," in Cox, Guelke, and Stephen, *A Farewell to Arms?*, 154–69.

24. Powell, *Great Hatred, Little Room*, 81.

25. George J. Mitchell, *Making Peace* (New York: Random House, 1999), 35–36. The argument against preconditions is also advanced in Powell, *Great Hatred, Little Room*, 317, and was the negotiating position of the Irish government under Bertie Ahern. See Ken Whelan and Eugene Masterson, *Bertie Ahern: Taoiseach and Peacemaker* (Edinburgh: Blackwater Press, 1998), 182.

26. The potential problems of parties to a negotiation with mediators are reviewed in Kyle Beardsley, "Intervention without Leverage: Explaining the Prevalence of Weak Mediators," *International Interactions* 35 (3) (2009): 272–97, and Oliver Richmond, "Devious Objectives and the Disputants' View of International Mediation: A Theoretical Framework," *Journal of Peace Research* 35 (6) (1998): 707–22.

27. See Gerald W. Schlabach, *Just Policing, Not War: An Alternative Response to World Violence* (Collegeville, MN: Liturgical Press, 2007).

28. Alan Bryden and Heiner Hänggi, *Security Governance in Post-Conflict Peacebuilding* (Münster, Germany: LIT Verlag, 2005); Anja H. Ebnöther and Philipp H. Fluri, *After Intervention: Public Security Management in Post-Conflict Societies—From Intervention to Sustainable Local Ownership* (Vienna: GKS, 2005); Caroline Hartzell, "Explaining the Stability of Negotiated Settlements to Intrastate Wars," *Journal of Conflict Resolution* 43 (1) (1999): 3–22; Albrecht Schnabel and Hans-Georg Ehrhart, *Security Sector Reform and Post-Conflict Peacebuilding* (Tokyo: United Nations University Press, 2006); and Mark Sedra, "Security Sector Reform in Afghanistan: The Slide towards Expediency," *International Peacekeeping* 13 (1) (2006): 94–110.

29. For the best overviews of police reforms in Northern Ireland, see chapter 6 and John Doyle, *Policing the Narrow Ground: Lessons from the Transformation of Policing in Northern Ireland* (Dublin: Royal Irish Academy, 2010). For more on policing in Northern Ireland, see Brice Dickson, "New Beginnings? Policing and Human Rights after the Conflict," in Cox, Guelke, and Stephen, *A Farewell to Arms?*, 170–86; Roger Mac Ginty, "Policing and the Northern Ireland Peace Process," in *Politics and Performance in Contemporary Northern Ireland*, ed. John P. Harrington and Elizabeth J. Mitchell (Amherst: University of Massachusetts Press, 1999), 103–21; Kieran McEvoy and John Morison, "Beyond the 'Constitutional Moment': Law, Transition, and Peacemaking in Northern Ireland," *Fordham International Law Journal* 26 (2003): 961–95; John McGarry and Brendan O'Leary, *Policing Northern Ireland: Proposals for a New Start* (Belfast: Blackstaff Press, 2000); Aogan Mulcahy, *Policing Northern Ireland: Conflict, Legitimacy and Reform* (Cullompton, Devon:

Willan Publishing, 2006); Robert Perry, "The Devolution of Policing in Northern Ireland: Politics and Reform," *Politics* 31 (3) (2011): 167–78; Mary O'Rawe, "Policing Change: To Reform or Not to Transform," in *Northern Ireland after the Troubles: A Society in Transition*, ed. Colin Coulter and Michael Murray (Manchester: Manchester University Press, 2008), 110–32; and Joanne Wright and Keith Bryett, *Policing and Conflict in Northern Ireland* (London: Macmillan, 2000).

30. See Niall Ó Dochartaigh, "Territoriality and Order in the North of Ireland," *Irish Political Studies* 26 (3) (2011): 313–28.

31. For Monica Duffy Toft's theory on the failure of negotiations to lead to successful settlement of civil wars based on statistical analysis, see "Ending Civil Wars: A Case for Rebel Victory?," *International Security* 34 (4) (2010): 7–36, and *Securing the Peace: The Durable Settlement of Civil Wars* (Princeton, NJ: Princeton University Press, 2010).

32. Toft, "Ending Civil Wars," 32.

33. For more on security-sector reform, see chapter 6.

34. Toft, "Ending Civil Wars," 34.

35. Karl Cordell and Stefan Wolff, *Ethnic Conflict: Causes—Consequences—Responses* (Cambridge: Polity, 2010); Dennis J. D. Sandole, *Peacebuilding* (Cambridge: Polity, 2010); and Barbara F. Walter, *Committing to Peace: The Successful Settlement of Civil Wars* (Princeton, NJ: Princeton University Press, 2002). Third parties tend to delay the resolution of civil wars. See Patrick M. Regan, "Third-Party Interventions and the Duration of Intrastate Conflicts," *Journal of Conflict Resolution* 46 (1) (2002): 55–73. This is the case because third parties have their own independent or separate agenda. See Dylan Balch-Lindsay, Andrew J. Enterline, and Kyle A. Joyce, "Third-Party Intervention and the Civil War Process," *Journal of Peace Research* 45 (3) (2008): 345–63, and David E. Cunningham, "Blocking Resolution: How External States Can Prolong Civil Wars," *Journal of Peace Research* 47 (2) (2010): 115–27.

36. Christopher Mitchell, "Mediation and the Ending of Conflicts," in *Contemporary Peacemaking: Conflict, Violence and Peace Processes* (New York: Palgrave Macmillan, 2003), 77–86.

37. See Kyle Beardsley, "Agreement without Peace? International Mediation and Time Inconsistency Problems," *American Journal of Political Science* 52 (4) (2008): 723–40.

38. Jonathan Powell, "Security Is Not Enough: Ten Lessons for Conflict Resolution from Northern Ireland," in Cox, *The Lessons of Northern Ireland*, 22. See also Frederic Pearson and Marie Olson Lounsbery, "Post-Intervention Stability of Civil War States," in *Critical Issues in Peace and Conflict Studies*, ed. Thomas Matyók, Jessica Senehi, and Sean Byrne (Boulder, CO: Lexington Books, 2011), 43–60.

39. Blair, *A Journey*, 188.

40. For the positive role third-party states can play in diplomatic intervention, see Patrick M. Regan and Aysegul Aydin, "Diplomacy and Other Forms of Intervention in Civil Wars," *Journal of Conflict Resolution* 50 (5) (2006): 736–56. For the importance of mediation, even in the most intractable cases, see Jacob Bercovitch, "Mediation in the Most Resistant Cases," in *Grasping the Nettle: Analyzing Cases of Intractable Conflict*, ed. Chester

A. Crocker, Fen Osler Hampson, and Pamela Aall (Washington, DC: United States Institute of Peace Press, 2005), 99–121.

41. Andrew H. Kydd, "When Can Mediators Build Trust?," *American Political Science Review* 100 (3) (2006): 449–62. Regan had previously found that neutral interventions were less effective than biased ones. See Regan, "Third-Party Interventions and the Duration of Intrastate Conflicts."

42. Chester A. Crocker, Fen Osler Hampson, and Pamela Aall, "Conclusion: From Intractable to Tractable—the Outlook and Implications for Third Parties," in Crocker, Hampson, and Aall, *Grasping the Nettle*, 379.

43. Maney, Ibrahim, Higgins, and Herzog, "The Past's Promise," 192. This is especially the case when the third parties can strengthen the commitments of the parties to the peace agreement (like the United States did in the case of the Northern Ireland conflict) and use their influence to guarantee the interests of "their" side in the negotiations. See Isak Svensson, "Bargaining, Bias and Peace Brokers: How Rebels Commit to Peace," *Journal of Peace Research* 44 (2) (2007): 177–94, and Isak Svensson, "Who Brings Peace? Neutral versus Biased Mediation and Institutional Peace Arrangements in Civil Wars," *Journal of Conflict Resolution* 53 (3) (2009): 446–69.

44. For the importance of timing in successful diplomatic interventions, see Regan and Aydin, "Diplomacy and Other Forms of Intervention in Civil Wars."

45. Paul F. Diehl and Gary Goertz, *War and Peace in International Rivalry* (Ann Arbor: University of Michigan Press, 2000), 205–15.

46. Paul Wilkinson contends that international actors can make a difference in "How Significant Was International Influence in the Northern Ireland Peace Process?," in *Combating Terrorism in Northern Ireland*, ed. James Dingley (London: Routledge, 2009), 245–57. The key to success for third parties in mediating conflicts between enduring rivalries is intervening when the parties are ready to accept a negotiated settlement. See J. Michael Greig, "Moments of Opportunity: Recognizing Conditions of Ripeness for International Mediation between Enduring Rivals," *Journal of Conflict Resolution* 45 (6) (2001): 691–718. This argument is supported by the literature on the settlement of civil wars. See Hartzell, Hoddie, and Rothchild, "Stabilizing the Peace after Civil War," 203.

47. There is a voluminous literature on the US role, much of which is critically examined in chapter 7. See also Paul Arthur, "American Intervention in the Anglo-Irish Peace Process: Incrementalism or Interference," *Cambridge Review of International Affairs* 11 (1) (1997): 46–62; Feargal Cochrane, "Irish America, the End of the IRA's Armed Struggle and the Utility of 'Soft Power,'" *Journal of Peace Research* 44 (2) (2007): 215–31; John Dumbrell, "'Hope and History': The US and Peace in Northern Ireland," in Cox, Guelke, and Stephen, *A Farewell to Arms?*, 214–22; John Dumbrell, "The New American Connection: President George W. Bush and Northern Ireland," in Cox, Guelke, and Stephen, *A Farewell to Arms?*, 357–66; William Hazleton, "Encouragement from the Sidelines: Clinton's Role in the Good Friday Agreement," *Irish Studies in International Affairs* 11 (2000): 103–19; Timothy J. Lynch, "The Gerry Adams Visa in Anglo-American Relations," *Irish Studies in International Affairs* 14 (2003): 33–44; Timothy J. Lynch, *Turf War: The*

Clinton Administration and Northern Ireland (Burlington, VT: Ashgate, 2004); Roger Mac Ginty, "American Influences on the Northern Ireland Peace Process," *Journal of Conflict Studies* 17 (2) (1997): 31–50; Conor O'Cleary, *The Greening of the White House: The Inside Story of How America Tried to Bring Peace to Ireland* (Dublin: Gill and Macmillan, 1996); and Niall O'Dowd, "The Awakening: Irish America's Key Role in the Irish Peace Process," in Elliott, *The Long Road to Peace in Northern Ireland*, 64–74. The importance of third parties, like the United States in Northern Ireland, in helping to implement peace agreements is stressed in Fen Osler Hampson, *Nurturing Peace: Why Peace Settlements Succeed or Fail* (Washington, DC: United States Institute of Peace Press, 1996).

48. See Stephen M. Saideman, "Discrimination in International Relations: Analyzing External Support for Ethnic Groups," *Journal of Peace Research* 39 (1) (2002): 27–50.

49. Bush assured the parties to the conflict of his willingness to help. In addition to Clancy's analysis in chapter 7, Jonathan Powell makes this argument in *Great Hatred, Little Room*, 190.

50. See also Mary Alice C. Clancy, "The United States and Post-Agreement Northern Ireland, 2001–6," *Irish Studies in International Affairs* 18 (2007): 155–73.

51. See especially Burcu Savun and Daniel Tirone, "Foreign Aid, Democratization, and Civil Conflict: How Does Democracy Aid Affect Civil Conflict?," *American Journal of Political Science* 55 (2) (2011): 233–46.

52. See Zeynup Taydas and Dursun Peksen, "Can States Buy Peace? Social Welfare Spending and Civil Conflicts," *Journal of Peace Research* 49 (2) (2012): 273–87, for this argument.

53. The external aid to support the peace process has been significant. John Brewer, in *Peace Processes: A Sociological Approach* (Cambridge: Polity, 2010), 169, estimates that approximately £1 billion has been provided to Northern Ireland and the border counties. For more on the effectiveness of the aid program to Northern Ireland, see chapter 8 in this volume and Sean Byrne, *Economic Assistance and the Northern Ireland Conflict: Building the Peace Dividend* (Madison, NJ: Farleigh Dickinson University Press, 2009). See also Elham Atashi, "Peace Dividends: The Role of External Aid in Peacebuilding," in *Building Peace in Northern Ireland*, ed. Maria Power (Liverpool: Liverpool University Press, 2011), 209–27; Sandra Buchanan, "Transforming Conflict in Northern Ireland [UK] and the [Irish] Border Counties: Some Lessons from the Peace Programmes on Valuing Participatory Democracy," *Irish Political Studies* 23 (3) (2008): 387–409; and Andrew Wilson, "'Doing the Business': Aspects of the Clinton Administration's Economic Support for the Northern Ireland Peace Process, 1994–2000," *Journal of Conflict Studies* 23 (1) (2003): 155–76.

54. In the context of the EU, the foreign assistance to Northern Ireland can provide a "connective effect" to improve the prospects for peace. It also can assist groups in Northern Ireland in redefining their identity as Wiedenhoft Murphy and Peden argue in chapter 4. See Thomas Diez, Stephan Stetter, and Mathias Albert, "The European Union and Border Conflicts: The Transformative Power of Integration," *International Organization* 60 (2006): 582 and 585.

55. Roger Mac Ginty, *International Peacebuilding and Local Resistance: Hybrid Forms of Peace* (New York: Palgrave Macmillan, 2011).

56. Chris Gilligan, "Peace or Pacification Process? A Brief Critique of the Peace Process," in *Peace or War? Understanding the Peace Process in Northern Ireland*, ed. Chris Gilligan and Jon Tonge (Aldershot: Ashgate, 1997), 32.

57. For a good overview, see Helmut Anheier and Jeremy Kendall, "Interpersonal Trust and Voluntary Associations: Examining Three Approaches," *British Journal of Sociology* 53 (3) (2002): 343–62.

58. While anarchy is a common assumption in theories of conflict in international relations, Lake demonstrates that a variety of hierarchical relationships exist between different actors and states. See David A. Lake, "Escape from the State of Nature: Authority and Hierarchy in World Politics," *International Security* 32 (1) (2007): 47–79. Communications is critical to preventing unnecessary war in this world of anarchy. See Robert F. Trager, "Diplomatic Calculus in Anarchy: How Communication Matters," *American Political Science Review* 104 (2) (2010): 347–68. Jack Snyder has argued that integrating material, institutional, and cultural approaches using complex systems theory will best allow us to understand the nature of anarchy and its implications in world politics. See Jack Snyder, "Anarchy and Culture: Insights from the Anthropology of War," *International Organization* 56 (1) (2002): 7–45.

59. Nurit Shnabel and Arie Nadler, "A Needs-Based Model of Reconciliation: Perpetrators Need Acceptance and Victims Need Empowerment to Reconcile," in *Prosocial Motives, Emotions, and Behavior: The Better Angels of Our Nature*, ed. Mario Mukilincer and Phillip R. Shaver (Washington, DC: American Psychological Association, 2010), 409–29.

60. Pierre Hazan, *Judging War, Judging History: Behind Truth and Reconciliation*, trans. Sarah Meyer de Stadelhofen (Stanford, CA: Stanford University Press, 2010), 9.

61. For an examination of how loyalist paramilitaries see a truth commission as a means of promoting a republican agenda, see Bill Rolston, "Dealing with the Past: Pro-State Paramilitaries, Truth and Transition in Northern Ireland," *Human Rights Quarterly* 28 (3) (2006): 652–75.

62. Ahern, *Bertie Ahern*, 231–33. As Ahern indicates, this is especially true in the wake of the Omagh bombing. For the pursuit of justice in this case, see Ruth Dudley Edwards, *Aftermath: The Omagh Bombing and the Families' Pursuit of Justice* (London: Vintage Books, 2010).

63. Patricia Lundy and Mark McGovern, "Attitudes towards a Truth Commission for Northern Ireland in Relation to Political Party Affiliation," *Irish Political Studies* 22 (3) (2007): 321–38, and Marie Smyth, "Putting the Past in Its Place: Issues of Victimhood and Reconciliation in Northern Ireland's Peace Process," in *Burying the Past: Making Peace and Doing Justice after Civil Conflict*, ed. Nigel Biggar (Washington, DC: Georgetown University Press, 2001), 123–25.

64. Feargal Cochrane, *Ending Wars* (Cambridge: Polity Press, 2008), 151; Erin Daly and Jeremy Sarkin, *Reconciliation in Divided Societies: Finding Common Ground* (Philadelphia: University of Pennsylvania Press, 2007); Ryan Gawn, "Truth Cohabitation: A Truth Commission for Northern Ireland?," *Irish Political Studies* 22 (3) (2007): 339–61; Patricia Lundy and Mark McGovern, "Telling Stories, Facing Truths: Memory, Justice and

Post-Conflict Transition," in *Northern Ireland: After the Troubles*, ed. Colin Coulter and Michael Murray (Manchester: Manchester University Press, 2008), 33; Terrence McCaughey, "Northern Ireland: Burying the Hatchet, Not the Past," in Biggar, *Burying the Past*, 261–65; Norman Porter, *The Elusive Quest: Reconciliation in Northern Ireland* (Belfast: Blackstaff Press, 2003); and Ronald A. Wells, "Northern Ireland: A Study of Friendship, Forgiveness, and Reconciliation," in *The Politics of Past Evil: Religion, Reconciliation, and the Dilemmas of Transitional Justice*, ed. Daniel Philpott (Notre Dame, IN: University of Notre Dame Press, 2006), 189–222.

65. David Bloomfield, Teresa Barnes, and Luc Huyse, *Reconciliation after Violent Conflict: A Handbook* (Stockholm: International Institute for Democracy and Electoral Assistance, 2003), 13. The need for this reconciliation is recognized even by the politicians who negotiated the Agreement and the effort to implement it. See Powell, *Great Hatred, Little Room*, 308.

66. Bew, *The Making and Remaking of the Good Friday Agreement*, 142; Powell, *Great Hatred, Little Room*, xi; and Powell, "Security Is Not Enough," 24. Powell especially recognizes the courage of Bertie Ahern in his pursuit of peace during the negotiations in *Great Hatred, Little Room*, 94. For the general argument that diplomatic engagement is the key to creating peace, see Charles A. Kupchan, *How Enemies Become Friends: The Sources of Stable Peace* (Princeton, NJ: Princeton University Press, 2010).

67. The important role played by Mo Mowlam is stressed in Powell, *Great Hatred, Little Room*, 80.

68. Blair, *A Journey*, 166.

69. Mitchell, *Making Peace*, 126 and 143–45. The use of a deadline in the Northern Irish experience conforms to the general finding that time pressure helps yield broad agreements but defies the more common trend that time pressures negatively affect complex negotiations and tend to yield less durable settlements. See Marco Pinfari, "Time to Agree: Is Time Pressure Good for Peace Negotiations?," *Journal of Conflict Resolution* 55 (5) (2011): 683–709.

70. Landon E. Hancock, "There Is No Alternative: Prospect Theory, the Yes Campaign and Selling the Good Friday Agreement," *Irish Political Studies* 26 (1) (2011): 95–116.

71. This argument is made in the Northern Ireland context in Niall Ó Dochartaigh, "Together in the Middle: Back-Channel Negotiation in the Irish Peace Process," *Journal of Peace Research* 48 (6) (2011): 767–80.

72. Anthony Oberschall and L. Kendall Palmer, "The Failure of Moderate Politics: The Case of Northern Ireland," in *Power Sharing: New Challenges for Divided Societies*, ed. Ian O'Flynn and David Russell (London: Pluto Press, 2005), 77–91.

73. Tonge, "Nationalist Convergence?," 59–76.

74. James Greer, "Paisley and His Heartland: A Case Study of Political Change," in *From Parnell to Paisley: Constitutional and Revolutionary Politics in Modern Ireland*, ed. Coimhe Nic Dháibhéid and Colin Reid (Dublin: Irish Academic Press, 2010), 224–49. Not only have the parties changed, but a generational shift has occurred among voters in Northern Ireland, where younger cohorts who are slightly more moderate than previous generations

are more likely to vote for the more "extreme" parties. See James Tilley and Geoffrey Evans, "Political Generations in Northern Ireland," *European Journal of Political Research* 50 (5) (2011): 583–608.

75. For the conceptualization of extremist parties outbidding the moderates in their own community, see Andrew H. Kydd and Barbara F. Walter, "The Strategies of Terrorism," *International Security* 31 (1) (2006): 76. This conforms to the general argument that hawks or extremists are more likely to make enduring settlements of conflicts. See Kenneth A. Schultz, "The Politics of Risking Peace: Do Hawks or Doves Deliver the Olive Branch?," *International Organization* 59 (1) (2005): 1–38. In the Northern Irish context, see Paul Mitchell, Geoffrey Evans, and Brendan O'Leary, "Extremist Outbidding in Ethnic Party Systems Is Not Inevitable: Tribune Parties in Northern Ireland," *Political Studies* 57 (2) (2009): 397–421. People in Northern Ireland tend to agree more than disagree with the proposition that "it is the job of our politicians to fight the corner for the community that they come from." See the 2010 Northern Ireland Life and Times Survey, http://www.ark.ac.uk/nilt/2010/Political_Attitudes/CORNER.html (accessed December 21, 2011). The Northern Ireland experience conforms to the more general argument that moderate voters will vote for more extreme parties and candidates to achieve what they perceive as balance in parliament or better representation of their position. See Orit Kedar, "When Moderate Voters Prefer Extreme Parties: Policy Balancing in Parliamentary Elections," *American Political Science Review* 99 (2) (2005): 185–99.

76. The role of spoilers is further explored in chapter 3 and in Stephen John Stedman, "Peace Processes and the Challenges of Violence," in *Contemporary Peacemaking: Conflict, Violence and Peace Processes*, ed. John Darby and Roger Mac Ginty (New York: Palgrave Macmillan, 2003), 103–13.

77. This point was stressed by Seán Ó hUiginn in comments made at the Brendan Duddy Archive Symposium held on November 22, 2011, at the National University of Ireland, Galway, and is supported by Maney, Ibrahim, Higgins, and Herzog, "The Past's Promise," 196.

78. See John Darby, *The Effects of Violence on Peace Processes* (Washington, DC: United States Institute of Peace, 2001), 118–20, and O'Kane, "Learning from Northern Ireland?," 241–52.

79. Kevin Bean, "'New dissidents are but old Provisionals writ large'? The Dynamics of Dissident Republicanism in the New Northern Ireland," *Political Quarterly* 83 (2) (2012): 210–18; Martyn Frampton, "Dissident Irish Republican Violence: A Resurgent Threat?," *Political Quarterly* 83 (2) (2012): 227–37; Martyn Frampton, *Legion of the Rearguard: Dissident Irish Republicanism* (Dublin: Irish Academic Press, 2011); and Jonathan Tonge, "'No-one likes us; we don't care': 'Dissident' Irish Republicans and Mandates," *Political Quarterly* 83 (2) (2012): 219–26.

80. Dixon, *Northern Ireland*, 286. Nuala O'Loan agrees that peacemaking, like that in Northern Ireland, requires choreography. See O'Loan, "What Lessons Have We Learned from Our Troubled Past in Planning for a Peaceful Future?" This choreography corresponds to what Broome identifies as "relational empathy," necessary to make peace. See

Benjamin J. Broome, "Building Relational Empathy Through an Interactive Design Process," in *Handbook of Conflict Analysis and Resolution*, ed. Dennis J. D. Sandole, Sean Byrne, Ingrid Sandole-Staroste, and Jessica Senehi (London: Routledge, 2009), 184–200.

81. Cathy Gormley-Heenan, *Political Leadership and the Northern Ireland Peace Process: Role, Capacity and Effect* (Basingstroke: Palgrave Macmillan, 2007).

82. Rick Wilford, "Northern Ireland: The Politics of Constraint," *Parliamentary Affairs* 63 (1) (2010): 134–55. Kaufman concludes that this has meant that a return to war is extremely unlikely. See Eric Kaufmann, "The Northern Ireland Peace Process in an Age of Austerity," *Political Quarterly* 83 (2) (2012): 203.

83. See Thomas Hennessey, *The Northern Ireland Peace Process: Ending the Troubles?* (Dublin: Gill and Macmillan, 2000), 6.

84. Despite some similar international shocks, Guelke emphasizes that Sharon's decision to discard the Oslo Peace Accords and the breakdown of the peace process in the Middle East are similar in some ways to unionist thinking in the wake of the Agreement. See Adrian Guelke, "Political Comparisons: From Johannesburg to Jerusalem," in Cox, Guelke, and Stephen, *A Farewell to Arms?*, 367–76.

85. Blair, *A Journey*, 158.

86. See Cathal McCall, *Identity in Northern Ireland: Communities, Politics and Change* (Basingstroke: Macmillan, 1999).

87. David E. Schmitt, "The US War on Terrorism and Its Impact on the Politics of Accommodation in Northern Ireland," in *Global Change, Civil Society and the Northern Ireland Peace Process: Implementing the Political Settlement*, ed. Christopher Farrington (New York: Palgrave Macmillan, 2008), 54–72.

88. For the role of political discourse in the context of the peace process in Northern Ireland, see Katy Hayward and Catherine O'Donnell, *Political Discourse and Conflict Resolution: Debating Peace in Northern Ireland* (London: Routledge, 2011), and Katy Hayward, "Convergence/Divergence: Party Political Discourse in Northern Ireland's Transition from Conflict," *Dynamics of Asymmetric Conflict* 4 (3) (2011): 196–213.

89. Powell, *Great Hatred, Little Room*, 309–10.

90. See Paul Arthur, "'Quiet Diplomacy and Personal Conversation': Track Two Diplomacy and the Search for a Settlement in Northern Ireland," in *After the Good Friday Agreement: Analysing Political Change in Northern Ireland*, ed. Joseph Ruane and Jennifer Todd (Dublin: University College Dublin Press, 1999), 71–95; Diana Chigas, "Negotiating Intractable Conflicts: The Contributions of Unofficial Intermediaries," in Crocker, Hampson, and Aall, *Grasping the Nettle*, 123–58; Niall Ó Dochartaigh, "The Role of Intermediary in Back-Channel Negotiation: Evidence from the Brendan Duddy Papers," *Dynamics of Asymmetric Conflict* 4 (3) (2011): 214–25; and Harold H. Saunders, *A Public Peace: Sustained Dialogue to Transform Racial and Ethnic Conflicts* (New York: St. Martin's, 1999). The effectiveness of these private intermediary efforts is enhanced when they support existing efforts by state actors to promote peace. See Tobias Böhmelt, "The Effectiveness of Tracks of Diplomacy Strategies in Third-Party Interventions," *Journal of Peace Research* 47 (2) (2010): 167–78.

91. See Suzanne Werner and Amy Yuen, "Making and Keeping Peace," *International Organization* 59 (2) (2005): 261–92.

92. Anderson, "Partition, Consociation, Border-Crossing," 85–104. The need to go beyond partition as a means to end civil wars is supported in Nicholas Sambanis and Jonah Schulhofer-Wohl, "What's in a Line? Is Partition a Solution to Civil War?," *International Security* 34 (2) (2009): 82–118.

93. Martin Mansergh, comments made at the seminar "Lessons Learned from the Northern Ireland Peace Process," sponsored by Xavier University and held at Bansha Castle, Bansha, Co. Tipperary, June 18, 2010. This same argument was also made by Jonathan Powell in *Great Hatred, Little Room*, 4, and Seán Ó hUiginn in comments made at the Brendan Duddy Archive Symposium held on November 22, 2011, at the National University of Ireland, Galway.

2   "Look at Northern Ireland"

Lessons Best Learned at Home

WILLIAM A. HAZLETON

> When I go now to other troubled places I point to you [Northern Ireland] as proof that peace is not an idle daydream, for you peace is real, and it resonates around the world. . . . Now when I meet Palestinians and Israelis, I can say, don't tell me it's impossible, look at Northern Ireland. . . . When I hear what the Indians and Pakistanis say about each other over their religious differences, I say, don't tell me you can't work this out, look at Northern Ireland. . . . Your work is the world's work. And everywhere in every corner there are people who long to believe in our better selves, who want to be able to say for the rest of their lives, in the face of any act of madness born of hatred over religious, or racial, or ethnic or tribal differences—they want to be able to shake their fists in defiance and say, do not tell me it has to be this way, look at Northern Ireland.
>
> President Bill Clinton

Like other peace processes that are widely regarded as "successful," Northern Ireland is frequently cited as a worthy example for peacemaking in other parts of the world. For as John Darby has pointed out, there is considerable "borrowing and lending" among peace processes owing to the many constructive insights that can be gleaned from their varied experiences.[1] Without questioning the value and usefulness of specific strategies, procedural mechanisms, and institutional arrangements that have been employed in Northern Ireland, there is a danger of placing too much emphasis on precedents, models, and similarities with other conflicts, in that conspicuous patterns and wide-ranging observations often neglect important contextual differences and pronounced discontinuities that will affect desired outcomes. When the literature speaks of "lessons," they likely refer to ameliorative prescriptions that individuals, far removed from the day-to-day consequences, wish to teach, rather than the lessons that participants on the ground may have learned, albeit in a more particularistic fashion, from what transpired around them. The complex and contested origins of the Northern Ireland conflict, with its many twists and turns over thirty-plus years, created a Rubik's Cube of competing grievances, interests, and aspirations that was reflected in the wide-ranging interpretations of its fundamental causes and how to accurately address them.[2] The same dilemma applies to assessing the outcome and relevance of the Northern Ireland peace process; that is, one's basic understanding of events surrounding the Agreement, and quite possibly one's own place within those developments, ensures multiple interpretations and explanations, along with different, and at times totally incompatible, conclusions. Like previous accounts of the conflict, there are aspects of the peace process that remain unknown or largely obscure to participants and analysts, in addition to those developments for which they had little sympathy and thus are likely to dismiss or ignore. Under such conditions, deriving universally accepted lessons or a coherent transferable model from Northern Ireland's experience becomes unrealistic, if not immaterial.[3] Simply put, different actors, as well as analysts of the peace process, have come away from Northern Ireland with varied lessons. This is not to say, however, that examining what transpired in Northern Ireland has little or no real value. As a case, it contains many of the classic features and seemingly insurmountable obstacles found in ethnonational conflicts; an extensive array of conflict management approaches were employed over the years; and despite disappointments and setbacks in its implementation, the Agreement marks a considerable accomplishment, with the prospect of conflict resolution rarely found in similar postconflict situations. Given the polemics and vagaries encountered in analyzing Northern Ireland's peace process, this chapter charts a cautionary course where lessons are not seen as imparting explicit answers or stock solutions but rather assisting participants and analysts to ask more informed and probing questions about what possibly can and should be done to bring peace to other conflict situations.

Why Look at Northern Ireland?
Interpretations and Expectation

In the early years following the 1998 Good Friday Agreement, the Northern Ireland peace process was held up as a model for conflict resolution in many parts of the world. The Northern Ireland Assembly welcomed delegations from places like Sri Lanka, Burundi, and Iraq, and several of its members attended peace conferences or served as external advisers or facilitators. Of the political parties, Sinn Féin has been the most active in terms of peace outreach, most notably with Deputy First Minister Martin McGuinness joining South African counterparts in discussions with Iraqi politicians in Finland and later participating, alongside members of the Alliance and Ulster Unionist parties, in a dialogue of national reconciliation in Baghdad.[4] Likewise, Sinn Féin president Gerry Adams has had a visible presence in ending the armed campaign of ETA, the Basque separatist group.[5] Even, Ian Paisley Jr. MP, whose Democratic Unionist Party (DUP) boycotted the negotiations leading up to the Agreement, accepted an invitation to be a mediator in Guinea-Bissau's peace and reconciliation process by expressing his intentions to apply "the Northern Ireland experience" in an African context.[6] Permanent institutions and hands-on programs have also been created or planned. In 2007 the Irish government launched a Conflict Resolution Unit in the Department of Foreign Affairs to build, in part, on its role in the peace process and share the lessons of Northern Ireland. In 2012 European funding was secured for constructing a conflict resolution center at the former Maze prison site, outside Belfast, which will provide educational and research facilities, exhibition space, and an archive as well as offer a place for visitors to exchange views on conflict transformation. These visits, exchanges, and the promotion of peaceful settlement are just a sample of what has been done to provide, in the words of former Irish foreign minister and taoiseach Brian Cowen, "a ray of hope to those who find themselves in seemingly hopeless situations."[7]

Speaking less than a month after the deadly 1998 Omagh bombing, President Clinton employed "look at Northern Ireland" as a rallying cry to reassure his audience that the Agreement popularly endorsed in the July referendum would not only survive but also serve to inspire others to turn away from hatred and violence. Northern Ireland was a success story, the people of Northern Ireland had achieved something great, and despite Omagh, their peace journey was worth emulating. In a larger sense

Clinton's inspiring remarks reflected America's characteristic optimism in a better future, its pragmatic spirit and faith in human progress, and its deep-seated belief in universal understanding and conflict transformation. These traits were seen in George Mitchell, Clinton's special envoy to Northern Ireland, who confided to a colleague while later working on the Israeli-Palestinian question that he believed "any conflict created by human beings could be resolved by them."[8] In 2009 Secretary of State Hillary Clinton reiterated her husband's optimistic message, telling the Stormont press corps how she had seen firsthand Northern Ireland "become a model for conflict resolution and reconciliation," and that "people who are determined to choose peace and progress over violence and division look toward you."[9] Models, and the lessons that accompany them, are alluring because they normally promise a fresh perspective, a desired escape from the past, a possible way out, and assurances of a better future. However, narratives charting inevitable progress commonly glance over the unpleasant realities of the here and now, offering instead a bold compass that points from where you have been to where you desire to go, managing to obscure how difficult the roadmap will be to read once the journey has begun.

Lessons, analogies, metaphors, and historical examples supply comfort and advocacy in making decisions.[10] On the one hand, they offer reassurance, reinforcement, and a way to tackle the unpredictability of the future. On the other hand, they instill a sense of empowerment, impart a direction to follow, or warn of paths better avoided. For the Clintons and many others, Northern Ireland became something of a missionary endeavor, that is, the desire to achieve good out of the suffering of others through the teaching of a story of redemption and transformation. Moreover, the peace process came with a convenient tool kit where one could unpack helpful procedures, interventions, confidence-building mechanisms, structural arrangements, and negotiating techniques and venues, all certified as tried and true. For many academics and commentators, "lessons" convey added weight to their interpretations of key events and credibility for their conclusions. Or from a more cynical perspective, lessons and analogies can be highly self-serving, providing powerful justifications for particular decisions and actions or, after the fact, claiming vindication, apportioning blame, or settling old scores. In short, lessons help stake out a position.

In the case of Northern Ireland, a dominant narrative has emerged that advocates an inclusive approach to peacemaking, an Irish "model," a key element of which is "talking with terrorists" without preconditions.[11] Such sweeping narratives, whose lessons may be "superficial and glib," can nevertheless become "hegemonic" and, in the eyes of critics, embody perceived truths that elicit unconditional acceptance, amounting to convenient folklore.[12] Here lessons become a type of shorthand, all-inclusive explanations, self-evident without need for elaboration or justification, for instance "lessons learned the hard way," which can be effortlessly invoked in discussing multiple conflict situations. Hegemonic narratives, like the liberal peace, can be quite comforting, for as John Gray observed: "When you're inside a myth it looks like fact, and for those who were inside the myth of the end of history it seems to have given a kind of peace of mind."[13] In constructing their narratives different actors in the peace process, mindful of the sensibilities of wider audiences, carefully cleanse those things we may not wish to know or shroud paths that we would prefer not to take. Mistakes were made, yes, and unfortunate, abhorrent things did happen for whatever reason; yet for a compelling narrative they are best forgotten and written out in an act of collective amnesia.[14]

Why, then, look at Northern Ireland's experience? An obvious reason is its successful outcome. While skeptics and dissidents challenge this conclusion, Northern Ireland constitutes a rare case where participants in a seemingly intractable conflict did reach an accord. Its lessons therefore are retrospective, looking back not only to identify what happened but also to interpret when, why, and how crucial events unfolded. The tendency has been to presume that over the course of events the participants learned the requisite skills, acquired the appropriate tools, and found the motivation to achieve peace, all of which is validated by Northern Ireland's success. Yet, even when the threshold for what constitutes "a lesson" appears to have been set fairly low, the results are assumed to represent answers that have transferable value. Rushing to judgment so that others are spared from repeating Northern Ireland's mistakes risks failing to understand that history's lessons "are rarely unambiguous."[15] Rather than divulging lessons that provide answers, history lends itself, to quote Sinn Féin press spokesman Danny Morrison, to "war but by other means."[16] Or as the noted Irish historian Joe Lee writes: "The appeal to history has nothing to do with a search for historical truth, and everything to do with the use of history as a weapon in the power struggles of the present."[17] This is not to say that little of value can be gained from assessing competing narratives of Northern Ireland's peace process but rather to be cognizant of the polemics and a priori solutions that may distort our understanding of how and why the historic Agreement was reached and eventually put into place.

Northern Ireland in the Wider World:
Comparisons and Borrowing

Over the last several decades Northern Ireland's experience has been the subject of numerous comparisons, ranging from scholarly publications and official reports to casual observations. A sampling of these include conflict situations in Bosnia-Herzegovina, the Basque Country, Corsica, Cyprus, Guatemala, Kashmir, the Middle East, South Africa, and Sri Lanka. While academic and journalistic accounts seek to draw contrasts between the similarities and differences involved, the presumption is that Northern Ireland and the entity or entities in question obviously share something in common; otherwise, making the comparison would be rather pointless. More importantly, from a practical perspective, several characteristics of these comparisons tend to stand out. The first, noted by Fred Halliday, is that "comparison is often more easily made from outside," that is, looking, for example, to Northern Ireland for "inspiration" or "in sympathy," or "for support" of a strategy or position.[18] A second, obviously related characteristic of comparisons is their use for polemical purposes, with comparisons and analogies serving as imprimaturs to enhance the credibility of an argument or validity of a contemplated action.[19] Last, comparisons often highlight trends and thus, implicitly or explicitly, impart predictions concerning future political developments. However, just as *likeness* should not be mistaken for *likelihood*,[20] Adrian Guelke cautions, "*identifying* a trend is not the same thing as *explaining* it."[21] To have salience in a particular setting, the forces that produced the trend must be dissected and analyzed to determine not only if they exist but also in a larger sense whether they would persist. Thus, despite perceived similarities between Northern Ireland and other conflict situations, most comparisons and analogies fall short of the mark, leaving their applicability and potential feasibility much to one's imagination when it comes to concrete application.

In an age of increased globalization, where intervention by outside third parties has gained increased currency, to ignore international trends and/or localize disputes may appear unfashionably provincial and totally misguided, especially among experts and elites. Not surprisingly then, individuals such as Jonathan Powell, Downing Street chief of staff, who served as Blair's point person on Northern Ireland, usually begin with the caveat that "Northern Ireland is of course *sui generis*," and that "facile parallels can be misleading," before drawing parallels and humbly tendering lessons for conflicts elsewhere, "so that they can make their own mistakes rather than repeating ours."[22] But even though Northern Ireland's *sui generis* generally warrants mention, along with examples of its exceptionalism, its relevance in the area of peace and conflict resolution is firmly rooted in its likeness, interconnectedness, and lessons learned for a wider world.

The differences in the Northern Ireland case, however, can be surprisingly stark. For example, the conflict did not occasion the collapse of the state, thus allowing for the continuation of rule of law and administrative functions and services; Northern Ireland remained part of a larger and stable liberal democracy; it was in a desirable neighborhood, part of a relatively wealthy postindustrial country inside the European Community and the European Union; despite its contested sovereignty, the immediate neighbors on the whole proved supportive; the violence itself was eventually contained, with a comparatively low casualty rate; and post-Agreement spoiler attacks have been largely restrained.[23] Obviously, Northern Ireland was not a failed or collapsed state, like Sudan or Somalia, nor did it endure ethnic violence on the scale of Rwanda, Bosnia, or Iraq. In Northern Ireland, external involvement by Dublin and London proved highly beneficial; in Cyprus and Kashmir external involvement led to war. Not all comparisons are as extreme, but in relation to other civil wars and ethnic conflicts of the period, conditions in Northern Ireland were far more favorable for reaching a peace accord.

Comparisons tend to highlight categories of similarities; for example, real and potential causes of ethnic conflict. These could include: contested sovereignty, political discrimination, government repression, human rights abuse, the absence of protection for minorities, cultural hegemony, and a host of socioeconomic grievances. While some could be identified as contributors to any conflict like that in Northern Ireland, there are still notable contextual differences that necessarily explain when and what drove people to violence. Taking this view, that understanding the local context is critical, English states: "The emergent Provisional IRA was very firmly rooted in the lives lived in the experience of particular streets, and only the disaggregation of terrorism into such localities will allow us to explain it. If this was a story with many actors—British and Irish states which had failed to appeal to their respective nationalist and unionist minorities; civil rights activists who had prompted divisive turbulence; loyalist aggression born of insecurity and threat; police and governmental failures of response when the crisis arose; military heavy-handedness from the British Army, and serious violence from the IRA: all were involved—

then it is also a tale which makes sense only in its intimately hostile Ulster locality."[24] While this argument may be dismissed as naively parochial or the product of fatalistic imaginations that "their" conflict is unique, the explanatory value of local context brings into question the appropriateness and value of broad cross-comparisons as well as the transferability of specific lessons.

While Northern Ireland was not isolated from or entirely immune to conflict transformation strategies and international geopolitical developments, their influence was most often indirect, and their promotion and/or application was typically elite driven. In the peace process, borrowing mainly came in the form of ideas or approaches, along with the requisite terminology, technical expertise, and mechanisms to facilitate the process, and was frequently accompanied by external mediators and observers to guide, counsel, and instill confidence and assurance. For example, as in other post-conflict situations, Northern Ireland needed ways to sort out the status of former combatants and their weapons, raising the issue of prisoner releases, the decommissioning of weapons, the demobilization of paramilitary groups, and their reintegration into society. Although much had previously been accomplished in these areas, when Northern Ireland took up similar measures, Rolston notes that their implementation demonstrated a profound lack of *political will*, which had been the chief criterion for successful disarmament, demobilization, and reintegration (DDR) programs around the world.[25]

In meetings with foreign delegations and experts, much attention was paid to facilitating the negotiating process, and Northern Ireland's parties did adopt, as one of the ground rules for the talks, the idea of *sufficient consensus* that the South Africans had devised to prevent smaller parties from having a potential veto over the progress of negotiations. Though generally endorsed as helpful, David Trimble, head of the Ulster Unionist Party, found *sufficient consensus* critical to his negotiating strategy of reaching a deal with the Social Democratic and Labour Party, the majority nationalist party, without necessarily risking a republican veto or having to directly engage with Sinn Féin.[26] Among those lending expertise, advice, and guidance, the contribution of particular individuals, like former US Senator George Mitchell, Finland's former prime minister, Harri Holkeri, and Canadian General John de Chastelain, stood out, in no small measure, because of their seemingly infinite patience and perseverance.

The borrowing, therefore, was confined mainly to mechanical or procedural issues, but there were exceptions, the most notable of which was Sinn Féin's relationship with the African National Congress (ANC) and the end of apartheid in South Africa. Guelke contends that comparisons with South Africa and to a lesser extent with Israel/Palestine by the republican movement are "a rare instance of an analogy (or perhaps analogies) that has exercised an influence on the course of events."[27] A new generation of republicans, led by Gerry Adams and Martin McGuinness, had begun to internationalize Sinn Féin's image as a party of national liberation engaged in an anticolonial struggle, but in the wake of the Cold War, the strategy of the ANC and Palestine Liberation Organization (PLO) shifted toward conflict resolution, which, according to Martyn Frampton, carried "both 'push' and 'pull' implications for the republican leadership."[28] On the one hand, it made the continuation of the IRA's armed struggle harder to justify outside republican ranks, and on the other hand, the acceptance by other revolutionary groups of a conflict resolution paradigm added credence to those contemplating an end to the armed campaign. However, Frampton adds the important caveat that "whereas events beyond Ireland's shores created an 'enabling movement' for the decision to halt the IRA's campaign, the direct roots of that decision were internal to the island, and, indeed, the republican movement itself."[29]

The republican leadership would later call on the ANC to lend legitimacy to endorsing the Agreement by asking its representatives to persuade Sinn Féin members to approve the accord, and a South African delegation went into the Maze prison to convince republican prisoners of the benefits that peace would bestow.[30] Thus, while external factors may have broadly influenced republican thinking, they were most apparent on select occasions and invariably used to buttress and legitimize decisions made by the leadership. More recently, interviews with former republican prisoners have underscored the elite-driven nature of these comparisons and affiliations. While incarceration admittedly restricted their access to information, few prisoners saw a connection between the peace process and "far-reaching global changes," and there was only a slight increase in those making a connection between Ireland's peace process and those in other corners of the world. The authors conclude: "Although the republican leadership may have made such connections, for most prisoners endogenous, parochial and community-oriented explanations of the process were more important than exogenous factors."[31]

From another perspective, Roger Mac Ginty holds up a mirror to the United Kingdom's liberal internationalist policies and goals in Afghanistan and Iraq and contrasts them to those it pursued in Northern Ireland.

The result for Northern Ireland was what he terms *liberal-peace-lite*, "a generous and largely consensual form of peacemaking based on negotiation, electoral endorsement and a good dose of Keynesianism."[32] It was a hybrid model, created in large part for pragmatic considerations that demanded compromises and concessions on liberal ideals that were found unachievable; nevertheless, British officials have appeared neither capable nor willing to draw from their own experience in Ulster in dealing with Afghanistan or Iraq.[33] While British actions may smack of hypocrisy, they also raise broader questions about not just what is borrowed and its relevance but also about the feasibility of replicating lessons learned from one context to another.

While policy transfer and lesson drawing across political borders have not received the attention they deserve, the general literature does offer several relevant insights.[34] For example, research has found that the export of lessons is less likely to occur through informal actors than formal networks comprised of nongovernmental organizations (NGOs), consulting firms, think tanks, and academics. Moreover, it is helpful to distinguish between policy (or social) learning and instrumental (or tactical) learning, in that the former implies a more coherent transfer of ideas, approaches, institutional arrangements, and practices while the latter is seen primarily as the ad hoc and incremental replication of these items. As for implementation, the approaches, mechanisms, procedures, et cetera, that are transplanted to new locales may produce very different, and even unanticipated, outcomes; to all intents and purposes, they become *indigenized*.[35] Nevertheless, underlying most studies is the optimistic assumption that transfers will result in successful implementation, rather than policy failure.[36] Dolowitz and Marsh, however, point out that this is clearly not always the case, citing problems of insufficient information about conditions in the country from which the policy is transferred (i.e., *uninformed transfer*), or elements vital to the policy's success in the originating country may not be transferred or fully transferable (i.e., *incomplete transfer*), or miscalculating or ignoring the differences between socioeconomic, political, and/or ideological contexts in the recipient and originating country (i.e., *inappropriate transfer*).[37]

Guelke provides a telling example of the inappropriateness of policy transfer in the campaign for creating an equivalent to South Africa's Truth and Reconciliation Commission in Northern Ireland to address the painfully slow process of reconciliation after the Agreement. The idea did enjoy a considerable measure of popular support and won the backing of groups in the voluntary sector. While its rejection was blamed on vociferous opposition from both unionist and nationalist politicians, none of whom were willing to countenance an official history of the Troubles, Guelke identifies several practical considerations that also emerged. For instance, unlike South Africa, many victims had already recounted their stories in the press and other media outlets, and the earlier release of paramilitary prisoners under the Agreement had supplanted the need for a commission to grant amnesty in return for admissions of wrongdoing or guilt. However, the question that most had overlooked was whether the Truth and Reconciliation Commission had been the primary agent in healing South Africa's postapartheid wounds or whether it was something else. Guelke believes the latter, that is, the commission played an important, but supplementary, role to a South African president whose exemplary conduct in office and deep personal commitment advanced genuine reconciliation. What Northern Ireland needed was a Mandela, not a commission.

Despite problems of application and implementation, there is a value in comparisons, as Guelke recognizes in his conclusion: "The South African analogy is helpful in understanding the importance of reconciliation to the peace process and transitions, but it is less helpful as an example of how it can be achieved in the case of Northern Ireland."[38] At the risk of oversimplifying and overgeneralizing, comparisons can and do provide helpful pointers as well as constructive warnings, particularly with regard to major problems and possible avenues for addressing them. In the case of what Northern Ireland borrowed, or has to lend, attention has focused on process, the mechanics of peacemaking, and its lesson-drawing appeal has largely been confined to elites and/or attentive elements of the nongovernmental sector and professional and academic communities. There were international contacts and connections, but their impact was usually indirect and limited. For example, the Provisional IRA saw itself as a national liberation movement, but the connection changed over time and eventually was conveniently dropped. Even though interaction with other national liberation fronts may have been relatively inconsequential, it was the legitimacy that the comparison bestowed on armed struggle, righteousness by association if you will. Comparisons, in a broad sense, can also give comfort, encouragement, and with them, sorely needed optimism. Despite acknowledging their problems and imperfections, Fred Halliday took a certain solace in such comparisons in ruminating: "As ever, Ireland is not alone, or unique, whatever its communities, as well as those who despair of it overcoming its nationalism, may sometimes think."[39]

Looking Back at Lesson Learning

It is conceivable that the emphasis devoted to promoting the lessons that Northern Ireland has to teach has diverted attention away from questioning what is, and is not, known about how it came to learn those lessons in the first place and why. Policy learning reflects a process of cognitive change in which causal relationships and interests are disassembled, reevaluated, and redefined on the basis of new knowledge that has brought into question the ideas and assumptions that underlie the policy and that can possibly affect the content, direction, and/or tactics of the policy in the near future.[40] Studies usually examine this process in a relatively controlled and isolated environment, most commonly a governmental decision-making unit or in some other institutional context.[41] Even then conditions under which learning takes place are hardly ever ideal; rather, decision makers commonly find themselves plagued by uncertainty and overwhelmed by events, handicapped by deficient or ambiguous information of questionable validity, and subjected to a cacophonous array of interpretations and options. Understandably, this type of learning environment makes the process, or more accurately processes, appear even more confusing and unpredictable when analyzing a political jigsaw puzzle like Northern Ireland. Policy "learning" is frequently described as a fundamental rethink of the core ideas and beliefs that had previously determined the choice of ends and means, often triggered by a traumatic event or drastic change in the policy environment. For example, Frampton asserts that fundamental shifts in the international political arena as well as within British politics during the early 1990s created an atmosphere in which the "IRA's armed campaign could be contemplated afresh" and that one event in particular, Margaret Thatcher's departure from the premiership, "was an important precursor to the new fluidity that entered republican thinking thereafter."[42]

Another form of learning, "adaptation," involves the reconsideration of ends-means relationships but does not directly question the policy's ends. Adaptation, sometimes associated with the notion of muddling through, tends to produce sporadic and incremental changes in the policy's approach and/or tactics it employs. Of the two types of learning, adaptation is the more common.[43] For those outside decision-making circles, policy learning can also take place through "introspection," a more unstructured process of evolutionary thinking that is stimulated by changing circumstances, new information, mutual discussion, and reflection. Introspection may spawn new rationales and alternative tactics, but these are assimilated without seriously challenging accepted ideological beliefs and professed ends. Introspective learning is more difficult to detect and chronicle, especially in a context where hostilities appear frozen in time; however, Tonge, Shirlow, and McAuley found that "ideological flexibility and political adaptability were apparent among [republican and loyalist] combatants, even as they prosecuted their 'war,' and at no point was their armed struggle ever static in terms of method or rationale."[44]

Haas refers to lessons as "consensual knowledge," a generally accepted understanding about cause-and-effect linkages that is incorporated into the decision-making process. Consensual knowledge is socially constructed and therefore neither factual nor flawless nor fully complete but rather subject to the vagaries of human interaction, individual idiosyncrasies, and political interests and influence.[45] Consensual knowledge is shared within a particular confine, be it institutionalized or loosely self-identified; rarely, if ever, is it universal. Thus, like too many cooks, Northern Ireland's political fault lines ensured that the participants concentrated primarily on concocting their own recipe for peace. Nor does the acquisition of consensual knowledge, particularly in cases of adaptation, necessarily imply that the learning process will follow a straight line. In a dynamic environment, elements of consensual knowledge will remain contentious and contested, and when confronted by new circumstances, political constraints, and/or implementation failures, ends-means calculations may be swiftly revised or rejected, causing policies to lurch in unanticipated directions. Thus, clichés like "learning from one's mistakes" should be questioned, along with presumptions of some linear trajectory for policy development, as in Séamus Mallon's famous quip that the Agreement was "Sunningdale for slow learners."[46] Consensual knowledge, in Haas's view, "is constantly challenged from within and without and must justify itself by submitting its claims to truth tests considered generally acceptable."[47] In other words, lessons must not only prove their worth but should also be continually subject to "question-asking" and "presumption-probing"—valuable advice for the practitioner as well as the analyst.[48]

One of the problems of lessons, however, is that we tend not to question or probe. Especially when it comes to using comparisons or analogies, decision makers (and analysts) often prefer broad generalities, and with little concern for details of causation, the predictable result is concentrating "more attention to *what* has happened than to *why* it has happened."[49]

Policies perceived as failures are summarily orphaned without investigating whether a better alternative existed or whether another action would possibly have made the situation worse. Likewise, in a successful outcome, Jervis observed, "relatively little attention is paid to the costs of the policy, the possibility that others might have worked even better, or the possibility success was largely attributable to luck and that the policy might just as easily have failed."[50] Consequently, rather than a thoughtful and deliberative process, policy learning (as distinguished from identifying lessons) can at times be a rather superficial, indiscriminate, and hasty process, where the end result, consensual knowledge, is justified through post hoc reasoning.[51]

Lessons imply a relationship between knowing and acting; that is, consensual knowledge is something that is both useful and useable. This raises questions of relevance, reception, and feasibility in terms of application and implementation. Relevance most often comes into question when a policy is perceived as a mistake, while feasibility is subject to pragmatic considerations that gauge the policy's performance in terms of efficiency and effectiveness. Reception or acceptance, however, involves political calculations of whose interest is served and measured in real time. For instance, in weighing the contribution of external actors to the Agreement, Tannam concluded that the general receptiveness of Northern Irish policy makers to external influences and their ability to incorporate them into policies was "a necessary factor in allowing policy change to occur."[52] In the early 1990s the loyalist Ulster Volunteer Force (UVF) became a willing partner in this process by reaching out to Dublin and Washington because, as its chief negotiator David Ervine later confessed, "we [UVF] did not fully understand the game," so "the UVF forced its way in . . . to take part in the game." After Gerry Adams received his visa from the Clinton administration, Ervine and his politically astute cohorts saw it not as a setback but as an opening to be seized. For an American visa, according to Ervine, bestowed an element of legitimacy, "which fuelled the belief in Adam's constituency that what he was advocating was of value. And it wasn't dissimilar for Loyalism." As a result, the UVF's political wing immediately set out to get theirs.[53]

Knowing that consensual knowledge may fail to attract sufficient acceptance creates a lesson in its own right. For example, the former deputy leader of the Ulster Unionist Party, John Taylor, who had been a member of the last Stormont government, defended his party's response to the civil rights campaign at the start of the Troubles by saying: "In politics sometimes the logical thing is not necessarily what the people will allow you to do. And in Northern Ireland such are the intense feelings and deep-seated fears that what an outside observer might consider logical is not the kind of thing you can deliver politically. And that we must always take into account."[54] Accepted understandings about cause-and-effect relationships remain highly conditional as new opportunities arise and others are lost, causing decision makers to search for alternative ways of coping with ambiguity and uncertainty. For example, years later, David Trimble recalled his impatience during the negotiating rounds before Good Friday: "Our problem, as is sometimes the case with unionists, was that we were very clear about what we did not want, but not so clear about how to achieve what we wanted."[55] His dilemma was not unique. Gerry Adams was even more succinct: "I have learnt that the toughest negotiation is with your own side. It isn't with your opponents."[56]

The frustration echoed by Trimble and Adams reflects their multiple roles as political leaders. They and others had to operate in different contexts (or at different levels) and appeal to different audiences simultaneously.[57] At particular stages of the peace process certain roles would necessarily become a priority. But with the exception of paramilitary organizations, the levels and venues were hard to separate or keep self-contained, which meant that whatever was said or done at one level might, and often did, affect, diverge from, or even contradict what was being pursued in another. For example, John Major and Bertie Ahern had to be mindful of the concerns of their parliamentary parties. In Major's case, establishing a political dialogue with Sinn Féin required great caution if the defection of Unionist and Conservative backbenchers at Westminster was to be prevented.[58] Meanwhile, Ahern's challenge in the Dáil was to keep his party, Fianna Fáil, informed and on board regarding possible revisions to Articles 2 and 3 of the Irish Constitution.[59] Gerry Adams, in proceeding along the negotiation path, assuaged the doubts of hard-liners in the IRA with assurances that "if the process failed, then war would and could resume."[60] Whereas, Sinn Féin's entry into the talks, after the IRA's ceasefire, caused David Trimble to undertake a two-month consultation exercise with his party as well as the grassroots "in order to inform them and change the whole public atmosphere," so that his base "felt comfortable" with the Ulster Unionists taking their place at the table.[61] In short, Northern Ireland's political leaders had responsibilities to protect the interests of their constituents—to engage with opponents in securing a deal, to reassure and deliver their constituents if a deal was agreed—and, one could argue, responsibilities to the broader community in bringing about peace.[62] This is no easy feat when all of these roles had to be performed more or less in tandem.

The need to manage these incompatibilities and contradictions reminds one that peace processes are neither solely top down nor exclusively elite driven. Ironically, parties with the greatest weight, like the British government in Northern Ireland, may find their ability to maneuver highly constrained because of the need to address so many audiences, in this case both external and internal, and take into account their disparate interests, opposing preferences, and divergent expectations.[63] McGrattan, for example, contends that given the situation on the ground after the collapse of the power-sharing Sunningdale Agreement in 1974, the dilemma facing the Wilson government was "what to do that would not make the situation any worse."[64] Another example was the widely criticized foot dragging of unionist leaders during the laborious twenty-one-month talks process, with Trimble often portrayed as irresolute and weak despite having to convince a party that was increasingly skeptical and nervous. One of the guidelines for peacemakers, put forward by Darby and Mac Ginty, states that "the primary function of leaders is to deliver their own people. Assisting their opponents in the process is secondary."[65] However, in this case, the problem was not Trimble's alone to solve, as Jonathan Powell later conceded: "This zero-sum game dogged us right through the negotiations and we only finally got to a settlement when the Republicans realised they had to think about the constituency on the other side as well as their own and participate in selling the agreement to that other constituency."[66] The intersections between various levels and venues, plus the interaction occasioned by multiple roles, meant not only that political leaders could be challenged and constrained but also that it was within the province of their fickle constituents to ignore, subvert, renegotiate, or amend the consensual knowledge upon which the policies and actions of party elites were based.[67]

Policy learning, then, implies a retrospective process of reevaluation and adjustment to new circumstances. It does not specify what ought to be learned, nor in most cases does it involve jettisoning or seriously questioning ideological beliefs that inspire the policy's end goal. Rather, it usually takes the form of a corrective action that entails a reexamination of means and purpose in search of more beneficial and/or effective alternatives, as the following description of Sinn Féin's political strategy indicates: "The pragmatism of the Adams–McGuinness leadership stems from a capacity to: make realistic appraisal of the situation facing the republican movement;

evaluate the movement's ability to achieve its objectives on that basis; and to act accordingly. Where those objectives have appeared unattainable, the leadership has altered course and embraced a new approach. . . . The leadership's pragmatism, therefore, does not reflect any eagerness to discard its underlying commitment to the key republican objective of Irish unity. On the contrary, on that fundamental issue the central figures of the leadership are avowed ideologues."[68] Thus, there were conspicuous elements of continuity during the Northern Ireland conflict, even though events on the ground constantly changed. Only a few policy initiatives marked shifts of historic proportions, while the vast majority constituted a maze of twists and turns as policy makers, their constituent groups, and public opinion reassessed their options in light of changing circumstances and attempted to respond by modifying their aims and realigning their strategies and expectations. For an outsider, these changes were frequently difficult to comprehend, let alone accurately predict until well after the fact, which means in terms of policy transfer, that Northern Ireland's peace process would be nigh on impossible to replicate.

Asking Questions and Probing Presumptions

Scholars studying the Northern Ireland peace process have, and rightly should, take up Neustadt and May's advice to practitioners when it comes to employing analogies and lessons of history, that is, question and probe what was done, scrutinize how and why that particular policy was selected, and, given the circumstances, ask if it could have been done any better.[69] The peace process was highly complex, multilayered with participants performing multiple roles, and never stood still. Like fragments of a mosaic where some pieces get distorted or misplaced and others eventually turn up or fall into place, what happened in Northern Ireland will never comprise a complete picture. If analysts and commentators are tempted to straighten out the mess or push ahead with an outcome specifically in mind, they run the risk of filling in the blank spaces or presuming that everything was just so. Consequently, like conventional wisdom, dominant narratives and the lessons they impart deserve an unconventional degree of scrutiny, so that possible half-truths, omissions, and misinterpretations can be filtered out and a fuller appreciation for what happened realized. There is much to be learned from the Northern Ireland case—perhaps not obvious lessons in the form of answers that can fill the pages of peacemaking manuals or conflict mediation guides, but highly instructive lessons in formulating better-informed questions to ask in seeking to bring peace to other conflict situations.

In learning about peace processes, Northern Ireland has a unique advantage. Outside the Middle East, and possibly South Africa, there is probably no other localized conflict that has received as much attention or been chronicled and documented to the extent of Northern Ireland. Innumerable memoirs and behind-the-scenes accounts fill library shelves; journalists and commentators have left an impressive record in press cuttings and television footage; and academic works on the subject appear on countless resumes. The conflict and resulting peace process has also generated periodicals, like *Fortnight*,[70] thousands of reports, political pamphlets and handbills, party manifestos, posters, and photographs, plus a fascinating array of ephemera ranging from miniscule messages smuggled out of prison to commemorative chess sets and Christmas cards. At the Linen Hall Library in Belfast, the Northern Ireland Political Collection has amassed over a quarter of a million items since 1969.[71] Other important collections are maintained at Boston College, which has documents detailing paramilitary decommissioning and the Belfast Project oral histories of republican and loyalist combatants, and at the National University of Ireland, Galway, which recently acquired the papers of Brendan Duddy, who facilitated secret contacts between the IRA and the British government from 1975 to 1993. The treasure trove of material on Northern Ireland promises to become richer through the annual release of the British and Irish state papers covering the period.

These accounts and the events they portray are not without problems, however. Much of the material was contemporary, "instant history" that was recorded "more or less in real time," and according to Mac Ginty, "The implication of this instant—or perhaps premature—history of the peace process is that it may be at risk of drawing lessons from an inaccurate account of the peace process."[72] More documents, such as intelligence reports, have yet to be released, and some accounts are no doubt lost or remain shrouded in secrecy or references and information concealed or removed. Consequently, Ó Dochartaigh, who has used the Duddy collection on back-channel negotiations, warns of a continuing struggle to dictate the peace narrative and cautions: "All of these accounts and records and interviews must be analysed as interpretations seeking to shape perceptions rather than as transparent evidence, as accounts situated in, and shaped by, a particular time and political context."[73] Under such conditions, where parts of the puzzle are unclear, coded, or missing, the analyst as well as the practitioner would be remiss to take the presumed for known.[74]

While scholars and practitioners confront some of the same constraints and concerns, those researching the peace process have a different perspective from those on the ground. This is due in large measure to the fact that analysts start at the end, or more accurately a specific point in the peace process, and essentially work backward and employ a theoretical framework, specific rationale, and condensed timeframe that gives coherence and clarity to their findings. Assumptions of bounded or procedural rationality frequently lead analysts to identify the problem that is being addressed in terms of the outcome, that is, the dominant inference pattern presumes that the actions taken were designed to ameliorate a particular situation, whereas the practitioners' perception of "the problem" may have been incomplete, imprecise, or ambiguous or may have undergone a metamorphosis over time.[75] Scholars may be too quick to discard alternatives that practitioners considered but did not pursue or too prone to unconditionally accept those that they did adopt where another could possibly have been better. By necessity analysts assess the interests, motivations, and intentions of decision makers in light of their actions. However, they have the advantage of doing so ex post facto, unlike practitioners, who can neither escape the urgency and risk involved nor avoid the frustration of having to comprehend, influence, and communicate with those "at the other side of the hill."[76]

In tackling a peace process as long and complicated as that in Northern Ireland, scholars have dissected it into manageable pieces that concentrate on specific actors (e.g., elites, governments, parties, movements, etc.), relationships between select participants, episodic or single events, or discrete issue areas. Yet, to analyze these pieces as if they were removed from the larger conflict, or somehow self-contained, ignores another reality facing practitioners: that each piece remains part of a complex puzzle and therefore is potentially affected by how other pieces have and will play out. Some analysts have used Northern Ireland as a case study for testing conflict resolution theory. The results, according to O'Kane, have been "rather mixed," but "whether this is due to the unsuitability of the theory to the case, a lack of application thus far or the uniqueness of the conflict remains to be seen."[77] Bew is more blunt. "Northern Ireland has been either oversimplified or over-conceptualized in a way that fails to acknowledge the ragged edges of real historical experience."[78]

Without denying that the peace process was, to a significant degree, elite driven, the contribution of key actors can be overstated. The lessons learned in memoirs and personal accounts of the talks are sometimes more revealing of the authors' self-perception than in offering guidance to those in similar situations. For example, at crucial junctures of the peace talks, Blair believed that his effectiveness was enhanced by his "capacity for absorbing abuse"[79] (surely he was not alone), while his secretary of state for Northern Ireland, Mo Mowlam, learned to go with her instincts: "Sometimes there is nothing else to guide you."[80] A common theme, echoed in Jonathan Powell's "bicycle theory,"[81] was the need to keep negotiations moving ahead through procedural dexterity and innovation, frequently referred to as "constructive ambiguity."[82] Armed with a cluttered tool box lacking much specificity and of questionable practical utility, the three British participants resorted to stressing the need to develop interpersonal relations, gain trust, exercise flexibility, make accommodations, grant concessions, and above all else, demonstrate dogged stick-to-itiveness.[83] From an elite perspective, at least within Blair's immediate circle, the apparent lesson is that intelligent people, with the appropriate skills and right attitude, can bring peace to troubled regions when they want to; however, it also reveals how far removed elites might be from the face of conflict, operating as it were in a bubble, and their lack of appreciation of previous efforts that, while not deemed successful, had helped advance the peace process.

There are other, and far better, ways to learn from Northern Ireland's experience that incorporate not only the complexity of the peace process but also capture the inconsistencies, perplexity, and uncertainty that enveloped participants and events. It requires digging down through the layers and probing deeper into what has become generally known and presumed about Northern Ireland's peace process and testing it in light of new information as it becomes available. Since the Agreement, several of Northern Ireland's popularly accepted truths have been subjected to increased scrutiny. Some conveniently forgotten or deliberately distorted elements of the conflict have been brought into sharper focus, and standard interpretations are increasingly debated and reassessed. This question asking has produced snippets of new consensual knowledge, but more importantly, it has also stimulated more thoughtful and probing questions. The following are but a few examples of the areas of inquiry that the Northern Ireland peace process has generated, which may aid others in framing their strategy and objectives in moving toward peace: In talking with terrorists, how necessary are preconditions, and more importantly, are they desirable if peace negotiations are to be inclusive? How can socio-economic investment and political reform not so much drain the terrorist swamp as give minority communities confidence, and how can their perceived benefits allow terrorists a way out? What constitutes a mutually hurting stalemate, and is a military stalemate a crucial ingredient for negotiating peace? If Northern Ireland's peace was constructed on a very tenuous middle ground, what measures were required to allow the center to hold firm? In the postconflict stage, is the incorporation of more extreme political elements inevitable if peace is to be consolidated? In deeply divided societies, are feasible alternatives to consociational arrangements available, and is it necessarily desirable to prioritize reconciliation over communal security? Pursuing broad questions like these has further advanced our understanding of the Northern Ireland peace process, and with sufficient indigenization, the findings can inform and assist the asking and probing of those seeking to manage or resolve other conflict situations. Northern Ireland's contribution thus becomes a useful laboratory for the kinds of questions that continually need to be asked, not a rough template of what to do. That, others will have to learn for themselves.

Conclusion

Lessons, along with comparisons and analogies, can be seductive, but they are also highly problematic. Lessons can be thinly disguised answers that are not a response to bona fide questions or, no less alarming, promoted without any rigorous questioning. Even though it is possible to find patterns and make comparisons, the underlying reasons for a particular outcome are complex and not reducible to broad generalizations. Nor does the label "lesson," or "likely comparison," guarantee that a policy will win broad acceptance or attain successful application. As English has pointed out, "locally rooted analysis and explanation is crucial" in understanding why violence breaks out and how conflicts can be sustained or brought to an end.[84] Thus, lessons in the form of policy transfers can be mistaken or inappropriate or can instill a false sense of certainty that results in unintended consequences. In reality, peace processes like that in Northern Ireland are a great deal more complicated, and so much more refractory, than we would otherwise wish them to be; yet in the advocacy of lessons, and the presumed comfort they afford, our predilections often govern our understanding and acceptance. A helpful antidote, recommended by Neustadt and May, is to exercise "conservatism in expectation, caution in conduct" when employing lessons or historical analogies.[85]

Unquestionably, many lessons were "learned" and "applied" within the context of Northern Ireland. Key decision makers in political parties, paramilitary organizations, and external governments continuously reevaluated linkages between their objectives and means, at times adopting new policy approaches, abandoning others, or making slight course corrections in light of changing circumstances and new information. For most of the Troubles' thirty-odd years, movement on the ground appeared painfully slow and at best sporadic and incremental, with little in the way of forward progress. The meaning and intentions behind such adjustments were not always apparent, perhaps even to the parties who initiated them, but rather served as tentative, exploratory steps to gauge whether a policy shift might better advance their objectives. There were, however, some truly historic moments, like the 1985 Anglo-Irish Agreement, that created a fundamental change in basic relationships and necessitated that Northern Ireland's political parties rethink, reconstruct, and subsequently realign their policies in light of the new configuration.[86] Be it lesson learning or adaptation, the process never ceased as events, large and small, continually unfolded.

The Agreement's lengthy and contentious implementation has dampened enthusiasm for transferring the Irish model to other parts of the world. O'Kane, Guelke, and Clancy believe that it is still premature to derive lessons from Northern Ireland because the peace process narrative is not complete and more needs to be known.[87] Mac Ginty deems the Northern Ireland experience an "outlier, an atypical peace process," because "consent and inclusion played very significant roles," correspondingly making him skeptical about deriving any wider lessons.[88] Bew, Frampton, and Gurruchaga find no prescriptive lessons to apply elsewhere; nevertheless, they single out several potentially useful factors that shaped the conflict and peaceful resolution efforts.[89] Along similar lines, this chapter has argued that Northern Ireland's experience, while offering no easily identifiable model or guaranteed policy approach, provides considerable insight into the kinds of problems and opportunities to look for in making peace and, in this way, informs others of critical questions that may need to be asked in resolving their own conflict. In looking at Northern Ireland, President Clinton got it right: the Agreement and subsequent transition to normal politics, though not yet complete or universally accepted, does serve as a source of inspiration for others ensnared in conflicts across the globe.

NOTES

The epigraph to this chapter is drawn from President Clinton's remarks to "A Gathering for Peace," [on the Mall in] Armagh, Northern Ireland, September 3, 1998 (The White House, Office of the Press Secretary, 1998).

1. John Darby, "Borrowing and Lending in Peace Processes," in *Contemporary Peacemaking: Conflict, Violence and Peace Processes*, 2nd ed., ed. John Darby and Roger Mac Ginty (New York: Palgrave Macmillan, 2009), 339–51.

2. For well-informed accounts of competing interpretations of the Northern Ireland conflict, see John McGarry and Brendan O'Leary, *Explaining Northern Ireland: Broken Images* (Oxford: Blackwell, 1995); Joseph Ruane and Jennifer Todd, *The Dynamics of Conflict in Northern Ireland: Power, Conflict and Emancipation* (Cambridge: Cambridge University Press, 1996); John Whyte, *Interpreting Northern Ireland* (Oxford: Clarendon Press, 1991); and Frank Wright, *Northern Ireland: A Comparative Analysis* (Dublin: Gill and Macmillan, 1987).

3. Qualifying Northern Ireland's lessons, Anderson states: "The lessons for other conflicts are negative as well as positive, though they may apply only at a rather general or abstract level of underlying structural problems, for every national conflict has its own detailed particularities." See James Anderson, "Partition, Consociation, Border-Crossing: Some Lessons from the National Conflict in Ireland," *Nations and Nationalism* 14 (1) (2008): 85.

4. Tom Hayden, "Northern Ireland, South Africa in Secret Iraq Peace Talks," *The Nation*, September 28, 2007, available at http://www.thenation.com/article/northern-ireland-south-africa-secret-iraq-peace-talks, accessed September 30, 2011, and BBC News, "Iraq Talks Possibly in Ireland," July 7, 2007, available at http://news.bbc.co.uk/gp/pr/fr/-/2/hi/uk_news/northern_ireland/7489785.stm, accessed September 30, 2011.

5. BBC News, "NI Peace Politicians at ETA Conference," October 17, 2011, available at http://www.bbc.co.uk/news/uk-northern-ireland-15331304, accessed October 17, 2011.

6. BBC News, "From Ballymena to Guinea-Bissau," January 10, 2012, available at http://bbc.co.uk/news/uk-northern-ireland-16487406, accessed January 10, 2012.

7. Quoted in Noel Whelan, "Bracing Wine of Reality Continues to Blow in FF's Policy on the North," *Irish Examiner*, October 16, 2003.

8. Aaron David Miller, "The False Religion of the Mideast Peace," *Foreign Policy* 179 (2010): 50–57.

9. Hillary Clinton, "Joint Press Statements with First Minister Robinson and Deputy First Minister McGuinness," Stormont Castle, October 12, 2009, available at http://www.state.gov/secretary/rm/2009a/10/130489.htm, accessed January 21, 2012.

10. Richard E. Neustadt and Ernest May, *Thinking in Time: The Uses of History for Decision-Making* (New York: Free Press, 1986), xii.

11. See Eamonn O'Kane, "Learning from Northern Ireland? The Uses and Abuses of the 'Irish Model,'" *British Journal of Politics and International Relations* 12 (2) (2010): 239–56, and John Bew, "Collective Amnesia and the Northern Ireland Model of Conflict

Resolution," in *The Lessons of Northern Ireland*, ed. Michael Cox (London: LSE IDEAS Special Report 008, November 2011), 16–20.

12. Roger Mac Ginty, "Bad Students Learning the Wrong Lessons?," in Cox, *Lessons of Northern Ireland*, 25–29.

13. John Gray, "A Point of View: The Endless Obsession with What Might Be," *BBC News Magazine*, December 25, 2011, available at http://www.bbc.co.uk/news/magazine-16245250, accessed December 29, 2011.

14. See Bew, "Collective Amnesia and the Northern Ireland Model of Conflict Resolution," 16–20.

15. Ernst B. Haas, *When Knowledge Is Power: Three Models of Change in International Organizations* (Berkeley: University of California Press, 1990), 32.

16. Quote available at http://sluggerotoole.com/2012/01/09/if-history-is-war-by-other-means-is-truth-the-first-casulty/, accessed January 12, 2012.

17. Joe Lee, "Peace and Northern Ireland," in *Re-Imagining Ireland*, ed. Andrew Higgins Wyndham (Charlottesville: University of Virginia Press, 2006), 222.

18. Fred Halliday, "Peace Processes in the Late Twentieth Century: A Mixed Record," in *A Farewell to Arms? From Long War to Long Peace in Northern Ireland*, 2nd ed., ed. Michael Cox, Adrian Guelke, and Fiona Stephen (Manchester: Manchester University Press, 2000), 275.

19. See David Brian Robertson, "Political Conflict and Lesson-Drawing," *Journal of Public Policy* 11 (1) (1991): 55–78.

20. See Neustadt and May, *Thinking in Time*, 57.

21. Adrian Guelke, "Political Comparisons: From Johannesburg to Jerusalem," in Cox, Guelke, and Stephen, *A Farewell to Arms?*, 367–68.

22. Jonathan Powell, "Security Is Not Enough: Ten Lessons for Conflict Resolution in Northern Ireland," in Cox, *The Lessons of Northern Ireland*, 21. See also Jonathan Powell, *Great Hatred, Little Room: Making Peace in Northern Ireland* (London: Bodley Head, 2008), 4–5.

23. See Adrian Guelke, "Lessons of Northern Ireland and the Relevance of the Regional Context," in Cox, *The Lessons of Northern Ireland*, 10, and Mac Ginty, "Bad Students Learning the Wrong Lessons?," 27.

24. Richard English, *Terrorism: How to Respond* (New York: Oxford University Press, 2009), 68.

25. Bill Rolston, "Demobilization and Reintegration of Ex-Combatants: The Irish Case in International Perspective," *Social & Legal Studies* 16 (2) (2007): 274.

26. David Trimble, "Anthony Alcock Memorial Lecture," University of Ulster, April 24, 2007, 4, available at http://www.davidtrimble.org/speeches.htm, accessed October 24, 2011.

27. Adrian Guelke, "Comparatively Peaceful: The Role of Analogy in Northern Ireland's Peace Process," *Cambridge Review of International Affairs* 11 (1) (1997): 34.

28. Martyn Frampton, *The Long March: The Political Strategy of Sinn Féin, 1981–2007* (New York: Palgrave Macmillan, 2009), 81.

29. Ibid., 82.

30. Ibid., 113–14.

31. Peter Shirlow, Jonathan Tonge, James McAuley, and Catherine McGlynn, *Abandoning Historical Conflict? Former Political Prisoners and Reconciliation in Northern Ireland* (Manchester: Manchester University Press, 2010), 100. For an analysis that stresses the relevance of international factors, see chapter 10 of this volume.

32. Mac Ginty, "Bad Students Learning the Wrong Lessons?," 27.

33. See Roger Mac Ginty, "The Liberal Peace at Home and Abroad: Northern Ireland and Liberal Internationalism," *British Journal of Politics and International Relations* 11 (4) (2009): 690–708.

34. Policy transfer refers to "the process by which knowledge about policies, administrative arrangements, institutions and ideas in one political system (past or present) is used in the development of policies, administrative arrangements, institutions and ideas in another political system." David P. Dolowitz and David Marsh, "Learning from Abroad: The Role of Policy Transfer in Contemporary Policy-Making," *Governance* 13 (1) (2000): 5.

35. Diane Stone, "Learning Lessons and Transferring Policy across Time, Space and Disciplines," *Politics* 19 (1) (1999): 56–58.

36. The literature on assessing policy success or failure is also quite limited. Fawcett and Marsh contend that success should be measured in three different categories: process success (i.e., the legitimacy gained through constitutional or quasi-constitutional procedures), programmatic success (i.e., the attainment of intended policy objectives), and political success (i.e., the advancement of the electoral prospects, reputation, and/or governing competence of a political entity). Paul Fawcett and David Marsh, "Policy Transfer and Policy Success: The Case of the Gateway Review Process (2001–10)," *Government and Opposition* 47 (2) (2012): 164–66.

37. Dolowitz and Marsh, "Learning from Abroad," 17.

38. Adrian Guelke, "The Lure of the Miracle? The South African Connection and the Northern Ireland Peace Process," in *Global Change, Civil Society and the Northern Ireland Peace Process*, ed. Christopher Farrington (New York: Palgrave Macmillan 2008), 88–89.

39. Halliday, "Peace Processes in the Late Twentieth Century," 287.

40. See Haas, *When Knowledge Is Power*, 23–24, and Stone, "Learning Lessons and Transferring Policy across Time, Space and Disciplines," 52.

41. For example, see Graham Allison, *Essence of Decision: Explaining the Cuban Missile Crisis* (Boston: Little, Brown, 1971).

42. Frampton, *The Long March*, 79–80.

43. See Haas, *When Knowledge Is Power*, 33–35.

44. Jonathan Tonge, Peter Shirlow, and James McAuley, "So Why Did the Guns Fall Silent? How Interplay, not Stalemate, Explains the Northern Ireland Peace Process," *Irish Political Studies* 26 (1) (2011): 14.

45. Haas, *When Knowledge Is Power*, 20–21.

46. See Cillian McGrattan, "Learning from the Past or Laundering History? Consociational Narratives and State Intervention in Northern Ireland," *British Politics* 5 (1) (2010): 92–113.

47. Haas, *When Knowledge Is Power*, 21.

48. Neustadt and May, *Thinking in Time*, xv.

49. Robert Jervis, *Perception and Misperception in International Politics* (Princeton, NJ: Princeton University Press, 1976), 228.

50. Ibid., 232.

51. Ibid., 228. See also Ernest R. May, *"Lessons" of the Past: The Uses and Misuses of History in American Foreign Policy* (New York: Oxford University Press, 1973), xi.

52. Etain Tannam, "Explaining the Good Friday Agreement: A Learning Process," *Government and Opposition* 36 (4) (2001): 514.

53. Ed Moloney, *Voices from the Grave: Two Men's War in Ireland* (London: Faber and Faber, 2010), 450–51.

54. From an interview in *The Irish Times*, September 27, 1989, in Frank Millar, *Northern Ireland: A Triumph of Politics, Interviews and Analysis, 1988–2008* (Dublin: Irish Academic Press, 2009), 51.

55. Trimble, "Anthony Alcock Memorial Lecture," 7.

56. Quoted in Johann Hari, "Gerry Adams: Unrepentant Irishman," *The Independent*, September 9, 2009.

57. This is referred to as double-edged diplomacy in the literature. See Peter B. Evans, Harold K. Jacobson, and Robert D. Putnam, *Double-Edged Diplomacy: International Bargaining and Domestic Politics* (Berkeley: University of California Press, 1993).

58. John Major, *John Major: The Autobiography* (New York: HarperCollins, 1999), 432.

59. Bertie Ahern, *Bertie Ahern: The Autobiography* (London: Hutchinson, 2009), 213–14.

60. Ed Moloney, "The Peace Process," in Wyndham, *Re-Imagining Ireland*, 212.

61. Trimble, "Anthony Alcock Memorial Lecture," 2.

62. See Cathy Gormley-Heenan, "Abdicated and Assumed Responsibilities: The Multiple Roles of Political Leadership During the Northern Ireland Peace Process," *Civil Wars* 7 (3) (2005): 195–218.

63. For example, Prime Minister Major recalled the period after 1993: "We had to move forward on a wide front, and take account of legitimate interests of all groups, not just one. That was particularly important for the British government as the constitutional authority for Northern Ireland. Other participants—the recognized parties, the Irish government—could take a partial view, as, in an extreme fashion, did the paramilitaries on both sides. We alone had to look at every aspect of the problem, and bear the responsibility for the decisions we took and any mistakes that resulted." See Major, *John Major*, 440–41.

64. McGrattan, "Learning from the Past or Laundering History?," 95.

65. John Darby and Roger Mac Ginty, "Conclusion: Peace Processes, Present and Future," in Darby and MacGinty, *Contemporary Peacemaking*, 365.

66. Powell, "Security Is Not Enough," 24.

67. See Roger Mac Ginty, "Six Observations on the Northern Ireland Peace Process," School of Politics, Queen's University Belfast, June 2008, available at http://st-andrews.academia.edu/RogerMacGinty, accessed January 26, 2012.

68. Frampton, *The Long March*, 188.

69. Neustadt and May, *Thinking in Time*, xiv–xv.

70. *Fortnight* ceased publication after 478 issues, spanning over forty years, in January 2012.

71. See http://www.linenhall.com/northernIrelandPoliticalCollection.asp, accessed January 3, 2012.

72. Mac Ginty, "Bad Students Learning the Wrong Lessons?," 25–26.

73. Niall Ó Dochartaigh, "Together in the Middle: Back-Channel Negotiation in the Irish Peace Process," *Journal of Peace Research* 48 (6) (2011): 771.

74. Neustadt and May, *Thinking in Time*, 56–57.

75. See Allison, *Essence of Decision*.

76. Quote attributed to the Duke of Wellington: "All the business of war, and indeed all the business of life, is to endeavour to find out what you don't know by what you do; that's what I called 'guess what was at the other side of the hill.'"

77. O'Kane, "Learning from Northern Ireland?," 254.

78. Bew, "Collective Amnesia and the Northern Ireland Model of Conflict Resolution," 16.

79. Tony Blair, *A Journey: My Political Life* (New York: Knopf, 2010), 164.

80. Mo Mowlam, *Momentum: The Struggle for Peace, Politics and the People* (London: Hodder & Stoughton, 2002), 331.

81. See Powell, *Great Hatred, Little Room*, 332.

82. For example, see David Mitchell, "Cooking the Fudge: Constructive Ambiguity and the Implementation of the Northern Ireland Agreement," *Irish Political Studies* 24 (3) (2009): 321–36.

83. At certain points Blair admits he "was throwing concessions around like confetti." See Blair, *Journey*, 170.

84. English, *Terrorism*, 90.

85. Neustadt and May, *Thinking in Time*, xv.

86. See Arthur Aughey and Cathy Gormley-Heenan, "The Anglo-Irish Agreement: 25 Years On," *Political Quarterly* 82 (3) (2011): 389–97.

87. O'Kane, "Learning from Northern Ireland?," 254; Guelke, "Lessons of Northern Ireland and the Relevance of the Regional Context," 7; and Mary-Alice Clancy, "Special Relationship: An Examination of the Bush Administration and the 'Internationalization' of Northern Ireland," *Ethnopolitics Papers* 6 (December 2010): 21, http://www.ethnopolitics .org/ethnopolitics-papers/ethnopoliticspapers-volume01-2010.htm, accessed September 16, 2011.

88. Mac Ginty, "Bad Students Learning the Wrong Lessons?," 28.

89. John Bew, Martyn Frampton, and Iñigo Gurruchaga, *Talking to Terrorists: Making Peace in Northern Ireland and the Basque Country* (New York: Columbia University Press, 2009), 239.

3   Peace from the People

Identity Salience and the Northern Irish Peace Process

LANDON E. HANCOCK

Of all the attempts made to resolve deep-rooted ethno-sectarian conflicts over the last few decades, only Northern Ireland has been moderately successful in implementing an agreement that calls for power sharing. The fact that its peace process has held, despite many fits and starts, is notable and worth study. Despite several suspensions, the Northern Irish Assembly shows a level of resilience unusual in peace processes. If we can identify what engendered this resilience and why, we may be able to apply our knowledge to other peace processes.

Salience, Roles, and Conflict Termination

One of the problems inhibiting the peaceful resolution of violent ethnic conflicts is the tenacity of "enemy images" held by conflicting parties. During a conflict's escalation, these enemy images become a part of each group's identity, polarizing views of the other.[1] I argue that the salience of individual and group identities moves from polarized extremes when the impact of significant events associated with the peace process allows a wider choice of identities and engenders a change in discourse that promotes the acceptability and desirability of these identities. The widening of identity choice, combined with the increased acceptability of nonpolarized identities, leads to a reordering of identity salience hierarchies for individuals.[2] This reordering decreases the salience of polarized identities vis-à-vis their newer, nonpolarized counterparts. The reordering of identity salience hierarchies is manifested through behavioral change, leading to attitude changes toward out-groups. Finally, these behavioral and attitude changes may impact attitudes toward the overall peace process, generating what has become known as a "groundswell effect" pushing for peace.

Previous research identified two major events, the 1994 paramilitary cease-fires and the 1998 Agreement, as the most significant events of the peace process.[3] This work will concentrate on the impact of these events and will cover two separate analyses. The first, identity widening, illustrates how these events allowed and encouraged the widening of identity choices, leading to a shift in salience in the primarily socialized identities of many in the general population. The second will address the changes in attitudes and behavior between the communities.

Each analysis relies on three data sets: a series of in-depth, open-ended interviews with twenty-five local community representatives from both sides of the conflict;[4] 1,800 newspaper editorials drawn from Northern Ireland's two morning dailies, the Belfast *News Letter* and the *Irish News*, spanning the course of the peace process from August 1994 through October 2001;[5] and the survey results from the Social and Community Planning Research group and the Northern Ireland Life and Times (NILT) from 1989 through 2000.[6]

The reasoning behind the use of three different data sets is to allow the strengths of each to help cover the weaknesses of the other two. The interviews were designed to collect a great deal of rich data about the impact of significant events in terms of how much of the community was impacted and what types of impact were more prevalent. The editorial data set was designed to determine the impact of certain events in terms of communal response and relies on an argument that newspaper editorials both reflect the values of their readership community and attempt to direct those values on occasion.[7] The survey data set is designed to allow connections between the individual responses and editorial themes and the attitudes of the general public. Despite the recognition that any transition from individual narrative to large-scale statistical data will contain some slippage, the use of these three sets helps to create a strong foundation for understanding how individual identities may have changed as a result of the peace process.

Identity Widening

Interview, newspaper, and survey data provide differences in the manner in which identity is described. This is largely because each examines identity at different levels. Survey data, for instance, tend to focus on two levels of identity—the state level (Irish or British) and the national or political levels (unionist or nationalist). Newspaper editorials tend to use the same set of identities but are more flexible in how they are interpreted. My interview questions focused on identity at multiple levels, including the everyday roles of a person's identity. Although this analysis is unable to show that the identity changes described by interview subjects are the same changes that have taken place for the entire population, it will show that the environment changed enough to widen the range of identity choices available to the population. This linkage will be shown through examples of more available identity roles, a reduction in the threat associated with certain identities, flexibility in how a particular identity is defined, and increased acceptance of "the other." Shifts in identity salience can be inferred directly from changes in these surrogates and are likely to be indicated by changes in levels of commitment, in terms of time or resources, among available identities.[8]

INTERVIEW RESULTS

Interviewees were asked about their perceived identities, how those were created, and how they had changed since the beginning of the peace process. They were then asked whether they thought elements of the peace process were responsible in some sense for that identity change. All the respondents indicated that their identities had changed over the course of time, and three of them directly linked these changes to aspects of the peace process. One subject, Hugh,[9] self-identified as a loyalist, had been involved in anti-republican movements. For Hugh the most important macrolevel impacts on microlevel changes occurred in response to the acceptance of the Agreement by supporters of republicanism. "I think the biggest thing for me was republicans buying into the notion of a partitionist settlement, if you like. Accepting Northern Ireland's existence and participating in the mechanisms of government here. Which before, was a total anathema to republicanism. I never envisaged the day I would see republicans sitting in Stormont administering British rule." When pressed on this point about why the republican acceptance of the Agreement was so important, Hugh responded that "yeah, really it was the most overt signal from the republican movement that at least in the interim they're willing to accept the status quo, well not the status quo but something, a partitionist settlement while still albeit it enables them to champion their cause for a united Ireland in a peaceful manner as well. But you know, I think it was a very important step in enabling any sort of political institutions to develop here."

Although Hugh's answers to how his self-identity had changed related primarily to impacts caused by the conflict, rather than the peace process, there are some grounds to believe that a change in his conception of the other has taken place in response to republican acceptance of the Agreement. In particular, Hugh initially described himself as deeply enmeshed in the conflict as a member of a loyalist paramilitary organization. When asked how his identity had changed, Hugh stated: "Even today, I still [identify as very] much British and unionist. I don't think I would be very difficult to deal with in terms of a political settlement. I would be very open to, and very much in support of the Good Friday Agreement. What I feel gives all political opinion a chance to air their views or campaign for whatever they would like for the island of Ireland. *If the people of Northern Ireland came to a democratic decision that their future lay in an all-Ireland, I certainly wouldn't be violently opposed to it. But, it would have to come about democratically*" (emphasis added).

This indicates a change in attitudes and perceptions regarding the vision of the other as untrustworthy and only interested in violence. If, in fact, the other (in this case republicans) are willing to "play by democratic rules," then the willingness to enter into a united Ireland without violence—even if some are not exactly ecstatic about the idea—can be seen as a measure of a change in the perception of the other as anathema.

A second subject, Rose, who described herself as a nationalist as opposed to being a republican, spoke about a lessening of the political role in her everyday life as a result of the Agreement. In Rose's opinion the Agreement legitimized being a nationalist and, to a lesser extent, being a republican pursuing a united Ireland by peaceful means: "I think at some point the political identity had to be larger. Because it was always . . . a fight to be legitimate. You had to fight to be legitimate as a nationalist, in the eyes of the ruling class. It was the ruling class at the level that I understood it back then was unionism. And unionism didn't recognize my right to be a nationalist, or in fact my right to have a political ideology other than the United Kingdom. . . . So that took up I think a larger part of my identity. Whereas with the agreement I do see that having shifted because I'm now freely and legitimately entitled to be a nationalist and to politically strive if I choose to and if I want to, to strive toward a united Ireland." When pressed on this point and its connection to the Agreement, Rose responded: "I think yes, the Agreement itself because it enshrined. It enshrined equality and it enshrined human rights. And it also legitimized not only nationalism but republicanism to some level. . . . So I don't see right now my political identity as being the be all and end all of me. I do see the most important things in my life as being improving the relationships with job, my family, [and] the city that I live in."

This symbolic change directly allowed more roles to assert themselves. Rose's freedom from "defending" her identity as a nationalist, as well as republicans feeling legitimized in their identities, leaves room for other identities to take root. This widens the identity field and allows familial and work-related identities to take more precedence. Rose provides a direct link between the reduction in identity threat and a shift in her identity commitment from being a nationalist to focusing on family concerns.

EDITORIAL RESULTS

There are difficulties inherent in trying to take the answers to specific questions found in the interviews and expanding them to the social level through the lens of newspaper editorials. One of the main difficulties is that, unlike the interview subjects, editorials tend to speak of identities in only national terms, instead of recognizing national identities as one among many available to individuals. This section examines how national identities are described in relation to one another and whether those identities are seen as mutually exclusive and monolithic or whether they are seen as diverse aspects of a mutually tolerant society.

Of nearly 1,800 editorials examined, only 28 discuss identity diversity. Of those, only 5 are in the Belfast *News Letter*. All of these were written after the Agreement, with the first coming over a year later, in May 1999. Despite this limited number of editorials, what they say is quite interesting. For example, a May 20, 1999, *News Letter* editorial notes the socioeconomic factors of national identity, described as tribal with a caveat. "People in less prosperous areas have a higher emotional investment in their tribal identity, a disposition all too easily exploited by tribal politicians. Yet much of the drive for cross-community endeavour and for the celebration of diversity has come from within those tribally delineated areas. It is more than a matter of wry amusement that whereas wall murals were seen, not so long ago, simply as aggressive acts of tribal vandalism, now they may be the subject of grant-aid, where the end-product is a well-produced expression of cultural heritage."[10] The editorial goes on to note that these types of changes are "what the Good Friday Agreement and the Assembly have provided for" in the sense of seeking accommodation rather than confrontation.[11] The main focus of this editorial is on the necessity and the valuation of accommodation and diversity among individuals and groups with differing national identities. Of particular note is the explicit link that the editorial makes between the drive for accommodation and the impact of the Agreement.

On April 13, 2001, the *News Letter* notes the impact of the Agreement on unionists' sense of Britishness: "Our Britishness has been diminished, they say, but is that really so? Who among unionists really feels any less British than they did three years ago? . . . Look at the rest of the UK today: pluralist, liberal, equitable. A place where people of every faith and culture have found a welcoming home. Where identity is not just about being British, but about being Northern Irish (or any kind of Irish), Welsh or Scots, Asian or Chinese, Jew or Gentile, or none of the above. Britain is less British today in the traditional understanding of that proud allegiance, but then Ireland is less Irish, too. That is not to say that people cannot be proud to be either, or both."[12]

In acknowledging the impact of the Agreement, the editorial says that the nationally based identities of British (unionist) and Irish (nationalist) are not threatened, by implication indicating that these national identities may have decreased in salience enough to share allegiance with other types of ethnic, cultural, or religious identities, or with each other. This is in direct contrast to several editorials written in 1997, which indicate that dealing with Sinn Féin or relenting on the right to parade would constitute a threat to unionists' sense of British identity. The change from the August 5, 1997, editorial titled "The Right to Parade Must Be Upheld" lies in the signing and implementation of the Agreement, which guarantees Northern Ireland's place in the United Kingdom (UK), until such a time as a majority in the province vote otherwise.[13]

The analysis of the changing use of identity in newspaper editorials uncovers a number of interesting developments. The first is that there is a trend for the acceptance of the other as a legitimate part of the Northern Irish community. Of the sixty-nine editorials that examined or described communal identity, fifty-two of them described the term in inclusivist or diverse terms as opposed to exclusionist or monolithic terms. The dates of those using the latter terms were almost entirely from before the signing of the Agreement. According to the editorial sources and the interviews, the Agreement created a new environment wherein the reduction in salience for mutually exclusive identities was called for and made possible.

Interview respondents indicated that identity change was based on the cease-fires and the Agreement. The editorial analysis indicating a change in identity definition, however, focused on the impact of the Agreement alone as the event most directly impacting this change. From these sources, we can posit a number of changes we expect to find in responses to certain survey questions. Among these there are two significant types of changes. The impact of the cease-fires should be greater in the realm of Northern Ireland's social atmosphere, while the impact of the Agreement should be greater in terms of attitudes toward Northern Ireland's social and governmental structure.[14] For examining the cease-fires in a social atmospheric sense one could predict that they produced a significant change not only in how Catholics and Protestants saw each other in regard to the past but more importantly how each community viewed future relations with the other. To test whether the significance of the paramilitary cease-fires uncovered by the interview and editorial data can be generalized to the wider population, I rely on two questions drawn from the community relations portion of the surveys. The two questions are:

1. Does the respondent believe that relations between Protestants and Catholics five years into the future will be better, worse, or the same as current relations?
2. Does the respondent believe that religion will always make a difference in the way people feel about each other?

The results of a time-series analysis for the percentage of those respondents to question 1 who felt that relations in five years would be better than the present are shown in figure 3.1, and the results for the percentage of those respondents to question 2 who felt that religion would always make a difference in how people feel about each other are shown in figure 3.2. In both figures there is a sharp upward spike in the 1995 survey, the first to take place after the 1994 paramilitary cease-fires. By contrast the downward spike in figure 3.2 does not take place until the 1998 survey, coinciding with the Agreement. In table 3.1 a comparison of the analyses of variance (ANOVA) for the same response to question 1 that relations will continue to get better in the future shows a very significant .004 shift for the cease-fires but an insignificant .153 shift for the Agreement.

As described, figure 3.2 shows the percentage decline in the number of respondents who believed that religion would always make a difference

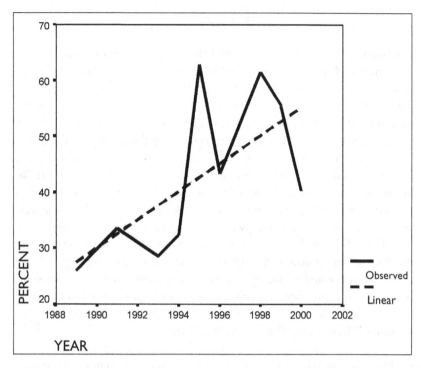

Figure 3.1. Time-series analysis of relations better in five years

Table 3.1. Comparison of future relations

Relations will be better five years from now	N	F	Significance
Across 1994 cease-fires	9	17.018	0.004
Across 1998 Good Friday Agreement	9	2.566	0.153

in the way people felt about each other. Table 3.2 shows the ANOVA confirming that the drop following the cease-fires is insignificant .063 (n = 9 years), while the drop after the Agreement is very significant .002 (n = 9 years).

Reviewing these results, we can see that the future relationships between Protestants and Catholics showed a significant shift following the paramilitary cease-fires, while whether one's religion will always make a

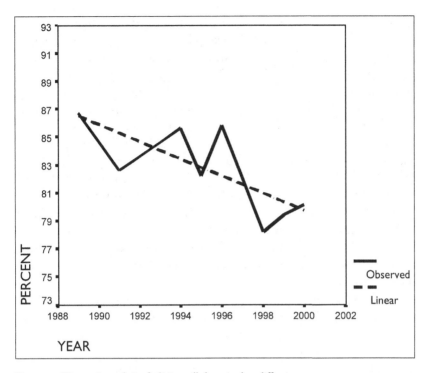

Figure 3.2. Time-series analysis of religion will always make a difference

Table 3.2. Comparison of religious difference

Religion will always make a difference	N	F	Significance
Across 1994 cease-fires	9	4.855	0.063
Across 1998 Good Friday Agreement	9	21.713	0.002

difference in how one views others, addressing social and governmentally structural issues, showed a significant shift following the Agreement. These findings support the proposition that the impact of the cease-fires was stronger in a social atmospheric sense and that the impact of the Agreement was stronger in a structural sense.

Our third measurement of change affecting identity can be found in changes in the answers to a survey question asking whether or not the respondent would classify him- or herself as a unionist, nationalist, or neither. We would expect to find two spikes in the number of individuals self-identifying as nationalist, but the jump associated with the Agreement should be much more significant. The atmospheric change generated by the cease-fires may have created a sense of relief, but it did not explicitly make being a nationalist, or to a lesser extent a republican, a socially accept-able identity. The acceptability of these identities, however, was enshrined in the Agreement, which stated that the participants to the Agreement "acknowledge[d] that . . . a substantial section of the people in Northern Ireland share the legitimate wish of a majority of the people of the island of Ireland for a united Ireland" and "recognise[d] the birthright of all the people of Northern Ireland to identify themselves and be accepted as Irish or British, or both, as they may so choose."[15] This difference in legitimate status would impact respondent willingness to self-identify as nationalist because of the fact that all the surveys were conducted by official govern-ment personnel.

Looking at figure 3.3, we can see that this is the case. There are indeed two jumps, with the second jump appearing much larger. Table 3.3 shows the numerical difference in the two jumps, with the 1994 jump significant at .037 (n = 10) and the 1998 jump much more significant at .008 (n = 10). The highly significant rise of those self-identifying as nationalist is mirrored in the very significant (p = .003, n = 10) drop in those respondents who chose neither as their self-identification, indicating a direct shift from one choice to the other in response to environmental changes, which represents the increasing legitimacy of the nationalist identity following the Agreement.

Viewing an increase in survey respondents self-identifying as national-ist as a sign of identity widening is counterintuitive. However, when we compare these survey responses to the interview responses, the link be-comes clearer. Recall the interview respondent who said, "I think at some point the political identity had to be larger. . . . You had to fight to be legit-imate as a nationalist, in the eyes of the ruling class. It was the ruling class at the level that I understood it back then was unionism. And unionism didn't recognize my right to be a nationalist, or in fact my right to have a political ideology other than the United Kingdom. . . . So that took up I think a larger part of my identity; whereas with the agreement I do see that having shifted because I'm now freely and legitimately entitled to be a na-tionalist." This indicates that the increase in those who self-identified as nationalist corresponds to the increased legitimacy of that response. If this is so, we can posit that if these respondents feel that they no longer have to

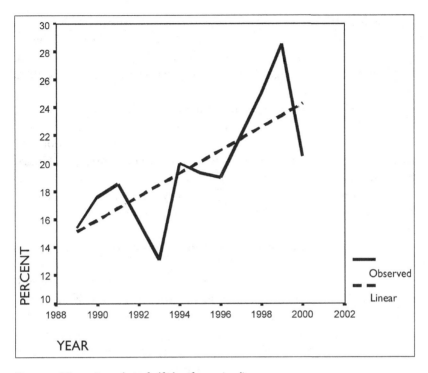

Figure 3.3. Time-series analysis of self-identify as nationalist

Table 3.3. Comparison of self-identify as a nationalist

Self-identify as a nationalist	N	F	Significance
Across 1994 cease-fires	10	6.258	0.037
Across 1998 Good Friday Agreement	10	12.367	0.008

fight to be legitimate, then their political identity as nationalists will have lessened in salience vis-à-vis other available identities.

Both events, the cease-fires and the Agreement, had a significant impact on respondents' willingness to self-identify as nationalists. Additionally, the much larger jump following the Agreement reflects the added legitimacy that the Agreement bestowed on the nationalist community as outlined in the interviews and editorials. The added legitimacy to the nationalist identity provided by the Agreement can be seen as a structural impact because it clearly changed the social and political structure of Northern Irish society in, at least, two ways. It explicitly legitimized the nationalist identity and its aspirations for a united Ireland. It created new social and political structures to regulate intercommunal relations and, hopefully, manage future conflicts in a peaceful manner. These two structural changes to Northern Irish society had the impact of lessening the threat to nationalist identity. By doing so, they lessened the amount of commitment—in time and resources—necessary for individuals to maintain their nationalist identities and, thus, opened the way for a widening of identity possibilities for these individuals. The result is that the nationalist identity may have *reduced* in salience for some nationalists as they engaged with and adopted some of the newly available identities.

Changes in Attitudes and Behaviors

Our next analysis examines the changes in attitudes toward interaction between Catholics and Protestants as a result of the peace process. Interview questions asked about interaction with members of the other community and how this has, or has not, been affected by specific events during the peace process. The editorial results examined changes in recommendations and exhortations regarding the issue of dialogue surrounding the annual sectarian parades. The focus for this analysis is the encouragement or discouragement of interaction with members of the opposite community. The results of the interviews and editorials will be used to analyze changes in attitudes toward interaction in the surveys.

INTERVIEW RESULTS

For this analysis each interview respondent was asked a series of questions regarding their interaction with individuals from the other community. Essentially, these questions asked them to provide a description of the amount, quality, and tone of their intercommunal interaction while at work and while socializing. Then, each respondent was asked whether any changes in their patterns of interaction had taken place since the beginning of the peace process and whether or not those changes resulted in an increase or decrease of the component in question. Finally, the respondents were asked if they felt the peace process was involved in their changes in interaction and, if so, what specific event, policy, or agreement contributed most to that change.

There were several positive responses indicating that there was an increased amount of interaction during the course of the peace process. In some instances respondents indicated that this was location dependent, with those in the neutral areas having more interaction and those in more traditional neighborhoods having limited interaction. Susan indicated that she thought it had increased: "Particularly for people . . . who would go to city center. The city centers are normally a neutral environment. Certainly in Belfast here, and there'd be a lot of interaction at that level where all the entertainment, the nightclubs, whatever there'd be a lot of. People from both traditions would go to the same places. But it's when you move into . . . their immediate social environment it's very much one or the other, there'd be virtually no interaction there."

However, Thomas, from Derry/Londonderry, indicated that this increase may not affect everyone. Part of this is structural, with the city center being on the "Catholic" side of the river, and part is policy oriented, with political discussions being actively discouraged by employers: "Until society begins to change and until government begins to make it worth someone's while to create incentives for the creation of the shared space, then peoples' general interactions with the other side will continue to be the same, which is not very much and not very often. . . . They don't have any quality conversations, they're superficial, they talk about the weather, about the football match, whatever. It's not evolved, and they avoid getting into any deep conversations." Overall, while the amount of interaction between the communities has increased in some circumstances and for some age groups, there are still structural and social impediments to increased mixing. These impediments include segregated neighborhoods and a social attitude discouraging political or sectarian discussions in the workplace.[16]

Turning to perceptions of increases or decreases in interaction quality, several respondents indicated that the peace process had a definite effect. In particular, Liam noted that "in work terms it has moved upwards in that people are looking forward rather than being stuck in positions of aggravation as they would say it. Before the cease-fires, people in either community were locked into particular positions of having grievances to a considerable degree against the other side. The cease-fires and then the Good Friday Agreement liberated, or began to liberate thinking from that grievance mentality into what might be possible." The interviews make it appear that the quality of interaction has improved, even to the extent that arguments that were impermissible at one time are no longer cause for extreme concern.

For the editorial analysis of how interactions and attitudes toward them have changed, we turn to a series of editorials regarding parades. In Northern Ireland, each summer brings the marching season, wherein mostly Protestant groups proclaim their allegiance to tradition by staging thousands of parades across the province. Most of these events take place with little notice and no trouble, but there are a few that have been considered contentious by both sides and have been flash points for violence. For Protestant groups such as the Orange Order and the Apprentice Boys of Derry these parades pay respect to their tradition and express their right as a free people in a free society to march peaceably along public roads. For Catholics, especially those living in areas where these marches pass, the issues include respect for their own sensitivities, abhorrence of perceived triumphalism on the part of the marchers, and a desire to have their views placed on an equal footing with those of the dominant majority.[17]

This analysis will not delve into the quagmire of the issues involved, nor will it dwell too much on what each side says to the other. Instead, this analysis will concentrate on what each newspaper says to its own community about their behavior and engaging in dialogue to resolve contentious marches. In a January 24, 1997, editorial in the Belfast *News Letter* it is clear that the editor promotes dialogue as the only viable solution to the ongoing Drumcree standoff. "The Drumcree church parade stand-off in Portadown will only be settled by dialogue. It is absolutely essential that every effort is made to avoid a repetition of the horrendous events which surrounded the impasse of the past two years and which cost Northern Ireland so much in financial terms and in standing internationally as a stable peaceful society."[18] This ostensibly positive view of dialogue as the answer is diluted because of the *News Letter*'s "understanding" of the Orange Order's unwillingness to meet with the Garvaghy Road residents solely because their spokesperson may have had connections to Sinn Féin or the Irish Republican Army (IRA).

Nowhere in the ensuing 1997 editorials is the issue of dialogue raised again. Instead, the *News Letter* concentrated on calling for restraint by all parties and on chastising nationalists for rioting in response to the Royal Ulster Constabulary (RUC) reversal on the Portadown parade. In this instance the RUC reversed an earlier decision to ban the parade because of fears of loyalist violence. Instead, mobile security units were required to clear the residents from the road for the parade, sparking nationalist riots across the province. Several *News Letter* editorials dated just after the confrontation depicted the Portadown Orange Lodge as marching "peacefully, in a dignified manner,"[19] and characterized those who opposed the marches as "militant republicans" who engage in "sinister activities" designed "to have lawful parades banned or re-routed," while making no mention of the loyalist threat of violence.[20]

The tone regarding the usefulness of dialogue and the manner in which the two sides engage in it changed substantially after April 10, 1998, the date of the Agreement. The first sign of this change came in an August 4, 1998, editorial that began, "Common sense has prevailed in Londonderry, where, after many weeks of intensive dialogue, the Apprentice Boys and local residents have thrashed out an acceptable formula for Saturday's spectacular Siege of Derry commemorations."[21] The editorial also noted a different tone regarding the Parades Commission, noting its helpful role in facilitating dialogue between the local residents and the Apprentice Boys, concluding that the agreement reached is a model for others, particularly the contentious parade from Drumcree down the Garvaghy Road.

Throughout the parade season of 1999 the *News Letter* published a number of editorials that retained their suspicion of nationalists and affirmation of unionists, but there was one distinct change. When unionists were praised, it was generally because they engaged, or were willing to engage, in dialogue with nationalists, with the latter being disparaged for being unwilling to engage in dialogue or for setting too many preconditions on their engagement. One group that was given a lot of praise was the aforementioned Apprentice Boys of Derry, who yearly celebrate the beginning of that city's siege by the forces of Catholic King James following the shutting of the city gates by a group of Protestant apprentices. In an editorial published on April 6, 1999, the *News Letter* states: "The Apprentice Boys of Derry have set an example to other loyal institutions by behaving courageously and responsibly in relation to their traditional parades. On a number of occasions, they have defused tensions by entering into wide-ranging talks and negotiations with the aim of achieving an outcome based on compromise instead of confrontation."[22]

While continuing to staunchly support the Orange Order and other loyalist institutions, the *News Letter* subtly shifted its rhetoric to advocate engagement in dialogue and negotiations as preferable to standing solely upon traditional rights to march when and where the organizations wish. When commenting on a mediator's report that no Drumcree solution for 2000 was likely to take place, a March 7, 2000, editorial recommended that "the Orange Order should review its attitude to the new [reformed Parades] Commission. Previously it has refused to engage in talks, but the Order played an important role in establishing the need for a review of its operation. Having succeeded in this respect, it should now test the objectivity and fairness of the current Commission by participating fully in any discussions which might assist the body in reaching fair and balanced conclusions."[23]

The *News Letter*'s stance toward nationalists changed little, but its stance toward groups in the Protestant community shifted in emphasis from the right to parade to the necessity of dialogue, even if only for the sake of "doing the right thing" before a ruling by authorities. On the issue of Drumcree, a June 27, 2001, editorial encouraged the Portadown Lodge of the Orange Order to relent in its traditional stance and engage in direct talks with the Garvaghy Road Residents' Association. Although the editorial points out that the residents may be using their demand for direct talks as a stalling tactic, the editorial promotes engagement in these talks despite their belief that the leader of the residents' association is a former republican. The editorial concludes that engaging in talks is a good tactical as well as a good strategic move.[24]

The changes in the *News Letter* editorials following the Agreement indicate a shift in the promotion of dialogue as the preferred means for the resolution of parade disputes and away from the approval of intransigence in the face of perceived abuse of traditional rights. Those rights, specifically the right to freely march along the queen's roads, are still recognized, but the concerns of the nationalist community are also being recognized as legitimate. The clearest example of this legitimization of the other rests in the shift of rhetoric from describing the nationalist associations as "extremist" to the recognition that the Orange Order should enter into direct dialogue with individuals they feel are repugnant because those individuals are "the appointed" spokespeople of their communities. Clearly, the moral valuation of talking has risen higher than the traditional value of rights.[25]

SURVEY RESULTS

In analyzing changes in interaction between Catholics and Protestants, one can identify aspirations of each community based on their responses to survey questions about Protestant-Catholic mixing. Questions ask respondents about general mixing, mixing in educational settings, and mixing in workplaces and living areas. Questions were asked by all the

Northern Ireland Social Attitudes (NISA) surveys from 1989 through 1996. These surveys allow us to analyze the impact of the paramilitary cease-fires. Unfortunately, because these questions were discontinued in the Life and Times Survey, which dates from late 1998, this study is unable to measure the impact of the Agreement. Instead, this study examines a number of the self-completion questions that ask the respondents about their belief that better relations will come from more mixing or more separation and whether they would be in favor of more mixing or more separation in a variety of settings.[26] For this analysis we will focus on shifts from one response to another, indicating a change in attitudes either toward or away from sentiment in favor of mixing.

Figure 3.4 shows the results of a time-series analysis of the survey response, indicating a belief that more mixing will result in better relations between Catholics and Protestants. The figure shows a clear and significant upward jump from the 1993 to the 1994 survey, indicating a rise in the number of respondents willing to engage in more mixing to create better intercommunal relations. As shown in table 3.4 an analysis of variance using the break point from just before the 1994 self-completion survey confirms the significance of the upward shift in figure 3.4. The level of significance shown is just above the .01 level, at .011 (n = 6), and is matched by an equally significant downward shift in the number of respondents who believed that better relations between Protestants and Catholics would only be achieved through more separation.

This change from a preference for more separation to a preference for more mixing affirms the impact that the paramilitary cease-fires had not only on the perception of improved intercommunal relations but also on how those relations could continue their improvement. This sense that mixing in general would be beneficial to improved relations was supported by responses to questions about mixing in a number of specific social areas.

Table 3.5 shows three significant findings in the analyses of variance measurements in attitudes toward mixing in educational settings.[27] While the upward shift in much more mixing at the primary school level reaches the .05 level of significance, the downward shifts—in keeping the primary schools and secondary/grammar schools as they are—are both significant at the .01 level, indicating a strong correlation between the impact of the cease-fire and the willingness of people to engage in more mixing at both school levels. This indicates a willingness by those respondents who were parents to have their own children attend mixed schools or mixed student functions.

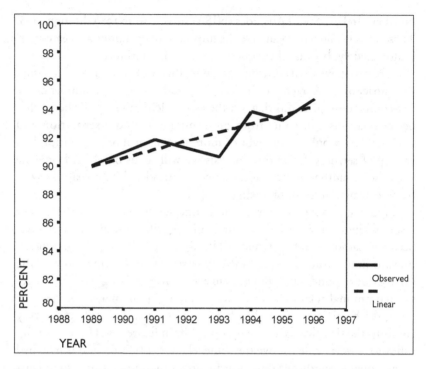

Figure 3.4. Time-series analysis of better relations through more mixing

Table 3.4. Better relations through more mixing or separation after 1994

	N	F	Significance
Better relations through more mixing	6	20.447	0.011
Better relations through more separation	6	19.811	0.011

Table 3.5. Mixing or separation in education after 1994

	N	F	Significance
Primary school much more mixing	6	8.206	0.046
Primary school keep as is	6	23.252	0.009
Grammar/Secondary school keep as is	6	32.617	0.005

The key element here is not the overall prevalence of respondents choosing the much more mixing category but the significant shifts. While the overall preference can be—to some extent—attributed to demand characteristics of the question,[28] the significant shifts are most attributable to the impact of the paramilitary cease-fires and their creation of a sense of hope in the general populace. People were more willing to consider living in a mixed neighborhood as a method for improving intercommunal relations. The numerical value of this rise in response is found in table 3.6 below, where the significance level is pegged at .014 (n = 6 years) and is mirrored by a significant (.019, n = 6 years) reduction in the number of those who responded that relations would improve with much more separation. Table 3.6 also shows a significant rise in the number of respondents who felt that relations would improve with much more mixing in the workplace (significance = .05, n = 6 years), indicating that, like the responses to mixing in living areas, people felt more positive about the prospect of mixing and interacting in workplaces.[29] The issue of mixed marriages is problematic for Northern Irish society, often resulting in the ostracizing of one of the two individuals and sometimes resulting in violence. While the numbers in this case are not large (a less than 2 percent shift), it is interesting to note the analysis of variance is very significant (.002, n = 6 years), indicating a reduction in the level of disapproval following the implementation of the paramilitary cease-fires.

The paramilitary cease-fires had an effect on respondents' perceptions of the value of mixing with members of the other community both in general and in specific arenas. While it is difficult to say precisely why this should be so, it seems reasonable to assume that the reduction in intercommunal paramilitary violence—punishment beatings tend to be intracommunity—allowed members of the two communities to mix more or to be more relaxed and less fearful in their daily interactions. The impact of events on patterns of behavior as shown by the interview results are

Table 3.6. Mixing or separation at work and home after 1994

	N	F	Significance
Living area much more mixing	6	17.336	0.014
Living area much more separation	6	14.45	0.019
Workplace much more mixing	6	7.712	0.050
Marriage much more separation	6	58.368	0.002

duplicated to some extent in the editorial results and confirmed by significant shifts in attitudes toward associational behavior in the surveys. The interview results show that positive changes in intercommunal interaction were a direct result of the peace process, with the paramilitary cease-fires encouraging an increase in interaction and the Agreement encouraging discussion of difficult issues that had, heretofore, been avoided.

These findings link directly to the survey results showing that the cease-fires had a positive impact on peoples' perceptions that mixing in a traditionally segregated society would improve relations between the groups. It is reasonable to assume that the respondents understood that much more mixing in general, at school, at home, and at work, would entail much more dialogue and discussion with members of the opposite community. Additionally, through the medium of newspaper editorials, the general population was told that constructive negotiation and talking on a face-to-face basis was the preferred method of resolving the most contentious of issues regardless of traditions, rights, or the perceived incompatibilities between the parties.

Identities, Roles, and Salience

The findings highlighted above illustrate several important lessons from the Northern Ireland peace process. The interviews explained how events in the peace process affected the sense of self and other. Interviewees indicated that the paramilitary cease-fires and the Agreement reduced the threat felt to their primarily socialized identities and allowed subjects to spend more time engaging with other role activities. In effect, interviewees indicated that their primary identities had decreased in salience as a result of the peace process because many of them felt that these identities were less important and elicited less commitment than before the process. A few respondents traced this change to the impact of events in the peace process, most specifically the Agreement and, to a lesser extent, the paramilitary cease-fires.

The editorial data, by contrast, spoke to a change in how groups defined their identities. Before the Agreement these identities were monolithic and exclusionist, with individuals choosing either one or the other of the identities or, more likely, having it chosen for them. After the Agreement the definition of these identities shifted from a monolithic sense to become more inclusive and flexible. The notion of British and Irish shifted from being an either/or proposition to the idea that a single individual could have both British and Irish allegiance. Additionally, the idea of a diversity of identities and traditions coexisting peacefully began to take hold in the editorial tone of both newspapers. This change was especially apparent in the Protestant newspaper's willingness to recognize the legitimacy of nationalist identities and its call for unionists to accommodate nationalist identity and accept their own Irishness.

The survey findings indicate that not only did the cease-fires and the Agreement impact the view of future and past relations between Protestants and Catholics, but they also changed the belief that religion would always be an important factor in how members of the two communities viewed each other. The perception that relations between the two communities had gotten better and would continue to do so in some sense reflects the atmospheric changes stemming from the cease-fires. The change in perception of the importance of religion, long considered the most salient social division in Northern Ireland, seems to reflect the structural changes brought about by the Agreement. An additional, and perhaps more important, effect of the Agreement was the counterintuitive increase in the number of respondents who chose to self-identify as nationalist. Nationalists believe their identity is protected by the Agreement. Since it is no longer threatened, individuals can safely reveal their sense of nationalist identity. Survey findings corroborate interview results that the reduction in threat to nationalist identity was a possible reduction in salience for that identity. We can conjecture, therefore, that the significant rise in the number of individuals who feel safer in self-identifying as nationalist may translate into a significant number for whom nationalist identity has subsequently become less salient as they have had more time and resources to devote to other identities. Overall, the evidence suggests that the indirect, environmental impact allowed and encouraged a process whereby a wider set of identities and roles could flourish. This process of identity-widening led to a reduction in the salience of primarily socialized identities.

The process of identity salience change has its theoretical foundations in symbolic interactionism and Stryker's argument that each individual's composite identity is made up of the various identities and roles that the individual acts out.[30] The concept of salience derives from the amount of commitment, in time or resources, that each identity or role receives from the individual and his or her environment.[31] Stryker's salience hierarchy describes the amount of commitment that each identity or role receives in a descending order. For identity salience hierarchies to change (by shifting the salience of one or more of the identities or roles), the individual needs to be able to access and actualize a number of different roles or identities. In Northern Ireland, the peace process allowed and encouraged a "widening" in these available roles and identities. Following this widening, the shifting of identity salience hierarchies reflects the lessening salience of conflict-oriented identities by virtue of a lessening of the individual and communal commitment to those identities. This does not mean that those identities disappear or become unimportant, merely that they become less important in relation to other available roles and identities. It is entirely conceivable that, if the environment should shift back to one of high threat and violent conflict, these identities could regain their preeminent position in the hierarchy.[32]

The findings of the identity-widening analysis are illustrated by the types of identities and roles that appear to have increased in commitment and salience as a result of this process. For the most part these identities are at what one would call the subnational level, rather than at the national or supranational level. Most interview subjects spoke of an increase in family, community, or professional roles, not supranational roles such as being European citizens. It is not that these interview subjects felt that they were any less Protestant, Catholic, unionist, or nationalist; it is that other aspects of their lives—work, home, family, local community—had gained enough in stature to become the primary identification in a less threatening environment.[33]

This finding was mirrored to some extent in the editorial and survey data, reflecting the impact of a widening of available roles and a subsequent reordering of identity salience hierarchies. The redefinition of nationally oriented identities as flexible, plural, and no longer monolithic in the editorial data is an indirect sign of the identity-widening process, leading to a shift in identity salience hierarchies. The process of identity widening leading to the reordering of identity salience hierarchies in the survey data emphasized the reduction of threat to nationally oriented identities.

This emphasis on subnational as opposed to national or supranational identities is novel in a number of ways. The first is that much of the social identity literature concerned with ameliorating intergroup conflict has focused on the creation of superordinate identities through controlled contact and the creation of superordinate goals. Limitations recognized by Brewer and Gaertner et al. include the difficulty of recategorizing group identities or creating group identities that will have any lasting effect outside of the episode or context of the controlled contact in which they first take place. However, a reordering of identity is necessary for shifting attitudes of members of one former group toward the other.[34] The evidence gathered in this study suggests something slightly different. One of the effects of the identity reordering was a shift in attitudes toward associating with members of the other community. This indicates that the creation of a superordinate identity may not be necessary to impel a shift in attitudes toward "former out-group members" but that a reduction in threat toward primarily socialized identities may encourage an identity-widening process that results in the positive shift in attitudes toward the other.

One area where the work of social psychologists on multiple categorization showed promising findings was in a review of moderating influences on reducing bias and discrimination.[35] Chief among these influences was the social inclusion pattern. In a cross-categorization study where all crossed groups are evaluated positively, double in-groups and partial groups are evaluated more positively than double out-groups. When a pattern of social exclusion exists, where any group that has out-group elements is evaluated negatively, then partial groups and double out-groups are evaluated more negatively than the double in-group. Essentially, these positive or negative evaluations of groups are seen by Crisp and Hewstone as the presence or absence of threat to a particular social identity. Crisp and Hewstone found that a reduction in identity threat resulted in an increase in social inclusion, reducing bias and discrimination.[36] This is remarkably similar to our findings that a reduction in threat to existing national identities promoted a reordering of identity salience hierarchies, with the priming effect in the experiments perhaps being comparable to the explicit recognition of both communal identities in the Agreement and the positive valuation of both identities found in the newspaper editorials.

Attitudes and Behavior toward Association

Identity widening had the effect of creating significant shifts in behaviors and in attitudes toward engaging with the other community.[37] The data from the interview, editorial, and survey data sets can be tied together by using Ajzen and Fishbein's theory of reasoned action.[38] This theory suggests that the subject's attitude toward a particular behavior is the most proximate predictor of whether or not the subject engages in that behavior.[39] The first stage of the theory has two main components, the attitude toward the behavior and the subjective norms, which feed into the subject's intention to perform that behavior and, finally, to the performance of the behavior.

One can further break down the source of attitudes toward behavior as stemming from beliefs that the behavior would lead to certain outcomes and an evaluation that these outcomes would be desirable. The breakdown of the sources of subjective norms stems from the belief that specific referents (people or institutions) think the subject should or should not perform the said behavior and from the subject's motivation to comply with those referents.[40] In a large number of experimental and quasi-experimental studies, researchers have concluded that there is a strong link between intention as a dependent variable and attitude toward behavior and subjective norms as independent variables. The link between intentions and behavior can be less strong if the behavior is not volitional or possible. With respect to purely volitional behavior Ajzen and others have found a strong correlation between intention to perform a specific behavior and its actual performance.[41] What this means is that if a Catholic in a mixed workplace intends to start a political discussion with her Protestant counterparts, then she will probably do so, unless that type of discussion is prohibited, making it nonvolitional.[42]

While the data deriving from the analysis of *Changes in Attitudes and Behavior* may not be definitive in terms of actual behavioral change in Northern Ireland, by using the framework of Ajzen and Fishbein's theory of reasoned action, we can assess how unionists and nationalists relate to each other. For instance, the interviews highlight both the intention of some of the respondents as well as a change in behavior. One respondent, in particular, embodied this by describing both the intention and increase in interaction, the behavioral change, as a result of the effects of the Agreement: "One of the things I decided to do was to begin to do more work within the Protestant community and particularly within the working class loyalist community. So my interactions increased with that grouping and with people who identified themselves as such."

The survey data highlighted the shift in attitudes, and this could be seen as both attitudes toward a specific behavior and the intent to actualize that behavior. The limitation of this view is that the surveys did not measure actual behavior, nor did they directly ask whether the respondent intended to actualize that behavior, merely whether they thought that people in general should engage in the specified behavior.

Finally, the editorials identified subjective norms and provided commentary on intentions and behaviors. The editorial promotion of dialogue between Protestant marching groups and Catholic residents' groups represents a change in the subjective norms, which make up a part of the independent variables affecting the creation or change of intentions. The validity of these editorials as a part of a community or group's subjective norms is strengthened by looking at only those editorials that were intracommunal in nature. By speaking to "their own communities" rather than across communal lines, these editorials were explicitly trying to change the subjective norms surrounding specific sets of attitudes and behaviors. The subjective norm of the Protestant community of upholding the right to parade slowly changed and lessened in importance when compared with the subjective norm for engaging in dialogue as a way of resolving the parade disputes. Along with this change in norms came a change in the view of the other and the norms for both respecting the rights of the other community and for engaging in dialogue despite possible paramilitary affiliations on the part of the other community's interlocutors.

The editorials also provide negative and positive valuations of specific behaviors taken by Protestant marching groups at specific points. While this too is a part of the change of subjective norms, it can also be seen as speaking toward actual behaviors taken as a result of the intentions of those groups or individuals. The positive valuations of behavior could be seen as a reinforcement mechanism contributing to a possible consistency and stability in attitude change through the change in subjective norms. The negative valuations of behavior, naturally enough, sought to change attitudes toward the behaviors by reinforcing the notion that subjective norms had changed and that those who wanted positive valuation needed to change their attitudes and behaviors in response.

Using the theory of reasoned action helps to explain the links between the results of the different data sets and strengthens the link between the analyses in the sense of showing how the process of environmental change had an impact on subjective norms and how the identity shift process had an impact on attitudes toward behavior. These two impacts could result in a change in both intentions and behaviors with regard to interacting with members of the other community.

Lessons Learned

There are a few lessons that have been learned and are worth considering both in terms of the Northern Irish peace process and in terms of peace processes in general. To maintain support for the peace and to provide the space for further shifts in identity salience, and hopefully conflict transformation, the government of Northern Ireland should focus on two specific policy areas. The first would be to reduce the focus on political concerns. It is not as though highly contentious political issues are going to disappear, nor are they going to become easier to solve. However, the more that the politicians from leading parties predicate their participation in government on contentious political issues to the detriment of bread and butter ones, the more they will tend to alienate themselves from the general population and the more they may contribute to a sense that the peace process is stalling instead of moving forward.[43]

A second major policy area that should be tackled by actors at all levels is the increasing perception on the part of the working-class unionist community that it is not benefiting equally from the peace process. One can argue that some of the economic benefits following normalization and deriving from the peace process are a form of implementation for the Agreement. Therefore, the growing perception that Protestants are not benefiting enough from the peace process may be part of the reason that the loyalist enclaves in North and East Belfast continue to be flash points for violence. It is not so much the monetary or economic benefits that are of issue in this case as it is the perception by these communities that they are being left out or exploited for political or economic gain, often by middle-class unionist politicians. The overwhelming sentiment in this community is that they were on the front lines of the fight in the Troubles—most members of the Protestant paramilitary groups were working-class loyalists—and that after doing the "dirty work" for the Protestant community they have been tossed aside. A concentrated effort to assist these communities, especially from a participatory and elicitive standpoint, could go a long way toward ameliorating feelings of alienation and persuading unionist communities that they have a future in the new Northern Ireland.[44] Looking back at the results of the identity-widening analysis, where a reduction in identity threat took place, space for identity widening and a shift in salience followed. This was especially true for the nationalist community but is less apparent for the unionist community.

The success of policies aimed at the general populace in Northern Ireland leads us to make some more general recommendations for other peace processes. First and foremost, to secure the support of the population for any peace process the public needs to feel the positive effects of that process on a daily basis. This usually means a return to—or the creation of—a sense of normal life with a reduced level of threat to the communal identities of both, or all, sides.[45] Differing circumstances in different conflicts will determine the type of impact sought or available, but some generalizations can be made.

The first is that for any cease-fire to have a long-term impact on the general population, it should be followed as rapidly as possible by some form of normalization. This would probably entail the removal of some security forces from the streets and the dismantling or scaling back of checkpoints, security sweeps, and the like. While one could argue that such a security "de-mobilization" only plays into the hands of spoiler groups, it could also be argued that increased security or maintaining high levels of security would probably do little to deter spoilers and would only have the effect of failing to convince the subordinate community that positive changes are here to stay.[46]

A second generalization has to do with the types of agreements made and their relation to the communal identities of the parties to the conflict. One of the effects of the Agreement was to lessen the threat felt to communal identities for most of the nationalist community and much of the unionist community. The idea that both these communal identities were given explicit legitimacy within the framework of the Agreement in large part allowed these identities to reduce in salience vis-à-vis other, less polarized identities, beginning the process outlined above. While terms of normalization may differ greatly depending on circumstance, it is possible for policy makers to pay attention to the identity needs of communities in conflict and address these needs in a manner that reduces the perceived threat to the identities of both communities, allowing space for their reduction in salience and, hopefully, opening a pathway to future conflict transformation. This was done in Northern Ireland by expressly protecting the legitimacy of both communities in the Agreement and the legitimacy of their goals for either remaining in the United Kingdom or uniting with the Republic of Ireland. Policy makers and deal negotiators should try to take into account the needs of the greater communities at large and not just the political activists who support the parties at the table, because it requires the support of a majority of all the people to sustain any peace process for the long haul.

Conclusion: The Groundswell Effect or Not?

What level of support did the general population of Northern Ireland have for the peace process? Did this support create a "groundswell" effect that would affect the willingness and motivation of leaders inside and outside Northern Ireland to push ahead with the process despite its many difficulties?[47] While some have stressed that the peace process was an elite-led negotiation, there is some evidence, anecdotal though it may be, that members of the Northern Irish Assembly have heard "the will of the people" and have attempted to work together on basic issues, despite continuing difficulties. A February 8, 2000, editorial in the *News Letter* notes, "Our elected representatives are fulfilling the overwhelming will of the people, even if the Members do not have over-arching influence on the issues which threaten the entire apparatus."[48] This editorial gives life to the contention that at least some members of the Northern Irish Assembly are aware that the will of the people is that they "get on with governing" and worry less about the political issues. The fact that they are attempting to do so may be an indicator of a type of "groundswell" wherein the politicians—who must eventually stand for reelection—are receiving messages of support for the process from their constituents and are paying attention to them.[49]

However, the support of Northern Ireland's population for the current peace process is not necessarily a "done deal." As long as the process continues to have an overall positive impact on ordinary people, then it is likely to have their support. However, if the population feels little or no positive impact for too long, then the process will likely lose the population's support and may indeed fall prey to spoilers, manipulative politicians, general discontent, or any number of threats that could derail the process and signal a return to conflict. Barring any specific example of a groundswell effect, what we as academics, and hopefully policy makers, should seek to do is ensure that any peace process, in Northern Ireland or elsewhere, creates and sustains that overall positive impact for a majority of the population. After all, isn't that what peace is supposed to be all about?

NOTES

1. The need for conflict resolution to go beyond the Agreement to transforming the images of the other in society is found in Daniel Bar-Tal, "From Intractable Conflict through Conflict Resolution to Reconciliation: Psychological Analysis," *Political Psychology* 21 (2) (2000): 351–65. In addition, for identity polarization, see Terrell Northrup, "The Dynamics of Identity in Personal and Social Conflict," in *Intractable Conflicts and Their Transformation*, ed. Louis Kriesberg, Terrell Northrup, and Stuart Thorson (Syracuse, NY: Syracuse University Press, 1989), 55–82. Extensive work on enemy images can be found in

the works of Vamik Volkan, most notably *Bloodlines: From Ethnic Pride to Ethnic Terrorism* (New York: Farrar, Straus and Giroux, 1997) and *The Need to Have Enemies and Allies* (Northvale, NJ: J. Aronson, 1994). A more comprehensive review of ethnicity and identity can be found in Landon E. Hancock, "Ethnic Identities and Boundaries: Anthropological, Psychological and Sociological Approaches," in *The International Studies Encyclopedia*, ed. Robert A. Denmark (Oxford: Blackwell, 2010), 1657–76.

2. Sheldon Stryker and Richard T. Serpe, "Commitment, Identity Salience, and Role Behavior," in *Personality, Roles, and Social Behavior*, ed. William Ickes and Eric S. Knowles (New York: Springer-Verlag, 1982), 199–218.

3. Landon E. Hancock, "Significant Events in the Northern Irish Peace Process: Impact and Implementation," in *From Power Sharing to Democracy: Post-Conflict Institutions in Ethnically Divided Societies*, ed. Sid Noel (Montreal: McGill-Queen's University Press, 2005), 67–84.

4. My interviews were conducted in person in Northern Ireland in the fall of 2001. Interviewees were selected on the basis of two criteria. First, because the research focus of this work was on the street-level impact of the peace process, elites, people associated with political parties involved in the peace process, current members of paramilitary groups, and academics were ineligible for subject interviews—though some did provide background information. Second, because I was asking for in-depth personal information about the subjects' personal histories, I relied on personal introductions and followed up with a snowball sampling technique. The fact that all of my interviewees were willing to share further contacts with me indicates that, as personal as the interview processes were, they felt comfortable sharing their life histories and perceptions of the peace process with me.

5. The two newspapers, the Belfast *News Letter* and *Irish News*, were selected because they represent two of three provincewide dailies, produced in the province for its inhabitants. The *News Letter* speaks mostly to a Protestant/Loyalist audience while the *Irish News* caters to the Catholic/Nationalist community. The third major daily, the *Belfast Telegraph*, is an evening paper catering more to the business community. Rolston notes that the two morning dailies, in particular, are noted for their strong communal representation, reflecting the concerns of moderate nationalists and working-class loyalists. For more on the editorial personalities of each paper, see Philip Elliott, "Reporting Northern Ireland: A Study of News in Great Britain, Northern Ireland, and the Republic of Ireland," in *Ethnicity and the Media* (Paris: UNESCO, 1977), 263–76, and Bill Rolston, "News Fit to Print: Belfast's Daily Newspapers," in *The Media and Northern Ireland: Covering the Troubles*, ed. Bill Rolston (London: MacMillan, 1991), 152–86.

6. Survey data was aggregated from the raw data sets of nine separate surveys conducted by two groups. The first survey set is the Northern Ireland Social Attitudes Survey (NISA), collected in 1989, 1991, 1993, 1994, 1995, and 1996 by the Social and Community Planning Research Group. The second survey set is drawn from the Northern Ireland Life and Times survey (NILT), which separated from the NISA survey in 1997. The NILT surveys used for this analysis were drawn from 1998, 1999, and 2000. While many questions remained the same throughout all surveys, some changed, which limited some of the analyses that could

be run. Answers for each question were aggregated by year, giving a maximum N of 9 years.

7. The newspaper editorials were coded based on Adriana Bolívar's scheme for dissecting editorial language into *lead* statements, which draw the reader's attention to important themes, *follow* statements, which support the lead, and *valuate* statements, which transmit an evaluation of the topic at hand and may lay out recommendations for the reader. Editorials are viewed as both reflecting the community that they serve—else they would go out of business—and also attempting to persuade their community. For more see Adriana Bolívar, "The Structure of Newspaper Editorials," in *Advances in Written Text Analysis*, ed. Malcolm Coulthard (London: Routledge, 1994), 276–94.

8. Sheldon Stryker and Richard T. Serpe, "Commitment, Identity Salience, and Role Behavior."

9. Because my interview data required individuals to divulge a great deal about their personal experiences and histories, I have given interviewees pseudonyms and omitted background information.

10. "Work Needed on the Walls of Our Minds," *News Letter*, May 20, 1999. For more on the interaction between identity transformation and the modification of loyalist murals, see Lee Smithey, *Unionists, Loyalists and Conflict Transformation in Northern Ireland* (New York: Oxford University Press, 2011), and Wiedenhoft Murphy and Peden in chapter 4 of this volume.

11. "Work Needed on the Walls of Our Minds," *News Letter*, May 20, 1999.

12. "Three Years On, and the Fight for Democracy Is Far from Over," *News Letter*, April 13, 2001.

13. "The Right to Parade Must Be Upheld," *News Letter*, August 5, 1997.

14. Hancock, "Significant Events in the Northern Irish Peace Process."

15. From subsections (iii) and (vi) of the constitutional issues section of the text of the Agreement, signed April 10, 1998. Text cited from online version of the agreement at http://cain.ulst.ac.uk/events/peace/docs/agreement.htm, accessed October 31, 2002.

16. For more on the difficulty of bridging the communal divide and its importance in promoting peace, see chapter 9.

17. For more on contentious parades in Northern Ireland, see Dominic Bryan, *Orange Parades: The Politics of Ritual, Tradition, and Control* (London: Pluto Press, 2000); Neil Jarman, *Material Conflicts: Parades and Visual Displays in Northern Ireland* (Oxford: Berg, 1997); Neil Jarman and Dominic Bryan, *Parade and Protest: A Discussion of Parading Disputes in Northern Ireland* (Coleraine: Centre for the Study of Conflict, 1996); John Wilson and Karyn Stapleton, "Voices of Commemoration: The Discourse of Celebration and Confrontation in Northern Ireland," *Text* 25 (5) (2005): 633–64; and Smithey, *Unionists, Loyalists and Conflict Transformation in Northern Ireland*.

18. "Drumcree Impasse Needs to Be Broken," *News Letter*, January 24, 1997.

19. "The Search for Accommodation Must Not End," *News Letter*, July 7, 1997.

20. "Time for Cool Heads and Voices of Sanity," *News Letter*, July 8, 1997.

21. "An Air of Hope in Londonderry," *News Letter*, August 4, 1998.

22. "Credit to the Boys," *News Letter*, April 6, 1999.

23. "Marching Season Off on Wrong Foot," *News Letter*, March 7, 2000.

24. "If Talking Means Walking It Ought to Be Considered," *News Letter*, June 27, 2001.

25. These findings are supported by Todd's assertion that loyalists, particularly members of the Orange Order, "can no longer count on wider Protestant support" for their activities and by Smithey's analysis showing that the Orange Order is shifting toward a more inclusive celebration of the twelfth in order to address falling membership—particularly in urban areas—and the perception of the Order as out of touch. For more see Smithey, *Unionists, Loyalists and Conflict Transformation in Northern Ireland*, and Jennifer Todd, "Social Transformation, Collective Categories, and Identity Change," *Theory and Society* 34 (4) (2005): 429–63.

26. Both the NISA and the NILT were administered by a face-to-face survey with respondents. In addition, respondents were asked to fill in and submit a self-completed questionnaire, whose answers were then added to the oral responses.

27. The time-series analyses showing a rise in the number of respondents supporting much more mixing in primary school and significant decreases in those supporting current relations in primary and grammar/secondary schools were not included in order to save space.

28. Given that the NISA studies were funded by government support, as a part of the British Studies Association surveys, it is reasonable to assume that questions on education might exhibit some demand characteristics.

29. Again, the time-series analyses associated with table 3.6 were not included in order to save space.

30. Sheldon Stryker, "Identity Theory: Developments and Extensions," in *Self and Identity: Psychosocial Perspectives*, ed. Krysia Yardley and Terry Honess (New York: John Wiley & Sons, 1987), 89–103; Sheldon Stryker and Peter J. Burke, "The Past, Present, and Future of an Identity Theory," *Social Psychology Quarterly* 63 (4) (2000): 284–97; Stryker and Serpe, "Commitment, Identity Salience, and Role Behavior"; and Sheldon Stryker and Richard T. Serpe, "Identity Salience and Psychological Centrality: Equivalent, Overlapping, or Complementary Concepts?," *Social Psychology Quarterly* 57 (1) (1994): 16–35.

31. This is primarily a sociological definition. Psychological definitions stress the distinctiveness, prominence, or obviousness of a phenomenon and stem largely from analyses of perception and cognition. Although referring to a social-psychological process of self-identification, this work relies upon Stryker's use of commitment-producing salience.

32. Similar findings are expressed by Jennifer Todd, Theresa O'Keefe, Nathalie Rougier, and Lorenzo Cañás Bottos, "Fluid or Frozen? Choice and Change in Ethno-National Identification in Contemporary Northern Ireland," *Nationalism & Ethnic Politics* 12 (3/4) (2006): 323–46.

33. This finding is mirrored in Todd's analysis of a series of articles in a special issue of *Nations and Nationalism*, where she indicates that "key aspects" of identity change in post-Agreement Northern Ireland have been "sub-political" and "sub-ideological," noting

that "everyday constructions of national identity are subtly changed" by individual choice in minor situations and that even though these shifts can be constrained by communal norms they are also "capable of underpinning collective change." See Jennifer Todd, "Introduction: National Identity in Transition? Moving Out of Conflict in (Northern) Ireland," *Nations & Nationalism* 13 (4) (2007): 565–71, esp. 569.

34. Marilynn B. Brewer, "Superordinate Goals versus Superordinate Identity as Bases for Intergroup Cooperation," in *Social Identity Processes: Trends in Theory and Research*, ed. Dora Capozza and Rupert Brown (Thousand Oaks, CA: SAGE, 2000), 117–32, and Samuel L. Gaertner, John F. Dovidio, and Jason A. Nier, "The Common Ingroup Identity Model for Reducing Intergroup Bias: Progress and Challenges," in Capozza and Brown, *Social Identity Processes*, 133–48.

35. See Richard J. Crisp and Miles Hewstone, "Multiple Categorization and Social Identity," in Capozza and Brown, *Social Identity Processes*, 149–66.

36. Crisp and Hewstone, "Multiple Categorization and Social Identity," 161.

37. Hancock, "Significant Events in the Northern Irish Peace Process."

38. See Icek Ajzen, *Attitudes, Personality, and Behavior* (Chicago: Dorsey Press, 1988).

39. Alice H. Eagly and Shelly Chaiken, "Attitude Structure and Function," in *The Handbook of Social Psychology*, ed. Daniel T. Gilbert, Susan T. Fiske, and Gardner Lindzey (Boston: McGraw Hill, 1998), 269–322.

40. Ajzen, *Attitudes, Personality, and Behavior*, 299.

41. Ibid., 113.

42. Research on cross-community interaction in workplaces has shown that policies promoting mixed workplaces have largely been successful, with basic contact in the workplace engendering levels of comfort and tolerance of the other. However, as Kelly notes, this may have come at the expense of being able to address sectarian issues, indicating that the workplace is now often seen as a "sterile zone," where issues of conflict and sectarian division are not able to be discussed. For more on this, see Gráinne Kelly, "Progressing Good Relations and Reconciliation in Post-Agreement Northern Ireland," INCORE, University of Ulster, Office of First Minister and Deputy First Minister, 2012, and David A. Dickson and Owen D. W. Hargie, "Relational Communication between Catholics and Protestants in the Workplace: A Study of Policies, Practices and Procedures," Jordanstown: University of Ulster, Funded by the Office of First Minister and Deputy First Minister—Equality Unit—Research Branch, 2002. For more on the limitations of contact in the Northern Irish context, see Ed Cairns, *A Welling Up of Deep Unconscious Forces: Psychology and the Northern Ireland Conflict* (Coleraine: Centre for the Study of Conflict, 1994).

43. This assertion is supported by Cochrane's analysis indicating that in terms of issue transformation in Northern Ireland, a 2010 opinion poll showed that the three most important issues of concern for both communities were jobs, health, and education, indicating in Cochrane's estimation that "most people are focusing on public policy and service-delivery issues rather than on . . . ethnonational dogma." See Feargal Cochrane, "From Transition to Transformation in Ethnonational Conflict: Some Lessons from Northern Ireland," *Ethnopolitics* 11 (2) (2012): 182–203.

44. For more detail on this issue, see Landon E. Hancock, "Belfast's Interfaces: Zones of Conflict or Zones of Peace," in *Local Peacebuilding and National Peace: Interaction between Grassroots and Elite Processes*, ed. Christopher R. Mitchell and Landon E. Hancock (New York: Continuum, 2012), 111–32.

45. For further analysis of the need for security and the lessons from the Northern Ireland peace process, see Landon E. Hancock, "There Is No Alternative: Prospect Theory, the Yes Campaign and Selling the Good Friday Agreement," *Irish Political Studies* 26 (1) (2011): 95–116; Smithey, *Unionists, Loyalists, and Conflict Transformation in Northern Ireland*; and Doyle, chapter 6 in this volume.

46. For the role of spoilers in peace processes, see Andrew H. Kydd and Barbara F. Walter, "The Strategies of Terrorism," *International Security* 31 (1) (2006): 72–76; Edward Newman and Oliver Richmond, *Challenges to Peacebuilding: Managing Spoilers During Conflict Resolution* (New York: United Nations University Press, 2006); and Stephen John Stedman, "Spoiler Problems in Peace Processes," *International Security* 22 (2) (1997): 5–53. Greenhill and Major modify the spoiler thesis by emphasizing the capabilities of potential spoilers to affect the peace process. See Kelly M. Greenhill and Solomon Major, "The Perils of Profiling: Civil War Spoilers and the Collapse of Intrastate Peace Accords," *International Security* 31 (3) (2006/2007): 7–40.

47. For more on the sense that a groundswell for peace existed, see Helena Cobban, *The Moral Architecture of World Peace: Nobel Laureates Discuss our Global Future* (Charlottesville: University Press of Virginia, 2000); Landon E. Hancock, "The Northern Irish Peace Process: From Top to Bottom," *International Studies Review* 10 (2) (2008): 203–38; Charles A. Reilly, *Peace-building and Development in Guatemala and Northern Ireland* (Basingstoke: Palgrave Macmillan, 2009); and Sean Smith, "Hume Says Popular Support for Peace in Northern Ireland Has Strengthened," *Boston College Chronicle*, March 14, 1996.

48. "Assembly Band Keeps Playing Bravely On," *News Letter*, February 8, 2000.

49. This argument for the need for peace from below is stressed in chapter 9 of this volume.

4   Ulster-Scots Diaspora

Articulating a Politics of Identification
after "the Peace" in Northern Ireland

WENDY ANN WIEDENHOFT MURPHY and
MINDY PEDEN

This chapter explores the emerging Ulster-Scots identity in the context of the peace process in Northern Ireland. The peace process offered unionists and loyalists an opportunity to rethink their political positions as well as reimagine their identity.[1] This was owing to the fact that the Agreement moved the conflict from being one over territory to one of culture and identity.[2] The provision of greater equality to the nationalist community unfroze historic conceptions of unionist identity and allowed a transformation to begin.[3] Despite significant evidence that religious and political identities continue to divide the people of Northern Ireland,[4] we contend that unionism may be more malleable than many assume. Some scholars argue that this identity lacks political and cultural saliency because it is being formed in opposition to the empowerment of Irish Catholics or that it is reactionary because of a sense of betrayal by the British government.[5] We stress, in contrast, that this identity may be more constructive than oppositional or reactionary,[6] particularly if it opens up an opportunity to articulate an affirmative understanding of identification. One potentially constructive articulation of this identity is its relation to the Ulster-Scots diaspora in the United States.[7] We argue that the recent turn to the Ulster-Scots diaspora in the United States has intensified in Northern Ireland as an attempt to navigate the uncertainty of the peace process and a desire to construct an identity that is constituted by a dynamic history and culture instead of an entrenched sectarianism.

We begin this chapter by exploring the relationship between the Ulster-Scots identity and loyalism and unionism in the context of the peace process in Northern Ireland. Next, we provide a historical account of the dispersals of the Ulster-Scots from Scotland to Ulster and subsequently from Ulster to the United States. Since we are most interested in the latter dispersal, we emphasize the various themes that have informed the construction of the Ulster-Scots identification in the United States over time. We then analyze these themes in relation to the diasporic imaginings of the Ulster-Scots in Northern Ireland today, positing that these imaginings constitute a third dispersal from the United States back to Ulster. Finally, we explore the possibilities of what these diasporic imaginings offer in terms of Ulster-Scots identifications in Northern Ireland. These possibilities suggest the prospect that the Ulster-Scots identity can and will learn important lessons of the peace process articulated by White in chapter 1 of this book by emphasizing inclusivity, the role of third parties, and the significance of reconciliation in future articulations of their distinctiveness. Thus, rather than seeing the evolving identification of the Ulster-Scots as part of a "continuation of conflict by other means,"[8] we see it as at least in part a genuine attempt to move forward from a complex conflict in which identifications are often essentialized in such a way as to prevent inclusivity and reconciliation. Moreover, the turn to the diaspora reveals historical realities of identification that undermine the intractable essentialisms so embedded in the conflict.

Loyalism, Unionism, and the Peace Process: Ulster-Scots Possibilities

Historically Ulster-Scots identity was subsumed under a general allegiance to the British Crown and a belief that Northern Ireland should remain part of the United Kingdom in the forms of loyalism and unionism. Though loyalism is frequently used to refer to individuals, usually working class, who identify primarily with Ulster and unionism to individuals who identify primarily with Britain,[9] both identities intersect with Protestantism and an antagonism toward the possibility of a united Ireland. This opposition to a united Ireland and to republicans and nationalists who were fighting for it fueled loyalists and unionists during the "Troubles" in Northern Ireland. While until 1973 unionist politicians had historically engaged in gerrymandering to maintain their position of privilege and political power, loyalist paramilitaries resorted to violence "to impress upon Britain and Irish nationalism that political appeasement of republicanism was not a violence-free option."[10] Loyalist and unionist opposition to a united Ireland has been accompanied by anti-Catholicism and the attendant fear of being marginalized as minorities on an island with a clear majority of Catholics. This fear is one reason why loyalists and unionists have been unable to "come to terms with [their] cultural location on the Island of Ireland" and to develop "an alternative indigenous cultural synthesis."[11] If, as some scholars argue, loyalists and unionists are experiencing an "identity crisis" or "alienation" because of a weakening interest of the British government in the future of Northern Ireland, then the failure to establish a secure space on the island is particularly problematic.[12]

The emerging Ulster-Scots identity in Northern Ireland may fill the present void in loyalist and unionist identities and become a source of political and cultural assurance on the island of Ireland.[13] Scholars have suggested that after devolution many Ulster-Scots would like to see their identity be conceptually equaled to, not derivative from, an exclusive British, Irish, or Scottish identity.[14] This is perhaps not surprising in the context of devolution if, as Wilson and Stapleton claim, many "British" citizens are "now arguably more likely to draw upon national or regional (or indeed 'ethnic' or 'cultural') identity categories."[15] Nor is it surprising in the context of the peace process in Northern Ireland, especially after the 1994 cease-fire, which Finlayson argues "created a space" for loyalist identity "in which lines of discourse are being redrawn and in which the possibilities of new forms of identification can be glimpsed."[16] The Ulster-Scots form of identification may be one of these possibilities, a space between the Irish and English dichotomy that is neither inherently anti-British nor anti-Irish as Graham claims.[17]

While the peace process has increased the insecurity of loyalists and unionists, it has also created the opportunity for the Ulster-Scots identity to strengthen. The 1985 Anglo-Irish Agreement, an agreement between the British and Irish governments that circumvented local politics in Northern Ireland, resulted in a strong sense of British betrayal for loyalists and unionists. Loyalists and unionists were offended that the Irish government would now have a limited role in the affairs in Northern Ireland and viewed the agreement as supporting Irish unity and implicitly rewarding the violence of the republicans.[18] However, the Anglo-Irish Agreement included a recognition of the "rights and identities of the two traditions in Northern Ireland," including cultural heritage, which offered an opening for loyalists and unionists to "reactively reflect" on whether or not Ulster-Scots identity could be a "cultural booster" that would put them on par with Irish identity and culture.[19] This recognition of a "parity of esteem" between the two traditions in Northern Ireland was endorsed in the 1998 Agreement, and cross-border bodies were created in 1999 to promote the Ulster-Scots language and culture in the North and South of Ireland.[20] The Agreement provided institutional support for the Ulster-Scots identity through the creation of the Ulster-Scots Agency (U-SA), which is funded by the Department of Culture, Arts, and Leisure in Northern Ireland and the Department of Community, Rural, and Gaeltacht Affairs in the Republic of Ireland.[21] The U-SA has been a significant actor in promoting Ulster-Scots language and culture, emphasizing in particular the Ulster-Scots diaspora in the United States in a series of glossy pamphlets, commissioned murals, and its monthly newspaper. It is precisely this gaze from Ulster to the United States that we suggest needs to be analyzed for what it may or may not offer in terms of transcending loyalist and unionist insecurity and past sectarianism and encouraging political, social, and cultural confidence. To understand why the diasporic imaginings of the U-SA are important, we first look carefully at the dynamic history of two major dispersals of the Ulster-Scots, the first from Scotland to Ulster and the second from Ulster to the United States.

"Brewed in Scotland, Bottled in Ulster, Uncorked in the United States": Locating the Ulster-Scots Dispersals

THE FIRST DISPERSAL FROM SCOTLAND TO ULSTER

Self-identified Scottish settlers had inhabited sections of the north of Ireland for centuries, particularly County Down and County Antrim, but the large-scale settlement or plantation of Ulster took off in 1609 after the last native Irish earls of Tyrone and Tyrconnell fled Ireland permanently.[22] Plantation was a British colonial policy in which land was confiscated from indigenous Irish Catholics and placed under the control of planters (or colonizers depending on one's political perspective) from Scotland and England. Though planters were "drawn from every class of British society," they were stereotyped as "the scum of both nations [Scotland and England], who, for debt or breaking and fleeing from justice, or seeking shelter, came thither."[23] The Scots, in particular, were viewed as troublemakers owing to their dissenting religious convictions and adherence to Presbyterianism. The majority of Scottish planters brought their Presbyterian faith with them to Ulster, but their status was not recognized by the Church of Ireland, which was controlled by Anglicans, and like the Catholic Irish, they did not have full political rights. Furthermore, like the Catholic Irish, the Ulster-Scots suffered religious intolerance and dispossession of their land from the English Crown and Parliament.[24] Though most were not as financially well off as Anglican Protestants and were more likely to rent than own land, many Ulster-Scots did have enough economic independence to not be completely subordinated by the Anglican power structure.[25] It is estimated that by 1633 one-half to two-thirds of all planters in Ulster were Scottish and that by 1715 approximately 200,000 of the 600,000 people living in Ulster were Presbyterians.[26]

Repression of Presbyterianism in Scotland during the 1670s and 1680s, including the Black Act of 1670, which made field preaching illegal and punishable by death, and the Test Act of 1681, which forced rebels of the Black Act to renounce their Presbyterian faith, stimulated another round of migration from Scotland to Ulster. However, this attraction to Ulster did not last long after the Catholic King James II came to the throne in 1685. James II enacted policies in Ireland to empower the Catholics at the expense of the Protestant establishment, resulting in a Catholic-dominated army and civil administration. Many Ulster Protestants, including Presbyterians, abandoned their homes in Ulster during 1688 and fled to Scotland and England, fearing that Catholics in Ireland would stage a repeat of the 1641 massacre of Irish Protestants.[27] Many of those who did not leave Ulster dispersed internally to the Protestant strongholds of Derry and Enniskillen. According to Chepesiuk, 30,000 Protestants left Antrim and Lisburn to relocate in Derry, burning their homes and crops before they left.[28] This movement of people certainly strained the food supply and amplified the suffering during the Siege of Derry in 1689. According to Bardon, "the fate of the Protestant settlement in Ulster depended on Derry's ability to hold out" against King James's army.[29] The triumph over King James at Derry reinforced the resolve that Ulster Protestants would not surrender even under the most adverse circumstances—a theme that has continued to inform Protestant identity formation in Northern Ireland to this day.

After the triumph of the Protestant King William of Orange over King James II in 1690, Ulster-Scots could again feel politically and economically secure in Ireland, and approximately 50,000 Scots migrated to Ulster between 1690 and 1697. New policies were enacted—such as the Test Act of 1704, which forced all public office holders, soldiers, members of municipal corporations, and civil servants to take communion in the Church of England—that were aimed at suppressing Catholics in Ireland but also affected Presbyterians. For example, Ulster-Scot Presbyterian ministers no longer had legal standing and could not officiate marriages and in some cases funerals;[30] however, they were still paid a royal stipend of £1,200 per year.[31]

In addition to religious intolerance, Ulster-Scots also suffered economic inequality, particularly from trade laws that restricted exports from Ireland. The severe regulation of the wool trade left only England and Wales as possible destinations for export from Ireland, limiting this once lucrative industry.[32] The British did encourage the linen industry in Ulster because it "did not conflict with English commercial interests."[33] However, the success of the linen industry set the stage for the Ulster-Scot dispersion to the United States. Flaxseed from the American colonies fueled the linen industry in Ulster, stimulating trade and providing a somewhat predictable pattern of travel for those interested in leaving Ulster. Although some Ulster-Scots prospered from the linen industry, many faced financial stress because rents on land intensified. Some refused to bid on overpriced land when their leases expired and lost their property; others sold the interest in their holdings and used the money to immigrate to the United States.[34]

In sum, even though Ulster-Scots facilitated the extension of British power in Ireland,[35] they were not privileged to the same opportunities as Anglican Protestants. Indeed, at certain points in time they were treated with the same contempt as Irish Catholics, classified under the category of "Dissenters" and viewed with suspicion. The insecurity of their political, economic, and religious position on the island of Ireland convinced hundreds of thousands that immigration to America, even though it too was under British rule, could be the path to stability and freedom.

THE SECOND DISPERSAL FROM ULSTER TO THE UNITED STATES

According to Kirkham, English-speaking households in Ulster most likely first became aware of America as a possible place to migrate in the early

1680s.[36] This initial awareness was due to recruitment efforts by Quakers in Pennsylvania, promotional literature published by Scottish Quakers of East New Jersey, and Covenanter merchants and gentry in southwest Scotland.[37] It is estimated that from the 1680s to 1776 more than 250,000 people migrated from Ulster to the American colonies and that another 500,000 arrived after the American Revolution.[38] Other scholars, such as Griffin, suggest a more conservative number of 100,000 emigrants from Ulster to America between the years of 1718 and 1776; however, Griffin acknowledges that even this number represented the single largest movement of any group from the British and Irish Isles to British North America during the eighteenth century.[39] Most arrived in Philadelphia and settled in Pennsylvania, but large numbers also arrived via Boston and set up households in Massachusetts and New Hampshire.[40] According to Devine, Ulster-Scot immigrants to America significantly outnumbered emigrants from Scotland and approximately two-thirds of all immigrants to America from the island of Ireland before 1815 were Presbyterian.[41] Most Ulster migration during the early 1700s consisted of families rather than single individuals; many were not destitute and were able to sell their interests on leases they held to pay for their passage to America. This pattern of migration had consequences on both sides of the Atlantic as families that departed Ulster left a visible void in their local communities while those arriving in America were noticeable in the regions where they concentrated, initially in New England and Pennsylvania.[42] Subsequently, large numbers migrated into the Appalachian regions of North Carolina, South Carolina, Tennessee, and West Virginia.[43]

A variety of reasons for this large-scale migration have been debated, including religious intolerance, increasing rents, deficient harvests, and a population spike, but scholars have concluded recently that transatlantic trade was the key development that opened up the opportunity structure for this second dispersal.[44] The linen industry in Ulster stimulated this transatlantic trade in the 1720s, and by 1775 approximately 75 percent of all flaxseed imports to Ulster arrived from America. Many Ulster-Scots emigrants left on ships returning to America with finished linen goods.[45] According to Bardon, "vessels carrying casks of flaxseed to Ulster from the colonies were eager to take on passengers for the return journey," and "shipping companies sent their agents into all the leading marketing towns with enticing stories of cheap land and prosperity."[46] By the mid-1700s emigration had become a commercial enterprise, with shipping agents and American land promoters actively advertising their services to Ulster-Scots in newspapers.[47] The consensus that transatlantic trade was a key factor that made mass emigration from Ulster to America possible is not surprising. However, it is most likely that the reason why so many Ulster-Scots decided to leave was economic pressure caused by rising rents on land and religious obligations in the form of tithes to the Church of Ireland, which they were required to pay even after the Toleration Act of 1719 officially recognized Presbyterianism in Ireland.[48]

While economic pressure and religious intolerance in Ulster are significant themes in the construction of the Ulster-Scots diaspora, a sense of betrayal by the British Crown and government plays an important role as well. According to Green, "the Scotch-Irish came to this country [United States] full of bitter feeling toward the government of Great Britain. They had been oppressed by that government and they believed that it had wickedly broken faith with them."[49] This bitterness toward Britain is cited as one of the reasons why Ulster-Scots were so enthusiastic to fight as patriots during the American Revolution.[50] It is also a reason why Ulster-Scots were differentiated from Scottish emigrants, as the Scots were "reviled by the colonial patriots as a nation of unreconstructed loyalists and the treacherous allies of the imperial state."[51] According to Hall, British Crown agents believed that "a Presbyterian conspiracy was at the heart of the [American] revolutionary movement," with one agent going so far as to call the American Revolution a "Scotch-Irish Presbyterian Rebellion."[52] In a response of appreciation to American Ambassador Whitelaw Reid's opening address to the Edinburgh Philosophical Institution in 1911, Lord Rosebery credited the success of the American Revolution to the efforts of the Ulster-Scot diaspora but notes that their "motive was not entirely connected with liberty of the subject in the United States . . . but with a fixed and rooted animosity against the reigning dynasty in England."[53] Of course, the Scotch-Irish were quick to point out their affinity for Britain if they were compared to the Irish Catholics. This was expressed by the Ulster-Scot Rev. James MacGregor, who settled in Londonderry, New Hampshire. "We are surprised to hear ourselves termed Irish people, when we so frequently ventured our all for the British Crown and liberties against the Irish Papists."[54] This leads to another theme in the construction of the Ulster-Scots diaspora, the contentiousness over the legitimacy of the category of Scotch-Irish.

The category of Scotch-Irish was not used by the Ulster-Scots that first migrated to America.[55] Indeed, some shunned the category because it implied that they were "mere" Irish. They preferred to identify as "frontier inhabitants" or "northern dissenters," but as Griffin notes, the latter category meant little in America where Presbyterians were free to practice their religion.[56] It was not until the mass arrival of Irish Catholic immigrants in the 1840s that the category of Scotch-Irish became more widespread in America, although it still carried negative connotations of an implied "Irishness."[57] The concern of being mistaken as Irish Catholic encouraged the formation of the Scotch-Irish Society of America in 1889 as a means to "preserve the history and perpetuate the achievements of the Scotch-Irish race in America."[58] Although the Society claimed that it was nonpartisan, the organization helped to construct the Scotch-Irish as a distinct racial category to differentiate Scotch-Irish from the Irish Celtic "race."[59] However, there was some controversy over whether or not Scotch-Irish was an authentic racial or ethnic category. Thomas Hamilton Murray wrote several letters published in various Massachusetts newspapers in 1895, criticizing the notion that the Scotch-Irish existed independent of the Irish. According to Murray, Scotch-Irish was simply a "fad" that he found an "unutterable bore," and he could not understand why "anybody of Irish birth or descent should try to sink his glorious heritage and seek to establish himself as Scotch rather than Irish."[60] J. D. O'Connell went so far as to write a monograph, originally published in the *New York Sun*, to explain why the Scotch-Irish category was a "delusion."[61] Others, like Michael J. O'Brien, the director of the American Irish Historical Society during the early 1900s, argued that the category of Scotch-Irish was nothing more than "anti-Irish propaganda."[62]

Although the themes of economic pressure, religious intolerance, British betrayal, and ethnic/racial controversy are important components of the construction of the Ulster-Scots diaspora, what is most pronounced is the celebration of their achievements in the United States, especially the contributions they made to the founding of the nation.[63] From fighting as soldiers to win the American Revolution to printing the Declaration of Independence, conquering the Native Americans and settling the frontier, and becoming presidents of the United States, the emphasis on the successes of the Ulster-Scots and their descendants in the United States occupies a central place in the diasporic imaginings being constructed in Northern Ireland today. In the following section we explore several examples of these diasporic imaginings, suggesting that they may constitute a third dispersal— not of people, but of ideas and collective identifications—from the United States to Ulster, one that has been particularly engaged from the beginnings of the Irish peace process.

TOWARD A THIRD DISPERSAL
FROM THE UNITED STATES TO ULSTER

Following Tölölyan, we think of diasporas "not as the name of a fixed concept and social formation but as a process of collective identifications and form of identity."[64] Because the Ulster-Scots' turn to their diaspora in the United States has taken place in the context of a shifting political and social landscape, the status of its identification should not be seen as beholden to past or present essentialisms. The current gaze from Ulster to the United States may be constructive if "positive articulations of diaspora identity" have the capacity to "reach outside the normative territory and temporality (myth-history) of the nation-state."[65] Unlike republicans, loyalists and unionists did not look to the Ulster-Scots diaspora in the United States as a "resource" of financial or ideological support during the Troubles, even though the majority of Americans who identify as Irish are Protestants.[66] Indeed, according to Wilson, loyalists and unionists "have viewed American involvement in Northern Ireland as biased towards nationalists."[67] This is why, in the aftermath of the Agreement, the choice to emphasize transatlantic connections between Ulster and the United States is curious and may represent an important shift away from the essentialisms of loyalist and unionist identifications and toward the potentially more inclusive, hybrid Ulster-Scots identity. In the following part of this chapter we provide some evidence of this shift by examining the various promotions in Northern Ireland of the Ulster-Scots diaspora in the United States.

The most public displays of the Ulster-Scots diaspora are found in several murals. Murals were politically salient instruments of expressing ideological positions and making territorial claims during the Troubles, a function that they continue to serve to this day.[68] Paramilitary images dominated loyalist and unionist murals during the Troubles, but in recent years some of these violent and sectarian images have been painted over with historical and cultural depictions of the Ulster-Scots.[69] One of the repainted paramilitary murals that we observed in a working-class, loyalist housing estate in Newtownards represents a clear gaze toward the Ulster-Scots diaspora in the United States. This Ulster-Scots mural was funded by the U-SA, and children from the estate youth club, who are depicted in the stars in the lower left corner, assisted the artist of the mural.[70] The first section of the mural illustrates the Ulster-Scots migration from Ulster, over the Atlantic, to New York. What is interesting about this portrayal of the second dispersal from Ulster to the United States is the image of the

Statue of Liberty, which is in New York and not in Boston or Philadelphia, where the majority of this dispersal landed. However, the symbolic value of choosing the Statue of Liberty to represent the United States is not surprising as it would be difficult to find a symbol from Boston or Philadelphia that would be as familiar.

The major section of the mural pictures Davy Crockett ("hero of the Alamo"), holding his gun and waving his raccoon-tailed hat, and Daniel Boone ("led the Ulster-Scots pioneers into Kentucky"), sitting on a saddle and leaning against his gun, and are clearly less threatening than a picture of a masked man with a semiautomatic weapon. However, violence is not absent, as the guns pictured with Crockett and Boone signify their successes at defeating the Native Americans and Mexicans. Furthermore, the theme of violence is expressed in the mural through the quote by Rev. W. F. Marshall: "Hi Uncle Sam! Wherever there was fighting, Or wrong that needed righting, An Ulsterman was sighting, His Kentucky gun with care: All the road to Yorktown, That Ulsterman was there." The reference to Yorktown signifies the location of the British Army's surrender during the American Revolutionary War. Also depicted in the scene are Uncle Sam and United States Presidents James Buchanan and Andrew Jackson, whose ancestors were from Ulster. Several pioneer women are included, along with what looks like an American Revolutionary soldier (although the coloring of his "red coat" puts him on the side of the British, which the Ulster-Scots supposedly fought against) and a Scottish drummer and bagpiper.

Whether the projected Ulster-Scots history in the mural, such as arriving in New York or the color of the colonial soldier's coat, is true or false is beside the point. What is of interest is that the identification is styled as transatlantic connections to the achievements of what Americans are taught are "their" national heroes. What is of further interest is how the local community views the change in the mural. According to community activist Charlie Kincaid, "The community thinks this is fantastic. Hopefully in the long-term we can move away from the paramilitary mural images to incorporate more of our re-claimed history into the murals of Northern Ireland."[71]

Another example of this third dispersal of collective imaginings from the United States to Ulster is a series of murals, called "From Pioneers to Presidents," that depict United States Presidents George Washington, Theodore Roosevelt, and James Buchanan. All three murals are located in

Londonderry. The same mural of Buchanan also appears off the Shankill Road, a loyalist area in Belfast.

The mural of George Washington quotes him saying, "If defeated everywhere else I will make my final stand for liberty with the Scotch-Irish (Ulster-Scots) of my native Virginia." This quote signifies the contribution of Ulster-Scots soldiers and officers, who some argue made up more than half of all colonial soldiers and officers during the American Revolutionary War. Roosevelt is illustrated with a quote stating: "My forefathers were the men who had followed Cromwell and who shared in the defense of Derry and in the victories of Aughrim and the Boyne." The reference to Cromwell, the British military commander, is paradoxical in relation to Washington's celebration of the Ulster-Scots defeat of the British in the American colonies. However, it is not so peculiar considering that Cromwell's violent military campaign in Ulster in 1649 was to subjugate the native Irish and exact revenge for the massacre of Ulster Protestants in 1641.[72] While the Washington and Roosevelt murals make explicit references to violence grounded on war successes, the mural of Buchanan is more subtle. Buchanan is quoted saying, "My Ulster blood is my most priceless heritage." The implication of this quote is that there is something essentialist or primordial about the Ulster-Scots identity, of heritage based on blood. Interestingly, Buchanan witnessed the establishment of the Confederacy during his presidency. However, he did not support the right of the Southern states to secede and dismissed Confederate sympathizers from his cabinet.

Diasporic imaginings of the American Civil War are explicitly portrayed in a different mural located in a loyalist housing estate in North Belfast. This mural clearly celebrates the Confederacy, betraying a position about the nature of the war itself by referring to it as the "War of Northern Aggression." Those who call it the War of Northern Aggression favor states' rights as the primary issue of the war, while those who call it the Civil War think of it as the battle to end slavery or as an economically motivated war. For much of the Southern United States, identification as an American coexists with a feeling of great personal and regional loss. Thus, the war was not so much a civil war as a war of aggression by one region on another. Stonewall Jackson and Jefferson Davis figure prominently in this mural, and it is noted that Jackson's ancestors emigrated from Ulster to the United States in 1748. These identifications point to a cultural characteristic of independence and self-sufficiency, but as in the case with overidentification with the Confederacy in the United States being linked to racism, there is also a subtext of "us versus them." Superimposing the "Dixie" flag of the Confederacy on the red hand from the Ulster flag in the mural is intriguing, perhaps signifying the desire by Ulster-Scots to secede from the United Kingdom. A similar message can be read by the fact that the British flag partially portrayed on the mural is dwarfed by the red hand of Ulster. The juxtaposition of the American Civil War and the 1912 Ulster Covenant against Home Rule in the mural also emphasizes that independence is a route to civil and religious freedoms. Similar to the other murals we have described, this one glorifies war, albeit a war that was not successful.

The contributions that Ulster-Scots made in the founding of the United States is a central theme of one of the main organizations involved in producing this third dispersal of diasporic imagining from the United States to Ulster, the U-SA.[73] A series of glossy pamphlets, published by the U-SA, describe "how the Ulster-Scots or Scots-Irish came to America," "how men with Ulster connections helped shape America through battle," "the Ulster-Scots and America's proudest moment—the signing of the Declaration of Independence," and "Presidents with Ulster connections who helped shape America." Other pamphlets emphasize how Presbyterianism "defined church life in America," the ways in which the Ulster-Scots influenced folk and country music in the United States, and the naming of American towns and cities after places in Ulster. A pamphlet on the "Ulster-Scots in the USA today" captures the spirit of the agency's diasporic imaginings: "The personal ambitions and remarkable attainments of the sturdy Scots-Irish (Scotch-Irish) immigrants from Ulster and, their descendants, have become an integral part of the great American dream which still shines brightly with peoples in this land of the free and radiates back across the Atlantic to those who passionately claim the bonds of kinship."[74] This passage further illustrates our conceptualization of how ideas and collective forms of identification, such as "personal ambitions" and "remarkable attainments," constitute a third dispersal from the United States to Ulster.

The success of the Ulster-Scots and their ancestors in the United States is also disseminated by the U-SA in its monthly newspaper, *The Ulster-Scot*. An article in 2008 identified the Ulster ancestry of 40 percent of all US presidents and, in particular, the County Antrim roots of Republican candidate John McCain as well as the Irish ancestry of Democratic candidate Barack Obama. "Regardless of who wins the White House in 2008, the Scots-Irish and Irish once again will be well represented in the top job in the world."[75] Another article describes US president Theodore Roosevelt's Ulster ancestry, which the author claims the president learned about when his mother's family, Confederate sympathizers, moved from Georgia to New York during the American Civil War. Roosevelt "would have fitted well among his ain [own] folk," as he was "a rough and ready individual, someone prone to action rather than waiting around."[76] Less popular figures of Ulster-Scot ancestry, such as Daniel McCook and Robert McCook, Union Army officers during the American Civil War (the latter of whom became the governor of the North Dakota Territory); Gilbert Christian, who envisioned the first "professionally planned city" in Tennessee; and John Kinley Tener, a major league baseball pitcher who became the president of the National League as well as a US congressman and a governor of Pennsylvania, are regularly featured in the newspaper.[77] In addition to publicizing the successes of past Ulster-Scots, the U-SA has worked with the Young Ambassador's Program that brings twelve young adults from the United States to Northern Ireland to learn about Ulster-Scots culture, Irish culture, and the legacy of Saint Patrick.[78] In the summer of 2008 the U-SA, with the support of other groups, initiated an Ulster-Scots tour from Belfast to Carrickfergus that features a tour of Andrew Jackson's ancestral home.

The presence of the Ulster-Scots Agency suggests both the promises and perils of the Ulster-Scots identification. On the one hand, the agency is a part of the crucial work that is done in diasporas to maintain contacts, promote identity and belonging, and advocate within and across nation states. On the other hand, the mere promotion of successes, especially if emphasizing war heroes and ethnic blood ties, could result in an essentialist notion of identity that reproduces the past parochialism of loyalism and unionism. As Richard Zumkhawala-Cook has pointed out in the case of Scottish heritage in the United States, there is the possibility of "preserving identities of privilege through narratives of history, race, and national pride."[79] The prominent role of guns and fighting in the diasporic imaginings of the Ulster-Scots discussed earlier mirrors a cultural connection grounded in war successes. In both the context of Northern Ireland and the United States, any war successes for the Ulster-Scots can be narrated by someone else as a war failure and a site of great human loss. Furthermore, like the murals we analyze, the U-SA's emphasis on the successes of the Ulster-Scots and their descendants in the United States tends to overshadow the fact that many were "poor and mobile" and "scratched a precarious existence out of the woods beyond the reach of the law and polite society."[80] Indeed, Protestants of Irish descent have lower levels of education and family incomes compared with Catholics of Irish descent in the

United States today.[81] It makes sense why the successes of the Ulster-Scots are being emphasized in Northern Ireland; however, this could encourage a static temporality of the diaspora that fails to address how the Ulster-Scots diaspora in the United States has changed since its inception in the early eighteenth century. The fact that the U-SA is a cross-border organization that transcends the territory of Northern Ireland opens up the possibility that an Irish dimension to the Ulster-Scots identity could be recognized, which is something that has not transpired through loyalist or unionist forms of identifications.

Another example of the diasporic imaginings to the United States is the Ulster American Folk Park (UAFP), located in County Tyrone on the ancestral homestead of the Ulster-Scot Mellon family that immigrated to Pennsylvania in 1816. The UAFP was established in 1976 to commemorate the United States' bicentennial and was awarded the 2008 Northern Ireland Award for Visitor Attraction of the year. The UAFP includes a Center for Migration Studies where visitors can research their genealogies not just from Ulster but the entire island of Ireland as well. The most popular events at the UAFP include its annual Fourth of July celebration, which last year interestingly included a reenactment from the American Civil, not Revolutionary, War, and its annual Appalachian and Bluegrass Music Festival, which includes musicians from the United States. While the UAFP does take an all-Ireland approach to emigration, the Ulster-Scots and the culture of their descendants in Appalachia is stressed. Though war reenactments take place at the UAFP, and some of its American collection includes American rifles and military clothing and a life-size display of an Ulster-Scot settler fighting a Native American, much of its focus is on portraying Ulster-Scots pioneer lifestyle, including material artifacts like rope-making equipment, cooking utensils, and log cabins.[82] Like the other imaginings we have discussed so far, the successes of the Ulster-Scots diaspora in the United States are displayed at the UAFP. However, the focus on Appalachian and pioneer lifestyles implicitly acknowledges the difficulties the Ulster-Scots faced when settling the frontier as well as their austere lifestyle. The promotion of Appalachian music and dance at the UAFP moves away from a static temporality of the Ulster-Scots diaspora by bringing over Ulster-Scots currently engaged in the active production of culture. Furthermore, by including stories of immigrants not just from Ulster but also from the entire island of Ireland, the UAFP alludes to the "hybridity" of what most Americans refer to as the "Irish" diaspora.[83]

Conclusion

It is precisely the recognition of the hybridity and diversity of the Irish diaspora—not just in the United States, but also in Canada, Australia, New Zealand, and other locations throughout the world where emigrants from the island of Ireland have concentrated—that could provide another way for Ulster-Scots in Northern Ireland to reconcile competing identifications of "Britishness," "Scottishness," and "Irishness" and transcend the parochialism of loyalism and unionism.[84] Multiple levels of identity at play are characteristic of diasporas,[85] of which the Ulster-Scots constitute one in Ireland. Interviews conducted by Wilson and Stapleton of self-identified Ulster-Scots in Northern Ireland expressed a broad range of hybridity: "'Not Irish' / 'British, but Ulster Scots first' / 'British, but not English' / 'Scottish, not Irish' / 'Scottish, not English' / 'Commonality with the Irish' / 'Scottish and Irish.'"[86] Though one of the key features of any diaspora is self-conscious identification with a homeland, our historical narrative of the migrations, however, complicates any straightforward identification with either Ireland or Scotland or Britain as the homeland for Ulster-Scots. This is perhaps one reason why the multiple levels of identification in the Irish diaspora may be arriving from the imaginings of the third dispersal from the United States to Ulster. That this articulation is intensifying now suggests that the peace process has provided an opportunity for inclusivity and reconciliation in the realm of identity communication as well as a strategic awareness of the role of third parties, in this case the diaspora. It may be that we are learning that the intractable identifications that fueled conflict are neither intractable nor as historically straightforward as they seemed during the Troubles.

NOTES

1. See John D. Brewer, "Continuity and Change in Contemporary Ulster Protestantism," *Sociological Review* 52 (2) (2004): 265–83; Claire Mitchell, "Protestant Identification and Political Change in Northern Ireland," *Ethnic and Racial Studies* 26 (4) (2003): 612–31; David Officer and Graham Walker, "Protestant Ulster: Ethno-History, Memory and Contemporary Prospects," *National Identities* 2 (3) (2000): 293–307; Norman Porter, *Rethinking Unionism: An Alternative Vision for Northern Ireland,* updated ed. (Belfast: Blackstaff Press, 1998); and Neil Southern, "Britishness, 'Ulsterness' and Unionists Identity in Northern Ireland," *Nationalism and Ethnic Politics* 13 (1) (2007): 71–102. For a good overview of the present status of unionist and loyalist identity in Northern Ireland, see

Feargal Cochrane, *Unionist Politics and the Politics of Unionism since the Anglo-Irish Agreement*, new ed. (Cork: Cork University Press, 2001); Christopher Farrington, *Ulster Unionism and the Peace Process in Northern Ireland* (New York: Palgrave Macmillan, 2006); Bernadette C. Hayes, Ian McAllister, and Lizanne Dowds, "The Erosion of Consent: Protestant Disillusionment with the 1998 Northern Ireland Agreement," *Journal of Elections, Public Opinion and Parties* 15 (2) (2005): 147–67; James W. McAuley, *Ulster's Last Stand? Reconstructing Unionism after the Peace Process* (Dublin: Irish Academic Press, 2010); James W. McAuley and Jonathan Tonge, "Britishness (and Irishness) in Northern Ireland since the Good Friday Agreement," *Parliamentary Affairs* 63 (2) (2010): 266–85; James W. McAuley, Jonathan Tonge, and Andrew Mycock, *Loyal to the Core? Orangeism and Britishness in Northern Ireland* (Dublin: Irish Academic Press, 2011); Henry Patterson, "Unionism after Good Friday and St. Andrews," *Political Quarterly* 83 (2) (2012): 247–55; Peter Shirlow, "A Prosperity of Thought in an Age of Austerity: The Case of Ulster Loyalism," *Political Quarterly* 83 (2) (2012): 238–46; and Graham Spencer, *The State of Loyalism in Northern Ireland* (New York: Palgrave Macmillan, 2008). For the more general argument that identity reconstruction can promote peace and reconciliation, see Donna Hicks, "The Role of Identity Reconstruction in Promoting Reconciliation," in *Forgiveness and Reconciliation: Religion, Public Policy, and Conflict Transformation*, ed. Raymond G. Helmick, S.J., and Rodney L. Petersen (Philadelphia: Templeton Foundation Press, 2001), 129–49.

2. Cathal McCall, "From 'Long War' to 'War of the Lilies': 'Post-Conflict' Territorial Compromise and the Return of Cultural Politics," in *A Farewell to Arms? Beyond the Good Friday Agreement*, 2nd ed., ed. Michael Cox, Adrian Guelke, and Fiona Stephen (Manchester: Manchester University Press, 2006), 302–16.

3. Jennifer Todd, "Equality as Steady State or Equality as a Threshold? Northern Ireland after the Good Friday (Belfast) Agreement, 1998," in *The Challenges of Ethno-Nationalism: Case Studies in Identity Politics*, ed. Adrian Guelke (New York: Palgrave Macmillan, 2010), 147.

4. John Coakley, "National Identity in Northern Ireland: Stability or Change?" *Nations and Nationalism* 13 (4) (2007): 573–97, and Orla T. Muldoon, Karen Trew, Jennifer Todd, Nathalie Rougier, and Katrina McLaughlin, "Religious and National Identity after the Belfast Good Friday Agreement," *Political Psychology* 28 (1) (2007): 89–103.

5. Brian Graham, "The Past in the Present: The Shaping of Identity in Loyalist Ulster," *Terrorism and Political Violence* 16 (3) (2004): 483–500, and Cathal McCall, "Political Transformation and the Reinvention of the Ulster-Scots Identity and Culture," *Identities: Global Studies in Culture and Power* 9 (2) (2002): 197–218.

6. Karyn Stapleton and John Wilson, "Ulster-Scots Identity and Culture: The Missing Voices," *Identities: Global Studies in Culture and Power* 11 (4) (2004): 563–91, and John Wilson and Karyn Stapleton, "Identity Categories in Use: Britishness, Devolution and the Ulster-Scots Identity in Northern Ireland," in *Devolution and Identity*, ed. John Wilson and Karyn Stapleton (Aldershot: Ashgate, 2006), 11–32.

7. The ethnic category "Scotch-Irish" is more commonly used in the United States than "Ulster-Scot." The category "Scots-Irish" is also used by some to refer to Ulster-Scots.

For an elaboration of these different categories, see Michael Montgomery, "Nomenclature for Ulster Emigrants: Scotch-Irish or Scots-Irish?," *Familia* 20 (2004): 16–36. For the historical process within the United States of naming this group, see Kerby A. Miller, "The New England and Federalist Origins of 'Scotch-Irish' Ethnicity," in *Ulster and Scotland, 1600–2000: History, Language and Identity*, ed. William Kelly and John R. Young (Dublin: Four Courts Press, 2004), 105–18. For the difficulty in mobilizing the Scotch-Irish as a parallel diaspora for unionists as Irish Catholic Americans who have served as a continuing source of support, see Niall Ó Dochartaigh, "Reframing Online: Ulster Loyalists Imagine an American Audience," *Identities: Global Studies in Culture and Power* 16 (1) (2009): 102–27.

8. Lee A. Smithey, *Unionists, Loyalists and Conflict Transformation in Northern Ireland* (Oxford: Oxford University Press, 2011), 7.

9. Ulster is one of the four provinces of Ireland, historically composed of nine counties (Antrim, Armagh, Cavan, Derry, Donegal, Down, Fermanagh, Monaghan, and Tyrone). The partition of Ireland in 1920 included only six of these counties (Antrim, Armagh, Derry, Down, Fermanagh, and Tyrone) as the North of Ireland, which ensured a Protestant and unionist majority. For how the creation of the border affected unionist and loyalist identity, see Graham Dawson, *Making Peace with the Past? Memory, Trauma and the Irish Troubles* (Manchester: Manchester University Press, 2007), 209–28. For more on the construction of unionist and loyalist identity, see Alan Finlayson, "Nationalism as Ideological Interpellation: The Case of Ulster Loyalism," *Ethnic and Racial Studies* 19 (1) (1996): 88–112; Graham, "The Past in the Present"; and Jennifer Todd, "Two Traditions in Unionist Political Culture," *Irish Political Studies* 2 (1987): 1–26.

10. Marc Mulholland, *Northern Ireland: A Very Short Introduction* (Oxford: Oxford University Press, 2002), 89. The targets of much of this violence were Catholic civilians. Close to seven hundred Catholic civilians were killed by loyalist paramilitaries during the Troubles.

11. Brian Graham, "The Imagining of Place: Representation and Identity in Contemporary Ireland," in *In Search of Ireland: A Cultural Geography*, ed. Brian Graham (New York: Routledge, 1997), 197.

12. Arthur Aughey, *Under Siege: Ulster Unionism and the Anglo-Irish Agreement* (New York: St. Martin's Press, 1989); Claire Mitchell, "Protestant Identification and Political Change in Northern Ireland," *Ethnic and Racial Studies* 26 (4) (2003): 612–31; Neil Southern, "Protestant Alienation in Northern Ireland: A Political, Cultural and Geographic Examination," *Journal of Ethnic and Migration Studies* 33 (1) (2007): 159–80; and Graham Spencer, "The Decline of Ulster Unionism: The Problem of Identity, Image and Change," *Contemporary Politics* 12 (1) (2006): 45–63.

13. Graham, "The Past in the Present," and McCall, "Political Transformation and the Reinvention of the Ulster-Scots Identity and Culture."

14. Michael Hall, *Is There a Shared Ulster Heritage?* (Belfast: Island Publications, 2007); Peter Shirlow and Mark McGovern, "Introduction: Who Are 'the People'? Unionism, Protestantism and Loyalism in Northern Ireland," in *Who Are "the People"? Unionism,*

Protestantism and Loyalism in Northern Ireland, ed. Peter Shirlow and Mark McGovern (London: Pluto Press, 1997), 1–15; Stapleton and Wilson, "Ulster-Scots Identity and Culture"; and Wilson and Stapleton, "Identity Categories in Use."

15. Wilson and Stapleton, "Identity Categories in Use," 11.

16. Alan Finlayson, "Discourse and Contemporary Loyalist Identity," in Shirlow and McGovern, *Who Are "the People"?*, 88. The significance of the 1994 cease-fires in allowing unionists (and nationalists) to redefine their identity is also stressed by Hancock in chapter 3 of this volume.

17. Graham, "The Past in the Present," 396. See also Stapleton and Wilson, "Ulster-Scots Identity and Culture," 81.

18. Mulholland, *Northern Ireland*, 117, and Jonathan Tonge, *Northern Ireland: Conflict and Change* (New York: Longman, 2002), 127–33.

19. McCall, "Political Transformation and the Reinvention of the Ulster-Scots Identity and Culture," 199–200, and Tonge, *Northern Ireland*, 130.

20. McCall, "Political Transformation and the Reinvention of the Ulster-Scots Identity and Culture"; M. Nic Craith, "Politicised Linguistic Consciousness: The Case of Ulster-Scots," *Nations and Nationalism* 7 (1) (2001): 21–37; Katie Radford, "Creating an Ulster-Scot Revival," *Peace Review* 13 (1) (2001): 51–57; and Stapleton and Wilson, "Ulster-Scots Identity and Culture." The UK Committee of the European Bureau of Lesser-Used Languages recognized the Ulster-Scots dialect in 1993, and the British government acknowledged Ulster-Scots as a category of the Scots language in the 2000 European Charter for Regional and Minority Languages. There is controversy whether Ulster-Scots is a dialect or language. See Radford, "Creating an Ulster-Scot Revival," 53, and Stapleton and Wilson, "Ulster-Scots Identity and Culture," 565. Loyalists removed bilingual street signs in East Belfast because they mistakenly thought the Ulster-Scots renditions were Irish, leading to questions about whether loyalists or unionists in Northern Ireland can actually speak and/or understand the language (see McCall, "Political Transformation and the Reinvention of the Ulster-Scots Identity and Culture," 206).

21. See http://www.ulsterscotsagency.com/aboutus-overview.asp.

22. Jonathan Bardon, *A History of Ulster* (Belfast: Blackstaff Press, 1992); Henry Jones Ford, *The Scotch-Irish in America* (Princeton, NJ: Princeton University Press, 1915); James Graham Leyburn, *The Scotch-Irish: A Social History* (Chapel Hill: University of North Carolina Press, 1962); M. Perceval-Maxwell, *The Scottish Migration to Ulster in the Reign of James I* (London: Routledge and Kegan Paul, 1973); and James Barkley Woodburn, *The Ulster-Scot, His History and Religion* (London: H.R. Allenson Limited, 1914). "Brewed in Scotland, Bottled in Ulster, Uncorked in the United States" is the slogan of ScotchIrish .net, which is an Internet community that promotes Scotch-Irish history and culture.

23. Bardon, *A History of Ulster*, 127–28.

24. Ronald Chepesiuk, *The Scotch-Irish: From the North of Ireland to the Making of America* (Jefferson, NC: McFarland & Company, 2001), 68.

25. S. C. Connolly, "Ulster Presbyterians: Religion, Culture, and Politics, 1660–1850," in *Ulster and North America: Transatlantic Perspectives on the Scotch-Irish*, ed. H. Tyler

Blethen and Curtis W. Wood Jr. (Tuscaloosa: University of Alabama Press, 1997), 30, and Patrick Griffin, *The People with No Name: Ireland's Ulster-Scots, America's Scots Irish, and the Creation of a British Atlantic World, 1689–1764* (Princeton, NJ: Princeton University Press, 2001), 3.

26. Chepesiuk, *The Scotch-Irish*, 49 and 70, and R. J. Dickson, *Ulster Emigration to Colonial America, 1718–1775* (London: Routledge & Kegan Paul, 1966), 3.

27. Chepesiuk, *The Scotch-Irish*, 70–74. There is a debate regarding the magnitude of this massacre (see Bardon, *A History of Ulster*, 138). However, it plays a role in contemporary narratives of the history of Protestants in Ulster, though today it is sometimes referred to as the "ethnic cleansing" or genocide.

28. Chepesiuk, *The Scotch-Irish*, 77.

29. Bardon, *A History of Ulster*, 154.

30. Chepesiuk, *The Scotch-Irish*, 93–95; Connolly, "Ulster Presbyterians," 26–27; and Woodburn, *The Ulster-Scot*, 213–14.

31. Bardon, *A History of Ulster*, 171.

32. Woodburn, *The Ulster-Scot*, 213–14.

33. Bardon, *A History of Ulster*, 180.

34. Ibid., 178; Chepesiuk, *The Scotch-Irish*, 96–98; Woodburn, *The Ulster-Scot*, 221.

35. Griffin, *The People with No Name*, 1.

36. Graeme Kirkham, "Ulster Emigration to North America, 1680–1720," in Blethen and Wood, *Ulster and North America*, 78.

37. Kirkham, "Ulster Emigration to North America," and Leyburn, *The Scotch-Irish*.

38. H. Tyler Blethen and Curtis W. Wood Jr., "Introduction," in Blethen and Wood, *Ulster and North America*, 3.

39. Griffin, *The People with No Name*, 1.

40. Samuel Green, *The Scotch-Irish in America* (Worcester, MA: Press of Charles Hamilton, 1895), and Griffin, *The People with No Name*.

41. Thomas Martin Devine, *Scotland's Empire and the Shaping of the Americas, 1600–1815* (Washington: Smithsonian Books, 2004), 97.

42. Benjamin Franklin estimated in 1776 that Ulster-Scots and their descendants constituted one-third of Pennsylvania's 350,000 inhabitants (see Bardon, *A History of Ulster*, 210).

43. Devine, *Scotland's Empire and the Shaping of the Americas*, and Kirkham, "Ulster Emigration to North America."

44. Devine, *Scotland's Empire and the Shaping of the Americas*; Kirkham, "Ulster Emigration to North America"; and Griffin, *The People with No Name*.

45. Chepesiuk, *The Scotch-Irish*, 96–98.

46. Bardon, *A History of Ulster*, 210.

47. Ibid.; Chepesiuk, *The Scotch-Irish*, 105; and Kirkham, "Ulster Emigration to North America," 92.

48. Bardon, *A History of Ulster*, 173 and 178.

49. Green, *The Scotch-Irish in America*, 24. Green was a leading figure in the movement to establish public libraries in the United States. His comments on the Scotch-Irish are

from a report he delivered at the Council of the American Antiquarian Society's semiannual meeting on April 24, 1895. A synopsis of this report was published in several Boston newspapers, which initiated a number of critical letters to the editors that were published in these newspapers and subsequently included in the appendix of Green's *The Scotch-Irish in America*.

50. Green, *The Scotch-Irish in America*, and Hall, *Is There a Shared Ulster Heritage?*

51. Devine, *Scotland's Empire and the Shaping of the Americas*, 181.

52. Hall, *Is There a Shared Ulster Heritage?*, 19.

53. Whitelaw Reid, *The Scot in America and the Ulster-Scot* (London: Harrison and Sons, 1911), 55. Some scholars claim that this hatred of England may be exaggerated and that some Ulster-Scots emigrants were either neutral or supported the Crown during the American Revolution (see Devine, *Scotland's Empire and the Shaping of the Americas*, 157).

54. Quoted in Reid, *The Scot in America and the Ulster-Scot*, 22–23.

55. Leyburn, *The Scotch-Irish*, xi and 327.

56. Griffin, *The People with No Name*, 2.

57. Devine, *Scotland's Empire and the Shaping of the Americas*, 143.

58. Ibid.

59. See Proceedings of the Second Scotch-Irish Congress, 1889 and 1890, and Devine, *Scotland's Empire and the Shaping of the Americas*.

60. Green, *The Scotch-Irish in America*, 56 and 58.

61. Jeremiah D. O'Connell, *The "Scotch-Irish" Delusion in America* (Washington, DC: American-Irish Publications, 1897). This monograph was a response to an article that Charles Eliot, president of Harvard University, published in the *Atlantic Monthly* in 1896. Eliot's article, "Five American Contributions to Civilization," failed to mention the Irish, but did specify the Scotch.

62. Michael Montgomery, "Nomenclature for Ulster Emigrants: Scotch-Irish or Scots-Irish?," *Familia* (20) (2004): 21.

63. Charles Bolton, *Scotch Irish Pioneers in Ulster and America* (Boston: Bacon and Brown, 1910); John Walker Dinsmore, *The Scotch-Irish in America: Their History, Traits, Institutions and Influences* (Chicago: Winona Publishing Company, 1906); Green, *The Scotch-Irish in America*; Griffin, *The People with No Name*; Montgomery, "Nomenclature for Ulster Emigrants"; Reid, *The Scot in America and the Ulster-Scot*; and James Webb, *Born Fighting: How the Scots-Irish Shaped America* (New York: Broadway Books, 2004).

64. Khachig Tölölyan, "The Contemporary Discourse of Diaspora Studies," *Comparative Studies of South Asia, Africa, and the Middle East* 27 (3) (2007): 649–50.

65. James Clifford, "Diasporas," *Cultural Anthropology* 9 (3) (1994): 307.

66. For how diasporas can serve as resources, see Emmanuel Ma Mung, "Dispersal as a Resource," *Diaspora* 13 (2) (2004): 211–26. The fact that most Americans who identify as Irish are Protestant is explained in Michael P. Carroll, "How the Irish Became Protestant in America," *Religion and American Culture* 16 (1) (2006): 25–54, and Brian Walker, "The Lost Tribes of Ireland: Diversity, Identity and Loss among the Irish Diaspora," *Irish Studies Review* 15 (3) (2007): 267–82.

67. Andrew J. Wilson, "The Ulster Unionist Party and the U.S. Role in the Northern Ireland Peace Process, 1994–2000," *Policy Studies Journal* 28 (4) (2000): 858.

68. Jean Abshire, "Northern Ireland's Politics in Paint," *Peace Review* 15 (2) (2003): 149–61; Neil Jarman, *Material Conflicts: Parades and Visual Displays in Northern Ireland* (New York: Berg, 1997); and Bill Rolston, *Politics and Painting: Murals and Conflict in Northern Ireland* (London: Associated University Presses, 1991).

69. In 2007 £3.3 million in government funds were earmarked to repaint paramilitary murals with historical and cultural images and sports stars. Some of the murals include depictions of the Titanic, which was built in Belfast, images from the books of C. S. Lewis, who was born in Belfast, and football star David Healy.

70. The authors observed this mural in the summer of 2006 and were able to meet two of the children who helped the artist.

71. Charlie Kincaid, quoted in a comment posted at http://www.scotchirish.net /forum/index.php?showtopic=1938, November 29, 2004.

72. Bardon, *A History of Ulster*, 140–41. See also http://www.scotchirish.net/scots%20 irish%20murals.php4 and http://www.scotchirish.net/Revolution%20and%20Civil%20 War.php4.

73. Diasporic imaginings of the Ulster-Scots in the United States is but one of many ways that the U-SA is encouraging Ulster-Scots identity in Northern Ireland. It is also focused on making connections between the Ulster-Scots diaspora in Northern Ireland and its homeland in Scotland. Much of its work involves creating and supporting Ulster-Scots language and culture programs for children and organizing Ulster-Scots festivals in both the North and South of Ireland throughout the year. Interestingly, the U-SA is attempting to reinvent the annual July 11 and July 12 Orange Order bonfires and parades into Ulster-Scots "celebrations of culture" and "Ulster-Scots Family Fun and Educational Awareness Days." Long a bastion of loyalist and unionist identities, the Orange Order is an exclusively Protestant organization that is viewed by republicans and nationalists as inherently sectarian.

74. B. Kennedy, "The Ulster-Scots in the USA Today," December 17, 2009, http:// www.ulsterscotsagency.com/fs/doc/new_range_of_ulster-scots_booklets/US_in_USA_ Today_BK2_AW_6.pdf, accessed March 26, 2013. Most of these pamphlets were written using historical research by Billy Kennedy, a popular historian who has written many books on the Ulster-Scots. Kennedy is a lead writer for the *Belfast News Letter* and the editor of the U-SA's monthly newspaper, *The Ulster-Scot.*

75. Fred Brown, "Ulster Dimension in the Presidential Race," *The Ulster-Scot*, April 2008, 15.

76. David Hume, "Anniversary Year for the Irvines of the Gleno Valley," *The Ulster-Scot*, May 2008, 13.

77. Alister J. McReynolds, "Exploits of the Fighting McCooks," *The Ulster-Scot*, March 2006, 13; Fred Brown, "Clerics Who Were Influence for Good," *The Ulster-Scot*, March 2008, 15; and Colin McAlpin, "Ulsterman with a Focus on American Baseball," *The Ulster-Scot*, July 2008, 11.

78. Billy Kennedy, "Trans-Atlantic Perspective on Our Culture," *The Ulster-Scot*, March 2008, 1.

79. Richard Zumkhawala-Cook, "The Mark of Scottish America," *Diaspora* 14 (1) (2005): 111.

80. Griffin, *The People with No Name*, 3.

81. Walker, "The Lost Tribes of Ireland," 271.

82. For more on the folk park, see http://www.nmni.com/uafp/collections.

83. Mary J. Hickman, "'Locating' the Irish Diaspora," *Irish Journal of Sociology* 11 (2) (2002): 8–26.

84. Ibid., and Walker, "The Lost Tribes of Ireland."

85. Jacob Bercovitch, "A Neglected Relationship: Diasporas and Conflict Resolution," in *Diasporas in Conflict: Peace-Makers or Peace-Wreckers*, ed. Hazel Smith and Paul Stares (New York: United Nations University Press, 2007), 19–20.

86. Wilson and Stapleton, "Identity Categories in Use," 11.

5 The Victory and Defeat of the IRA?

Neoconservative Interpretations of the Northern Ireland Peace Process

PAUL DIXON

> Burke is the best model for what might be called politicians of the possible. Politicians who seek to make a working peace, not in some perfect world that never was, but in this, the flawed world, which is our only workshop.
>
> David Trimble, Nobel Peace Prize Speech, 1998

The Northern Ireland peace process appears to represent a successful case of two democratic governments— the British and Irish—negotiating with "terrorists" to achieve an accommodation. The peace process has achieved an inclusive power-sharing accommodation that has led Sinn Féin and the Irish Republican Army (IRA) to moderate their political positions, enter government, and decommission weapons. This has led to a major reduction in the level of violence.

Various actors with competing political agendas claim to have discovered "the lessons" of Northern Ireland for other areas in conflict. The British government's orthodox interpretation, widely shared in Ireland and the United States, argues that it is always, or nearly always, a good idea to talk to the enemy. Key figures in the British Labour government who negotiated the peace process have promoted the orthodox interpretation, arguing that the key lesson to be drawn from Northern Ireland is that talking to the enemy is generally a good idea.[1] This is because a peace process can provide a nonviolent path to accommodation, and once the paramilitaries become involved in talks and negotiations it is more difficult for them to extricate themselves from the democratic process and return to violence. They argue that politicians should not believe their own demonizing propaganda about the evil, criminality, or pathology of terrorists but instead work pragmatically to draw paramilitary organizations and their supporters away from violence. This involves a realist approach tempered by idealism in which political skills or lies and manipulation are justifiable because the end justifies the means.[2] After the decline of the moderate parties, the "extreme" Democratic Unionist Party (DUP) and Sinn Féin were brought into a power-sharing government in 2007, an accommodation that was more stable because it could not be outflanked by hard-liners.

This orthodox interpretation is probably the dominant explanation of the peace process because it overlaps with the account of powerful actors who negotiated it in Britain and Ireland. Notably, this also includes the realist practice of John Major's Conservative governments toward Northern Ireland from 1990 to 1997.[3] The orthodox interpretation has been criticized for underplaying the conditions that were placed on paramilitaries for entering democratic politics, overindulging paramilitary organizations in the ongoing negotiations of the peace process, and for failing to sufficiently support the moderate parties.[4]

Since 2007 a neoconservative interpretation of the peace process has challenged the orthodox account. It argues that the lesson of Northern Ireland is the necessity of defeating terrorists before talking to them or negotiating with evil. Neoconservatives have made a radical critique of Labour's orthodox interpretation of the peace process because their ideological position is hostile to negotiating with terrorists, whether in Northern Ireland, the Middle East, or Afghanistan (i.e., Hamas, Hezbollah, the "Sunni" militias in Iraq, Al Qaeda, and the Taliban). Neoconservatives present the world as a Manichaean struggle between good and evil in which you are either with us or against us on this ideological crusade. This certainty leads to moral clarity and a refusal to compromise on fundamental principles. Neoconservatives proclaim their idealism and contrast themselves with the realism of their critics, who are prepared to compromise their principles, appease, talk to terrorists, and negotiate with evil.[5]

The Northern Ireland peace process is a difficult case for neoconservatives because talking to terrorists has, apparently, helped to bring about a major transformation in a terrorist organization from pursuing armed struggle to participating in the democratic process and wielding executive power. Labour's orthodox interpretation of the peace process can be a powerful example of why engaging with insurgent groups and making concessions to them might be a more effective way of dealing with political violence than attempting to defeat them militarily.

David Trimble, leader of the Ulster Unionist Party (UUP) from 1995 to 2005, played a key role in bringing peace to Northern Ireland.[6] Elected as a hard-line candidate for the leadership of the UUP, he entered all-party talks with republicans in September 1997 and then supported the Agreement in April 1998. Arguably, the Labour government failed to give moderates sufficient support in the post-1998 period by, for example, insisting on IRA decommissioning. In 2003 the UUP were defeated by the DUP at the polls and the "Trimbleistas"—supporters of the UUP leader—began to take a more skeptical view of the peace process, probably in an attempt to out-flank the DUP and win the battle for unionism. After 2003 they began to argue that the reintroduction of direct rule might be preferable to the attempts to negotiate power sharing between Sinn Féin and the DUP. The success of these negotiations and other signs of progress undermined the anti–peace process unionist camp, which was reduced to the ultra-hard-liners of Traditional Unionist Voice and some on the right of the British Conservative Party. Since 2007 the Trimbleistas have gravitated to a more "orthodox" neoconservative position, which is articulated in Bew, Framp-ton, and Gurruchaga's book, *Talking to Terrorists: Making Peace in Northern Ireland and the Basque Country*, published in 2009.

The evolution of the Trimbleistas has created some confusion in the neoconservative narrative. This is illustrated in the writings of Bew and Frampton (2004–12), who were founding members of the neoconservative Henry Jackson Society (2005), which takes a hawkish view on military intervention and is hostile to negotiating with terrorists. There are three strands to the neoconservative narrative on the peace process:

1. *Trimbleistas (supporters of the Ulster Unionist Party leader, David Trimble), 1995–2003.* They argue conflict between the British government and the IRA was deadlocked. The peace process was, therefore, a difficult negotiating process requiring pragmatic realism to overcome the divisions between the parties and the constraints affecting political leaders. The Agreement represented a victory for unionism, but the Labour government subsequently failed to support the moderate parties sufficiently. Trimble's pragmatic realism during this period makes it questionable whether this perspective is neoconservative.

2. *An anti–peace process unionism.* The IRA won the war, and the British government and the UUP entered a surrender process in which they capitulated to the IRA rather than preserve democratic principles and ideals.
3. *An "orthodox" neoconservatism.* The British government defeated the IRA because it used hard power and the dirty war to defeat the IRA before talking to it: guns first, talks later.[7] The British government also laid down strict conditions for negotiating with the IRA and refused to compromise core principles and democratic norms. The peace process represents a victory for the British government and the triumph of idealism over realism. The international lesson to be drawn from Northern Ireland is to use hard power to defeat terrorists before negotiating their surrender.[8]

This chapter will argue that Bew and Frampton's writings on Northern Ireland represent an attempt to reconcile elements of these three, incompatible, neoconservative narratives on the conflict in order to capture the Northern Ireland case for neoconservatism in the debates on how to deal with terrorism. This reflects the neoconservatives' attempts to win over two contrasting audiences.

- First, in Northern Ireland they employed a unionist, anti–peace process perspective to outflank the DUP electorally, which in the period 2003–7 showed signs of negotiating a power-sharing deal with Sinn Féin.
- Second, since 2007 an "orthodox" neoconservative analysis has been deployed to win international support for the proposition that you should defeat terrorists through dirty war and hard power before talking to them. Neoconservatives argue that Northern Ireland is the exception to the rule and that you should nearly never talk to the enemy.

The unionist anti–peace process and orthodox neoconservative narratives provide moralistic, ideologically driven, and inaccurate accounts of the peace process from which lessons are derived. These lessons emphasize the efficacy of military force in achieving victory over terrorism. By contrast, I argue that the peace process represented a triumph of nonviolent politics, involving political engagement, negotiation, and compromise. These negotiations were marked by a considerable degree of pragmatic realism demonstrated, not least of all, by Trimble's record during the period 1995–2003. The British government did not dictate terms to republicans during the peace process because there is little evidence that the IRA was either defeated or had won. Since the conflict between the British state and the IRA was deadlocked, the peace process did not represent the victors imposing their will on republicans. Rather a complex process of negotiation—choreography and cooperation among elites as well as conflict—involved uncertainty and contingency and was characterized by a considerable degree of pragmatism, compromise, and deception. Trimble declared his Burkean realism in negotiating the peace process, and it was only when the UUP were no longer negotiating the peace process that the Trimbleistas gravitated toward the idealism of anti–peace process unionism and orthodox neoconservatism.

This chapter will first describe neoconservative attitudes toward talking to terrorists and then elaborate Trimble's realist position (1995–2003) and that of anti–peace process unionists. It will then critique the orthodox neoconservative interpretation of the peace process, arguing that there is insufficient evidence to suggest that the dirty war was effective or that the IRA was defeated. The success of the peace process was more the result of a pragmatic realism than the neoconservatives' fundamentalist idealism. Finally, I comment on the problem of drawing lessons from the Northern Ireland peace process.

Neoconservatives: Nearly Never Talking to Terrorists

The definition of neoconservatism is controversial. Vaisse has argued: "Discontinuity, heterogeneity, and contradiction are an integral part of neoconservatism, a word that is in danger of losing any precise meaning."[9] For the neoconservatives, the United States is in permanent crisis, whether from the Soviet threat, terrorism, or Islamofascism. This justifies an ever-increasing military budget. Neoconservatives are "strict universalists" and "can be compared to the Jacobins of the French Revolution because of their revolutionary zeal to transform states through US military intervention."[10]

Neoconservatives take a Manichaean view of the world, and this is reflected in their policy prescriptions. This moral clarity explains neoconservative opposition to the peace processes both in Northern Ireland and the Middle East. In the Middle East, Ross and Makovsky argue, the neoconservatives start from the assertion that "the Arabs categorically reject Israel, and peace is not possible as a result. The corollary is that if the Arabs prove themselves in terms of accepting Israel, then peace can be possible, but until that point there is no reason for US engagement on peace. Engagement is futile at best and counterproductive at worst, and as a result, disengagement is the right policy prescription."[11]

In 1996 several neoconservatives published "A Clear Break" for the incoming Netanyahu government, urging the Israeli prime minister to abandon the peace process. The Bush administration opposed even using the term "peace process." For neoconservatives the peace process represented the Palestinian Liberation Organization's (PLO's) deceptive and tactical use of the armed struggle to bring about Israel's destruction, and they believed that peace or compromise in the Middle East was an illusion.[12] Irving Kristol claimed that the Middle East peace process was an appeasement process and that the reason peace processes in Cyprus and Northern Ireland get nowhere "is that no mediator can envisage an end situation satisfactory to both parties."[13]

Moral relativism, neoconservatives claim, leads to negotiation, the appeasement of evil, and defeatism. This encourages terrorists to exploit the weakness of the good and undermines nonviolent moderates and democrats by demonstrating that the gun is more effective than the ballot box. Negotiations are perilous because terrorists may use them to win concessions, rearm, regroup, and destroy democracy. Negotiations are also dangerous because they encourage terrorists to increase violence in the belief that they are winning. Talks should only be considered once terrorists have been defeated. The defeat of the terrorists will be achieved by demonstrating resolution in the battle of wills between good and evil. In this struggle, repressive or tough measures may be justified. Some neoconservatives may take a less hard-line approach but insist on certain stringent preconditions before talking to terrorists.[14] Neoconservatives tend to draw a sharp contrast between their idealism and the unprincipled conservative or liberal realism of their opponents. This dichotomy does not do justice to the complexity of neoconservatism, which draws on both idealist and realist traditions. Some argue that neoconservatism's idealist rhetoric disguises its realist US nationalism and imperialist ambitions.[15]

David Trimble and the UUP, 1995–2003: Deadlock and Realism

The conservative unionist David Trimble initially argued that the conflict in Northern Ireland was deadlocked and that there was a real danger of a split in the IRA and a threat from republican dissidents.[16] In 1998, while negotiating the peace process and defending his support for the Agreement, Trimble invoked Edmund Burke, who is usually associated with prudence and political realism. Trimble appealed to realism, for a peace within the realms of the possible rather than pursuing the idealistic fantasies of complete victory pursued by anti-peace-process unionists. Godson's remarkable biography of Trimble provides fascinating evidence of the UUP leader's backstage concern for the political survival of the Sinn Féin leadership, his front-stage enemies. There is no evidence that Trimble believed that the IRA had been defeated. Indeed, Godson provides important evidence of the extent to which Trimble carried on a remarkable private dialogue with republicans. He attempted to help the Sinn Féin leadership manage the republican movement and was concerned about the physical threat to Adams and McGuinness.[17]

The UUP leader struggled to demonstrate the benefits of the peace process to unionists, who particularly resented Sinn Féin's success in securing reform of the Royal Ulster Constabulary (RUC), the release of their prisoners, and their entry into government before the IRA carried out any decommissioning. After the DUP overtook the UUP as the dominant party within unionism and became the key unionist negotiators of the peace process, the Trimbleistas shifted toward a more idealist, anti-peace-process unionism and then an orthodox neoconservatism.

Anti-Peace-Process Unionists: The IRA's Victory, Idealism, and the Rejection of the Northern Ireland Model

The most notable advocates of the anti-peace-process unionist position were Robert McCartney, the UK Unionist Party (UKUP) leader, the DUP (until 2007), hard-line members of the UUP (although the most prominent of these defected to the DUP in January 2004), and some on the right of the Conservative Party. Neoconservative ideology is most compatible with anti-peace-process unionism. This is because anti-peace-process unionists tended to oppose concessions or even talking to terrorists. The IRA was not defeated but employing the tactical use of the armed struggle to achieve its goals. The British government, they argued, was embarked on a surrender process of concessions to terrorists that corrupted core values and democratic norms. The British government had deceived about its back-channel contacts with republicans and was gradually extricating itself from Northern Ireland. Anti-peace-process neoconservatives argued that the surrender process was driven by the economic impact of the bombings in London in 1992, 1993, and 1996. They objected most vociferously to the way the peace process had corrupted democracy by allowing Sinn Féin into negotiations, and later into government, without decommissioning. It was on this principle that the DUP and UKUP walked out of talks in 1997. Anti-Agreement unionists attacked the Agreement and Trimble's UUP for undermining democracy and making concessions to terrorists. It was not so much the constitution but the law-and-order issues of prisoner releases and Sinn Féin in government without IRA de-commissioning as well as the reform of the RUC that most antagonized anti-Agreement unionists. They also attacked the political skills or lying and manipulation that were used to keep the peace process moving forward. The unionist anti-peace-process narrative resonated with popular unionist skepticism about the peace process, and this contributed to the DUP's electoral triumph in 2003.

There was, however, growing evidence that anti-peace-process unionism's interpretation of the republican movement's involvement in the peace process was flawed.

- In October 2001 the IRA began decommissioning.
- In July 2005 the IRA declared that its armed campaign was over and stood down.
- The IRA carried out its final act of decommissioning in September 2005.
- Sinn Féin endorsed the police and the rule of law in 2007.
- Sinn Féin entered power sharing with the DUP in May 2007, and this lasted for the full lifetime of the assembly and beyond.
- In March 2009 and April 2011, Sinn Féin leaders made strong attacks on the violence of republican dissidents.

The DUP's decision to share power with Sinn Féin in 2007 led to the marginalization of anti-peace-process unionism, which became reduced to ultra-hard-liners of Traditional Unionist Voice and some on the right of the British Conservative Party. Neoconservatives opposed to the peace process found themselves disarmed—just as neoconservatives had been by the collapse of the Soviet Union—by the failure of their alarmist predictions and the manifest success of the peace process in producing relatively stable, democratic government. This situation threatened to leave neo-conservatives unable to use the success of Northern Ireland in the rhetorical battle over how to deal with terrorism.

The Trimbleistas moved *toward* a unionist anti-peace-process position after losing power in 2003. Their position is distinct, however, because they had supported the Agreement and Trimble's record as UUP leader: "The Good Friday Agreement reflected the core democratic reality of unionist political power" and "the 1998 settlement was a triumph for moderation over extremism."[18] They are also distinct because they were attempting to outflank the DUP by suggesting that direct rule from Westminster might be better for unionists than Sinn Féin–DUP power sharing because the DUP were outnegotiated by a resurgent Sinn Féin. The Trimbleistas criticized the DUP for making concessions to republicans in the ongoing negotiations of the peace process. They argued that concessions were unnecessary because the republican leadership now had full control over their movement.

Bew and Frampton initially adopted an anti-peace-process unionist position and decried the realism and lack of principle demonstrated in the peace process. Bew argued that the IRA's Northern Bank robbery in December 2004 was "a glimpse of the future" and "seems to illustrate just how detached they [the IRA] are from the norms of any functioning democratic society."[19] Frampton suggested that the IRA's gunrunning, spying, and robbery showed that the IRA "does not believe the war to have been lost. On the contrary, the 'struggle' has . . . been displaced to another level."[20] By September 2005 the IRA had declared that the armed campaign was over and that it was preparing for a major act of decommissioning. Bew and Frampton argued that republicans "had been able to repeatedly extract the maximum number of concessions in return for that decommissioning" and "violence has been seen to 'pay.'"[21] By 2009 Frampton was still expressing this hard-line suspicion of the motives of Sinn Féin and the IRA in his book *The Long March: The Political Strategy of Sinn Féin, 1981–2007*. He argued that the IRA had *not* been defeated but continued to pursue its ideological goal of a united Ireland by other means: "[The] supposition that Sinn Féin and the wider republican movement have, to all intents and purposes, accepted defeat, runs, as this study will show, contrary to the evidence. Indeed, the 'defeat hypothesis' rests on an understanding of what the Good Friday Agreement represents to the republican movement, which is almost wholly at variance with the way Sinn Féin has acted since 1998."[22]

Frampton claimed that the republican movement sincerely believed that a shift from the armed struggle to the unarmed struggle would be more effective in achieving a united Ireland. Rather than being defeated, he argues, the republican leadership were able to successfully exploit the peace process to their advantage.[23] The Labour government was "playing over the odds for peace in Northern Ireland," and "concession after concession came the way of republicans in order to shore-up the supposedly vulnerable Adams-McGuinness leadership."[24] The thrust of this analysis is that the republicans are still a threat to the Union. The "screws" (slang for prison officers) are being lulled "into a false sense of security" so that victory can be achieved. The Agreement "was a bitter pill for republicans to swallow, but it too was to be seen as part of the effort by which republicans might yet inflict a terminal defeat on their ideological opponents."[25]

Talking to Terrorists: A British, Orthodox Neoconservative Interpretation of the Northern Ireland Peace Process

Bew and Frampton's *Talking to Terrorists* was widely reviewed among right-wing commentators, many of whom endorsed the neoconservative interpretation of the book: guns first, talks later.[26] The US neoconservative magazine *The Weekly Standard* published a lengthy and enthusiastic review by Gary Schmitt of the American Enterprise Institute. Schmitt criticized the British government's attempts to negotiate with terrorists and argued that, from the evidence of *Talking to Terrorists*, "it is difficult not to conclude that the 'talk first, guns later' strategy has things pretty much in reverse."[27]

The key claim in *Talking to Terrorists* is that the British state's repressive security policy and dirty war had defeated the IRA by the early nineties, and this explains why the British were able to impose an uncompromising, peace process on the IRA. British policy was consistent and clear red lines and conditions were laid down in their handling of terrorists, and it was this that prevented the erosion of democratic norms. British governments refused to compromise on core issues or make concessions to violence, and these stringent conditions explain the exceptional success of the peace process. "Robust insistence on democratic norms is a prerequisite to introducing terror groups into democratic dialogue."[28] The book's final sentence argues: "Ultimately, if talking to terrorists can be said to have had some success in Northern Ireland, this was only when the terrorists had come to accept the rules of the game and agreed to abide by them in the search for a settlement."[29]

This argument is important to neoconservatives because it seeks to establish that the British government succeeded without making concessions to violence. The reason that the British talked to terrorists is because the government was negotiating from a position of strength. The terrorists were not on the crest of a wave, and it was the IRA that approached the British.[30] The IRA's attacks on London in 1992, 1993, and 1996 are dismissed as the last gasp of a defeated organization, retreating on every front. While Bew, Frampton, and Gurruchaga acknowledge that the British government has a history of talking to terrorists, they argue that these talks in 1972, 1975–76, 1980–81, and up until the early nineties were, if anything, counterproductive because they encouraged the IRA to believe that it was winning, and this resulted in an increase in violence.[31] In the early nineties, by contrast, the British government was dealing with terrorists from a position of strength. They were, therefore, able to lay down strict conditions for the IRA to enter the peace process. The British government did not have to make concessions to the Sinn Féin leadership because Adams and McGuinness had full control over the republican movement.[32] The republican leadership simply had to be made to understand that they were losing and that unless they signed up to the British government's stern conditions their position would only get worse. There was, therefore, no dilemma for the British government. They did not have to appease the Sinn Féin leadership to help it keep its unruly supporters on board for the painful compromises that would have to be made during the peace process. The British government effectively managed the surrender of Sinn Féin/IRA, but this was mismanaged in the post-Agreement period by the Labour government, which undermined Northern Ireland's moderate parties.[33]

According to Bew, Frampton, and Gurruchaga, the strength of the British state's negotiating position from the 1990s derived in part, if not principally, from Britain's use of hard power. The dirty war waged against the IRA, rather than the permanent British state's propensity to negotiate, proved to be effective in forcing republicans to the negotiating table.[34] The dirty war is usually interpreted as including:

1. An alleged "shoot to kill" policy by the British state.
2. Some level of collusion between the British state and loyalist paramilitaries, who were provided with information to help them target republicans.
3. The use and abuse of informers within loyalist and republican paramilitary organizations, who were allowed to participate in murder to protect themselves.

Three reasons are given for republicans entering a peace process in the 1990s, all of which emphasize the importance of hard power:

1. War weariness.
2. The loyalist backlash in the late eighties and early nineties, which led to a "surge in loyalist activity [that] was baldly sectarian" but "also impacted on high level republicans."[35]
3. The "growing effectiveness of the security forces in infiltrating and interdicting the IRA's campaign was having an impact upon republicans. It is true that the British had been unable to achieve a *decisive* military victory over the IRA, but their policy of containment and attrition had undoubtedly taken a toll."[36]

Talking to Terrorists also emphasizes Britain's "highly effective unofficial war against the republican movement that was being carried out by the intelligence services. This had a decisive impact on what occurred subsequently."[37] The rate of attrition and infiltration of the republican movement meant that "although the IRA still posed a deadly threat into the 1990s, its capacity for 'war' seems to have been gradually curtailed."[38] Frampton contends: "All that can be said with certainty is that the 'dirty war' largely achieved its aims."[39] He also argues that "it seems irrefutable that this 'dirty war' saw agents of the State carry out the most serious violations of human rights, up to and including murder."[40]

There is also an attempt to rehabilitate the effectiveness of the policy of internment introduced in 1971, which despite its "deeply damaging impact on the political mood of the province" was "not, in purely military terms, a complete failure." Furthermore, "The reality was that the policy of internment—despite a disastrous start—had in fact taken a toll on the organisation."[41] The problem with this argument is that the military's objective is not military victory but rather the negotiation of a political settlement, and in this, internment failed as well as succeeding in alienating nationalists. Bew and his colleagues also try to attribute the violence during 1972 to the British government's talks with the IRA in July of that year in order to draw the international lesson that sometimes it is counterproductive to "talk to terrorists."[42] The introduction of internment in August 1971, Bloody Sunday in January 1972, the introduction of direct rule in March 1972, as well as the growing ambiguity of British policy from the autumn of 1971 and the loyalist backlash are among other plausible contributors to the violence in 1972. The decision to talk to the IRA in 1972 did not result in a surge in violence. Within a few weeks of the failure of the talks, the

British government launched "Operation Motorman," the biggest British military operation since Suez in 1956 to retake the "no-go" areas in Belfast and Derry. This led to a major decline in violence. Some have argued that Britain's more diplomatic approach and restraint on security gave the British the political advantage and created the environment in which Operation Motorman could be so successful.[43]

A Critique of the Orthodox Neoconservative Perspective: The Incompatibility of the Three Neoconservative Strands

The orthodox neoconservative perspective contrasts sharply with Bew and Frampton's simultaneous advocacy of the unionist anti-peace-process perspective. These two perspectives are incompatible with Trimble's record of negotiating the peace process (see table 5.1). The orthodox perspective also lacks evidence to suggest that the IRA was defeated. If the IRA was not defeated, then this diminishes the importance of hard power and the dirty war. In negotiating the peace process Trimble argued that the conflict was deadlocked and demonstrated an acute understanding of the problems facing the republican leadership, bravely trying to help Adams and McGuinness relinquish the armed struggle (rather than simply negotiating the IRA's surrender). It was this pragmatic realism that was more characteristic of the negotiation of the peace process than neoconservative idealism and moral clarity. Orthodox neoconservatives appear not to believe that the dirty war contradicts core values and democratic norms.

The Trimbleistas adopted an anti-peace-process position at the time when Sinn Féin made the transition to democratic politics by standing down the IRA and sharing power with the DUP in 2007. Bew and Frampton's anti-peace-process narrative contrasts sharply with their orthodox neoconservative defense of the Northern Ireland model. On August 31, 2005, they argued, "Notwithstanding Paisley's own strategic shortcomings, it is hard to avoid the conclusion that the worse the IRA have behaved since 1998, the more time they have been given in Downing Street and the more they have managed to strip from the government in the way of concessions."[44] This unionist anti-peace-process position decried the realism and lack of principle demonstrated in the peace process, in which "violence has been seen to pay" and the long march of republicans to victory continued.[45]

Table 5.1. Comparing and contrasting three irreconcilable neoconservative perspectives on the peace process

	Anti-peace- process unionism	Pro-Agreement unionism, David Trimble (1995–2003)	Orthodox neoconservatism
Heroes	Robert McCartney (UKUP), DUP (to 2007), Jim Allister (TUV)	David Trimble, UUP leader, 1995–2005, Trimbleistas	Roy Mason (Secretary of State for Northern Ireland, 1976–79), Airey Neave (Conservative Opposition Spokesman on Northern Ireland, 1975–79), Margaret Thatcher (British Prime Minister, 1979–90), Mitchell Reiss (US envoy to Northern Ireland, 2004–7), David Trimble (UUP leader post-2003)
Villains	Blair, Trimble (and everyone else in the peace process)	Republican dissidents, DUP, anti-Agreement UUP	Labour government (Blair and Powell), Sinn Féin/IRA
Approach to politics	Idealist	Realist (Edmund Burke)	Idealist
What was the nature of the peace process?	British government's surrender to the IRA	Agreement strengthened the Union	British government accepted the IRA's surrender

Was the IRA defeated in the early nineties?	No, it won	No, deadlock	Yes
Was there a threat from dissident republicans?	No	Yes, but Labour government made too many concessions	Not until 2006–10
Why did the British make concessions to the IRA/Sinn Féin?	Betrayal of the Union, IRA bombs in England, realism	To achieve a fair compromise, but Labour conceded too much	Labour government mishandled post-Agreement and undermined moderates
Did the governments show "moral clarity" during the peace process?	No, they (including Trimble) negotiated with the devil and were morally corrupted	Realist Trimble showed pragmatism, making peace within the realms of the possible	Idealist, yes, democratic norms and core principles were (generally) not compromised
Should one talk to terrorists?	No (or nearly never)	Yes, pragmatically	Nearly never
Is Northern Ireland a model for the rest of the world?	No, the Agreement compromised democracy and let terrorists into government	Yes	Yes, it shows that one should nearly never talk to terrorists

The orthodox neoconservative perspective, by contrast, claimed that the IRA was not winning but had lost in the early 1990s and was forced into a peace process. This meant that the British government could conduct the peace process without compromising core values and democratic norms. Violence was not seen to pay, and this was the lesson that the international community should draw from the Northern Ireland model.[46]

Bew and Frampton's attempt to straddle the three incompatible strands of neoconservatism lead them to confusion over whether the IRA won, lost, or drew the war and what the difference is between these outcomes.

- Frampton claims that the Ulster Defence Regiment and Royal Ulster Constabulary, with RUC Special Branch calling the shots, "helped bring about the *de facto defeat* of the Provisional IRA."[47]
- Bew and Frampton argue that the IRA was "to some extent *'strategically defeated,'* but still ideologically committed" (it has also been claimed that the IRA was "defeated at the political level," but we are not told what this means).
- *Talking to Terrorists* defines itself *against the stalemate thesis* but argues that there was a growing realization in the IRA leadership that the armed struggle had "reached a point of *deadlock*."[48] Stalemate and deadlock are synonyms and both mean draw. Whether Bew and Frampton believed the IRA was objectively defeated is rather beside the point if the IRA and other key actors in the peace process did not perceive that to be the case.
- Bew and Frampton endorse Hennessey's argument: "It was true that *the IRA were not defeated militarily*; but the British only needed a draw to win."[49]
- They also claim that *the IRA won* and Provisional republicanism was winning and "might yet inflict a terminal defeat on their ideological opponents." Frampton explicitly rejects the hypothesis that the IRA was defeated, which is "contrary to the evidence."[50]
- Bew and Frampton have also claimed that the defeat of the IRA is *debatable*, but then claim both that "the IRA was *forced* to end its campaign" (my emphasis) while simultaneously quoting Danny Morrison, an influential member of Sinn Féin in 1991: "I think we can fight on forever and can't be defeated." He also argued that if the IRA had fought on and been defeated then it wouldn't have been able to negotiate.[51]

Words are used precisely and carefully to more accurately convey meaning. The term "defeat" suggests that the enemy were beaten, conquered, vanquished, routed, or trounced.[52] To claim that governments or parties were defeated because they failed to achieve all their goals suggests that any peace process that involves negotiations and compromise involves the defeat of the participants. This not only seems to be a misleading use of the word but it is also likely to discourage diplomacy, negotiation, and compromise because these are defined as representing defeat, something politicians and soldiers are generally reluctant to embrace.

In a peace process it is important to present any compromise deal as a victory rather than a defeat (even if it is more accurately described as arising from a stalemate or deadlock) in order to shore up the peacemakers against hard-line opponents. The Agreement was designed so that all the supporters of the Agreement could claim victory.[53] During the negotiations of the Agreement, Blair told Adams: "Everyone could win, but everyone had to compromise."[54] Neoconservatives and republican dissidents, by defining out of existence the idea of stalemate, deadlock, and draw, leave behind only the choice of victory or defeat and seek the escalation of violence to achieve victory.

Was the IRA Defeated?

The point of criticizing the thesis that the IRA was defeated is that, based on the available evidence and arguments, it is an inaccurate description of the peace process. This undermines the neoconservative's militaristic arguments that hard power is the best way to defeat global terrorism. The security forces certainly played their role in containing the republican threat, but it was complex and morally difficult political negotiations and diplomacy that more convincingly explain the success of the peace process and the heroic role of moderate politicians. This explains why the peace process was not an IRA surrender process but involved tortuous negotiations, the compromising of democratic norms, and a high degree of uncertainty as to the intentions of the republican leadership and its ability to deliver their movement. The successful outcome represented the triumph of (nonviolent) politics over the gun.

There is evidence that the peace process was already emerging out of the stalemate of the 1980s and the early 1990s when neoconservatives claim the IRA was defeated. These developments included:

- Sinn Féin's shift to a more political and electoral path in 1981/82
- The Sinn Féin leadership beginning to look for a way out of the armed struggle in 1982
- The Anglo-Irish Agreement of 1985

- British contacts with Sinn Féin in 1986
- Sinn Féin's decision to end abstentionism and take seats in the Irish parliament in 1986
- Irish government contacts with Sinn Féin in the late 1980s
- SDLP/Sinn Féin talks in 1988
- Brooke's interview and speeches in 1989 and 1990
- The revival of the British government–Sinn Féin back channel in 1990
- The end of the Cold War, with its impact on British strategic calculations and US attitudes

There is little evidence that the IRA was defeated by the early nineties. Key actors involved in the peace process, including the republican leadership, did not believe they had been defeated and acted on that perception. In 1989 Peter Brooke, the secretary of state for Northern Ireland, made a public overture to republicans. He said that the security forces could contain the IRA, but he found it "difficult to envisage" its military defeat. This was in line with an influential view in British counterinsurgency thinking that the army could only hold the ring until a political settlement was found. If the terrorists decided that the game had ceased to be worth the candle, then it would be possible that the British government could sit down and talk with Sinn Féin. It is clear from the accounts of leading British and Irish figures involved in the peace process—John Major, Tony Blair, Peter Mandelson, Jonathan Powell, Albert Reynolds, and Bertie Ahern— that they did not believe that the IRA was defeated.[55] Michael Ancram, Conservative junior minister and minister of state in the Northern Ireland Office, 1993–97, has argued that the Conservative government's analysis was the following: "First, that the war could not be won. Second, that there could be no long-term solution to the problem we were confronting without the eventual involvement of those we were fighting. Third, that even as the fighting continued, we needed to find a means of engaging them. And fourth, that this could only be done by opening dialogue."[56]

Until very late in the peace process senior British policy makers were unsure of whether the IRA would relaunch its armed struggle. According to Blair, from the Agreement to October 2002, the IRA "were going to wait to see if the Unionists delivered their side of the bargain, and until then the IRA would hold the use of force in reserve."[57] David Trimble is one of the heroes of the peace process because he did not act as if the IRA had been defeated but as if the armed struggle had reached a deadlock.[58] This explains the UUP leader's courageous leadership in attempting to support the attempt of the Adams/McGuinness leadership to bring a united republican movement into a peace process and reach accommodation. During the negotiations the UUP leader did not claim that the IRA was defeated. "Undoubtedly, the IRA were not winning. They could do damage but they could not 'drive the British out.'"[59] Trimble argued that the armed struggle had reached deadlock but that the Sinn Féin/IRA leadership did not have complete control over its movement and that republican dissidents represented a real and physical threat to the republican leadership.[60] By 2004 Trimble was still not convinced the IRA would make the transition to purely peaceful methods.[61] If Trimble were to argue that the IRA was defeated, he might look foolish for having negotiated so sincerely with Sinn Féin. He argues that "concern was real enough" "about a serious split in the republican movement" and "that decommissioning became the lightning-rod issue going forward." Although the republicans manipulated this concern to their advantage, Trimble was worried enough that he was prepared to enter an executive order without decommissioning in December 1999.[62] It was only with the benefit of hindsight that Trimble argued that the Real IRA split in 1997 was "relatively modest in import" and that "the Adams/McGuinness leadership was secure."[63]

The security forces (British Army, RUC, and MI5) have an organizational interest in asserting that the IRA was defeated in order to bolster their reputation and power. The security forces used claims that the enemy had been defeated or was on the verge of defeat to pressure politicians into adopting the military's prescriptions to secure victory in 1971–72 and 1975–76. The claims of triumph over the IRA have tended to emerge since 2007 (after it was clear the IRA had not won), and there is a lack of contemporaneous evidence that the Army or the RUC believed that the IRA had been defeated. In November 1991 security chiefs (both military and RUC) were reported to believe that the security situation was dire and the "defeat of the IRA is not on the horizon while current security policies are maintained."[64] The IRA would ultimately be defeated, but this could take over ten years to achieve. A high-level military source stated: "The IRA terrorists are better equipped, better resourced, better led, bolder and more secure against our penetration than at any time before. They are absolutely a formidable enemy. The essential attributes of their leaders are better than ever before. Some of their operations are brilliant, in terrorist terms. If we don't intern, it's a long haul."[65]

After the IRA's cease-fire in 1994, the military elite were highly critical of the British government's attempts to demilitarize Northern Ireland because of the continuing security threat. Senior RUC officers did not believe the IRA had been defeated and acknowledged the difficult task the Sinn Féin leadership had in bringing the republican movement to political accommodation.[66] There also appears to be little evidence that MI5 considered the IRA to have been defeated.[67]

Claims about the defeat of the IRA are often related to the extent of the penetration of the republican movement by the British security forces. The republican movement, however, has always been penetrated by informers. The IRA had adopted countermeasures, and penetration had not prevented the IRA from running a highly effective military campaign. The IRA declared amnesties for informers in August 1974 and March 1982 in order to reduce the threat to their organization.[68] The IRA reorganized into a cellular structure in the late seventies to inhibit its penetration by informers. In spite of this, by the early eighties the IRA had been so penetrated that a member was as likely to be killed by his or her own organization as they were by the British. The "supergrass" trials of the early eighties may well have provided the security forces with further knowledge about the IRA. At least 450 people were charged on the basis of their evidence, and the IRA leadership was brought close to panic.

Although penetrated by informers, from 1989 to 1997 the IRA launched a bombing offensive against England. There were 204 bombings and 7 shootings during this period, resulting in the deaths of 11 civilians and 15 British Army and police personnel, with 718 injured.[69] The IRA bombed Downing Street (February 1991), the City of London (1992, 1993, and 1996), and Manchester (1996). It is estimated that the bombings caused over £2 billion worth of damage and caused considerable concern in the City of London.[70] In Northern Ireland the winding down of the violence between the British and the IRA in the early nineties may well have been an effect of the emerging peace process rather than signaling the defeat of the IRA. This was exemplified by the Derry initiative in the early 1990s, which led to the IRA and British Army making reciprocal gestures in order to build trust and reduce violence.[71]

The peace process would not have been so tortuous and so many concessions would not have been made to republicans if the IRA had been defeated and it was just a matter of negotiating its surrender. This undermines the neoconservative's universal lesson, which is that terrorists should not be negotiated with when they are on the crest of a wave but when they have been defeated. First, the peace process was successful even though the IRA was not defeated. Second, there is considerable difficulty in judging whether or not terrorists are on the crest of a wave. Third, we need to entertain the possibility that it is precisely when terrorists are on the crest of a wave, when their negotiating power is at its height, that they want to negotiate a political accommodation.

What is significant is that Bew and Frampton want to argue first that the IRA was defeated, and second that the dirty war was effective on the basis of such limited evidence and with little serious discussion of what effectiveness means. Since there is little evidence to suggest that the IRA was defeated, then the argument that the "dirty war" was effective is undermined. There is also little evidence presented for the effectiveness of the dirty war, certainly not enough to sustain the assertion that "all that can be said with certainty is that the 'dirty war' largely achieved its aims."[72] Bew and Frampton contradict themselves when they also argued in 2008 that "the extent to which the IRA was actually defeated will be debated for many years. It is difficult to measure the importance of the 'secret war' against other variables."[73] There is evidence that the republican movement was penetrated by the security forces and that key agents operated in the upper echelons of Sinn Féin and the IRA. However, this did not prevent the IRA carrying out devastating attacks on the City of London and Manchester. Neither did the intelligence services seem to have presented the British prime minister, Tony Blair, with conclusive evidence on Sinn Féin's bottom line in negotiations.[74] These difficulties suggest that there are problems for the government in assessing when it is appropriate to negotiate with the enemy. Bew and Frampton also see little irony in arguing that the British policy did not compromise core values and democratic norms while accepting that the British government's dirty war involved "the most serious violations of human rights."[75]

The Pragmatic Realism of British Policy

British policy toward Northern Ireland was characterized by a considerable degree of continuity but with "tactical adjustments."[76] This is not to claim that British policy was completely constrained and that there was no scope for change. British policy was shaped by what was perceived to be possible, and the parameters of policy were explored, particularly in the period 1969–76. This raises the question as to what Bew and others mean by a "core" commitment. If this implies an unalterable commitment, then this is clearly not the case. British governments have not been staunch defenders of the Union, and there has been willingness during the recent conflict to consider compromise on core issues such as the consent principle. From 1969 to 1976, British governments explored different options for managing the conflict: bringing Northern Ireland up to British standards as a way of addressing discrimination and nationalist grievances; the pursuit of power sharing with an Irish dimension; and the possibility of integrating Northern Ireland more closely into the Union. Leading figures in both the British Labour and Conservative parties, however, were prepared to investigate the possibility of overriding the consent principle and withdrawal. While it was open to British politicians to pursue any of these options, the predominant perception seems to have been that the costs of pursuing withdrawal, repartition, or integration were too high and that the most likely ground for a more peaceful Northern Ireland was power sharing, perhaps with an Irish dimension. In the period up to 2007 there was a threat by the Labour government to impose joint authority. This would also have been against the consent of the overwhelming majority in Northern Ireland.

British policy was strongly characterized by pragmatism rather than strong ideological support for the Union with Northern Ireland. The consent principle may have been democratic, but it was also a practical measure to reduce the constitutional insecurity that it was thought fueled violence. Behind the scenes, British politicians were considering all options in order to achieve stability, whether that left Northern Ireland in the Union or not. Ironically, the pragmatism of British politicians is illustrated also in the careers of neoconservative heroes Prime Minister Margaret Thatcher and opposition Conservative spokesperson on Northern Ireland Airey Neave. Prior to his murder and in the run-up to the 1979 British general election, Neave had been shifting away from a hard-line, integrationist position, and it looked unlikely even if he had lived that integration would have been implemented.[77] This is partly because integration was likely to undermine the position of moderate nationalists in the North to Sinn Féin's benefit, and both the government of the Republic of Ireland and Irish American opinion would have opposed the move.[78] Thatcher's uncompromising image belied her government's extensive negotiations with the Hunger Strikers in 1980–81 and her negotiation of the Anglo-Irish Agreement of 1985, which was seen as a great betrayal by unionists. Margaret Thatcher was willing to consider repartition and seemed preoccupied more by an English unionist/nationalist desire to protect "our boys" in the British Army than sympathy for Ulster unionism.[79] She also tolerated the contacts between her secretary of state Tom King and Gerry Adams, and it was on her watch that Peter Brooke, secretary of state for Northern Ireland, made his overtures to Sinn Féin and contacts were renewed in 1990. British neoconservatives try to preserve the hard-line reputation of Thatcher by blaming "British authorities," President Reagan, or the "permanent British state" in order to avoid facing up to the realism of their hero.[80]

There has been an attempt by neoconservatives to elevate the Bush administration and Mitchell Reiss, President Bush's envoy to Northern Ireland, as key players in achieving power sharing in 2007. It is asserted that Reiss's uncompromising stance toward republicans and the DUP— unlike the appeasing Irish and, particularly, British governments—forced them into the deal. The evidence for this comes largely from Reiss's own claims in his book *Negotiating with Evil* (2010) and anonymous interviews with Bush administration officials.[81] Similar to Bew, Frampton, and Gurruchaga, he has argued that you should not talk to terrorists "unless you're winning or unless you remove the hope that the other side has of winning."[82] Reiss has also emphasized the importance of pragmatism, because peacemaking could be messy, "with its inevitable errors, miscalculations, and squalid compromises. Few protocols or precedents exist to guide policymakers. Morality or high principles may offer no better guide, as negotiators often (and rightly) value pragmatism over all other considerations. [Jonathan] Powell's account [of the peace process] candidly reveals that not all grievances, no matter how legitimate, can be honoured equally or sometimes at all. It suggests that revulsion at unspeakable depravity must somehow be subordinated to the pursuit of larger goals."[83]

Realism was also strongly in evidence among all parties to the peace process, and it is difficult to identify a period when Labour and Conservative governments acted in the idealist, uncompromising manner identified by orthodox neoconservatives. This was because the IRA had not been defeated, and the various actors were negotiating a morally difficult, compromise accommodation. Political actors deployed various "political skills or lying and manipulation" to reassure their supporters and voters while bringing them toward an accommodation.[84] The Conservative government did explore backstage contacts with republicans while the IRA's violence continued and then deceived to cover this up. The Conservative then Labour governments' approach to decommissioning illustrates their willingness to take a pragmatic approach to advancing the peace process. Initially, decommissioning was to have taken place even before contacts between Sinn Féin and British officials. This position was compromised, so that IRA decommissioning did not take place until after prisoner releases had been completed and Sinn Féin were sitting in government. The Conservative government accelerated the pace of the peace process after the IRA broke its cease-fire in February 1996. This prompted criticism that the governments had only moved in response to violence.[85] Senior Labour figures publicly admitted that they deployed a pragmatic realism and even deception in driving the peace process forward, which involved uncomfortable compromises with paramilitaries. Mo Mowlam acknowledged, "Yes, it was an imperfect peace, but surely that is better than no peace at all?"[86] In October 2002 Blair recognized that constructive ambiguity had facilitated the peace process but that this had become an impediment. In his autobiography he admitted the use of deception during the peace process.[87]

The realism of the British government's and the UUP's approach helps to explain the appeal and success of the DUP's idealist stance. Anti-peace-process unionists and dissident republicans did have a point when they criticized the deceptive means by which leading actors drove the peace process forward, although this loudly proclaimed piety and idealism often concealed a brutal and violent political practice. The DUP was electorally successful partly because it took advantage of this populist, antipolitical view of "politicians as liars" and used it to their electoral advantage. Once dominant, they shifted toward a more realist narrative to justify power sharing with republicans.

Neoconservatives and the Peace Process

This chapter has argued that neoconservatives have attempted to capture the apparently favorable Northern Ireland case and apply its lesson of "nearly never talking to terrorists" to other conflicts.[88] Bew and Frampton's writings attempt to *simultaneously* combine elements of these three incompatible perspectives, and this produces problems in their analysis. These three perspectives clash over whether:

- The IRA drew, lost, or won
- The British government behaved with idealism or realism
- The Northern Ireland model is a good or bad model for the rest of the world
- Lessons from the Northern Ireland conflict should be drawn for conflicts elsewhere

Nonetheless, in spite of their different interpretations of the conflict, the unionist anti-peace-process perspective and the orthodox neoconservative perspective both come to the same policy conclusion: you should nearly never talk to terrorists and should concentrate on using hard power to defeat them. The idealism of these two perspectives contrasts sharply with Trimble's pragmatic conduct of the peace process and defense of his compromises. Since 2003 the Trimbleistas have distanced themselves from this honorable record of realism in the cause of peace and attempted to combine an anti-peace-process and orthodox neoconservatism. This is partly a result of attempts at winning over two contrasting audiences:

- First, the battle against the DUP for the unionist audience in Northern Ireland, leading the Trimbleistas to deploy their unionist anti-peace-process narrative in the period after 2003.
- Second, the attempt to win over the international audience to "guns first, talks later" after 2007, with claims that it is nearly never right to talk to terrorists.

The proclaimed idealism and moral clarity of the neoconservatives disguise their conservative realism:

- First, neoconservative opposition to terrorism conceals their support for non-state terrorists whose aims they agree with, against the Sandinistas in Nicaragua, by Cuban exiles against the Castro regime, or the MEK (The People's Mujahedin of Iran) against Iran.
- Second, neoconservatives claim to be championing democracy, human rights, and civil liberties and yet advocate state terrorism, which has involved extra-judicial murder by unaccountable members of the security forces.
- Third, there is an interesting symbiotic relationship between republican dissidents and orthodox (unionist) neoconservatives. They are both militaristic in their emphasis on the effectiveness of force. They are also united in their visceral hatred of the Sinn Féin/IRA leadership (and at points the peace process itself), and both argue that the Sinn Féin leadership lost the war and has been engaged in a surrender process. Orthodox neoconservatives have given prominence to republican dissidents and their arguments because it bolsters Trimble's reputation, is damaging to Sinn Féin, and emphasizes the threat from dissidents to justify unspecified and potentially counterproductive tougher security measures to defeat them.[89] Intriguingly, neoconservatives and republican dissidents also seem to share a fundamentalist, idealist outlook on the world: both claim to be "an enlightened elite, who alone truly understand the situation as it really exists. . . . They are the guardians of the revealed truth."[90]

- Fourth, the orthodox neoconservative account attempts to draw clear lessons from Northern Ireland, but this leads them to oversimplify and overmoralize the political process. In the orthodox neoconservative account, good behavior by the British government gets its just reward: the defeat of the IRA and a peaceful accommodation. The fundamentalist idealist does not face dilemmas; the moral course of action is always the most effective way to achieve moral goals. Nevertheless, as we have seen, this idealism conceals the realism practiced even by neoconservative heroes—Neave, Thatcher, Trimble, and Reiss—and recorded by leading neoconservative writers.[91] The loudly proclaimed idealism of anti-peace-process unionists and republicans has sometimes acted as a smokescreen to conceal the use of violence to achieve political ends.[92] The danger is that policy makers looking to learn the lessons of Northern Ireland mistakenly believe that the peace process was achieved by defeating the IRA through dirty war and by taking a rigid, moralistic stance on negotiating with terrorists. This is somewhat at odds with the empirical evidence and the realist and honorable political practice of David Trimble and other participants in the process, both unionists and nationalists. As Coady argued, "To turn everything you value into a matter of basic principle is not to show moral strength but moralistic inflexibility." Compromise may be practical and also respectful of "the conscientiously held values and the dignity of those who disagree with you."[93]

Whether or not neoconservative accounts of the peace process are incoherent and contradictory may be irrelevant if the point is not to explain or describe the world accurately but to change it. The contradictory neoconservative accounts of the peace process with their clear moral lessons—seized upon and amplified by sympathetic think tanks, academics, policy makers, and the media—may provide highly effective ammunition in the current rhetorical war of ideology over talking to the enemy.

Conclusion: Lessons?

There are two key pitfalls in drawing lessons from the Northern Ireland peace process for other areas in conflict. First, there is a tendency to claim that Northern Ireland is unique and that no lessons can be drawn from it. But this is usually accompanied by a simultaneous assertion that the lessons of Northern Ireland apply globally.[94] Those with a "mechanical" approach to comparison derive lessons from the Northern Irish case that should be applied directly to other conflicts with little regard to context (always talk to terrorists or never talk to terrorists). Those with a "contextualist" approach argue that there is something to be learned from Northern Ireland but emphasize the importance of context. The "mechanical" approach is more popular among academics and policy makers because it gives them an uncomplicated description of conflict and simple prescriptions. This gives such comparativists a license to prescribe for conflicts about which they know little. The "contextualists" argue that such a "mechanical" approach is dangerous because it ignores context and encourages overconfidence and the implementation of simplistic models on diverse and complex conflicts. Prescriptions appropriate in one conflict might not be appropriate in another. This is illustrated by the case of Iraq, where neoconservative prescriptions and expectations were "mechanically" imposed on the country with tragic consequences.

The "contextualists" emphasize the importance of the context in deriving lessons or making prescriptions. The decision as to whether or not to marginalize spoilers or include them in the peace process has to be taken with regard to the impact of the particular context and according to ideals that are tempered by realism. The exclusion and marginalization of Sinn Féin and the IRA because of the IRA's ongoing armed struggle made pragmatic sense for much of the conflict because it bolstered nationalist moderates and also created an incentive for republicans to give up their violence and enter the democratic process. This did not prevent low-level and deniable contacts and channels of communication from being maintained. Judging the right balance between exclusion and inclusion is a difficult political judgment that has to be carefully related to the wider political environment. The IRA was kept in the peace process after 1998 even though it had broken its cease-fire. This was a pragmatic move that probably helped to keep the process moving forward, but there are difficult moral and political judgments in trying to achieve peace without corrupting the democratic process too much.

The second pitfall in drawing lessons from Northern Ireland is the tendency toward morality tales, in which good action by governments or other actors results in good outcomes and bad action results in bad outcomes. Always or nearly never talking to terrorists leads to peace. Those with a "mechanical" approach to comparison tend more to morality tales because they assume that regularities exist across conflicts and believe that implementing their prescriptions will lead to predictable outcomes. "Contextualists" see politics as far more complex, contingent, and unpredictable. Appeasement or the use of force may work in some circumstances but not in others. This skepticism, arguably, provides a more realistic basis on which to make policy prescriptions by rejecting mechanical, overgeneralized prescriptions and seeking to understand the constraints and opportunities that affect the attempts of political and other actors in their particular context to achieve an end to violent conflict.[95]

NOTES

This chapter is an adaptation of Paul Dixon, "Guns First, Talks Later: Neoconservatives and the Northern Ireland Peace Process," *Journal of Imperial and Commonwealth History* 39 (4) (2011): 649–76; Paul Dixon, "Was the IRA Defeated? Neoconservative Propaganda as History," *Journal of Imperial and Commonwealth History* 40 (2) (2012): 303–20; Paul Dixon, "In Defence of Politics: Interpreting the Peace Process and the Future of Northern Ireland," *Political Quarterly* 83 (2) (2012): 265–76; and Paul Dixon, "Bew and Frampton: Recognisably Neoconservative," *Political Quarterly* 83 (2) (2012): 283–86.

1. Tony Blair, *A Journey* (London: Hutchinson, 2010); Mo Mowlam, *Momentum: The Struggle for Peace, Politics and the People* (London: Hodder and Stoughton, 2002); and Jonathan Powell, *Great Hatred, Little Room: Making Peace in Northern Ireland* (London: The Bodley Head, 2008), 313.

2. Blair, *A Journey*, 186; Paul Dixon, "Political Skills or Lying and Manipulation? The Choreography of the Northern Ireland Peace Process," *Political Studies* 50 (3) (2002): 725–41, and Powell, *Great Hatred, Little Room*, 9.

3. John Major, *John Major: The Autobiography* (London: HarperCollins, 1999), and Michael Ancram, "Dancing with Wolves: The Importance of Talking to Your Enemies," *Middle East Policy* 14 (2) (Summer 2007): 22–29.

4. Paul Dixon, *Northern Ireland: The Politics of War and Peace*, 2nd ed. (New York: Palgrave Macmillan, 2008), and Paul Dixon and Eamonn O'Kane, *Northern Ireland Since 1969* (New York: Longman, 2011).

5. John Bew, Martyn Frampton, and Iñigo Gurruchaga, *Talking to Terrorists: Making Peace in Northern Ireland and the Basque Country* (London: Hurst, 2009), and Mitchell Reiss, *Negotiating with Evil: When to Talk to Terrorists* (New York: Open Road, 2010).

6. Paul Dixon, "'Peace Within the Realms of the Possible?' David Trimble, Unionist Ideology and Theatrical Politics," *Terrorism and Political Violence* 16 (3) (2004): 462–82.

7. Gary Schmitt, "Peace, It's wonderful: But Winning It Is Hard Work," *Weekly Standard* 14 (45) (2009).

8. Bew, Frampton, and Gurruchaga, *Talking to Terrorists*.

9. Justin Vaisse, *Neoconservatism: The Biography of a Movement* (London: The Belknap Press, 2010), 6–7 and 271.

10. Vaisse, *Neoconservatism*, 2 and 78.

11. Dennis Ross and David Makovsky, *Myths, Illusions, and Peace: Finding a New Direction for America in the Middle East* (New York: Penguin, 2010), 91.

12. Ibid., chapter 4.

13. Irving Kristol, "Conflicts That Can't Be Resolved," *Wall Street Journal*, September 5, 1997.

14. Bew, Frampton, and Gurruchaga, *Talking to Terrorists*; Reiss, *Negotiating with Evil*; and Vaisse, *Neoconservatism*, 200.

15. Danny Cooper, *Neoconservatism and American Foreign Policy: A Critical Analysis* (London: Routledge, 2010), 8, and Vaisse, *Neoconservatism*, 278–79.

16. David Trimble, "Misunderstanding Ulster," 2007, available at www.davidtrimble .org, accessed March 17, 2011.

17. Dean Godson, *Himself Alone: David Trimble and the Ordeal of Unionism* (London: HarperCollins, 2004), 397, 398, and 517–18, and Dixon, "Guns First, Talks Later," 656–57.

18. Bew, Frampton, and Gurruchaga, *Talking to Terrorists*, 249.

19. John Bew, "Opening Editorial, Northern Ireland," March 15, 2005, http://web .archive.org/web/20060430144820/z0pe06.v.servelocity.net/hjs/organising_committee, accessed March 17, 2011.

20. Martyn Frampton, "Time for a Re-think?," April 12, 2005, http://web.archive .org/web/20060430144820/z0pe06.v.servelocity.net/hjs/organising_committee, accessed March 17, 2011.

21. John Bew and Martyn Frampton, "Belfast 2005: A Blast from the Past?" September 13, 2005, http://web.archive.org/web/20060430144820/z0pe06.v.servelocity.net/hjs /organising_committee, accessed March 17, 2011.

22. Martyn Frampton, *The Long March: The Political Strategy of Sinn Féin, 1981–2007* (Basingstoke: Palgrave, 2009), 6.

23. Ibid., 16, 17, 18, and 185–87, and Bew, Frampton, and Gurruchaga, *Talking to Terrorists*, 156–57.

24. Martyn Frampton, "Paying Over the Odds for Peace in Northern Ireland," *Parliamentary Brief*, May 9, 2008.

25. Frampton, "Agents and Ambushes," 89.

26. Dixon, "Guns First, Talks Later," 660, and Dixon, "Was the IRA Defeated?"

27. Schmitt, "Peace, It's Wonderful."

28. Bew, Frampton, and Gurruchaga, *Talking to Terrorists*, 139, 243, and 258–59.

29. Ibid., 259.

30. Ibid., 246 and 255.

31. Ibid., 253.

32. Ibid., 155–57 and 256.

33. Ibid., 164 and 250.

34. Ibid., 246–52, and Martyn Frampton, "Agents and Ambushes: Britain's 'Dirty War' in Northern Ireland," in *Democracies at War Against Terrorism: A Comparative Perspective*, ed. Samy Cohen, trans. John Atherton et al. (Basingstoke: Palgrave, 2008), 77–100.

35. Bew, Frampton, and Gurruchaga, *Talking to Terrorists*, 108.

36. Ibid., 109–10.

37. Ibid., 247.

38. Ibid., 110.

39. Frampton, "Agents and Ambushes," 96.

40. Ibid., 89.

41. Bew, Frampton, and Gurruchaga, *Talking to Terrorists*, 35 and 52, and Dean Godson, "The Real Lessons of Ulster," *Prospect* 140 (2007): 32–37, on rehabilitating internment.

42. Bew and Frampton, "Talking to Terrorists," and Bew, Frampton, and Gurruchaga, *Talking to Terrorists*, 43.

43. Dixon, "Was the IRA Defeated?," 309–10.

44. Bew and Frampton, "Where Do We Stand Now with the IRA," August 31, 2005, http://web.archive.org/web/20060430144820/zope06.v.servelocity.net/hjs/organising_committee, accessed March 17, 2011.

45. Frampton, *The Long March*.

46. Bew and Frampton, "Talking to Terrorists," and Bew, Frampton, and Gurruchaga, *Talking to Terrorists*.

47. Frampton, "Return of the Militants," 31.

48. Bew, Frampton, and Gurruchaga, *Talking to Terrorists*, 13 and 111.

49. Ibid., 246.

50. Frampton, *The Long March*, 6, 19, 184, 187, and 189.

51. Dixon, "Was the IRA Defeated?"

52. Ibid.

53. Mowlam, *Momentum*, 231.

54. Alastair Campbell, *The Alastair Campbell Diaries*, vol. 2 (London: Hutchinson, 2011), 350.

55. Dixon, *Northern Ireland*, 216–19 and 242–43. On British counterinsurgency thinking, see Paul Dixon, ed., *The British Approach to Counterinsurgency: From Malaya and Northern Ireland to Iraq and Afghanistan* (Basingstoke: Palgrave Macmillan, 2012).

56. Ancram, "Dancing with Wolves," 23.

57. Blair, *A Journey*, 189, and Powell, *Great Hatred, Little Room*.

58. Trimble, "Misunderstanding Ulster."

59. David Trimble, "Engaging Reality," Speech to the Young Unionist Conference, October 3, 1998.

60. Godson, *Himself Alone*.

61. Frank Millar, *The Price of Peace* (Dublin: The Liffey Press, 2004), 62 and 63–64.

62. David Trimble, "Belfast Talk," *American Interest* 5 (2) (2009): 90–91, and Godson, *Himself Alone*.

63. Trimble, "Belfast Talk," 90.

64. *Independent on Sunday*, November 17, 1991.

65. See, for example, *The Times*, January 11, 1992; *Sunday Times*, August 22, 1993; and Dixon, "Was the IRA Defeated?"

66. Dixon, *Northern Ireland*, 242–44.

67. Christopher Andrew, *The Defence of the Realm: The Authorized History of MI5* (London: Penguin, 2010).

68. R. Bourke, "British Army Penetration of IRA Shown in File Passed to Cosgrove," *Irish Times*, January 2, 2004.

69. Gary McGladdery, *The Provisional IRA in England: The Bombing Campaign, 1973–1997* (Dublin: Irish Academic Press, 2006), 229.

70. Ibid., 215–16.

71. Ed Moloney, *A Secret History of the IRA* (London: Penguin, 2002), chapter 13.

72. Frampton, *The Long March*, 96.

73. Bew and Frampton, "Talking to Terrorists," 8.

74. Powell, *Great Hatred, Little Room*.

75. Frampton, "Agents and Ambushes," 89.

76. Paul Dixon, "British Policy towards Northern Ireland, 1969–2000: Continuity, Tactical Adjustment and Consistent 'Inconsistencies,'" *British Journal of Politics and International Relations* 3 (3) (2001): 340–68.

77. *Guardian*, March 27, 1979, and *Daily Telegraph*, March 31, 1979.

78. Paul Dixon, "'The Usual English Doubletalk': The British Political Parties and the Ulster Unionists, 1974–94," *Irish Political Studies* 9 (1994): 25–40.

79. Dixon, *Northern Ireland*, 196–98.

80. Bew, Frampton, and Gurruchaga, *Talking to Terrorists*, 91, 98, and 116–17.

81. See Reiss, *Negotiating with Evil*, 67, for Reiss's belief that his invite to the McCartney sisters to the White House and the criticism of Senator John McCain turned the tide. See also Mary-Alice C. Clancy, "The United States and Post-Agreement Northern Ireland, 2001–6," *Irish Studies in International Affairs* 18 (2007): 155–73.

82. *Irish Times*, October 2, 2010.

83. Mitchell Reiss, "The Trouble We've Seen," *The American Interest* 3 (6) (2008): 100–104.

84. Dixon, "Political Skills or Lying and Manipulation."

85. Bew, Frampton, and Gurruchaga, *Talking to Terrorists*, 253.

86. Mowlam, *Momentum*, 269.

87. Blair, *A Journey*, and Powell, *Great Hatred, Little Room*.

88. This interpretation of *Talking to Terrorists* is consistent with the interpretation of conservative reviewers of the book. Dixon, "Was the IRA Defeated?"

89. Martyn Frampton, *Legion of the Rearguard: Dissident Irish Republicanism* (Dublin: Irish Academic Press, 2010), chapter 4, and 163 on the ambiguity of nonviolent republican dissidents' attitude toward violence. See also Frampton, "Return of the Militants."

90. Frampton, *Legion of the Rearguard*, 39.

91. Godson, *Himself Alone*.

92. Dixon, "Political Skills or Lying and Manipulation," 738–39.

93. Tony Coady, *Messy Morality* (Oxford: Oxford University Press, 2008), 20, 45, 62, and 74.

94. Dixon, "Bew and Frampton," and Powell, *Great Hatred, Little Room*.

95. Paul Dixon, "The Politics of Conflict: A Constructivist Critique of Consociational and Civil Society Theories," *Nations and Nationalism* 18 (1) (2012): 98–121.

6 The Transformation of Policing in Postconflict Societies

Lessons from the Northern Ireland Experience

JOHN DOYLE

The issues of power and status went to the heart of the conflict in Northern Ireland. Most symbolically and fundamentally this was represented in the debate on the constitutional status of Northern Ireland. However, the conflict also centered on the nature of governance, economic and social inequalities, and the application of state power through security and policing. Both at the beginning of the modern conflict and as it progressed, the policing of Northern Ireland was one of the mostly highly contested aspects of the conflict and was regarded as such by political actors and communities. Policing created an apparently unbridgeable divide between the two communities. Because of the changes that have come to policing, the new policing institutions are increasingly acceptable to both nationalists and unionists. This remarkable achievement and the process by which it was achieved can be instructive to other zones of ethnic and regional conflict in the world. Beyond the model of policing agreed in Northern Ireland, the question of the transformation of policing addresses a few other key issues for international debates on conflict resolution highlighted in the introductory chapter of this volume. Policing reflected key themes of the overall Northern Ireland case, first of all in the manner in which it was negotiated. All parties, including those who had previously supported armed attacks on the police during the conflict, were fully involved in the discussions. No one was excluded and there were no preconditions to the talks and no predetermined outcome, beyond requiring groups to commit themselves to seeking a peaceful way forward. As this chapter will show, the agreement on policing came slowly, long after the 1998 Agreement, the destruction of weapons, and the withdrawal of the British Army from the streets. However, it was negotiated by the parties and not imposed, and as others highlight in various chapters of this book, it was negotiated in advance of a wider societal process of reconciliation. Finally, this chapter argues that the question of policing followed a consociational logic in the nature of the accountability mechanisms and indeed in recruitment to the police service itself.

Some authors have portrayed the Northern Ireland peace process as following a model where nationalists effectively abandoned their goal of seceding from the United Kingdom (UK) and agreed instead to local power sharing. In return, nationalists were given reforms in the areas of civil and human rights, including policing.[1] This perspective has the effect of reducing the transformation of policing in Northern Ireland to the status of a lower-order concession to nationalists, which though resisted by unionists was finally agreed once unionists believed that they had secured their constitutional preferences. Contrary to the view of policing as a lower-order concession, given in return for the ending of an Irish nationalist challenge to the British state, this chapter argues that the transformation of policing, as much as the new institutions of government, reflected and indeed are a core element of the new constitutional framework enshrined in the consociational character of the 1998 Agreement and its institutionalized linkages between Northern Ireland and the Republic of Ireland.[2]

The issues involved in the transformation of policing in Northern Ireland are of enormous significance internationally and of broad interest to those involved in conflict resolution efforts elsewhere. Security sector reform is one of the most challenging issues in international conflict resolution. During the Cold War, when interstate conflicts dominated international relations, cease-fires were usually followed by a withdrawal of forces. Therefore, international involvement, if present at all, was generally limited to the interposition of peacekeepers along a cease-fire line. Civil wars, distorted by superpower interference, were also more likely to end militarily rather than by a negotiated settlement, as external support often exasperated and prolonged the local internal dynamics of conflicts. For as long as the Cold War lasted, in neither interstate nor civil wars was the need for security sector reform seen as an important part of the postconflict settlement. Since the mid-1990s, by contrast, most armed conflicts have been primarily internal wars, even if they often have a strong international or regional context. Post–Cold War civil conflicts are more likely to be the subject of international mediation efforts and are statistically more likely than conflicts in earlier eras to end in a negotiated peace agreement.[3] Peace agreements at the end of civil wars, almost by definition, leave previously hostile political groups and armed forces sharing the same political and geographical space. In this context, new forms of government at the national level—usually involving power sharing of some form—and security sector reform within the police and/or military have emerged as some of the most crucial elements of the content of peace agreements signed over the past twenty years. The international community continues to struggle, however, with the planning and execution of security sector reform. In that respect, the Northern Ireland case has significance beyond those interested simply in that specific conflict.

Civil conflicts generally involve a highly polarized relationship between the official security forces of the state and those nonstate actors challenging for state power or seeking to secede from the state. There will often be a long history of poor and conflictual relationships between security forces and sections of the population before an armed conflict emerges. Even in those cases where the security forces have not been a significant factor in the eruption of armed conflict, the nature and style of counterinsurgency operations in almost all conflicts has led to a sharp deterioration in relations between the police and army on the one hand and the communities within which challenging nonstate actors operate on the other. Northern Ireland was typical of many modern conflicts in this respect. By the time a peace agreement was negotiated, the community was highly polarized on the future of policing. For the British government and unionists, the Royal Ulster Constabulary (RUC), along with the British Army, was their defender, which had bravely guarded them against a terrorist insurgency. For Irish nationalists, even those who had strongly opposed the IRA, the police were part of the problem; they were an unrepresentative force with a poor human-rights record, had almost no support among the wider nationalist community, and could not provide a normal postconflict policing service.

This chapter is structured around a few key issues. First, it explores the perspectives on policing during the conflict to give a sense of the depth of divisions among the communal groups in society. Second, it examines the political process, including the role of the International Commission, chaired by Chris Patten, which led, over a period of about ten years, to a broad political agreement on the transformation of policing. Finally, this chapter explores the implications of those changes, and the manner in which they happened, for other conflict situations.

Divided Views of Policing during the Conflict

The attitudes of both communities to policing during the years of conflict in Northern Ireland demonstrate that this issue was inseparable from the wider constitutional question and from conflicting definitions of citizenship. Initially, in the late 1960s, the demands of the civil-rights movement focused on voting rights and equality of access to employment, housing, and policing.[4] For unionists, on the other hand, the police were defenders of the state against what they saw as an attempt at radical insurrection. The aggressive response of the police to the civil-rights protests from autumn 1968 onward radicalized and entrenched Irish nationalist hostility to the police and marked the beginning of international concerns with the RUC's human-rights record. The initial shock at the high level of intercommunal violence in Northern Ireland led to the deployment of British troops there in 1969. The escalating crisis saw the British government take full control of security, including policing, in 1972, leading to direct rule from London and the end of the devolved Unionist government and parliament in Northern Ireland. Unionists opposed the loss of local control over policing but in all other respects continued to support the RUC as "their" police force. In this, as in other respects, the overall political divisions between unionists and nationalists were reflected in the debates on policing.

The critiques of policing in Northern Ireland made by Irish nationalists during the conflict are taken from the view articulated by Sinn Féin and the Social Democratic and Labour Party (SDLP), as those parties between them secure the votes of almost 100 percent of the nationalist community (the SDLP being the larger party during the conflict but Sinn Féin becoming the dominant party since the 1990s).[5] Their positions and concerns regarding policing included counterinsurgency and the demand for politically impartial policing, the need to redress human-rights abuses by security forces, and the unrepresentative membership of the RUC.

Sinn Féin's core perspective on policing during the conflict centered on its opposition to the RUC as an instrument of repression and counterinsurgency, whose primary aim was to uphold British sovereignty over Northern Ireland. For Sinn Féin, this view of the RUC was reflected in its title, both the use of the word "Royal" linking it to the British Crown and the use of the geographical descriptor Ulster (favored by unionists) rather than the more neutral Northern Ireland. The terminology used in Sinn Féin statements and publications in the 1970s and 1980s reflected this perception of the force, with the police usually referred to as "Crown Forces."[6] While this view of the RUC as a force with a counterinsurgency mission was logical and consistent from the perspective of Sinn Féin— supporters of the insurgency—this form of critique of the RUC was widespread in the nationalist community.

The RUC was also fundamentally criticized by moderate nationalists for going beyond what was required for effective counterinsurgency and upholding the constitutional order (which was its legal duty) by effectively distorting its policing mission with an antinationalist bias.[7] Repeated examples of this type of differentiated policing of nationalist and unionist public protest reinforced nationalist opinion that the RUC was not simply keeping the law but was upholding unionists' power over nationalists. John Hume, the undisputed leader of moderate nationalism, when challenged at the time of the cease-fire as to whether the SDLP attitude to the RUC over the years of conflict had been a mistake, countered: "The basis of order in any society is agreement on how you govern. When that is absent . . . the police are going to be seen as being on one side or the other—which is what happens in Northern Ireland. . . . Until such time as the political problem was resolved our position was that we fully and unequivocally supported the police in upholding the rule of law. Our only qualification was that they should do so impartially."[8] The crucial point for Hume is that the RUC did not police impartially and therefore did not meet the basic criteria for SDLP endorsement.

Throughout the conflict both the SDLP and Sinn Féin made repeated and vocal criticisms of the RUC's human-rights record. The issues consistently raised by nationalists over the years were allegations of ill treatment and even torture during interrogation, summary executions, the reckless use of plastic bullets, and police collusion with killings by illegal loyalist paramilitary groups. These positions were reinforced by the actions of external actors. For example, in the early 1970s the Irish state brought the UK to the European Court of Human Rights over the treatment of people in police custody, while the Carter administration banned the sale of firearms to the RUC, citing human-rights concerns.[9] Human-rights abuses were extensively documented and analyzed.[10] While nationalist campaigns on human-rights issues, bolstered by international pressure, occasionally resulted in investigations into these issues and in some minimal reforms, none of these measures were successful in persuading members of the wider nationalist community that the RUC was a legitimate police service deserving of their support. Indeed, the conduct of these investigations into human-rights abuses and the limited and partial response to their findings tended to reinforce nationalist alienation from the police rather than mitigate it. The events around the "Stalker Enquiry" led by John Stalker, deputy chief constable of the Greater Manchester Police in England, in the early 1980s when the RUC was accused of a targeted assassination policy are one example where the perceived cover-up by security forces and the British government during the investigation made relations worse rather than better.[11]

Nationalists also criticized the RUC as an "unrepresentative force," not only because of the religious identity of its members but also as a result of what they saw as the antinationalist ethos of the RUC. In 1998, when the Agreement was signed, nationalists made up between 44 percent and 48 percent of the working-age population in Northern Ireland, but only 7.5 percent of RUC officers were Catholic and fewer still were likely to be Irish nationalists.[12] Nationalists argued that a police service that so under-represented its community could not, by its very nature, deliver policing in a manner acceptable to that community. Nationalist critiques also linked the makeup of the RUC to what they regarded as its unionist ethos. The RUC reflected a unionist culture and identity. Police stations displayed photographs of the British monarch and flew the Union Jack, and police officers were embedded in and had strong links with unionist communities. Nationalist communities were politically, culturally, and geographically perceived as the "other," reinforcing the gulf between the police and the nationalist community.

While nationalist critiques have been well documented and follow a familiar international pattern in divided societies experiencing conflict, less attention has been paid in the literature generally to the views of pro-state actors on policing in conflict situations. Unionist political parties were, and are, unanimous in their broad support for the police and in their rejection of nationalist critiques. It is a mistake, however, to reduce the views of pro-state actors to either a defense of their monopoly of well-paid jobs or even to the provision of security as a functional commodity. Unionists' views are more complex, and like nationalist perspectives they are strongly intertwined with their political positions. First, unionist parties rejected nationalist complaints about the pro-British ethos of the RUC. They insisted that the ethos of the RUC *should* reflect British sovereignty and further argued that it was the duty of every citizen (and every party) to support the RUC and to encourage people to join. Second, human-rights critiques were rebuffed, and unionists regularly called for more hard-line security tactics, such as capital punishment, assassination of Irish Republican Army (IRA) members, and internment without trial. Finally, the low percentage of nationalist recruits to the RUC was dismissed as being caused by IRA intimidation or by the nationalist community's support for terrorism.

Unionist politicians perceived Sinn Féin to be directly involved in an armed insurgency, and so they had no expectation that Sinn Féin or the party's support base would back the RUC. Criticisms of nationalist views on policing therefore focused on the more moderate SDLP. Criticism of the SDLP for its failure to support the RUC unambiguously, or to encourage nationalist recruitment, spans the entire unionist political spectrum and the entire time period of the conflict. Unionist politicians, including the most moderate in the Alliance Party, repeatedly argued that they would not take part in governmental power sharing with the SDLP without the party's full support for the RUC. This was usually linked to an insistence that supporting the police was a requirement of accepting British sovereignty over Northern Ireland.[13] The unanimity of unionist discourse on this issue is striking. Nationalists were not being offered power sharing in return for supporting the police. Nationalists had, in unionist eyes, an absolute duty to support the police. If nationalists refused to offer that support, then they had, in the unionists' view, excluded themselves from any right to hold public office. It is also an indication of the scale of nationalist alienation from the RUC that the SDLP could not endorse the service, despite the party's strong desire to agree on power sharing with unionists.

During the conflict, the widespread human-rights-based criticisms of the RUC from groups and individuals who were not supporters of an Irish nationalist agenda did not open up any space within the major unionist parties for nonpolitical critiques of policing based on legal values or even arguments that such abuses strengthened the IRA. The unionist parties attacked human-rights groups as being engaged in a campaign, deliberately or through naïveté, to undermine the state. After the cease-fire, Ulster Unionist Party (UUP) spokesperson on security Ken Maginnis, MP, continued to assert that even some of those involved in the law supported the gun and the bomb.[14] The unionist suspicions of the motivations of human-rights groups were accompanied by a rejection of the substantive criticisms made of the RUC. There was cross-party unionist opposition to any disciplinary action over the "shoot-to-kill" operations investigated by John Stalker.[15] There was near unanimous support, for example, for capital punishment and the use of ambush tactics against the IRA.[16] The extent of unionist rejections of human-rights-based critiques of the RUC meant that human-rights discourse did not provide a neutral or nonpolitical language for discussing police reform.

There was no recognition by unionist politicians that nationalists were alienated from the RUC because of its ethos or actions. Low levels of Catholic recruitment were explained, by unionists, as being caused by IRA intimidation[17] or the subversive nature of the nationalist community.[18] These two explanations are at least potentially contradictory, but the occasional public statements from unionist politicians, claiming that there existed a silent loyal Catholic grouping, is overwhelmed by the much larger number of unionist statements that clearly extend the definition of subversive to the entire nationalist community (or even to the Catholic community). In the House of Commons in 1991, David Trimble quoted as a form of precedent the practice of treating all enemy aliens as suspects during wartime.[19] The possibility that some aliens might actually sympathize with their host country was outweighed by the strategic and security imperative, and so all enemy aliens were to be treated as suspect. The implication was that all nationalists were enemy aliens and similarly were to be seen as a threat.

This rather lengthy discussion of the perspectives held during the period of conflict is included here to demonstrate that the later transformation of policing was no minor matter; rather, it was at the heart of the peace process. The extent of the shift is what makes the case interesting from an international perspective. It also provides a model for disaggregating the starting point for debates on police reform. Critiques by insurgent groups can be instrumental, as the police by definition oppose their aims as well as strategy. However, for the wider insurgent community, including moderates opposed to the use of armed force, demands for security reform are usually rooted in human-rights abuses, alienation from the force on political or cultural grounds, and the typically unrepresentative nature of police forces in contexts of armed political rebellion. Each of these issues needs to be addressed and will require separate solutions. Likewise for those actors and communities who support the state (or the status quo), the debate is often too dominated by crude characterizations of the employment resource and the instrumental power of security. These are important, but the police and army are also high-value political-cultural institutions reflecting the ideological power of a dominant bloc, and those issues remain crucial even after a peace process. Indeed, they are likely to become more difficult as a previously dominant community has to adjust to a more egalitarian society.

The Peace Process and the Transformation of Policing

The nationalist community in Northern Ireland did not believe any peace deal could be enduring if it did not deal with policing, because they believed policing was at the heart of the conflict.[20] The highly politicized nature of policing, the legacy of human-rights concerns, and the highly unrepresentative makeup of the RUC ensured that no nationalist party could endorse the police and retain political support. It was also impossible for the RUC to provide policing in nationalist areas without community support. The centrality of policing to the wider peace process was reflected in public debates that began in the immediate aftermath of the cease-fires. The importance of this issue was also clear in the public meetings held by the commission and in those published submissions made by a wide range of nationalist organizations.[21] The two nationalist political parties highlighted the issue of policing in regular statements. The SDLP made it very clear that it would not endorse a tokenistic reform program. A survey of party members indicated that over 94 percent of them sought radical reform of the RUC after the cease-fires.[22] Sinn Féin ran a high-profile, public campaign under the slogan "Disband the RUC," and its members supported this approach.[23] In contrast, mainstream unionism's position on policing led it to dismiss any requirement to consider RUC reform as part of the process of a political settlement for Northern Ireland. Even symbolic changes in the name and uniform were rejected by all unionist parties other than Alliance.[24]

Given the strength of these opposing perspectives, it was not surprising that all parties agreed, during the negotiations leading up to the 1998 Agreement, that a solution to policing could not be agreed at that time and that an independent commission should be established to make recommendations on policing, which would be "broadly representative" and have "expert and international representation."[25] The terms of reference for this commission stated that "its proposals on policing should be designed to ensure that policing arrangements, including composition, recruitment, training, culture, ethos, and symbols, are such that in a new approach Northern Ireland has a police service that can enjoy widespread support from, and is seen as an integral part of, the community as a whole."[26]

By establishing such a commission, the negotiators in 1998 created space for a peace agreement to be reached without finalizing a political agreement on policing. A similar procedure was used to make progress on the contentious issue of weapons held by illegal armed groups. The idea of a policing commission allowed the first hurdle to be crossed, but it did not resolve the underlying problems. Even if a peace agreement could be signed, it would not be sustainable for very long without agreement on the substantive issues that the Independent Commission on Policing for Northern Ireland had been asked to address. The commission therefore, once established, faced a hugely challenging task in drafting a report that would provide a basis for the transformation of policing in Northern Ireland and would meet the demands of its terms of reference, that a new police service "can enjoy widespread support from, and is seen as an integral part of, the community as a whole."[27]

The SDLP, Sinn Féin, and the Irish government had put considerable resources into achieving the strongest possible reform agenda for a commission on policing. Surprisingly, unionist negotiators did not seem as focused on this issue. Nationalist negotiators were prepared for a last-minute backlash from the UUP to reverse the text of the terms of reference for a policing commission, but it did not materialize. The UUP was hugely focused on limiting the North-South institutional linkages. Its negotiators were very influenced by an analysis of the collapse of the 1974 power-sharing institutions, which (over)emphasized the importance of the all-island Council of Ireland in explaining unionist opposition to that agreement. On policing, the UUP seemed to assume that a British-government-appointed commission would largely favor the status quo. The terms of reference were, however, fundamental to the direction given to the Independent Commission on Policing for Northern Ireland, and the International Commission interpreted its terms of reference as requiring it to produce recommendations for creating a policing system that "can enjoy widespread support"—effectively precluding any vision based only on limited or technical reforms. Indeed, commission member Peter Smith, a lawyer and former member of the UUP, assumed that part of the reasoning behind his appointment to the commission was to bring a unionist perspective to such a report, capable of receiving nationalist endorsement. He accepted that the unionist leadership would need to maintain some distance from their report. Having agreed to the terms of reference in the Agreement, he assumed the UUP leadership was prepared for a fundamental transformation of policing. Thus, Smith was both surprised and resentful of the later attacks on the commission by unionist leader David Trimble.[28]

Agreeing to establish the International Commission was only the very beginning of a process, and immediately its membership became an issue of contention. While the commission was technically established by the British government, under the terms of the Agreement, its composition required coordination with the Irish government, at least in spirit. The Irish government never commented on the commission membership during the establishment phase, but one commission member, Gerald W. Lynch from New York, subsequently claimed that none of the initially announced names had been reviewed by the Irish government and that he was added to the list following pressure from the Irish government.[29] Certainly, there was wider public comment on the membership once it was announced. Chris Patten, though later widely praised for his independence from the British government, was initially seen by nationalists as too much of a British insider to chair an independent and international commission. There was also concern by nationalists that there was no equivalent person associated with the Irish state. In addition, while Peter Smith was a former member of the UUP in addition to being a lawyer, his equivalent from within the Catholic community, former senior civil servant Maurice Hayes, would not have been perceived to be close to either of the nationalist parties. Certainly, there was no one even remotely perceived to be close to the republican community on the commission. In addition to Gerald Lynch, the other commission members from outside Ireland and Britain were the distinguished academic criminologist from South Africa Clifford Shearing and US Police Commissioner Kathleen O'Toole, and these members were crucial in securing nationalist acceptance of the commission. Finally, the other members were former deputy commissioner of the London Metropolitan Police and Lucy Wood, an expert in change management from the business world.

In addition to the challenges of producing a blueprint for reforming policing in Northern Ireland, the commission needed first of all to establish its bona fides with a unionist community essentially hostile to any reform and a nationalist community unsure if the membership of the commission was sufficiently international. The manner by which they conducted their work was crucial. The commission devoted considerable time to outreach meetings throughout Northern Ireland. More than forty public meetings were held with over 1,000 speakers, attracting over 10,000 people in a society with a population of only 1.5 million. The meetings were held in a diverse range of communities and without police protection, so that the commission was seen to put its trust in the communities that were most alienated from the police. Chris Patten himself highlighted the importance of these meetings for the commission, and they were certainly crucial in establishing the commission's independence and in building a relationship with the wider community, including all the political parties—a relationship that would be crucial once its report was issued.[30] The commission also made tremendous efforts, successfully in many cases, to persuade police officers that they had nothing to fear from the transformation of policing. The terms of reference set out in the Agreement, the international composition of the commission's members, its independence from government, and its representation of local views were essential components in laying a strong foundation on which the members of the Policing Commission could establish their credibility and ensure that their report would be broadly acceptable and difficult to ignore.

The publication of the report by the Policing Commission was, in many respects, as the title suggests, a "new beginning." It was not a solution or a settlement. It was to take another ten years for the institutional structure of accountability and control to be fully devolved from London to the local elected executive, but by that time many remarkable changes had already occurred—and indeed were an essential part of the confidence building that was necessary to allow rival unionist and nationalist political parties to reach agreement on sharing power. There are issues that remain to be resolved—not least that the new Police Service of Northern Ireland (PSNI) still does not fully reflect the demographic profile of Northern Ireland. However, the situation has been remarkably transformed. The political parties representing about 99 percent of nationalist opinion in Northern Ireland both support the police service and encourage nationalists to join. This was most illustrated visually and metaphorically in March 2009 when the Sinn Féin MP and former IRA leader Martin McGuiness, now deputy first minister of Northern Ireland, stood side by side with the unionist first minister Peter Robinson and the chief constable of the PSNI, Hugh Orde, in condemning the shooting of a PSNI police officer by a small IRA splinter group.[31]

The Patten Commission Report's most basic elements included a change of name, uniform, and badge to symbolize a fundamental alteration in policing.[32] It was also a report about policing, not the police, with considerable attention paid to accountability mechanisms, a human-rights culture, a police ombudsman to independently investigate allegations of police misconduct, and an international oversight commission to access progress on implementation and community acceptability. The report proposed a generous retirement package to both downsize the force and to make way for a new generation of recruits. This package was ultimately successful and crucial in both allowing an honorable way out for those who did not wish to be part of a different type of policing system and also in changing the representative base of the police in the sort of short-time scale that was needed to gain public confidence. New recruits would be drawn equally—50 percent each—from the nationalist and unionist communities. The commission was particularly original and insightful in dealing with the question of what to do after the publication of the *Patten Report*. Had they functioned like a standard government commission and simply disbanded, leaving the government to make political choices on which elements, if any, of the *Report* to implement, they would have fulfilled the letter of their mandate but perhaps not the spirit. On the other hand, it would have been impossible to appoint themselves as the overseers of the transformation. Thus, the proposal to establish an oversight commissioner from outside Ireland and the UK was a very significant decision, which provided an additional view, independent of government, on the degree to which the commission's proposals were implemented. The Office of the Oversight Commissioner was to play a crucial role as an independent verification mechanism in later years.

In the immediate aftermath of the publication of the *Patten Report*, public debate was dominated by unionist rejection of its proposals. The Democratic Unionist Party (DUP) was, at that point, still in opposition to the 1998 Agreement and predictably opposed the report, but UUP leader and first minister David Trimble also attacked it in very trenchant terms, rejecting its entire premise, calling it the "most shoddy piece of work I have seen in my entire life," and referring to the name change for the RUC as a "gratuitous insult." The SDLP welcomed the report, while calling for a more rapid and ambitious target for creating a representative police service. Sinn Féin welcomed the proposals for accountability but said that they could have gone further in some key areas. The main point emphasized by Sinn Féin in this period, however, was that it needed to know what the British government would do, and therefore it would reserve final judgment on whether it would urge people to join any new police service until it saw the appropriate legislation on implementing the report's recommendations.[33] Sinn Féin did not trust the British government to implement the report, and so it was wary that endorsing it might turn it into a nationalist wish list rather than an Independent Commission report, which did not, by any measure, represent all of Sinn Féin's demands.

In fact, when the British government's legislation (the Police Bill) and a parallel implementation plan, purporting to show how it would implement the commission's report, were published in May 2000, the British government had abandoned key recommendations in the report and did indeed seek to present their proposed legislation as a compromise between a nationalist-supported commission report and unionist opposition to change.[34] The British government proposals were roundly criticized not only by the two nationalist parties in Northern Ireland but by most significant human-rights groups, nationalist commentators, and civil society organizations.[35] The Irish government, too, signaled its displeasure that so many of the commission's 175 recommendations had been rejected by the British government.[36] John Hume called the Police Bill defective,[37] while Gerry Adams stated, "there is no way at this time that I, or Sinn Féin, could recommend to nationalists or republicans that they should consider joining or supporting a police force as described in that legislation."[38]

The deputy first minister and SDLP MP Seamus Mallon reacted to British secretary of state for Northern Ireland Peter Mandelson's depictions of his legislation as a compromise between nationalist support for the *Patten Report* and unionist opposition, saying that "*Patten* is itself a compromise. It is policing not in the image of unionism or nationalism."[39] Both the SDLP and Sinn Féin issued lengthy critiques of the bill.[40] Nationalist critiques focused on the insertion of the phrase "incorporating the RUC" in the formal title of the new PSNI; the potential continuation of the practice of flying the Union Jack on police stations; the weakening of oversight, human rights, and accountability mechanisms; the potential weakening of the commitment to 50:50 recruitment; provisions allowing the British government or chief constable to veto investigations into allegations of police malpractice; and the limitation of a new oath of office to new recruits only (rather than having it apply to all existing officers as recommended by the commission). Statements reflected all the traditional nationalist critiques of the RUC—the counterinsurgency priority, human-rights issues, and community representation.

The May 2000 Police Bill was seen as a victory for unionist lobbying. The bill included a significant weakening of the oversight, human rights, and accountability proposals made in the commission's report. While unionists did not oppose the British government's overturning of the commission's recommendations in these areas, there is little evidence of a vigorous unionist campaign. The motivation for rejecting the commission's recommendations on oversight and human rights seemed to come from the British government itself and the police and security agencies, rather than unionists in Northern Ireland—highlighting the multiactor nature of all attempts at security reform.

Following an extensive campaign of pressure from the nationalist parties, some British Labour backbenchers, senior US politicians, and human-rights groups as well as a series of interparty talks in Weston Park in England in 2001, the British government introduced a number of significant amendments to its own proposed legislation to bring it closer to the recommendations of the commission's report.[41] This was sufficient for the Irish government and the SDLP to support the new arrangements, and in August 2001 the SDLP agreed to join the new Policing Board.

Sinn Féin refused to join the Policing Board or support the PSNI at this time, arguing that the proposed legislation and the British government's implementation plan for police reform were still far weaker than the commission's recommendations. Although Sinn Féin had not given unqualified support to the commission's *Patten Report* when published, from this time Sinn Féin explicitly used the report as a benchmark against which to measure the transformation of policing.[42] Another very positive development at this time was the quality and detail of the reports of the first oversight commissioner, Tom Constantine. His very detailed performance indicators, judging action on policing in comparison to the commission's recommendations, ensured that the British government did not have a monopoly of authoritative information.[43] Sinn Féin, from this point onward, focused on the remaining gaps between the commission's recommendations and British government decisions—especially on accountability, human rights, and oversight, on retention of some key powers in London, and on control of the Special Branch and covert policing operations.[44]

Unionist parties, notwithstanding their opposition to elements of the reform agenda, agreed to join the new Policing Board and support the new police service. They highlighted two continuing priorities in announcing their decision to join. The first was to ensure that the police service's symbols would recognize Northern Ireland's constitutional position in the UK, indicating how important the police were to unionist definitions of the nature of the state. The second priority was the unionists' ongoing campaign to minimize the reduction in the size of the force.[45] The Policing Board unanimously agreed on a new PSNI symbol in December 2001.[46] While not strictly following the commission's recommendation of having a badge that was entirely free from any association with either the British or Irish states, the new badge was widely judged to be acceptable to both communities. This achievement was swamped, however, by the wider crisis in the peace process that led to the suspension of the power-sharing executive and Assembly in October 2002 as the UUP refused to continue sharing power with Sinn Féin without the handover or destruction of IRA weapons. New elections in November 2003 saw the DUP emerge as the largest unionist party and Sinn Féin as the largest nationalist party—entitling the leaders of these parties to hold the offices of first minister and deputy first minister, respectively.[47] No agreement on power sharing was possible, and the Assembly was immediately suspended. The key issues in dispute were unionists' refusal to share power with Sinn Féin without the IRA destroying its weapons and the IRA refusal to do so while the peace process was stalled.

Ultimately, the IRA agreed to put its weapons beyond use in a process overseen and observed by another international commission—this one on decommissioning, led by Canadian General John de Chastelain. This decommissioning was completed in September 2005 and was the key defining moment for Sinn Féin.[48] The destruction of IRA weapons was a major political decision. The initial IRA cease-fire could be interpreted (or sold) as an experiment. An IRA campaign could have been restarted and indeed was resumed (at a low level) between February 1996 and July 1997. However, symbolically the destruction of weapons was a clear signal that the IRA was not intending to restart its campaign and that Sinn Féin would pursue republican goals by exclusively peaceful means. The next logical step was support for policing. However, no wider agreement on power sharing with unionists or Sinn Féin support for the police was reached at this time.

Agreement seemed to have finally been reached in talks at St. Andrews in Scotland in October 2006.[49] The St. Andrews Agreement provided for a deal whereby the suspended Northern Ireland Executive and Assembly would be reconstituted; new elections would be held as a means of gaining community endorsement; new legislation on policing, human rights, and the Irish language was promised by the British government and that on policing would be passed by the end of 2006; and the British government guaranteed that there would be no executive role for the British secret service (MI5) in Northern Ireland—even on national security issues—when control of policing was devolved to Northern Ireland. In this context Sinn Féin was expected to endorse the police service.

Sinn Féin used considerable leadership resources in a dialogue with their party members and wider public supporters. They held over sixty meetings with party supporters across Ireland to gauge opinion on the question of supporting the PSNI and probably hundreds of internal meetings for party members.[50] A special party *ard fheis* (conference) was called with delegates from every local branch of the party, and the leadership needed to be certain that it would secure an overwhelming majority to avoid the danger of a split in the party. The debate within Sinn Féin was intense and relatively public—unusually so for a party whose internal discipline is legendary in Irish politics. Over 1,000 people attended a meeting, which the press were permitted to observe, in Gerry Adams's own constituency.[51] Letters for and against endorsing the PSNI were carried in the Sinn Féin newspaper *An Phoblacht*.[52] The newspaper also carried very prominent messages of support for the leadership position from former African National Congress chief negotiator Cyril Ramaphosa and the Palestinian ambassador to Ireland, Hikmat Ajjuri. Three thousand delegates attended the ard fheis, and the motion committing the party to fully support the PSNI was carried with an estimated 90 percent yes vote.[53] Throughout the peace process Sinn Féin's leadership engaged their base in an effort to build support and avoid a split, which is in sharp contrast to the negligible equivalent efforts within the UUP, where the party leadership never sought to manage the process of the party's changing positions, with disastrous consequences in terms of internal divisions and loss of support.

Following the Sinn Féin decision, elections to the Northern Ireland Assembly (the next step in the agreed process) were called for March 2007. Unionists were relatively subdued in their responses to the Sinn Féin change of policy, adopting a wait-and-see attitude. The March 2007 elections saw further significant gains for both Sinn Féin and the DUP, meaning that under the power-sharing rules they would take the positions of first minister and deputy first minister from a position of strength. Dissident republican candidates, standing on a platform of opposition to Sinn Féin's decision on policing, received only tiny levels of support.[54] In the end, the DUP agreed to form a power-sharing executive, with its leader Ian Paisley as first minister and Sinn Féin's Martin McGuinness as deputy first minister. The Assembly was restored in May 2007.[55] Sinn Féin then joined the Policing Board and nominated a former high-profile IRA prisoner, Martina Anderson, as one of its three nominees. This did not generate any significant unionist comment, with the DUP's Gregory Campbell saying, "We have to move on."[56]

As the deadline for agreement on the devolution of control of policing from London to Northern Ireland approached, unionist parties raised new objections: calling for the IRA leadership structures to be publicly disbanded,[57] demanding a veto over the ministerial nominee (to ensure it would not be a Sinn Féin minister),[58] and seeking further financial guarantees on public funding for policing from the British government.[59] Some of these issues were resolved with a financial package from the British government and an agreement between the DUP and Sinn Féin that neither would seek to hold the Justice portfolio during its first Assembly term. A report by a British-government-appointed Monitoring Commission that the IRA Army Council was not functional or operational and posed no threat to the peace process also assisted progress toward devolution.[60] The DUP's public position was that greater unionist confidence was required. In reality, the party seemed uncertain how such a decision would be received by its supporters. Ultimately, the party did endorse the agreement, and control of policing was transferred to Northern Ireland. The power-sharing executive appointed a moderate unionist from the Alliance Party as its first minister for justice. This minister would share the administration of policing with the Northern Ireland Policing Board (representing all the political parties and civil society).

Although the parties and British and Irish governments have come to an agreement on a devolved policing ministry in Northern Ireland, many challenges still remain. Northern Ireland remains a very underdeveloped economy with pockets of deep poverty in both nationalist and unionist working-class communities. In addition to the problems of postconflict transformation, the Police Service of Northern Ireland faces the same difficulties as police forces elsewhere in effectively policing communities where trust in the police is low, where there are very few police officers who grew up in those communities, and where there may be high levels of antisocial behavior and crime. The particular problems of being a postconflict police service, however, add an additional dimension. Graham Ellison provides a very perceptive analysis of community support for policing in the aftermath of Sinn Féin's decision to support the PSNI.[61] In recent years there is a relatively high level of generalized support for the police among Catholics and Protestants.

The other significant challenge to policing comes from those in the nationalist community who reject the peace process and support a resumption of a high-level armed campaign. There is negligible political support for these dissident republicans. While attacks on the police, including

Table 6.1. Performance of local police in Northern Ireland, 2007–9

Rating	Percentage of respondents											
	2007 Oct.			2008 Apr.			2008 Sept.			2009 Apr.		
	C	P	ALL	C	P	ALL	C	P	ALL	C	P	ALL
Very/Fairly good	54	67	62	56	60	58	59	64	62	59	69	64
Neither good nor poor	21	16	19	21	21	21	20	16	18	24	14	18
Very/Fairly poor	23	16	19	20	18	19	19	18	18	16	15	16
Don't know/Refusal	1	0	1	3	2	2	2	2	2	1	1	1

Source: Graham Ellison, "Police-Community Relations in Northern Ireland in the post-*Patten* Era: Towards an Ecological Analysis," in *Policing the Narrow Ground: Lessons from the Transformation of Policing in Northern Ireland*, ed. John Doyle (Dublin: Royal Irish Academy, 2010), 251.

attacks leading to deaths, have occurred, the number of such attacks is very small. It is more difficult, however, to judge how much lingering hostility to the peace process and the PSNI may exist among those who sympathize to some degree with IRA dissidents, even if they do not support their use of violence.

The Wider International Implications

The politics of policing transformation in Northern Ireland, the nature and timing of the agreements that created the atmosphere for such transformation, and the difficulty in reaching them are clear evidence that policing powers and structures are an integral part of the constitutional framework of contested societies and not a lower-order matter that can be more easily divided up as spoils of peace. Each step in the process of change, from the 1998 Agreement (including the terms of reference) to the debate on the International Commission's *Patten Report* and various interparty talks and agreements linked discussion about policing to other issues in the peace process. Both nationalists and unionists strongly linked police reform to the wider peace process, and progress on policing would have been impossible without agreement on an open-ended constitutional framework that did not require either political community to abandon their longer-term political goals. Nationalists did not and would not have abandoned their political campaign for a united Ireland in return for policing reform. Unionists would not have accepted the transformation of policing without a balanced constitutional and political agreement and without the IRA ending its armed campaign. Policing reform was not a causal result of peace nor was peace precipitated by police reform. Each was related to the other in a dynamic and complex set of interactions. None of these steps would have taken place had significant preconditions been put in place. Nor could they have been started if those aligned with armed groups were excluded from the process or if those in a position of leadership had waited for wider community reconciliation (or even trust between opposing political leaders).

The 1998 Agreement is essentially consociational in character.[62] It is based on an institutionalized model of power sharing, which shares executive power between the political parties based on their electoral support and commits the state to greater equality and greater recognition of nationalists' political identity. Traditional models of consociationalism, as developed by Arend Lijphart, are, however, almost exclusively internally focused and see external involvement in a conflict in largely negative terms. The Northern Ireland case extends or challenges Lijphart's original work, as external mediation and involvement is widely regarded as having played a very positive role in this case. This positive international dimension in the Northern Ireland case was visible at the level of process and in the substantive content of the 1998 Agreement. On process issues it was seen in the work of President Clinton, in the chairing of talks by George Mitchell, and in the international involvement of various experts and diplomats from South Africa, Finland, Canada, and the United States. These external actors were critical to monitoring cease-fires, decommissioning, and reforming the police via an international commission. In the substance of the Agreement, a fundamentally important international dimension was enshrined in the North-South Ministerial Council and the cross-border bodies and in the formalized cooperation between the Irish and British governments. Both of these dimensions—consociationalism and the international extension of that approach—were crucial to the transformation of politics and policing in Northern Ireland. The power-sharing model at executive level created a model for power sharing on the Policing Board and on local district policing partnerships. The logic of governmental-level power sharing also required some exceptional measures to deal with the unrepresentative nature of the police—ultimately leading to a period of fifty-fifty recruitment between Catholics and Protestants. The international dimensions of the peace process were critical in building support for compromises between previously conflictual positions on policing and many other matters and in creating a greater balance between the unionist and nationalist communities and the Irish and British governments.

Without a more general peace process in Northern Ireland there would have been no transformation of policing. Police reform was explicitly linked to the consociational power-sharing model at the heart of the new political structures in Northern Ireland and the interlinked institutions between the Northern Ireland executive and the government of the Republic of Ireland. These institutions saw political power shared between the political communities at the executive level and on the Policing Board. This power sharing reinforced the importance of equality—measured in particular, but not exclusively, as between the two national communities. The Agreement reflected nationalists' political identity and ambitions while guaranteeing unionists that a united Ireland would not be enforced without majority support within Northern Ireland itself.

Security sector reform is crucial in peace processes, and the commitment to create a widely acceptable policing system needs to be in the foundational peace agreement. The international dimension to the commission in Northern Ireland was so essential that the process may have ultimately collapsed without it. It provided a counterbalance to the institutional power of the British state and is a model that ought to transfer well to many other contexts. It gives the less powerful actors some confidence that they will not be outmaneuvered following a cease-fire. The international monitoring of implementation was equally important and should feature in best-practice models. Community relations are also important, and communities need to see themselves represented in an international commission's work, including opportunities for communities that experienced the worst of the conflict to make their cases directly. Progress on policing (and other crucial sectors) will also have to be linked incrementally to implementation of a broad peace process. Each can support the other incrementally, building confidence to allow the next phase of difficult decisions to be made in an ongoing process of change.

Policing transformation has its own particular agenda. Issues such as accountability, human rights, training, management, and police culture are all part of this agenda. The Northern Ireland case can add to our understanding of best practices in a number of these domains. However, most crucially as the Northern Ireland experience demonstrates, while you can have a police force without consent or agreement, you can only have community policing and a police service in postconflict societies if policing is embedded in a wider political agreement that deals with the political and social roots of the conflict. The structures, symbols, and ethos of policing and the composition of the police service all must reflect the ethos and spirit of the wider peace agreement. The Northern Ireland case clearly has its own unique character. The report of the Independent Commission on Policing for Northern Ireland is not a blueprint for every other postconflict situation, and the purpose of this chapter is not to suggest that it is. The Northern Ireland experience does, however, show that progress is possible, even in difficult circumstances, even where a community is almost totally polarized in its attitudes to the security forces, and even where the implementation of a peace agreement has many other challenges.

NOTES

1. See, for example, Ed Moloney, *The Secret History of the IRA* (London: Penguin, 2002), xv, and Paul Bew, *Irish Times*, May 15, 1998.

2. See John Doyle, "Governance and Citizenship in Contested States: The Northern Ireland Peace Agreement as Internationalised Governance," *Irish Studies in International Affairs* 10 (1999): 201–19. The Agreement was signed in Belfast on April 10, 1998. The full text of the document is available at http://foreignaffairs.gov.ie/uploads/documents/Anglo-Irish/agreement.pdf. For discussion of its content and the negotiating process, see John Doyle, "Towards a Lasting Peace? The Northern Ireland Multi-Party Agreement, Referendum and Assembly Elections of 1998," *Scottish Affairs* 25 (1998): 1–20, and John Doyle, "Re-examining the Northern Ireland Conflict," in *The Politics of Conflict: A Survey*, ed. Foukas Vassilis (London: Routledge, 2007), 132–46.

3. See, for example, Frank R. Pfetsch and Christopher Rohloff, *National and International Conflicts, 1945–1995: New Empirical and Theoretical Approaches* (London: Routledge, 2000), and Peter Wallensteen, *Understanding Conflict Resolution* (London: SAGE, 2007).

4. Sabine Wichert, *Northern Ireland since 1945* (London: Longman, 1999), 106.

5. See http://www.sinnfein.ie and http://www.sdlp.ie, accessed March 1, 2013.

6. See almost every issue of the Sinn Féin newspaper *An Phoblacht*, right through the 1970s and 1980s.

7. For example, see Seamus Mallon, *Irish Times*, January 6, 1987, January 28, 1985, October 5, 1984, and July 29, 1977.

8. Quoted in George Drower, *John Hume: Peacemaker* (London: Victor Gollancz, 1995), 74.

9. For a good overview of these issues, see Graham Ellison and Jim Smyth, *The Crowned Harp: Policing Northern Ireland* (London: Pluto, 2000).

10. For example, see Human Rights Watch, *Human Rights in Northern Ireland: A Helsinki Watch Report*; Christine Bell, *Peace Agreements and Human Rights* (Oxford: Oxford University Press, 2003); Brice Dickson, "Counter-Insurgency and Human Rights in

Northern Ireland," *Journal of Strategic Studies* 32 (3) (2009): 475–93; and Kadar Asmal, *Shoot to Kill* (Cork: Mercier Press, 1985).

11. John Stalker, *Stalker* (London: Penguin, 1989).

12. The proportion of Catholics published as being members of the RUC included Roman Catholics from outside Northern Ireland, who were unlikely to be Irish nationalists. Nationalists make up approximately 43 percent of the working-age population of Northern Ireland (see http://www.ofmdfmni.gov.uk/index/equality/equalityresearch/research-publications/labour-force-religion-reports.htm, accessed March 15, 2013). Most nationalists are culturally Roman Catholic (even if not personally religious), and likewise most unionists are culturally Protestant. The proportion of each community that supports the dominant political ideology of the other, that is, Roman Catholic unionists and Protestant Irish nationalists, is difficult to estimate, but voting trends and surveys suggest it is in the low single figures and similar for each community. At a macrostatistical level, therefore, figures for employment equality (which are collected as Catholic and Others/Protestant) are a close approximation for nationalist versus unionist, even if at an individual level the terms are not interchangeable. However, while unionist Roman Catholics were likely to support and join the police, Protestants who supported nationalist parties were ideologically less likely to do so. Therefore, the percentage of nationalists (of even the mildest form) in the RUC was likely to be significantly lower than 7.5 percent.

13. David Trimble, quoted in *Co. Down Spectator*, January 30, 1976. Trimble was then a leading opponent of power sharing and later was the leader of the UUP at the time of the 1998 Agreement. See John Cushnahan (Alliance Party leader), NI Assembly, vol. 16, p. 1024, June 29, 1983; and John Cushnahan, Conference Speeches, *Alliance News*, May 1986 and May 1987.

14. House of Commons, Report of Standing Committee B (NI Emergency Provisions Bill), col. 104, January 23, 1996.

15. For example, see statements from unionist MPs Paisley, Maginnis, and Kilfedder, House of Commons, vol. 128, cols. 427–28, February 25, 1988.

16. For example, see Ken Maginnis MP (UUP), House of Commons, vol. 204, col. 1099, February 27, 1992. See also David Trimble, *Irish News*, January 14, 1993.

17. For example, see Jim Kilfedder, House of Commons, vol. 849, col. 1497, January 31, 1973; Robert Bradford, House of Commons, vol. 959, col. 1564, December 6, 1978; William Ross, House of Commons, vol. 70, col. 655, December 20, 1984; Jim Molyneaux, House of Commons, vol. 203, col. 1156, February 13, 1992; Hugh Smyth, NI Forum, vol. 58, col. 39, January 23, 1998.

18. Robert Bradford, House of Commons, vol. 899, col. 283, November 4, 1975; Jim Molyneaux, House of Commons, vol. 922, col. 1961, December 17, 1976; William Ross, House of Commons, vol. 876, col. 1233, July 9, 1974; Ken Maginnis (UUP security spokesperson), House of Commons, vol. 303, col. 64, December 15, 1997.

19. House of Commons, Standing Committee B, col. 177, January 22, 1991.

20. For example, see "82 Per Cent of Catholics Believe That the RUC Must Be Reformed, Replaced or Disbanded," *Irish Times*, December 6, 1996. See also Seamus Mallon, House of Commons, vol. 303, col. 64, December 15, 1997, and Sinn Féin, "A

Policing Service for a New Future: Sinn Féin's Submission to the Commission on Policing," September 1998.

21. For example, see Falls Community Council, "A New Beginning: A New Police Service. A Submission to the Independent Commission on Policing," September 15, 1998.

22. Gerard Murray and Jonathan Tonge, *Sinn Féin and the SDLP: From Alienation to Participation* (Dublin: O'Brien Press, 2005), 206.

23. See Seamus Mallon (SDLP deputy leader), *Irish Times*, November 7, 9, and 21, 1994, for early SDLP responses to the IRA cease-fire, which was announced on August 31, 1994. For the Sinn Féin campaign, see regular articles in *An Phoblacht* in late 1994 and early 1995.

24. Ken Maginnis, *Newsletter*, November 5, 1996; Ian Paisley, *Irish Times*, May 5, 1997; John Taylor and Ian Paisley Jr., *Irish News*, February 3, 1996; David Trimble, House of Commons, vol. 303, col. 96, December 15, 1997.

25. *Agreement*, 27.

26. Ibid., Annex A.

27. Its ultimate report was published the following year. Independent Commission on Policing for Northern Ireland, *A New Beginning: Policing in Northern Ireland* (Report of the Independent Commission on Policing for Northern Ireland) (Belfast: HMSO Northern Ireland Office, 1999).

28. Peter Smith, "Policing and Politics," in *Policing the Narrow Ground: Lessons from the Transformation of Policing in Northern Ireland*, ed. John Doyle (Dublin: Royal Irish Academy, 2010), 68–78.

29. Gerald W. Lynch, "Human Rights and Police Reform," in Doyle, *Policing the Narrow Ground*, 41.

30. Chris Patten, "Personal Reflections on Chairing the Commission," in Doyle, *Policing the Narrow Ground*, 13–26.

31. See http://news.bbc.co.uk/2/hi/uk_news/northern_ireland/7934426.stm, accessed March 19, 2013.

32. See http://cain.ulst.ac.uk/issues/police/patten/patten99.pdf, accessed March 19, 2013.

33. See, for example, *Irish Times*, January 28, 2000, and Debate in Northern Ireland Assembly, January 24, 2000.

34. Implementation Plan, available at http://cain.ulst.ac.uk/issues/police/patten/nio190102.pdf; and the bill itself, available at http://www.parliament.the-stationery-office.co.uk/pa/cm199900/cmbills/125/2000125.htm.

35. *Irish Times*, May 18, May 22, and June 6, 2000.

36. See, for example, *Irish Times*, May 18, May 31, and June 1, 2000.

37. *Irish Times*, June 3, 2000.

38. *Irish Times*, May 22, 2000.

39. *Irish Times*, May 18, 2000.

40. *Irish Times*, June 13, 2000.

41. See, in addition to nationalist comments in earlier notes, Labour MP Kevin McNamara, *Irish Times*, May 31, 2000; Amnesty International and the Committee on the Administration of Justice, *Irish Times*, June 6, 2000; Senator Edward Kennedy, *Irish Times*,

October 11, 2000; Professor Paddy Hillyard, *Irish Times*, August 2, 2000; Professor Brendan O'Leary, *Irish Times*, July 28, 2000; and Paddy Hillyard and Mike Tomlinson, "Patterns of Policing and Policing Patten," *Journal of Law and Society* 27 (3) (2000): 394–415.

42. *Irish Times*, August 25 and November 27, 2001.

43. See the published summary reports available at http://cain.ulst.ac.uk/issues/police /source.htm, accessed March 19, 2013.

44. *Irish Times*, August 25, 2001.

45. *Irish Times*, September 22, 2001.

46. See http://news.bbc.co.uk/2/hi/uk_news/northern_ireland/1707059.stm, accessed March 19, 2013.

47. In fact, Sinn Féin became the largest nationalist party for the first time at the June 2001 British general (Westminster) election when it polled 21.7 percent compared with the SDLP's 21.0 percent of the vote. The gap widened over the following years, and in the 2003 Northern Ireland Assembly election Sinn Féin polled 23.5 percent to the SDLP's 17 percent. Election results are available at http://www.ark.ac.uk/elections, accessed March 19, 2013.

48. See http://news.bbc.co.uk/2/hi/uk_news/northern_ireland/4283740.stm, accessed March 19, 2013. For their reports, see http://cain.ulst.ac.uk/events/peace/decommission /iicdreports.htm, accessed March 19, 2013.

49. The full text of this agreement is available at http://www.dfa.ie/uploads/documents /st_andrews_agreement.pdf, accessed March 19, 2013.

50. *Irish Times*, November 3, 2006.

51. *Irish Times*, January 25, 2007.

52. For example, see *An Phoblacht*, January 11, 18, and 27, 2007.

53. *Irish Times*, February 1, 2007.

54. See, for example, *Irish Times*, March 10, 2007.

55. *Irish Times*, March 27, 2007.

56. *Irish Times*, April 24, 2007.

57. *Irish Times*, March 3 and September 4, 2008.

58. *Irish Times*, July 1 and October 27, 2008.

59. *Irish Times*, November 3, 2008. The Northern Ireland Executive has no tax-raising powers, and the DUP wanted agreement on a multiannual police budget from the British government.

60. *Irish Times*, September 4, 2008.

61. Graham Ellison, "Police-Community Relations in Northern Ireland in the Post-*Patten* Era: Towards an Ecological Analysis," in Doyle, *Policing the Narrow Ground*, 242–76.

62. Consociationalism is a model of power sharing for divided societies associated with the work of academic Arend Lijphart. See, for example, Arend Lijphart, *Democracy in Plural Societies* (New Haven, CT: Yale University Press, 1977). For analyses of consociationalism in Northern Ireland, see Doyle, "Governance and Citizenship in Contested States," and John McGarry and Brendan O'Leary, *The Northern Ireland Conflict: Consociational Engagements* (Oxford: Oxford University Press, 2004).

7   The Lessons of Third-Party Intervention?

The Curious Case of the United States in Northern Ireland

MARY-ALICE C. CLANCY

Since the signing of the Belfast, or Good Friday, Agreement in 1998, a veritable cottage industry has emerged seeking to export Northern Ireland's "lessons." One of the most frequently cited lessons is the role of "internationalization"[1] in conflict resolution and the importance of aligning international influence.[2] The lesson's import, however, is open to dispute. On the one hand, the international dimension is liable to be distorted by those seeking to secure their own legacy in Northern Ireland.[3] On the other hand, some have sought to downplay its importance, arguing that British, Irish, and American officials' disputes are carefully choreographed ruses.[4] This thesis, however, is undermined by a lack of primary evidence, and those authors who have engaged in field research on this question draw opposite conclusions.[5]

Focusing on the United States, this chapter aims to provide a nuanced assessment of the internationalization of Northern Ireland's peace and political processes.[6] It begins with a brief reassessment of the Clinton administration's role in Northern Ireland, arguing that its tendency to side with Dublin when disputes arose between the Irish and United Kingdom (UK) governments decreased the negative consequences associated with the Irish Republican Army's (IRA)'s continued failure to disarm. This partially expedited the enervation of Northern Ireland's political center ground by allowing the political extremes of unionism and nationalism—the

Democratic Unionist Party (DUP) and Sinn Féin, respectively—to capitalize on their "ethnic tribune" appeals.[7]

Examining the Bush administration's role, this chapter demonstrates that although US pressure was vital in securing the IRA's first act of decommissioning, the emergence of a pattern similar to that which emerged in the Clinton administration partially explains the triumph of Sinn Féin and the DUP in the 2003 Northern Ireland Assembly elections. The arrival of Mitchell Reiss as US special envoy altered this pattern because his decision to bar Sinn Féin officials from the White House during 2005–6 and restrict the party's ability to fund-raise in the United States incentivized the republican movement's decision to decommission in 2005 and to endorse policing in 2007, thus paving the way for the power-sharing deal in May 2007. While a cursory reading might suggest that UK officials welcomed Reiss's actions, a closer examination reveals that they did not support Reiss's wielding of the "stick." Despite the importance of Britain to the US-led "War on Terror," relations between US and UK officials vis-à-vis Northern Ireland were "nasty."[8] Reiss admitted that British officials "weren't reluctant to share their anger" with him.[9] The chapter then argues that the various crises in the Belfast Agreement's implementation stemmed from a credible commitment problem engendered by the inappropriate mix of concessions and sanctions offered by UK, Irish, and US officials to the republican leadership to facilitate IRA decommissioning. Having recast the Agreement's implementation problems in this manner, it concludes by examining the lessons that can be extracted from the internationalization of the peace process.

The Clinton Administration and
the Peace and Political Processes

As many accounts have noted, historically the US-UK "special relationship" usually trumped any American desire to intervene in Northern Ireland.[10] Although Ronald Reagan did put some pressure on Margaret Thatcher to sign the Anglo-Irish Agreement in 1985 in an effort to gain US Speaker of the House Thomas (Tip) O'Neill's acquiescence for funding for the *contras*,[11] the first real break with the policy of non-interference came with Bill Clinton's presidency.

Lynch explains the change in policy via Clinton's need to burnish his foreign policy record, his ability to circumvent various bureaucracies, and inadequate UK diplomatic power.[12] Seeking to grant Sinn Féin the legitimacy that would facilitate an IRA cease-fire and secure Sinn Féin's place at the talks, the Irish government began to lobby the White House to grant Sinn Féin president and republican leader Gerry Adams a US visa.[13] For White House officials, it soon became apparent that Northern Ireland was a win-win situation. It was a low-risk foreign policy initiative with domestic benefits, as it was likely to appease Irish American congressional Democrats disenchanted with Clinton's centrism.[14] Clinton's ability to reverse the policy can be explained by his diplomatic and bureaucratic skills, as they allowed him to override both State Department and UK officials' objections.

According to Dixon, British objections to Clinton's decision to grant a visa to Adams were vociferous.[15] In contrast to the Irish government, UK officials wanted no US visas issued to Sinn Féin until after its military wing, the IRA, declared a permanent cease-fire. The British feared that if US visas were issued prior to a cease-fire, republicans would continue to equivocate in order to gain concessions.[16] Evidence from the IRA's decision to call a second cease-fire in 1997 suggests that this is what it was trying to do. According to a British official, the republican leadership reinstated its cease-fire after discussions with Irish and US officials revealed that the two governments backed the British government's *aide mémoire* outlining its positions on the peace and political processes and thus would not support any further vacillation by republicans.[17]

The alliance of northern Irish nationalists, the Irish government, and—to a degree—the Clinton administration probably helped to legitimize the republican leadership's revision of republican shibboleths. This, in turn, "generated political confidence" within the movement.[18] Indeed, it is interesting that senior US and Irish officials active during the Clinton administration viewed the United States' primary role in the peace process as one of granting legitimacy to the republican movement.[19] With legitimacy, however, comes responsibility, and thus it was vital that the former should not have been prematurely bestowed. Conferring legitimacy prior to the declaration of a permanent cease-fire opened the way for republicans to determine the pace and content of the peace and political processes. While this strategy had obvious attractions, as all three governments had a keen interest in facilitating the republican movement's transition, acquiescing in it ignored the legitimate concerns of unionists and had the potential to destabilize any future peace settlement.

The problem of conferring legitimacy absent a negotiating framework that elicited reasonable expectations of reciprocity can be seen in the important, if misunderstood, role that former US Senator George Mitchell played in Northern Ireland. An official active in both the Major and Blair administrations argued that Blair found the Clinton administration's pro–Sinn Féin bias troubling, and some UK officials also became reluctant to share intelligence with the Clinton administration since they feared it might be shared with republicans.[20] Although Clinton did not always support Sinn Féin, on balance, he tended to support Irish nationalists. Clinton's exchanges with the historian Taylor Branch—wherein Clinton viewed Northern nationalists as akin to African Americans of the pre–Civil Rights American South and unionists as, at best, reluctant partners in peace and at worst, supremacist *colons*—suggest that Clinton fundamentally misunderstood the Northern Ireland conflict.[21] According to a British official, Mitchell's arrival in Northern Ireland—first as the head of an international commission on decommissioning, later as the chairman of the talks process that would lead to the Agreement—was viewed by UK officials as an opportunity to blunt Clinton's ability to intervene in Northern Ireland and to co-opt US officials onto their agenda.[22] Mitchell's presence also presented another opportunity. Just as his report in 1996 allowed the two governments to bypass the precondition of decommissioning prior to all-party talks, Mitchell's neutrality was a boon to the subsequent negotiations, as it could be utilized to pressure the various nationalist and unionist parties into signing the Agreement. The two governments asked Mitchell to present their final draft of what became the Agreement as his own work; in doing so, Moloney argues that both the nationalist Social Democratic and Labour Party (SDLP) and Ulster Unionist Party (UUP) would feel obligated to accept the Agreement because Mitchell's neutrality gave him the ability to credibly allocate blame should either party walk away.[23] As such, the SDLP and UUP's acceptance of the Agreement can be partially attributed to this exogenous pressure.

The two governments employed this tactic again when they asked Mitchell to chair a review to kick-start devolution, which was stalled over decommissioning. At the review's conclusion, Mitchell recommended that decommissioning begin after establishing devolution. In response, David Trimble decided to "jump first" and share power with Sinn Féin absent prior decommissioning. His parachute was a postdated letter of resignation as first minister should disarmament have not commenced by February 2000. Trimble's decision was partly motivated by the realization that unionism needed to shed the perception that it was intransigent by occupying the moral high ground. If decommissioning did not begin after power sharing, Trimble hoped that the onus would be on the governments to guarantee decommissioning and that republicans would be on the receiving end of local, national, and international opprobrium. Indeed, Clinton outlined this very scenario when trying to persuade Trimble to share power with Sinn Féin prior to Mitchell's review.[24]

This scenario, however, did not occur. When the secretary of state for Northern Ireland, Peter Mandelson, suspended power sharing to preempt Trimble's resignation, US officials joined the Irish in their condemnation of the suspension. Prior to Trimble's resignation taking effect, Blair's chief of staff Jonathan Powell asked Clinton to pressure Adams vis-à-vis decommissioning, but Adams told Clinton that this was counterproductive.[25] The former Irish taoiseach (prime minister) Bertie Ahern argues that unlike other secretaries of state for Northern Ireland, Mandelson had Blair's ear, making it "difficult to go over his head," an admission that partially explains Irish officials' decision to appeal to the United States for help.[26]

Trimble understood why the Irish government did not support the suspension. While the Irish government did not always side with northern nationalists and republicans during negotiations, it did have political and electoral reasons for favoring Sinn Féin. Politically, the Irish government had done little to discourage Sinn Féin's mistaken belief that the repeal of Section 75 of the 1920 Government of Ireland Act represented a diminution of UK sovereignty over Northern Ireland.[27] Thus, the empirical evidence against the Irish interpretation of Section 75's import raised the specter of political attacks from both republicans and Fianna Fáil's grassroots.[28] While Irish policy was not primarily driven by ideological concerns, there was also a sense that republicans could only be kept on board for the peace process if Irish policy was seen as being independent from London.[29] Trimble was more perturbed by the United States' decision to effectively side with nationalist Ireland, which appeared hypocritical in light of Clinton's comments during the Mitchell review and in light of Mitchell's own understanding, according to both the SDLP's Séamus Mallon and Jonathan Powell, that decommissioning should commence at the end of January.[30]

The end result of the Irish government's propensity to support northern nationalists and republicans—and the Clinton administration's tendency to support the Irish government when it came into conflict with the British government—was that Trimble's attempts to appropriate the moral high ground often left him right back where he started, with no real improvement to his position either within the UUP or unionism at large. This was also compounded by Blair and Powell's reluctance to apply pressure over decommissioning. While it is perfectly understandable that Blair and Powell would not want to undermine the republican leadership, evidence suggests that their fears stemmed almost entirely from Adams's and McGuinness's presentations of their positions. Adams and McGuinness consolidated their control over the republican movement by 1999, and the dissident threat was limited by the fact that the various dissident groups were disorganized and infiltrated by the security services.[31] Moreover, from 2005 onward, officials from the Department of An Taoiseach and the Irish Department of Justice (DOJ), US officials, and members of the British security services were aware of Adams and McGuinness's stability.[32] However, portraying themselves as vulnerable to internal overthrow and/or dissidents offered several benefits to the republican leadership. First, the republican leadership is alleged to have had a twin-track strategy, wherein devolved government was one of two acceptable outcomes, the other being the imposition of something akin to British-Irish joint authority. Few British or Irish officials were certain which track of the strategy predominated at any given time, but many also admitted that devolved government within the UK was hardly the republican movement's "great aim" and that the republican leadership appeared to be divided over its merits.[33]

The republican leadership's twin-track strategy can be characterized as a credible commitment problem. While settlements such as the Agreement are often signed by combatants, they often fall apart during their implementation. This is because agreements create incentives for signatories to renege on their commitments, and the inability of other signatories to punish defaulting parties can make a return to war—or at least an agreement's collapse—a preferred outcome.[34] Third parties, however, can alleviate credible commitment problems by offering a mix of side payments—to encourage desired actions—and credible sanctions should parties default. In the case of Northern Ireland, moderate unionists feared that if they agreed to share power, republicans would not reciprocate with decommissioning, leaving both moderate unionists and nationalists vulnerable to overthrow by their more extreme counterparts. Therefore, the UK, Irish, and US governments would need to apply an appropriate balance of sticks and carrots to make the joint authority track sufficiently unattractive.

Both the British and Irish governments' approach, however, centered on giving Adams and McGuinness carrots in the hope of expediting republicans' democratic transition. The continued provision of carrots in the absence of any reciprocity created a situation where it was logical for

Adams and McGuinness to delay decommissioning. This situation facilitated Sinn Féin's electoral rise in Northern Ireland, as any attempt by the party's nationalist rival, the SDLP, to compromise with the UUP could be used by Sinn Féin as evidence of its reputation as an "ethnic tribune," or the strongest defender of the nationalist community's interests.[35] Alternatively, attempts to outflank Sinn Féin by the SDLP in this environment were bound to meet an ignominious end. Beyond Northern Ireland, perpetual negotiations had the ability to keep Sinn Féin in the spotlight in the Republic, and they also burnished Adams's international statesman image, a key plank in the party's electoral strategy.

This environment also contributed to the UUP's electoral enervation. Trimble managed to sell the Belfast Agreement to the UUP, and the unionist electorate endorsed it by thin margins. It would be wrong, however, to confuse this reluctance with hostility toward the peace and political processes. As Aughey argues, a majority of unionists voted for the Agreement because they saw its potential to create a new, nonviolent beginning in Northern Ireland.[36] British officials acknowledge that painful concessions for unionists such as the release of paramilitary prisoners and police reform early on in the process needed to be counterbalanced by reciprocal concessions if unionists were to keep faith with the Agreement.[37]

Absent full decommissioning, Trimble was forced to rely on measures such as Assembly suspensions, nugatory concessions on policing, and banning members of Sinn Féin from meetings of the North-South Ministerial Council.[38] These measures upset nationalist Ireland, and it sought US support for its disenchantment. Therefore, during this period the three governments' unwillingness to confront the republican leadership and exogenous pressure that favored Irish nationalists created a framework that weakened Northern Ireland's political moderates. Continued enervation would depend on whether or not this framework was challenged through a realignment of exogenous forces.

Richard Haass, 8/11, and 9/11

At the beginning of George W. Bush's presidency, it appeared that the United States would adopt a more laissez-faire approach to Northern Ireland. The future national security advisor, Condoleezza Rice, told UK officials that she wished to see Northern Ireland "fixed" prior to the inauguration, and it is alleged that the incoming administration privately informed Downing Street that it considered Northern Ireland to be the UK's sole responsibility.[39] Bush's first special envoy, Richard Haass, had previously written about Northern Ireland, and his writings did not suggest that there would be extensive, high-level US involvement in Northern Ireland.[40] Although Haass gave the Clinton administration "one cheer" for its efforts, on balance he characterized its interventions as misguided and tendentious.[41] The Irish government soon picked up on Haass's sentiments. According to a senior official, the Irish establishment viewed Haass as someone "who wasn't really empathetic to Ireland. . . . He was seen as coming from an absolute neutral position. . . . They wanted the Teddy Kennedy, Democratic, sort of touchy feely approach to Ireland, and they didn't see that with Richard Haass."[42]

After IRA members were found in Colombia allegedly training the FARC on August 11, 2001,[43] empathy was not high on Haass's list of priorities. The idea of IRA members training FARC rebels in methods that could be used to murder US citizens and military personnel also did not sit well with the republican movement's congressional supporters like Ben Gilman (a Republican from New York). The "Colombia Three" rattled Congress and the Bush administration, and both signaled their anger by calling for congressional hearings and firmly supporting the SDLP's decision to endorse the newly reformed Police Service of Northern Ireland (PSNI).[44]

The IRA's alleged involvement with the FARC angered the Washington establishment, and it upset one of the republican movement's key US backers, Bill Flynn, who called on the IRA to disarm.[45] It was this message that Haass sought to reiterate when he traveled to the UK and Ireland on 9/11. On the eve of 9/11 Haass gave Adams and McGuinness a preview of the dressing down they would receive the next day, but the events of that day transformed Haass's words from a warning into an expletive-laden threat.[46] As Lynch notes, "9/11 provided a rhetorical context to turn the screws on Sinn Féin but it was 8/11 that forced a revised American posture."[47] According to both Irish and US officials present that day, Adams received Haass's message loud and clear, and his message was largely echoed by Bill Flynn and other prominent Irish Americans. Realizing that republicans were on the back foot, the IRA announced its first act of decommissioning six weeks later.[48]

Herein lay the promise of the pan-nationalist front created in the early years of the peace process. The republican movement's access to corporate Irish America came with a price. The desire to retain its esteem could be leveraged to get republicans to make concessions. Adams and McGuinness appeared well aware of Haass's significant clout, and that corporate Irish America most likely would not protest if Haass banned republicans from the United States if the IRA did not disarm. The endorsement of the reformed PSNI by two of Sinn Féin's traditional congressional supporters, Ben Gilman and William Delahunt (a Democrat from Massachusetts), also pointed to the prospect of a ban.[49] Thus, the temporary realignment in exogenous forces in 8/11 and 9/11's aftermath made it likely that the IRA would decommission. The only question that remained was the act's scale.

A lack of alignment between US tactics on the one hand and Irish and British tactics on the other meant that republicans were allowed to regain international respectability after having engaged in a minor act of decommissioning. Although one could hardly envision a more auspicious environment in which to make a demand for significant decommissioning, British and Irish officials demurred from this course of action, apparently because of concerns over the republican leadership's stability. Powell recounts meetings with Adams during this period wherein the latter told him that decommissioning had been extremely difficult and almost necessitated an Army Convention—despite the fact that the need for a convention had been abolished in 1999, the same year that the leadership consolidated its control over the republican movement.[50] British officials appeared to know of these changes, as Mandelson states that he was receiving intelligence from 1999 onward stating that republicans had taken the decision to decommission but were holding out for further concessions.[51] However, Powell admits that there was "no science" to judging Adams and McGuinness's bottom line,[52] and Blair also contends that while the intelligence services advised him that the republican leadership was well in control, he "took a different view."[53] Similarly, even though intelligence fed into the process from the Irish DOJ from 2002 onward suggested that the republican leadership faced no significant threat, Bertie Ahern states that he was skeptical of most of the intelligence he received.[54] This lack of exogenous alignment meant that only American officials brandished the "stick" on decommissioning, while British officials dangled "carrots" instead. Blair notified David Trimble eight days after 9/11 that Sinn Féin would not be excluded from the Assembly even if the IRA did not decommission, and he offered Sinn Féin Westminster allowances in the hopes of facilitating disarmament.[55] The act of decommissioning allowed Trimble to go back into government with Sinn Féin in October 2001, but with the parameters of the peace and political processes unaltered, this was more like a stay of execution. As the following sections will show, Haass's change of heart vis-à vis both Sinn Féin and the DUP further expedited the UUP and SDLP's demise.

Haass's *Volte-Face* and the Triumph of the Extremes

In addition to his sober view of the IRA, Haass appeared to take unionists' concerns seriously. In January 2002 Haass delivered a speech drafted by two of Trimble's advisors, which described the conflict as ethnonational, an admission that recognized the legitimacy of unionists' identities and undercut the notion that the IRA's armed struggle was about equality for nationalists/Catholics.[56] Haass's relationship with Trimble, however, soon soured, most likely because both men can be very difficult. Moreover, Haass's dissatisfaction coincided with a growing affinity between Haass and Adams, and US officials state that Haass became "enamored" of Adams.[57] While he appeared to share this fascination with Blair and Powell, he did not share their appreciation of David Trimble.

The Irish government shared Haass's frustration. Despair over Trimble led the Irish Department of Foreign Affairs (DFA), the UK Northern Ireland Office (NIO), and one Downing Street official to look at the viability of a deal between the DUP and Sinn Féin in 2002. However, British contemplation of such a deal had more to do with occasional annoyance with Trimble than serious policy. Blair possessed a degree of loyalty to Trimble, and he was uncomfortable with Paisley. Moreover, the NIO's contacts with the DUP suggested that a power-sharing deal was not viable in the short to medium term and might not occur at all.[58] While there were divisions within the Irish government—the DOJ appeared to share Downing Street's and the NIO's skepticism about the viability of a deal between the extremes—DFA officials admit that they contacted the DUP's "more progressive middle-rankers" and confirm US officials' contention that Haass came to prefer a Sinn Féin–DUP deal "about two seconds after Dublin did," around March 2002.[59]

While hindsight makes it tempting to commend Haass and the DFA's perspicacity, it is worth interrogating the assumptions that led them to promote this deal. While the DFA had contact with the DUP's "progressive middle-rankers," it was in both the DUP's and Sinn Féin's interest to promote themselves as amenable to a deal since Irish and US officials were more likely to push for elections that would place both parties at the head of their respective electoral blocs if they felt a viable alternative existed. In addition to concerns regarding DUP progressive middle-rankers' sincerity, there was also the problem of this group's relationship to the then party leader, Ian Paisley Sr. An official admits that the DFA's contact with the DUP was based on a mistaken assumed relationship between the then deputy leader, Peter Robinson, and Paisley, with the hope that the former could deliver the latter.[60] However, as Moloney notes, the relationship between Paisley and Robinson was far from perfect, and it was not reasonable to expect Robinson to deliver Paisley.[61]

US officials' support for a DUP–Sinn Féin deal appeared to rest on optimistic foundations. In addition to the DUP's and Sinn Féin's good intent, US officials also believed that unionist disenchantment with the Agreement stemmed not from its implementation but rather from Trimble's alleged poor salesmanship. However, survey evidence points to unionists' disillusionment with the Agreement's implementation.[62] Moreover, when Trimble attempted to better "sell" the Agreement by introducing confidence-building measures such as the Independent Monitoring Commission,[63] he was often stymied by the three governments' desire not to cause difficulties for republicans.[64] Therefore, the source of unionist disillusionment suggested that the DUP could not be any more flexible than Trimble in its demands. Given the republican leadership's alleged twin-track strategy, it also remained to be seen whether the DUP's electoral hegemony within the unionist bloc would make decommissioning any more likely.

With Downing Street and most of the NIO unwilling to promote a deal between the extremes, the British government postponed the 2003 Assembly elections twice after republicans failed to provide clear statements signaling their intention to complete their democratic transition. The suspension did not sit well with either Irish or US officials, and both pressured UK officials for elections. Ultimately, British officials found the pressure irresistible, and the election was held in November.[65] Once the republican leadership was guaranteed elections, it became logical not to modify the IRA's confidentiality agreement with the Independent International Commission on Decommissioning (IICD), and the opacity of the IRA's act of disarmament left Trimble in a poor position for the elections. In the Assembly elections, both Sinn Féin and the DUP became the head of their electoral blocs. The DUP won three more seats than the UUP, but its share of first preference votes only increased by 1.4 percent.[66] Although Blair's postelection fidelity to Trimble was considered "wacky" and "kooky" by some US officials, it was not entirely preposterous.[67] The

DUP's ascent was a harbinger of things to come, however, and Blair was eventually forced to contemplate a deal between the extremes.

Mitchell Reiss, Policing, and the St. Andrews "Agreement"

After resigning, Richard Haass was replaced by Mitchell Reiss in December 2003. Reiss differed from his predecessor. In addition to being less abrasive than Haass, Reiss made republicans' support for the PSNI the cornerstone of his tenure.[68] Haass had backed away from policing, and he had put much store in the alleged dissident threat to the republican leadership.[69] Reiss, on the other hand, was not convinced of the alleged dissident and internal threats to Adams and McGuinness; moreover, the Irish DOJ, the British Army, and the British security services supported his interpretation.[70]

Exogenous actors' prioritization of the peace process created an environment where it was logical for the republican leadership to delay concessions for as long as possible. The related tendency to ignore republicans' continued paramilitarism and criminality created a situation where they became ever more enmeshed in both activities. Therefore, Reiss and the Irish minister for justice, Michael McDowell, convinced the DUP's Peter Robinson that in addition to decommissioning, endorsing the PSNI and ending criminality were important metrics for judging republicans' bona fides.[71] Reiss identified these as the necessary conditions for a power-sharing deal, and he felt that their identification would also get the DUP to move toward embracing objective and tangible standards of progress.

Facilitating the DUP's move from abstract to concrete demands also bolstered the party's engagement with Irish America as the DUP's prior vague and subjective notions of progress reinforced some Irish Americans' assumption that the party was simply uninterested in sharing power. If the DUP could make it clear that it was willing to share power with republicans if they endorsed policing and abandoned criminality, US officials believed that Irish America could persuade Sinn Féin to deliver. Specifically, US officials felt that the desire to retain Irish Americans' esteem could be used as leverage to get Sinn Féin to endorse the PSNI.[72]

Republicans' continued involvement in paramilitarism and criminality arguably reached its nadir with alleged IRA involvement in the Northern bank robbery in December 2004 and the cover-up of the murder of Robert McCartney in January 2005.[73] Both incidents upset the three governments, as planning for the robbery appeared to be concomitant with negotiations to restore power sharing in 2004, but Irish DOJ and US officials were the most keen to make their anger known. McDowell named Adams, McGuinness, and Martin Ferris as Army Council members in February 2005, and Reiss banned all political parties from the Saint Patrick's Day festivities at the White House, inviting Mr. McCartney's family instead. Reiss also banned Sinn Féin members from fund-raising during Saint Patrick's Day. Although he still came to the United States, Adams was excoriated wherever he went. Senators John McCain and Edward Kennedy, Congressman Peter King, and the Friends of Ireland group all condemned the IRA's alleged actions and called for the organization to disband. Corporate Irish America yet again let Adams know how it felt, breaking into spontaneous applause when McCain delivered a blistering attack on the IRA. Senior Irish and US officials have argued that this had a "shattering" effect on Adams, as this audience had previously "adored" him.[74]

This atmosphere was replicated at home. Sinn Féin did not take SDLP leader Mark Durkan's seat in the Westminster elections, and local elections netted the party fewer seats than expected. The IRA answered positively to Gerry Adams's preelection call on April 6, nineteen days after his Saint Patrick's Day trip to the United States, to consider engaging in purely political and democratic activity. The IRA subsequently decommissioned a significant amount of weaponry in September.

For Reiss and McDowell, the lessons were clear. Decommissioning suggested that the republican leadership responded to pressure, and that it could cede concessions without any great upheaval. This was also underscored by McDowell's refusal to grant Adams further concessions to facilitate decommissioning, since the DOJ possessed intelligence indicating that Adams was already committed to disarming but was trying to wring out as many concessions as possible.[75]

This rationale underpinned Reiss's decision to continue denying fund-raising visas to Sinn Féin in order to expedite its endorsement of the PSNI. However, British and Irish officials—apart from the Irish DOJ— had been unhappy with Reiss's decision to ban the political parties from the White House on Saint Patrick's Day. Moreover, Downing Street and the NIO were extremely upset at the continued fund-raising ban, with the former unsuccessfully attempting to go over Reiss's head—at Adams's behest—to reverse the policy. Reiss characterized the incident as probably his "lowest point" as special envoy, and US officials state that relations between Reiss and British officials were "nasty" at this time.[76] Although

US officials assert that Reiss had the private support of the Department of An Taoiseach for the ban, publicly the Irish foreign minister stated that policing would not be a precondition for a deal, an announcement that led US officials to call Dublin for clarification.[77]

While British—and most Irish—officials' reluctance to make policing a precondition is ostensibly reasonable, it begs the question as to how the three governments felt that they could secure a deal in its absence, particularly given the republican leadership's alleged twin-track strategy. If the DUP were to convince skeptical unionist voters that power sharing was worthwhile, it would need to achieve more than the UUP if it were to retain its "ethnic tribune" appeal. While one could argue that decommissioning had been achieved on the DUP's watch, a US copy of minutes from Irish officials' meeting with Paisley on November 18, 2005, suggests that he was aware that decommissioning was incomplete, a fact alluded to in the Independent Monitoring Commission's eighth report.[78]

According to British officials, Paisley signaled his willingness to share power if the conditions—primarily, if Sinn Féin endorsed the PSNI—were right.[79] The toing and froing prior to the St. Andrews summit, coupled with British officials' lack of planning and a crisis created by a British general's remarks about Iraq during the final day, meant that little was achieved, apart from British and Irish officials' decision to market St. Andrews as an "agreement" in the hopes of pressuring the DUP and Sinn Féin to endorse it.[80] Although the DUP leadership indicated its willingness to consider a deal on the summit's final day, the amount of unease within the party's grassroots—evidenced by the chicanery employed to obtain its endorsement of St. Andrews—caused Paisley to retreat into his party's more uncompromising wing. It soon became clear that those keen for a deal (Paisley and Robinson) would have to compromise with members (Nigel Dodds, Gregory Campbell, and David Simpson) who required a credible testing period of Sinn Féin's commitment and a considerable gap between the restoration of Stormont and the devolution of policing and justice powers.[81] Although acceptance of the police continued to be a sine qua non of a deal, the issue remained mired in negotiations. A UK official argues that Blair's "endless phone calls to Adams and Paisley through the Christmas period were partly about the Prime Minister recognizing that Adams had real management issues on policing and that he needed support."[82]

Powell states that during this period, "we [the British] knew that the dissidents were desperately trying to kill someone."[83] This view, however, was not shared by US officials, the Irish DOJ, or even by Bertie Ahern at this point.[84] An IRA Convention backed policing in January, and following this a Sinn Féin *ard fheis* (annual meeting) endorsed policing with approximately 90 percent of the vote, albeit with the caveat that the endorsement was conditional upon establishing power sharing and a date for devolving policing and justice powers.[85] This caveat provided a means for the republican leadership to pursue its alleged twin-track strategy, as it appeared to do in late 2009 and early 2010. Nevertheless, on May 8, 2007, the British government restored devolution under the DUP and Sinn Féin's auspices.

The Lessons of Northern Ireland's Internationalization

What, if any, lessons does Northern Ireland's internationalization offer other conflict-affected regions? In one sense, there is a tremendous conceit in proffering lessons from a peace process about which we still know relatively little. The counterinsurgency tactics that brought the IRA to the negotiating table are still mired in confusion and secrecy and are likely to remain so. We do know, however, that by 1994, 80 percent of operations planned by the IRA's Belfast Brigade were being foiled by the police, and that both the former head of the IRA's Internal Security Unit and Sinn Féin's former US representative and director of elections were British agents for many decades. At the very least, this does not suggest that a mutually hurting stalemate prompted the republican leadership's decision to engage in negotiations.[86]

Nevertheless, there appear to be some salient lessons that can be extracted from Northern Ireland's internationalization. US intervention has been neither uniformly destructive nor constructive, nor has it always been in alignment with UK and Irish preferences. It can be further argued that US interventions both exacerbated and alleviated the credible commitment problem within the negotiating process. The two governments capitalized on George Mitchell's perceived neutrality to pressure the UUP and the SDLP to sign the Agreement. By pretending that the final draft of what became the Belfast Agreement was Mitchell's handiwork, the two governments raised the stakes vis-à-vis default: Mitchell's outsider status and his perceived neutrality would allow him to allocate blame in a manner far more convincing than the two governments, both of which were historically implicated in the conflict, ever could. Thus, as a third party, the United States could facilitate the political process by alleviating credible commitment problems. The republican leadership, however, had a twin-track strategy that engendered a new credible commitment problem during the Agreement's implementation. This problem centered on moderate unionists' fear that if they agreed to share power, republicans would not reciprocate and decommission, thus destabilizing both the Agreement and moderate unionists and nationalists. The Clinton administration's tendency to side with the Irish government, along with the primacy of the peace process, exacerbated this credible commitment problem, as it decreased the negative consequences associated with republicans' delay in delivering concessions. This contributed to the weakening of the more moderate political parties in Northern Ireland and made it attractive for the republican leadership to pursue both tracks of its twin-track strategy.

The pressure applied by US officials and corporate Irish America in 8/11 and 9/11's aftermath temporarily alleviated the credible commitment problem, but the three governments' lack of alignment meant that republicans' first act of decommissioning was relatively insignificant, and republicans continued with their twin-track strategy. Haass and Dublin's promotion of a deal between the extremes meant that the governments' tactics were yet again unaligned, and this only made it all the more logical for republicans to continue delaying decommissioning. Reiss and the Irish DOJ's condition-led approaches altered the incentive structure for decommissioning and republicans' endorsement of the PSNI. Their tactics, however, were not appreciated by most UK and Irish officials. Therefore, Reiss's own experience contradicts his claim regarding the importance of "unity among key stakeholders."[87] While the three governments were unified vis-à-vis outcomes, they employed different tactics. Tactical disunity was partially responsible for the DUP's and Sinn Féin's electoral ascendancy. Reiss's tenure, however, also points to the benefits of tactical disunity in alleviating credible commitment problems. Reiss's and the DOJ's condition-led approaches helped to facilitate a deal, and their focus on decommissioning and criminality allowed both issues to be brought to the fore without political consequences for the Department of An Taoiseach, a tendency best captured by a former DOJ official's contention that Bertie Ahern could always blame the "lunatic across the road"[88] (i.e., Michael McDowell) when he refused to acquiesce in Downing Street's desire to grant republicans further concessions. Thus, on balance, US interventions suggest that it cannot be unambiguously asserted that aligning international influence is an important lesson to be extracted from Northern Ireland.

Reframing the difficulties surrounding the Agreement and its implementation as a credible commitment problem challenges several oft-cited "lessons" of the peace process. Many critics of the Agreement's consociational, or power-sharing, institutions characterize them as inherently centrifugal, thus treating the DUP and Sinn Féin's electoral ascendancy as inevitable.[89] The assumed corollary here is that a voluntary coalition of moderates would have been more stable and would have blunted the rise of Northern Ireland's "extremes." Although this argument can be criticized on a number of grounds,[90] reframing negotiations in Northern Ireland as bedeviled by credible commitment problems makes it particularly problematic.

For instance, while a voluntary coalition of moderates appears intuitively more stable than institutions that automatically allow parties in government after they have obtained a certain number of votes, this line of reasoning omits that Northern Ireland was subject to both a political process and a peace process, and that republicans and loyalists would still have to be brought in from the cold regardless of the nature of any power-sharing arrangement. Thus, counterfactual reasoning suggests that a voluntary coalition of moderate unionists and nationalists would still be undermined by the dynamic (i.e., concessions to republicans with no meaningful reciprocity) that destabilized the Agreement. This reasoning is borne out in the notes of a US Foreign Service officer (FSO), who describes a meeting with the SDLP in the wake of the IRA's alleged involvement in the Northern Bank robbery in 2004 and the McCartney murder in 2005. Recounting this meeting at the US consulate in Belfast, the FSO states that SDLP members reiterated the conditions under which the party would go into a voluntary coalition with the DUP, conditions that it had already outlined to Prime Minister Blair. The SDLP, however, ultimately demurred from entering into this arrangement, fearing that Blair would undermine its position by continuing to offer republicans concessions in the hope that this would facilitate decommissioning.[91] Thus, we can see that power-sharing institutions are not inherently centrifugal, and their outcomes are heavily dependent on the incentives and sanctions provided by exogenous actors.

This line of reasoning also applies to those who are more sanguine about power-sharing effects in Northern Ireland.[92] While it is true that Northern Ireland's liberal form of consociationalism provided some incentives for Sinn Féin and the DUP to share power, this does not mean that liberal consociational institutions are inherently centripetal. Close readings of the negotiations proceeding the Sinn Féin and the DUP's electoral triumphs over their more moderate rivals in 2003 and 2005 demonstrate that power sharing under the auspices of these two parties was not a foregone conclusion. Again, a DUP–Sinn Féin deal was heavily reliant on the mix of incentives and sanctions provided by exogenous actors, such as US officials' denial of fund-raising visas to republicans until they endorsed the PSNI, a sine qua non of any power-sharing deal to which the DUP would agree. Acknowledging that a deal between the DUP and Sinn Féin heavily relied on—and continues to rely on—a mix of incentives and disincentives from outside actors also problematizes the evidence that Northern Ireland allegedly provides for the "lesson" that the only stable political deals are those that are agreed to by political "extremes," as only these parties cannot be outflanked by rivals.[93] Rather than focus on extracting lessons about the alleged deficiencies or benefits of various forms of power sharing, more fruitful lessons could be exported by examining how the lack of a negotiating framework that elicited reasonable expectations of reciprocity served to undermine moderate unionists and nationalists. Similarly, lessons could also focus on how the creation of such a framework by US and Irish DOJ officials from 2005 onward led Sinn Féin and the DUP to share power in 2007.

Focusing on the credible commitment problems that attended the Agreement's creation and implementation also calls into question the importance of "building trust" as a key element of the peace process's success. Although trust is often cited as an important lesson to be extracted from the peace process,[94] many key players questioned its importance, characterizing it as "over-rated"[95] at best; at worst, according to Reiss, it "fundamentally mischaracterizes what happens during negotiations."[96] According to Trimble, what is more important is ensuring that one can "do business"[97] with one's adversaries, again pointing to the importance of establishing a negotiating framework that elicits reasonable expectations of reciprocity.

In sum, the "lessons" of the internationalization of the Northern Ireland peace process are ambiguous. As demonstrated, the United States' third-party intervention has been both helpful and destabilizing: it has helped to alleviate credible commitment problems surrounding the Agreement and its implementation, but it has also exacerbated these problems. Focusing on the internationalization of the peace process also casts doubts about the many "lessons" about power sharing, be they positive or negative, that are predicated on the Northern Ireland experience. Focusing on how the incentives and sanctions offered by the UK, Irish, and US governments exacerbated and ameliorated credible commitment problems within the negotiating process provides a more convincing explanation as to why the DUP and Sinn Féin overtook their more moderate rivals and ultimately agreed to share power. Finally, the internationalization of the Irish peace process also suggests the limits of exporting the so-called Northern Ireland "model." While the UK, Irish, and US governments did come into conflict during the peace process, Northern Ireland is located within a region of the world that is quite stable, and this stability is buttressed by the fact that the Republic of Ireland only pays lip service to unity and is not genuinely irredentist. This alone makes Northern Ireland rather different from places such as Lebanon and Kashmir. Moreover, the UK government possesses both the constitutional and financial capacity to intervene in Northern Ireland whenever power sharing appears to falter, thus giving Northern Ireland a degree of stability unlikely to be found in other conflict-affected regions. Northern Ireland's unique international context, combined with a counterinsurgency campaign of which we still know relatively little, limits the lessons that can be successfully exported to other regions.

NOTES

1. "Internationalization" refers to the process by which individuals, governments, and organizations from outside the United Kingdom have become involved in the creation and implementation of the Agreement. This chapter is limited to examining the Irish and US governments' roles in facilitating and implementing the Agreement.

2. Peter Hain, "Peacemaking in Northern Ireland: A Model for Conflict Resolution?" (speech, Chatham House, June 12, 2007, published by the Northern Ireland Office, Belfast), 22–23, and Mitchell B. Reiss, "Lessons of the Northern Ireland Peace Process" (speech, Emmanuel College, Cambridge, September 9, 2005, http://www.state.gov/p/eur/rls/rm /54869.htm, accessed November 2, 2005).

3. See, for example, Toby Harnden, "Nobel Winner: Hillary Clinton's Peace Claims 'Silly,'" *The Telegraph*, March 8, 2008, http://www.telegraph.co.uk/news/worldnews/1581150 /Nobel-winner-Hillary-Clintonssilly-Irish-peace-claims.html, accessed August 10, 2010, and Niall O'Dowd, "The Awakening: Irish America's Key Role in the Irish Peace Process," in *The Long Road to Peace in Northern Ireland*, ed. Marianne Elliott (Liverpool: Liverpool University Press, 2002), 64–74.

4. Paul Dixon, "Rethinking the International in Northern Ireland: A Critique," in *A Farewell to Arms? Beyond the Good Friday Agreement*, 2nd ed., ed. Michael Cox, Adrian Guelke, and Fiona Stephen (Manchester: Manchester University Press, 2006), 418–19.

5. Mary-Alice C. Clancy, "The United States and post-Agreement Northern Ireland, 2001–6," *Irish Studies in International Affairs* 18 (2007): 155–73, and Peter R. Neumann,

Britain's Long War: British Strategy in the Northern Ireland Conflict, 1969–98 (New York: Palgrave Macmillan, 2003).

6. The *peace process* involves facilitating paramilitaries'—primarily the IRA—transition from violent to constitutional means. The *political process* describes attempts to get unionists and nationalists to share power. Although it is difficult to wholly separate these processes, it is useful to do so for explanatory purposes. It is also clear that in practice many British, Irish, and American officials make this distinction. See Mary-Alice C. Clancy, *Peace Without Consensus: Power Sharing Politics in Northern Ireland* (Burlington, VT: Ashgate, 2010).

7. Paul Mitchell, Geoffrey Evans, and Brendan O'Leary, "Extremist Outbidding in Ethnic Party Systems Is Not Inevitable: Tribune Parties in Northern Ireland," *Political Studies* 57 (2) (2009): 397–421.

8. Clancy, "The United States and Post-Agreement Northern Ireland," 171.

9. Mitchell Reiss, quoted in John Ware, "The Price of Peace: Dealing with Gerry," BBC Radio 4, March 2, 2008.

10. Paul Arthur, *Special Relationships: Britain, Ireland and the Northern Ireland Problem* (Belfast: Blackstaff Press, 2000); John Dumbrell, *A Special Relationship: Anglo-American Relations in the Cold War and After* (New York: Palgrave Macmillan, 2001); Joseph E. Thompson, *American Policy and Northern Ireland: A Saga of Peacebuilding* (Westport, CT: Praeger, 2001); and Andrew J. Wilson, *Irish America and the Ulster Conflict, 1968–1995* (Belfast: Blackstaff Press, 1995).

11. John A. Farrell, *Tip O'Neill and the Democratic Century* (Boston: Little, Brown, 2001), 623–24.

12. Timothy J. Lynch, *Turf War: The Clinton Administration and Northern Ireland* (Burlington, VT: Ashgate, 2004), 141–43. See also Taylor Branch, *The Clinton Tapes: Wrestling History in the White House* (New York: Simon & Schuster, 2009), 127; Edward M. Kennedy, *True Compass: A Memoir* (New York: Twelve, 2009), 462–64; and Albert Reynolds, *My Autobiography* (London: Transworld Ireland, 2009), 243 and 323–25.

13. Throughout this chapter references are made to the "republican movement" and the "republican leadership." Although in the past distinctions have been made between Sinn Féin and the IRA's leadership, this was a pragmatic distinction that facilitated republicans' entry into political dialogue in the early 1990s. However, the Sinn Féin president (Gerry Adams), an MP and then minister for education in Northern Ireland (Martin McGuinness), and a *teachta dála* (TD) (Martin Ferris) outed themselves as IRA members via their resignations from the IRA's Army Council in 2005. Adams and McGuinness's extensive hold over the Provisional republican movement—demonstrated by the fact that the Army Council was populated by Adams loyalists and the relative rapidity with which the IRA decommissioned and accepted the PSNI—suggests that there was little daylight between the IRA and Sinn Féin's positions. Therefore, the "republican movement" encompasses both Sinn Féin and the IRA. The "republican leadership" is synonymous with Gerry Adams and Martin McGuinness's leadership of the republican movement.

14. Kennedy, *True Compass*, 460; Lynch, *Turf War*, 55; and Andrew J. Wilson, "From the Beltway to Belfast: The Clinton Administration, Sinn Féin and the Northern Ireland Peace Process," *New Hibernia Review* 1 (3) (1997): 30.

15. Paul Dixon, "Political Skills or Lying Manipulation? The Choreography of the Northern Ireland Peace Process," *Political Studies* 50 (4) (2002): 725–41, and Dixon, "Rethinking the International in Northern Ireland." See also Branch, *The Clinton Tapes*; Kennedy, *True Compass*; John Major, *John Major: The Autobiography* (London: HarperCollins, 1999); Neumann, *Britain's Long War*; Jonathan Powell, *Great Hatred, Little Room: Making Peace in Northern Ireland* (London: The Bodley Head, 2008); Reynolds, *My Autobiography*; and Raymond Seitz, *Over Here* (London: Weidenfeld & Nicolson, 1998).

16. Reynolds, *My Autobiography*, 332–33.

17. Clancy, *Peace Without Consensus*, 73. See also Bertie Ahern, *Bertie Ahern: The Autobiography* (London: Arrow Books, 2009), 196, and Alastair Campbell, *The Blair Years: Extracts from the Alastair Campbell Diaries* (London: Hutchinson, 2007), 214–17.

18. Neumann, *Britain's Long War*, 165.

19. Clancy, *Peace Without Consensus*, 64.

20. Con Coughlin, *American Ally: Tony Blair and the War on Terror* (London: Politico's, 2006), 32–33 and 38; Dean Godson, *Himself Alone: David Trimble and the Ordeal of Unionism* (London: HarperCollins, 2004), 686; and Seitz, *Over Here*, 291.

21. Branch, *The Clinton Tapes*, 329, 500, and 641. Applying the US Civil Rights analogy to Northern Ireland obscures the conflict's ethnonational roots and mitigates paramilitaries' culpability for violence. Nationalists did not experience the levels of discrimination African Americans faced. In his meta study of discrimination in Northern Ireland, John Whyte argued that "the consensus among those who have looked at the evidence dispassionately is that the picture is neither black nor white, but a shade of grey." Discrimination was largely confined to three local councils west of the River Bann, and it was not solely practiced by unionists. Stormont's most grievous offense was that it did not seek to redress the discrimination that did occur at the regional level. John Whyte, "How Much Discrimination Was There under the Unionist Regime, 1921–1968?," CAIN, last modified April 1, 2012, http://cain.ulst.ac.uk/issues/discrimination/whyte.htm#chap1, accessed July 30, 2012.

22. Clancy, *Peace Without Consensus*, 77.

23. Ed Moloney, "His Wasn't the Central Role in the Northern Ireland Peace Deal," *Jerusalem Post*, February 4, 2009, http://www.jpost.com/servlet/Satellite?cid=1233304687555&pagename=JPost%2FJPArticle%2FShowFull, accessed November 25, 2009.

24. Joe Carroll, "Tragedy if Talks Break Down Over Sequencing, Says Clinton," *The Irish Times*, July 2, 1999, 9.

25. Powell, *Great Hatred, Little Room*, 168.

26. Ahern, *Bertie Ahern*, 263–64.

27. Irish officials such as Martin Mansergh—along with members of the republican leadership—appeared to believe that Section 75 of the Government of Ireland Act (1920)

asserted sovereignty over Northern Ireland. This was predicated on the mistaken belief that the Anglo-Irish Treaty (1921) had superseded the Act of Union (1801). As it did not, Section 75 served as a saving clause, with sovereignty asserted by the Act of Union. Thomas Hennessey, *The Northern Ireland Peace Process: Ending the Troubles?* (Hampshire: Palgrave Macmillan, 2001), 140–41.

28. Fianna Fáil, a party formed from the anti-Treaty IRA in the Irish Civil War's aftermath, governed the Republic of Ireland during most of the peace process.

29. Frank Millar, *David Trimble: The Price of Peace* (Dublin: Liffey Press, 2004), 115.

30. Millar, *The Price of Peace*, 109–10, and Powell, *Great Hatred, Little Room*, 167.

31. Clancy, *Peace Without Consensus*, 151–53 and 177, and Ed Moloney, *A Secret History of the IRA*, 2nd ed. (London: Penguin, 2007), 520.

32. Clancy, *Peace Without Consensus*, 164–65, 168, and 177.

33. Ibid., 90–92.

34. James D. Fearon, "Commitment Problems and the Spread of Ethnic Conflict," in *The International Spread of Ethnic Conflict*, ed. David A. Lake and Donald Rothchild (Princeton, NJ: Princeton University Press, 1998), 107–26.

35. Mitchell, Evans, and O'Leary, "Extremist Outbidding in Ethnic Party Systems Is Not Inevitable."

36. Arthur Aughey, *The Politics of Northern Ireland: Beyond the Belfast Agreement* (New York: Routledge, 2005), 103. See also Bernadette C. Hayes and Ian McAllister, "Who Voted for Peace? Public Support for the 1998 Northern Ireland Agreement," *Irish Political Studies* 16 (2001): 82.

37. Clancy, *Peace Without Consensus*, 84–85.

38. The North-South Ministerial Council is part of Strand Two of the Good Friday Agreement, which deals with relationships between Northern Ireland and the Republic of Ireland.

39. Coughlin, *American Ally*, 118, and Christopher Meyer, *DC Confidential* (London: Weidenfeld & Nicolson, 2005), 166.

40. Richard N. Haass, *Conflicts Unending: The United States and Regional Disputes* (New Haven, CT: Yale University Press, 1990).

41. John A. Farrell, "President, Adams Meet at Capitol," *Boston Globe*, March 17, 1995, 1; "Clinton's Foreign Policy," *Journal of Commerce*, November 4, 1996, 6A; and Richard N. Haass, "The Squandered Presidency," *Foreign Affairs* 79 (3) (2000): 136–41.

42. Clancy, *Peace Without Consensus*, 115.

43. FARC, known in English as the Revolutionary Armed Forces of Colombia, is a communist revolutionary group that is also deemed to be a narcoterrorist organization by the Colombian government, the US government, and the European Union.

44. Ray O'Hanlon, "Sinn Féin Faces US Political Backlash," *Irish News*, August 23, 2001, 8.

45. Henry McDonald, *Gunsmoke and Mirrors: How Sinn Féin Dressed Up Defeat as Victory* (Dublin: Gill and Macmillan, 2008), 161.

46. "Bush Envoy Set to Grill SF over Colombia Arrests," *The News Letter*, September 11, 2001, and McDonald, *Gunsmoke and Mirrors*, 159.

47. Timothy J. Lynch, "'We Don't Care if They're Terrorists': Sinn Féin in Anglo-American Relations, from Clinton to Bush," in *Public Diplomacy, Cultural Interventions & the Peace Process in Northern Ireland: Track Two to Peace?*, ed. Joseph J. Popiolkowski and Nicholas J. Cull (Los Angeles: Figueroa Press, 2009), 76. An American official concedes this point. See Clancy, *Peace Without Consensus*, 116.

48. Moloney, *A Secret History of the IRA*, 489–91.

49. Benjamin Gilman and William Delahunt, "Time to Lift Ban on FBI Training of Police Service of Northern Ireland," *Irish Times*, November 7, 2001.

50. Powell, *Great Hatred, Little Room*, 203. See also Moloney, *A Secret History of the IRA*, 518.

51. Nicholas Watt, "Carrots and Capitulation—Mandelson on Blair," *Guardian*, March 14, 2007, 13.

52. Powell, *Great Hatred, Little Room*, 163.

53. BBC, "Interview with Tony Blair," *Hearts and Minds*, April 20, 2008.

54. Ahern, *Bertie Ahern*, 199.

55. Robin Cook, *The Point of Departure* (London: Simon & Schuster, 2003), 69–71.

56. Richard N. Haass, "The Northern Ireland Peace Process," Address to the National Committee on American Foreign Policy, January 7, 2002, http://www.state.gov/s/p/rem /7300.htm, accessed November 7, 2005.

57. Clancy, *Peace Without Consensus*, 120.

58. Ibid., 128, and Godson, *Himself Alone*, 723 and 761.

59. Clancy, *Peace Without Consensus*, 121–24, and Godson, *Himself Alone*, 722.

60. Clancy, *Peace Without Consensus*, 122–23.

61. Ed Moloney, *Paisley: From Demagogue to Democrat?* (Dublin: Poolbeg, 2008), 415, 449, and 471. See also Clancy, *Peace Without Consensus*, 122–23.

62. See, for instance, ARK, "Political Attitudes," *Northern Ireland Life and Times Survey*, May 20, 2003, http://www.ark.ac.uk/nilt/2003/Political_Attitudes/NIAABOL.html, accessed June 18, 2007.

63. The Independent Monitoring Commission (IMC) was proposed as a means of restoring public confidence in the peace and political processes by having independent commissioners report on the state of paramilitary cease-fires. Officials initially resisted the idea because, according to a British official, they needed to make "nuanced assessments" about cease-fires. According to an Irish official, the Irish government resisted because the republican leadership "didn't want referees noting fouls all the time." See Clancy, *Peace Without Consensus*, 126. The UK and Irish governments established a modified IMC in 2004, but it was a case of too little, too late for Trimble.

64. Clancy, *Peace Without Consensus*, 126–27, and Godson, *Himself Alone*, 720.

65. Clancy, *Peace Without Consensus*, 134.

66. Colin Rallings and Michael Thrasher, "Voting at the Northern Ireland Assembly Election, 2003," *The Electoral Commission*, April 28, 2004, http://www.electoralcommission .org.uk/__data/assets/electoral_commission_pdf_file/0014/16133/Electionresults report-FINAL_13178-9766__N__.pdf, accessed September 13, 2007.

67. Clancy, *Peace Without Consensus*, 135.

68. Clancy, "The United States and Post-Agreement Northern Ireland," 168.

69. Clancy, *Peace Without Consensus*, 121, and Godson, *Himself Alone*, 720.

70. Clancy, *Peace Without Consensus*, 152–53 and 175–79.

71. Moloney, *Paisley*, 426.

72. Clancy, *Peace Without Consensus*, 149.

73. The British and Irish governments had good reasons for alleging IRA involvement. The Irish DOJ had the alleged bank robbers—an Irish businessman associated with the subsequent laundering of the £26.5 million and the republican leadership—under surveillance prior to the robbery. Although the IRA did not appear to order Mr. McCartney's murder, it did appear to order the subsequent cover-up. See Clancy, *Peace Without Consensus*, 147–49.

74. Reiss's comments are quoted in John Ware, "The Price of Peace." See also Clancy, *Peace Without Consensus*, 150.

75. Clancy, *Peace Without Consensus*, 151–52.

76. Clancy, "The United States and Post-Agreement Northern Ireland," 171, and Reiss quoted in Ware, "The Price of Peace." For further evidence of the distance between Reiss and some UK and Irish officials, see Mitchell B. Reiss, *Negotiating with Evil: When to Talk to Terrorists* (New York: Open Road, 2010), 246.

77. Clancy, "The United States and Post-Agreement Northern Ireland," 171; Frank Millar, *Northern Ireland: A Triumph of Politics* (Dublin: Irish Academic Press, 2008), 165–69; and Reiss quoted in Ware, "The Price of Peace." The idea that the Irish government did not believe that policing should be treated as a precondition also appears in US officials' private correspondence. The Department of An Taoiseach's private support for the ban must also be weighed against US correspondence suggesting that Irish officials put pressure on IMC commissioners throughout 2005 to give the IRA a clean bill of health in order to restore devolved government. See Clancy, *Peace Without Consensus*, 156.

78. Independent Monitoring Commission, "Eighth Report of the Independent Monitoring Commission," February 1, 2006, http://www.independentmonitoring commission.org/documents/uploads/8th%20IMC%20Report.pdf, accessed January 19, 2010. See also Clancy, *Peace Without Consensus*, 157.

79. Clancy, *Peace Without Consensus*, 160.

80. Ibid., 163.

81. Moloney, *Paisley*, 465 and 470–71.

82. Clancy, *Peace Without Consensus*, 164.

83. Powell, *Great Hatred, Little Room*, 300.

84. Clancy, *Peace Without Consensus*, 165.

85. Moloney, *A Secret History of the IRA*, 590, and Moloney, *Paisley*, 477.

86. I. William Zartman and Maureen R. Berman, *The Practical Negotiator* (New Haven, CT: Yale University Press, 1982), 66–78. For this conceptualization, see Jack Holland and Susan Phoenix, *Phoenix: Policing the Shadows* (London: Hodder & Stoughton, 1996), 391.

87. Reiss, "Lessons of the Northern Ireland Peace Process."

88. Author interview with former Irish Department of Justice official, September 2009.

89. Steve Bruce, *Paisley: Religion and Politics in Northern Ireland*, 2nd ed. (Oxford: Oxford University Press, 2007), 265. See also Rick Wilford and Robin Wilson, "Northern Ireland: A Route to Stability?," Economic and Social Research Council, 2003, http://www.devolution.ac.uk/pdfdata/Wilson_&_Wilford_Paper.pdf, accessed November 26, 2009.

90. See John Nagle and Mary-Alice C. Clancy, *Shared Society or Benign Apartheid? Understanding Peacebuilding in Divided Societies* (Hampshire: Palgrave Macmillan, 2010), 43–72.

91. This correspondence was included in the private papers of a Bush administration official that were left to the author. See Clancy, *Peace Without Consensus*, 148.

92. See, for instance, John McGarry and Brendan O'Leary, "Power Shared after the Death of Thousands," in *Consociational Theory: McGarry and O'Leary and the Northern Ireland Conflict*, ed. Rupert Taylor (London: Routledge, 2009), 15–84.

93. Powell, *Great Hatred, Little Room*, 312.

94. Irish Department of Foreign Affairs and Trade, "Opening Address by the Tánaiste and Minister for Foreign Affairs and Trade, Eamon Gilmore, TD," OSCE Conference 2012: Shared Future: Building and Sustaining Peace, the Northern Ireland Case Study, April 27, 2012, http://www.dfa.ie/uploads/documents/Political%20Division/OSCE/shared%20future%20t%C3%A1naiste%20address.pdf, accessed July 30, 2012.

95. David Trimble, "Agreeing to Differ," *Guardian*, April 5, 2008, http://www.guardian.co.uk/books/2008/apr/05/politics2, accessed July 30, 2012.

96. Reiss, *Negotiating with Evil*, 237.

97. Trimble, "Agreeing to Differ."

8 Peacebuilding, Community Development, and Reconciliation in Northern Ireland

The Role of the Belfast Agreement and the Implications for External Economic Aid

OLGA SKARLATO, EYOB FISSUH,

SEAN BYRNE, PETER KARARI, and

KAWSER AHMED

"Peacebuilding" is a term that incorporates a number of various initiatives and approaches, including reducing violence, conducting peacekeeping operations, and promoting capacity building and reconciliation, conflict transformation, and humanitarian and economic assistance.[1] Peace treaties and peace agreements play an important role when a cease-fire or the end of hostilities are declared by introducing measures (whether political, institutional, legal, or other) that would facilitate the transition of a country or region from conflict to peace. Peacebuilding, however, is a long-term process; it may commence during the conflict or after the conflict has ended and a peace treaty is signed.[2] The peacebuilding process involves a lasting commitment from the various actors involved in conflict transformation and in building a peaceful future for all citizens.[3]

In this chapter we analyze the tracks of peacebuilding that are both interrelated and complementary. First, we discuss the 1998 Good Friday Agreement, also known as the Belfast Agreement, which was signed by the British and Irish governments and endorsed by Northern Ireland's political parties. This Agreement introduced a power-sharing government in Northern Ireland and contributed to the deescalation of violence that afflicted Northern Irish society during the Troubles. Second, we present the quantitative data analysis of this Agreement in relation to peacebuilding and reconciliation in Northern Ireland. Third, we discuss the implications for international economic aid to Northern Ireland provided by the European Union (EU) Program for Peace and Reconciliation in Northern Ireland and the Border Counties of Ireland (Peace II) and the International Fund for Ireland (IFI). The funds were set up to support economic and social development, address the legacy of violent conflict, promote reconciliation between the nationalist and unionist communities, and shore up the institutions created by the Agreement.[4]

Our hypothesis is that strong and effective political institutions in a post-accord society supplemented by international economic assistance to peacebuilding and reconciliation efforts can assist in providing a solid foundation to a peace process. By examining the role of the Agreement in Northern Ireland's peace process, along with identifying the chief beneficiaries of the peace process and the beneficiaries of violence, we explore the connections between the Agreement and the peace process. This analysis can assist in gaining a deeper understanding of peacebuilding factors and approaches, which can potentially guide international economic assistance programs in other post-accord societies.

We also examine differences in perceptions of the Agreement by analyzing religious affiliation, economic class, and the gender of the respondents in our survey research. Conducting this analysis can assist in identifying demographic factors that contribute to the similarities and differences in perceptions among Northern Ireland's communities regarding the role of the Agreement in the reduction of violence and in building peace. Overall, by exploring these peacebuilding tracks—a multiparty Agreement that included new constitutional arrangements and introduced new political institutions along with international economic assistance programs—we reflect on the significance of these components within a peacebuilding and reconciliation framework and discuss the challenges and opportunities provided by these peacebuilding approaches.

Peacebuilding, Reconciliation, and the Agreement

In conflict analysis, as well as in peacebuilding, it is critical to examine the complex root causes of ethnic conflict in order to design and implement appropriate conflict transformation and peacebuilding processes.[5] The Northern Ireland conflict is rooted in a deep ethnonational antagonism between the unionist and nationalist communities.[6] Throughout the history of this conflict, Northern Ireland has suffered from sectarian politics impacted by segregation, social exclusion, inequality, unemployment, and poverty.[7] According to Hughes, violent conflict in Northern Ireland is the "product of historically rooted antagonisms derived from territorial partitions and repartitions, and systematic political and socioeconomic discrimination by privileged hegemonic groups against unprivileged subordinate groups."[8] Dixon also argues that while the terms "Catholic" and "Protestant" are often used to describe the two major groups in Northern Ireland, "the conflict is not to any great extent about religion or religious dogma."[9] Approximately 60 percent of Northern Ireland's population are unionists who support the idea of Northern Ireland remaining part of the United Kingdom (UK) and perceive themselves as British, and approximately 40 percent of the population are nationalists who "see themselves as Irish and aspire to be part of a united Ireland."[10]

The period in Northern Ireland's history between the late 1960s and the end of the 1990s commonly known as the Troubles was characterized by violent ethnopolitical conflict between the unionist and nationalist communities.[11] As a result, approximately 3,720 people were killed between 1966 and 2006.[12] The process that led to the signing of the Agreement in 1998 was a remarkable effort to build peace and promote reconciliation in Northern Ireland. However, the complexity and the multidimensional character of the Northern Ireland conflict calls for an integrated framework of peacebuilding that would go beyond the Agreement to address the underlying deep-rooted division of Northern Ireland's society.[13] True peace and reconciliation in Northern Ireland, according to Dingley, "would require an extensive programme of social and structural change that [would create] . . . a single community, interest, shared morality, and sense of legitimacy and the acceptance of a permanent state and its boundaries."[14] While this may be the ideal, the more practical challenge for the peace process in Northern Ireland was "to bridge the ideological gap between Unionists and Republicans . . . and bring sufficient,

200

cross-community elites, parties and voters to an agreement that would be sustainable."[15]

Peacebuilding theory and practice provide a number of creative approaches to addressing multiple issues that may contribute to conflict escalation in divided societies.[16] For example, the conceptual framework of *Multitrack Diplomacy* can assist peacebuilders in identifying and coordinating approaches within a multidimensional peacebuilding intervention.[17] In relation to the Northern Ireland conflict, multitracks that include government, nongovernmental organization (NGO), and private citizen involvement through advocacy, improved communications, funding, and other resources have a strong peacebuilding potential, especially if used in an integrated manner.[18] An integrated peacebuilding framework suggested by Lederach focuses on both immediate and long-term goals of reconciliation, building relationships, crisis management, and the prevention of further destructive conflict by addressing the conflict's root causes, the involvement of various actors (and specifically middle-range leaders), and the linkage of immediate issues with the broader systematic context of a particular conflict situation.[19] Moreover, conflict transformation is an integrative part of a comprehensive peacebuilding framework. In particular, Lederach views conflict transformation as a process that goes beyond conflict resolution and can be conceptualized through personal, relational, structural, and cultural dimensions.[20]

Further, in terms of peacebuilding by addressing violent conflict in divided societies, Jeong highlights the necessity of creating social spaces for facilitated dialogue between people with diverse identities and values in order to assist them in recognizing shared long-term interests and goals. Jeong also notes the significance of respecting the cultural and political identity of diverse members of society in a conflict transformation process.[21] The Agreement has addressed a number of these issues within the Northern Ireland context ranging from establishing new political institutions to declaring a commitment to the principle of nonviolence in resolving differences.

The Agreement supports the consent principle that the British and Irish governments will respect the choice of the majority of Northern Ireland's citizens to remain in the United Kingdom or opt out into a united island.[22] The Agreement also made provisions for a 108-member Assembly in Northern Ireland, a North-South Ministerial Council in Armagh City, a British-Irish Council, and a British-Irish Intergovernmental Conference, which signified the interdependency of these structures and the need to cooperate, as "the success of each depends on that of the other."[23] In this context, the Agreement set out a vision and a framework for political institutional change and the inclusion of the government of the Republic of Ireland within the political decision-making process.[24] The Assembly was given legislative authority on the issues devolved to government departments in Northern Ireland. Members of the Assembly are required to register a designation of identity—nationalist, unionist, or other—and a cross-community principle of consent is applied for major decisions made by the Assembly. The North-South Ministerial Council develops consultation, exchange of information, and cooperation between ministers from Northern Ireland and the Irish government on "matters of mutual interest within the competence of the Administrations, North and South."[25] The British-Irish Council comprises representatives of the British and Irish governments, devolved institutions in Northern Ireland, Scotland, and Wales, along with representatives of the Isle of Man and the Channel Islands. Its purpose is to consult, discuss, and exchange information on matters of mutual interest including but not limited to transport links, health, education, and approaches to EU issues. The Agreement also established the British-Irish Council to deal "with the totality of relationships" and bring the British and Irish governments together to promote bilateral cooperation at all levels of mutual interest also operating within a supranational EU framework.[26]

The participants who negotiated the Agreement declared their commitment to respect human rights and equality, their dedication to achieve reconciliation and mutual trust, as well as their "absolute commitment to exclusively democratic and peaceful means of resolving differences on political issues."[27] It is important to note that the constitutional principles of the Agreement were endorsed in referendums both in Northern Ireland and the Republic of Ireland on May 22, 1998. In Northern Ireland 71.1 percent approved the Agreement, and in the Republic of Ireland 94.9 percent supported the Agreement by "voting to erase the territorial claim on the North from their constitution."[28] The referendums and their outcomes not only added legitimacy to the peace process but also signified the considerable expectations associated with it by the people of Northern Ireland and the Republic of Ireland.

Moreover, the Agreement emphasized the significance of reconciliation, specifically in terms of the following elements: (1) acknowledging and addressing the suffering of the victims of violence, (2) building a peaceful and just society, in particular by supporting community-based initiatives, and (3) supporting the work of organizations that promote "reconciliation and mutual understanding and respect between and within communities and traditions, in Northern Ireland and between North and South."[29] Furthermore, the Agreement notes that "an essential aspect of the reconciliation process is the promotion of a culture of tolerance at every level of society, including initiatives to facilitate and encourage integrated education and mixed housing."[30]

Enhanced cross-border cooperation was identified by the Agreement as one of the important tasks to be developed in Northern Ireland and the border region. In particular, twelve areas of cross-border North-South cooperation were identified: agriculture, education, transport, environment, waterways, social security/social welfare, tourism, relevant EU programs, inland fisheries, aquaculture and marine matters, health, and urban and rural development.[31] Relevant EU Programs, as one of the areas of cross-border cooperation identified in the Agreement, establish a connection between the commitment to support cooperation between communities North and South and external international economic aid, including initiating and developing peacebuilding projects in Northern Ireland and the border counties. Presently, the Special EU Programs Body is managing cross-border EU Structural Funds programs in Northern Ireland and the border region, including the European Union's Program for Peace and Reconciliation (Peace I, II, and III) and the European Union's Cross-Border Program for Territorial Co-operation (INTERREG IVA Program).[32] In addition, the IFI, which was established in 1986 as an "independent international organization" by the governments of Britain and Ireland along with support and contributions from the United States, the EU, Canada, Australia, and New Zealand, provides funding to promote peacebuilding and reconciliation efforts in Northern Ireland and the border counties.[33] There is no doubt that both the IFI and the EU Peace Program have funded local projects that have fostered grassroots empowerment and confidence building.[34] However, the EU was criticized for being overtly bureaucratic, and the IFI for funding grandiose white elephant projects.[35] The findings are mixed.

Scholars, however, have debated the significance of the Agreement in fostering cross-border cooperation.[36] For example, Tannam discusses the extent to which cross-border institutional arrangements designed by the Agreement have contributed to increased cross-border cooperation in the economic and political spheres between the Irish Republic and

Northern Ireland and concludes that the Agreement has not provided "sufficient conditions for generalized and significant cross-Border co-operation to date."[37] In addition, O'Dowd and McCall note that while the "cross-Border dimension emphasizes economic cooperation with the Irish Republic, . . . [the] Agreement's emphasis on 'identity recognition' has enhanced the polarization of communal interests."[38]

Identity issues are very complex and have played a critical role in the conflict and for developing and implementing conflict resolution approaches.[39] There is potential for incorporating identity issues into the peacebuilding process. However, this potential requires a deep understanding of the historical context and current political and sociocultural dynamics as well as a genuine desire to promote peacebuilding and reconciliation between both conflicting groups.[40] The Agreement provides a number of examples that illustrate the significance of identity issues in Northern Ireland's political and social spheres. For example, members of Northern Ireland's Assembly have to designate themselves as unionist, nationalist, or other, as the cross-community decision-making principle within the Assembly is based on this mandatory expression of identity. Moreover, the Agreement has introduced the recognition of one's birth-right in Northern Ireland as British, Irish, or both, which also reveals the significance of recognizing a shared umbrella identity in efforts to promote reconciliation and peacebuilding between both traditions.

The Agreement also established a Northern Ireland Human Rights Commission to promote awareness of human rights throughout Northern Ireland, review existing laws and practices in the area of human rights, and advise the government on matters related to human rights. For example, Bell discusses the relationship between human rights, peace agreements, and conflict resolution based on a case study of Northern Ireland and concludes that "human rights measures can be useful to a peace process, not just because they address root causes of violence but because they can assist parties in finding agreement on issues such as political accommodation by reducing the zero-sum dimension to intercommunal power tussles."[41]

Despite the comprehensive and inclusive character of the Agreement, there are a number of critiques of the Agreement.[42] One key concern is the effectiveness of the implementation of the measures introduced into the Agreement. In particular, Dingley points out that the intractable nature of the Northern Ireland conflict, rooted in incompatible interests of nationalists and unionists regarding the political stance of Northern Ireland, is "hardly unlikely to alter for the sake of one Agreement."[43] According to

Dingley, the Agreement has not only failed to address the causes of the Troubles and the sectarian division in Northern Ireland but has even made them worse "by the way the Agreement institutionalized them."[44] The fact that the Assembly was suspended several times raises some concern about the long-term political effectiveness of the Agreement.

Another critique is tied to its consociational power-sharing character, a settlement that guarantees group representation for nationalists and unionists in the political domain on the basis of a power-sharing principle. For example, Rupert Taylor contends that the Agreement, "as a consociational settlement, rests on and promotes an ethnonational group-based understanding of politics that is inherently illiberal" and raises a concern that there are processes within consociational politics that are "inimical to liberal democracy."[45] In terms of Northern Ireland's political and social development, consociationalists favor segregation and argue that "antagonistic Unionist and Nationalist identities are either impossible or very difficult to change," while integrationists support an inclusive civil society approach, which promotes the ideas of contact and cooperation between both groups.[46]

Another significant critique is related to the so-called constructive ambiguity of the Agreement.[47] Coakley notes the "extraordinar[ily] broad and complex" character of the Agreement, which was expressed in "carefully crafted language whose meaning (perhaps deliberately) was not always clear."[48] According to Coakley, the Agreement "was designed as a master plan to resolve as many long-term issues as possible, while dealing with unresolved matters either through calculated ambiguity or provisions for alternative mechanisms for tackling them later."[49] While ambiguous language used to refer to important matters in general terms leaves room for negotiation and adjustments within the political decision-making process, it may also cause uncertainty and contribute to the inability of the Agreement to provide clear political and institutional guidance.

According to Bew and Gillespie, two problematic issues have the potential to undermine the Agreement—first, the "grey area" of the Agreement that "might be interpreted in such a way as to undermine the support of those who had initially backed the Agreement," and second, "the actions of some of those who had opposed the Agreement from the outset."[50] Further, Mac Ginty argues that while there is "little anticipation of a return to a large-scale violence," the Agreement requires considerable intervention from both the British and Irish governments to sustain the peace process.[51] At the same time, Mac Ginty notes that despite the flaws of the Northern

Ireland peace process it has "delivered significant quality-of-life benefits, addressed grievances and provided the mechanism for the sharing of power."[52]

Along with the criticisms of the Agreement, political and social development has been made in Northern Ireland since the signing of the Agreement. One such example is a connection between peacebuilding efforts through North-South cooperation and the relevant EU programs providing external financial assistance. International assistance can take various forms, including direct financial aid, institution-building, peacekeeping efforts aimed at strengthening civil society, cross-community cooperation, and the democratization process.[53] Economic aid may also play a significant role in assisting cross-community projects that promote building relationships and trust among members of conflicting communities.[54] At the same time, a study of the impact of cross-community cooperation on the reconciliation of Protestant and Catholic communities in Northern Ireland has revealed mixed perceptions. While some respondents believed that cross-community initiatives supported by Peace II and the IFI have made significant contributions to relationship building, others argued that "cross-community contact remained superficial."[55]

It can also be argued that one of the contributions of the Agreement to peacebuilding and reconciliation is in promoting cross-community contact and cooperation in Northern Ireland's government and politics.[56] International economic assistance has also contributed to building a peace dividend and promoting reconciliation in Northern Ireland through supporting and facilitating cross-community dialogue and relationship building, as well as through addressing socioeconomic inequality and unemployment by implementing initiatives aimed at capacity building and empowerment of both communities.[57] Therefore, both the institutional arrangements established by the Agreement and the international economic assistance programs may have contributed to building peace and reconciliation in Northern Ireland by focusing on cross-community relations as well as facilitating contact and cooperation in the political, social, and economic domains. People may now feel that they have ownership of local economies and politics in a participatory transformational democracy that is inclusive and transparent.[58] We now turn to presenting the findings of this study, which addresses the connections between the Agreement, the Northern Ireland peace process, and the implication for external economic aid programs.

Data and Methodology

This study is based on the quantitative analysis of a public opinion survey, which the third author commissioned Millward Brown Ulster (MBU) to carry out as part of its October Northern Ireland Omnibus Survey. Face-to-face interviews were conducted October 20–28, 2006, at forty-five randomly selected sampling locations in Northern Ireland. The respondents were quota-selected, and the final sample of 1,023 adults aged sixteen and older was fully representative of Northern Ireland's adult population. All interviews were consistent with the definitive standards of the Interviewer Quality Control Scheme, and further supervisory inspection of all questionnaires and a back check with 10 percent of respondents were conducted. All aspects of this research were in accordance with the Code of Conduct of the British Market Research Society. For our statistical analysis of the survey results, we use regression to examine the effect of religious affiliation, gender, and economic class on the perceived role of the Agreement on the peace and reconciliation process in Northern Ireland. In particular, we employ nonlinear regression models (i.e., probit models) because the dependent variables of our regression models are discrete binary variables. To facilitate the discussion, the results from the regression analysis are organized by themes.

Does the Agreement Support the Northern Ireland Peace Process?

More than 50 percent of the respondents across the population concurred that the Agreement supports the Northern Ireland peace process. This is indicative of the overall positive role of the Agreement on the peace and reconciliation process. How does this perception vary across the two major communities in Northern Ireland? We estimate a probability model (i.e., a probit regression model) to explore the effect of the different demographic variables on the perceived role of the Agreement on the Northern Ireland peace process. The dependent variable for our model is a binary variable, which assumes a value of 1 if a respondent agrees or strongly agrees that the Agreement supports the peace process in Northern Ireland and 0 otherwise. In the probit model, we include gender, religious affiliation, the economic class of respondents, the age of the respondents, and region as possible covariates.

Table 8.1. Probability models on reactions to the Agreement

	The Agreement supports the peace process (Marginal effects)	The Agreement will endure to promote peace and reconciliation (Marginal effects)
Religious affiliation:	0.280*	0.150*
Catholic	(0.118)	(0.030)
Economic class:	0.390*	0.120*
Professional	(0.120)	(0.040)
Economic class:	0.004	0.030
Skilled	(0.143)	(0.040)
Gender	-0.139	-0.080*
	(0.104)	(0.030)
Correctly classified (%)	76%	74%
Sample size	757	737

Source: Public Opinion Survey (2006).
Note: Standard errors are in parentheses. Age and regional residence of respondents were included but not reported.
*Statistically significant at 1% level.

The emphasis is on examining whether there is systematic difference between the two communities on the degree of agreement with the idea that the Agreement assists in promoting the peace process in Northern Ireland. It is well known that religion is an emblem of the identity of both communities in the Northern Ireland conflict.[59] To capture the effect of religion, the respondents were classified into three religious groups: Protestant, Catholic, and Other. However, since the focus is on the comparison of the Protestant and Catholic communities, the respondents with "other" religious affiliation were dropped out of the sample. Accordingly, we generated two dummy variables, representing the Protestant and Catholic religious affiliations.

A number of relationships are identified in this regression analysis. First, the probability of Catholic respondents agreeing that the Agreement supports the peace process in Northern Ireland is higher than their Protestant counterparts. This finding is noteworthy because it shows that the two communities in Northern Ireland differ in their perception of the role of the Agreement in supporting the peace and reconciliation process, which conforms to Hazleton's argument in chapter 2 that different actors and groups learned different lessons in the peace process. Moreover, the second column of table 8.1 indicates that Catholics are more likely than Protestant respondents to express agreement that the Agreement supports the point that the peace process will endure to promote peace and reconciliation. Catholic nationalists were discriminated against in the past and can gain more economically and politically from the Agreement and an inclusive peace process.[60] Protestants believe that the Agreement and the economic aid benefited Catholics to the detriment of unionists, whose culture, identity, and connection to the Union are now threatened.[61]

Second, respondents from the professional economic class believe that the Agreement supports the peace process much more than respondents from the semiskilled class. However, there is no statistically significant difference between respondents from the skilled and semiskilled economic class in their perception toward the role of the Agreement in supporting the peace process. Similarly, we find that the probability that someone from the professional economic class will agree that the Agreement will endure to promote peace and reconciliation is about 12 percent higher than respondents from the semiskilled economic class. Compared with other classes, those from the professional class have more to gain in terms of a better quality of life and are more likely to support the Agreement.[62] The professional economic class has the most to gain from economic opportunities in a peaceful milieu conducive to business and financial incentives.[63]

Finally, there is no statistically significant difference between men and women in evaluating the role of the Agreement in the peace process. With a voter turnout of over 80 percent in a referendum held in Northern Ireland on May 22, 1998, 77 percent of men and women voted in favor of the Agreement. The now defunct Northern Ireland Women's Coalition ensured that women's voices and concerns and social justice issues were built into the Agreement and that women were elected to the Northern Ireland Assembly.[64] Similarly, a previous study analyzing the impact of the IFI and EU Peace I Fund on building the peace dividend in Northern Ireland found no statistical difference between men and women.[65]

Beneficiaries of the Agreement

Our study also explores the chief beneficiaries of the Agreement and the international funding that has come to Northern Ireland and the border counties since the signing of the Agreement.

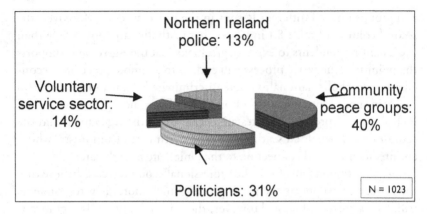

Figure 8.1. Top four organizations benefiting from the Agreement and/or international funding (UMS Survey [2006])

As expected, the chief beneficiaries of the Agreement are reported to be the community peace groups in Northern Ireland. This finding is indeed encouraging as the respondents perceive that local grassroots cross-community organizations are critical in facilitating peace and reconciliation processes. The survey reveals that the public also perceives politicians to have been the second greatest beneficiaries of the Agreement. This result indicates that there is a potential for politicians involved in the peace process to be occupied with the promotion of their own interests, which may not coincide with the prime objectives of the peace process. This finding calls for special attention to be given to designing and monitoring incentive mechanisms to motivate politicians not to deviate from the best interests of society. Northern Ireland's politicians must cooperate across party lines as they confront the political and economic issues facing society, and not continue the sectarian politics of the past. The police and voluntary service sector are also identified as benefiting from the Agreement.

Beneficiaries from Violence

We now turn to the issue of who benefits from the violence in Northern Ireland as summarized by table 8.2. The data in table 8.2 indicate that only 56 percent of the sample agrees that there are no groups who benefit from violence, suggesting the prevalence of some spoiler groups that would like to see the conflict unresolved or that continue to see violence as an effective means of achieving one's political goals in

Table 8.2. Level of agreement that there are no groups that benefit from the violence in Northern Ireland

	Strongly agree	Agree	Neither agree nor disagree	Disagree	Strongly disagree	Don't know
Gender						
Male	20%	35%	5%	12%	12%	17%
Female	26%	32%	3%	10%	10%	20%
Class						
Professional	24%	33%	4%	13%	13%	12%
Skilled	26%	34%	4%	11%	9%	16%
Semiskilled	20%	33%	3%	7%	10%	27%
Religion						
Protestant	26%	32%	4%	11%	11%	16%
Catholic	19%	37%	3%	11%	11%	19%
Other/Refused	26%	26%	2%	10%	5%	31%

Source: UMS Survey (2006).
Note: N = 1023.

Northern Ireland. Overall, this finding indicates that there could be certain spoiler groups that believe they benefit from the protracted conflict in Northern Ireland. These individuals who remain reluctant to renounce the efficacy of violence continue to be important opponents of the peace process. As far as the distribution of the level of agreement that there are no groups that benefit from the violence in Northern Ireland across socioeconomic groups is concerned, there is only a slight difference of opinion, which is not statistically significant to warrant further discussion. Socioeconomic groups express broadly similar opinions regarding the perception that there are no groups that benefit from violence. The slight difference of opinion is not statistically significant.

There are a number of explanations for the high level of agreement scored by respondents on the perceived role of the Agreement on the peacebuilding process in Northern Ireland. First, the Agreement has introduced significant changes within the political structures and institutions of Northern Ireland. According to Girvin, the Agreement "has had a significant impact on the polarized nature of the region's political system."[66] The Agreement was based on a number of specific principles including power sharing, cross-community cooperation, mutual respect, and the commitment to the nonviolent resolution of differences. It can be argued that the aforementioned principles contributed to the peacebuilding and reconciliation process in Northern Ireland in a number of ways, one of which was the Agreement's contribution to stopping the violence.

Second, the Agreement provided a constitutional framework that can be conceptualized as an institutional foundation with the potential to develop further political mechanisms aimed at peacebuilding and reconciliation in Northern Ireland. In this context the findings regarding the potential endurance of the Agreement and its contribution to promoting peace and reconciliation in Northern Ireland are significant. Further, by preventing violence and promoting peace, the Agreement also opened up the potential of economic assistance in nurturing peacebuilding initiatives in Northern Ireland. Some of these initiatives have in turn made further contributions to reinforcing peace, supporting the reconciliation process, and promoting cross-community dialogue, relationship building, and cooperation. There is a connection between the aforementioned contributions and the values spelled out in the Agreement, in particular, the commitment to cross-community cooperation within Northern Ireland and between Northern Ireland and the Republic of Ireland.

At the same time it is important to conceptualize peacebuilding in a multidimensional and integrative manner.[67] Having analyzed examples of transnational networks created in the framework of the EU Peace II program, O'Dowd and McCall, for example, concluded that "project-based transnational cooperation" can play a key role in combating territorialism and in encouraging a culture of cooperation, but these efforts need to be supported by a stable and durable institutional partnership framework capable of sustaining a long-term peacebuilding and reconciliation process.[68] It may be argued that the Agreement does provide such an institutional framework, but its effectiveness and sustainability are questionable. While the power-sharing principle is an important component within the political structure of Northern Ireland's government, it is critical to consider the significance of "complementarity of both the elite power-sharing and the grassroots participatory approaches" in order to build a lasting and sustainable peace in Northern Ireland.[69] Combining these two approaches, within a "multimodal complementarity approach at multiple levels of conflict intervention" can contribute to creating a peacebuilding framework for addressing the deep divisions caused by the nature of the protracted conflict.[70] Building on Lederach's conflict transformation and peacebuilding framework, which includes personal, relational, structural, and cultural dimensions, we suggest that for the conflict transformation process to be truly integrative there is a need to include an institutional dimension, which would ensure that political and institutional structures are involved in an integrated peacebuilding process. While this dimension partly correlates with the structural dimension suggested by Lederach, it is a more specific structural level primarily focused on political institutional arrangements put in place to maintain and support the peacebuilding efforts.[71] In terms of Northern Ireland's experience, the Agreement can be considered an attempt to implement an institutional dimension within the conflict transformation and peacebuilding process.[72]

It is also important to note that the respondents in this study perceived community peacebuilding groups to be the main beneficiaries of the international funding that followed from the Agreement, highlighting the connection between peacebuilding, economic aid, and the legacy of the Agreement. Other beneficiaries named by respondents were politicians, the voluntary service sector, and the Police Service of Northern Ireland. Politicians were named as the second largest beneficiary for two possible reasons. First, it may signify the hope held among the respondents that the Agreement's provisions as well as the support from both international funds can assist politicians in leading the peace process. In this context Flores and Nooruddin argue that it is very important for politicians to be committed to peace within the process of post-accord economic recovery and that their inability to do so inhibits peacebuilding investments.[73] Hughes and her colleagues also note that a "concerted effort on the part of policy-makers" is needed in order to address the ongoing realities of segregation and sectarianism in Northern Ireland. In particular, institutional arrangements, policies, and support are needed to promote "bridge-building, sharing and dealing with the legacies of the past."[74] Furthermore, Racioppi and O'Sullivan See raise the question of whether civil society and grassroots peacebuilding initiatives have the potential to "disrupt long-standing patterns of ethnic animosity" without "sustained institutionalized elite-level engagement."[75] Second, this finding may also signify the respondents' fears or suspicions that while politicians may have benefited from the Agreement and international funding, these benefits would not be extended toward promoting the peace process but rather to promoting their own self-interests. Only 56 percent of the respondents indicated that there are no groups that benefit from violence, suggesting that there are groups (Continuity IRA, Real IRA, Orange Defenders, Loyalist Volunteer Force) that may be interested in the continuation of conflict in Northern Ireland, and there is the potential for these spoiler groups to threaten the Northern Ireland peace process.

This study has also offered some insight into the debate regarding the Agreement and its critiques. The cross-community power-sharing principle in the Northern Ireland government system, which was established in the Agreement, is reinforcing both the political and the social division to some extent. For example, according to consociationalists, the Agreement has to be implemented by following consociational theory through "reinforcing communal pillars and creating separate provisions for each community."[76] At the same time, integrationists stress the significance of the civil society approach and question the effectiveness of reinforcing political divisions as a means of reconciliation. This may explain why Catholics, compared with Protestants, were found to be more optimistic about the role of the Agreement in the peace process.

Perhaps, while the power-sharing form of government may not be the most democratic, it is possibly the most effective transitional form of government in a region affected by a protracted ethnonational conflict.[77] This type of government seems to be able to manage the conflict, reduce violence, and introduce stable government structures as well as maintain the Northern Ireland peace process. As a transitional form of government from violence to peace it might just be the best option in particular historical circumstances. However, in terms of promoting peace and reconciliation within the political and sociocultural life of Northern Ireland's society, it is questionable whether the Agreement is successful because it is based on the idea of a fundamental division between unionists and nationalists within a political decision-making process of power sharing. In this context, Buchanan discusses the value of grassroots participatory democracy that should be incorporated into the decision-making process along with the mainstream political elite decision-making approach.[78] Supporting community peacebuilding initiatives through international funding assistance can empower the grassroots to be more active, not only through local involvement but also through their advocacy and political participation.

Finally, the Agreement has also opened up spaces for international economic aid to flow into Northern Ireland and the border counties to support their economic and social development as well as promote cross-community reconciliation and peacebuilding efforts. This is an important achievement, and coupled with internal peacebuilding efforts, international economic aid is assisting the civil society groups to nurture the peacebuilding process.

Having identified two major alternative narratives of post-Agreement development in Northern Ireland—a narrative of progress and a narrative of regress—Aughey argues that there is also a third, more complex narrative that combines both the elements of success and the elements of failure. The progress narrative includes the *peace dividend* in the form of political cooperation, economic development, and the reduction of violence, while the narrative of regress implies continued instability and polarization in both the political and social dimensions of Northern Ireland.[79] In terms of the "third" narrative based on the idea of the coexistence of success and failure in implementing the Agreement, a combination of sharing and segregation within Northern Irish politics and society can be noted. Thus, the Agreement has yielded mixed results. Moreover, both its intermediate successes and failures are important in terms of a long-term peacebuilding and reconciliation goal, whether as a learning tool, a guide for improvement, or for developing best practices.

In her reflections for peacebuilders, Fitzduff notes that there is not a shortage of solutions to the Northern Ireland conflict. "We have filing cabinets full of potential solutions, many of them intricately and intelligently crafted. . . . The problem was not so much in developing the solutions but in getting people to open the filing cabinets together and look at these possibilities together."[80] *Together* is a key idea here. The willingness of both unionists and nationalists to come together to craft solutions and design approaches to address the legacy of conflict, and then work together in implementing these solutions, is critical. In this context, the Agreement has provided a framework for such cooperation, while the international economic support supplemented internal efforts of funding cross-community cooperation in the economic and social spheres. However, for these initiatives to succeed there needs to be a real commitment by members of both communities—including government elites, middle-level leaders, grassroots, spoilers, and dissident republicans and loyalists—to work together toward building their relationships within a peace and reconciliation framework. Both funds will end in 2013, impacting grassroots peacebuilding as dissident spoiler groups—raising questions about whether peace is really being won in Northern Ireland and who owns the peace process in the wake of the global economic meltdown—take center stage. Neoliberal peacebuilding has its limitations, as economic aid on its own is not a panacea for transforming protracted ethnopolitical conflicts emerging from a violent past.[81] Rising expectations were not met in Northern Ireland, as unionists now perceive that nationalists have benefited from the peace while they have lost ground.[82] The peace process is also threatened by the sectarian politics surrounding the devolution of policing and justice and recent Continuity IRA attacks on Catholic PSNI officers. Peace is a process. People need time to heal from the trauma of past violence, to get to know each other, and to forge new opportunities and a political terrain that builds hope and trust, as well as a political future and a lasting peace for all citizens.[83]

Lessons Learned

What have we learned about the role and impact of external economic aid to an ethnic or civil conflict like that of Northern Ireland? The EU Peace I Fund provided a wide range of funding to a plethora of grassroots community groups and was perceived as more accessible than the IFI that funded large signature projects.[84] The first wave of funding created much excitement, as people on the ground bought into the peace process and started to reach across the communal divide as well as work on single-identity projects to build local capacity.[85] The EU Peace II Fund and the IFI were used effectively as part of the reconciliation and peace-building process, yet the number of EU Peace II funded projects began to dwindle as NGOs competed for the small trough of available grants.[86] As a result of corruption in some loyalist communities in projects perceived in some quarters as fronts for the Ulster Volunteer Force (UVF) and the Ulster Defence Association (UDA), a more highly bureaucratized EU Peace II application and reporting process emerged than the IFI's easily accessible and less bureaucratized process.[87] Some questioned if the funded projects were really creating a deep reconciliation and sustainable peace-building in a highly sectarian society or if this was a ploy by both governments, the United States and the EU, to support grassroots civil society NGOs and keep the paramilitaries in the peace process.[88] It is important to bear in mind that the British subvention to Northern Ireland far outweighs the economic assistance from both international aid agencies.[89] The external aid ends in 2013. Local grassroots NGOs are now competing for a smaller pot from the IFI and the EU Peace III Fund, raising concerns that only the "successful" projects that can be sustained are being funded while smaller NGOs are squeezed out of the funding process, which is creating internal competition and conflict between some grassroots peace-building and socioeconomic development NGOs.[90] For the people trying to escape decades of poverty in the wake of a turbulent and violent past, short-term investment in the voluntary sector to fund grassroots NGOs aimed at forcibly forging a peaceful society is unrealistic.[91] Moreover, the uneven class support for the Agreement and the imbalance between Protestant and Catholic support confirms previous research of vast differences between both opinions that may be attributed to the unequal distribution of the funding.[92] Perhaps what we learn from the Northern Ireland case is that local people must own the peace, and it may have been wiser to create a hybrid model whereby the economic resources are placed into a trust fund managed by a board comprising the funders, local politicians, and trusted elders in the grassroots. The external aid has nurtured much good work on the ground. Nevertheless, the process put in place by both funders is a top-down approach rather than top and bottom working together, with local people taking the lead. This reality fits in with the critique of the liberal peace approach offered by Mac Ginty, Williams, and Richmond.[93] There is no quick fix; a long-term peacebuilding process is needed to sustain cross-community relationships.

In chapter 1, White argued that the complexity and flexibility of the Agreement, with its inclusive process and open agenda, allowed everyone to read into it and get out of it what they desired. As Cox argues, the Agreement "is neither a solution to the Irish question nor a blueprint for government, it is a framework to build consensus."[94] The Agreement has successfully managed the relationship between the two communities. However, a process of deep reconciliation is not being built, as the trust to transform relationships just is not present. Bitterness and suspicions run deep in a society fraught with sectarian fissures and divisions. Unionists are pessimistic about the peace process, as consistently found in the Northern Ireland Life and Times Surveys carried out from 1998 to 2005, because they perceive that nationalists have gained more from the funding and the peace process.[95] The conflict is like an iceberg: what one does not see under the water is more important than what one sees above it. People continue to live in segregated neighborhoods and fewer than 5 percent of schools are integrated, so both communities are kept apart. Integrated education is a critical conflict transformation process that would create real cross-community engagement. Perhaps the time is ripe to integrate the education system in Northern Ireland as the US federal government did in the 1960s with the ending of the Jim Crow educational system in the American South.

In the introductory chapter White points out that the internal and external leaders took "risks for peace" because they did not desire sliding back over the abyss into the Troubles. Strong, fluid relationships among hard-line leaders are key to tackling deep-rooted issues. Hard-liners like Paisley and Adams were able to sell the Agreement to their DUP and Sinn

Féin constituents because of the trust built up with them over three decades. Unionists accepted the Agreement because "only by being generous now could they reconcile Nationalists to the Union and protect themselves against possible seismic shifts in the balance of demographic power."[96] Paisley (and Robinson) and McGuinness (the Chuckle Brothers) respected each other and were able to share political power, while the ultrarepublican and loyalist hard-liners who advocated armed struggle were marginalized. In addition, the Al Qaeda attacks of September 11, 2001, put pressure on mainstream loyalist and republican paramilitaries to take the gun permanently out of Northern Irish politics.[97] At this point in time in the conflict positive external regional and international leadership relationships also coincided with positive internal relationships. The EU and the United States in the role of primary mediators were able to provide resources (i.e., economic aid) and credible threats, while both external ethnoguarantors (the Irish and British governments) were able to work together in a cooperative partnership with their internal conationals (nationalists and unionists), with whom they have economic, historical, identity, political, and psychocultural ties, to enforce the Agreement and a cold peace.[98]

Conclusion

We have discussed some of the ideas and initiatives introduced in the Agreement, and we have explored some of its achievements as well as some of the areas that require further work and cooperation. While the Agreement may have failed at some levels, there are also areas in which it achieved progress and has contributed to the overall peace process in Northern Ireland. The achievements of the Agreement include its contributions to stopping the violence, its vision for the peaceful future of the unionist and nationalist communities in Northern Ireland, and a political institutional framework that may facilitate the implementation of this vision.

Peacebuilding projects financed by the IFI and the EU Peace II Fund have also made a number of contributions to cross-community development in Northern Ireland by focusing on building relationships and trust and encouraging cross-community cooperation and capacity building. Moreover, the peacebuilding and reconciliation agenda can be further advanced using the legacy of the Agreement along with the assistance of international economic aid. The Agreement provides a political framework of equity and the inclusion and parity of unionists and nationalists, while both external funders have provided the resources to nurture and support cross-community group projects at the grassroots level to build the peace dividend at the microlevel.

The question about the endurance of the Agreement in addressing the legacy of violent conflict with the contribution of various peacebuilding approaches is also critical. The progress made by Northern Irish society so far is encouraging. At the same time, a deep division, which keeps Northern Irish communities apart, is rooted in the legacy of sectarianism, segregation, the border, and mistrust. One of the key aspects of peacebuilding (perhaps *the* key one) that has the potential to address existing divisions is reconciliation. Without genuine reconciliation as discussed in chapter 9, sustainable and lasting peace is hardly possible. Dixon points to the challenge of bringing about reconciliation in Northern Ireland after having established elite power-sharing mechanisms.[99]

In terms of the Northern Ireland peace process, the Agreement has laid out a strategy and created a constitutional and institutional framework, but these efforts should be continuously supplemented by supporting initiatives aimed at building relationships and trust among the Protestant and Catholic communities as they move toward acknowledging the past and reconciling their differences. In this context, the support of the EU Peace II Fund and the IFI play an important role, especially as their missions include not only assisting economic and social development but also in promoting peacebuilding and reconciliation between both communities in Northern Ireland. Reconciliation is a critical peacebuilding approach that addresses the legacy of past conflict in order to create a vision for a brighter and safer future, as well as design peacebuilding structures and institutions that would make this vision a reality, for all the people of Northern Ireland.

NOTES

We are grateful to Jessica Senehi, Hamdesa Tuso, Tom Boudreau, and Timothy J. White for reading and commenting on a number of drafts of this chapter. The research for this chapter was supported by a three-year research grant from the Social Sciences and Humanities Research Council of Canada. This chapter is dedicated to the memory of Patricia Byrne (Sean's mom), who was buried in Teemore, Co. Fermanagh, on February 26, 2013.

1. Boutros Boutros-Ghali, *An Agenda for Peace* (New York: United Nations, 1995); Dennis Sandole, Sean Byrne, Ingrid Sandole-Staroste, and Jessica Senehi, *Handbook of Conflict Analysis and Resolution* (New York: Routledge, 2009); Graciana Del Castillo, *Rebuilding War-Torn States: The Challenge of Post-Conflict Economic Reconstruction* (Oxford:

Oxford University Press, 2008); and David Sorenson and Pia Christina Wood, *The Politics of Peacekeeping in the Post-Cold War Era* (New York: Frank Cass, 2005).

2. John Paul Lederach, *Building Peace: Sustainable Reconciliation in Divided Societies* (Washington, DC: United States Institute of Peace Press, 1997).

3. Ho-Won Jeong, *Peacebuilding in Postconflict Societies* (Boulder, CO: Lynne Rienner, 2005).

4. Sandra Buchanan, "Transforming Conflict in Northern Ireland and the Border Counties: Some Lessons from the Peace Programmes on Valuing Participative Democracy," *Irish Political Studies* 23 (3) (2008): 387–409.

5. Dennis Sandole, *Peacebuilding: Preventing Violent Conflict in a Complex World* (Cambridge: Polity Press, 2010).

6. Paul Arthur, *Special Relationships: Britain, Ireland and the Northern Ireland Problem* (Belfast: Blackstaff Press, 2000).

7. Sean Byrne and Cynthia Irvin, "A Shared Common Sense: Perceptions of the Material Effects and Impacts of Economic Growth in Northern Ireland," *Civil Wars* 5 (1) (2002): 55–86, and Paul Dixon, *Northern Ireland: The Politics of War and Peace* (New York: Palgrave Macmillan, 2008).

8. James Hughes, "Paying for Peace: Comparing the EU's Role in the Conflicts in Northern Ireland and Kosovo," *Ethnopolitics* 8 (3–4) (2009): 288.

9. Dixon, *Northern Ireland*, 2.

10. Ibid.

11. Paul Bew and Gordon Gillespie, *Northern Ireland: A Chronology of the Troubles, 1968–1999* (Lanham, MD: Scarecrow Press, 1999), and Tim Pat Coogan, *The Troubles: Ireland's Ordeal, 1966–1996, and the Search for Peace* (Boulder: Roberts Rinehart, 1996).

12. Dixon, *Northern Ireland*, 27.

13. Sean Byrne, Olga Skarlato, Eyob Fissuh, and Cynthia Irvin, "Building Trust and Goodwill in Northern Ireland and the Border Counties: The Impact of Economic Aid on Peace Process," *Irish Political Studies* 24 (3) (2009): 337–63.

14. James Dingley, "The Road to Peace? Northern Ireland after the Belfast Agreement: Causes of Failure," *Democracy and Security* 2 (2006): 280.

15. Paul Dixon, "Political Skills or Lying and Manipulation? The Choreography of the Northern Ireland Peace Process," *Political Studies* 50 (4) (2002): 732.

16. Jeong, *Peacebuilding in Postconflict Societies.*

17. Sean Byrne and Loraleigh Keashly, "Working with Ethnopolitical Conflict: A Multi-modal Approach," *International Peacekeeping* 7 (1) (2000): 97–120, and Louise Diamond and John McDonald, *Multi-Track Diplomacy: A Systems Approach to Peace*, 3rd ed. (West Hartford, CT: Kumarian Press, 1996).

18. Cathal McCall and Liam O'Dowd, "Hanging Flower Baskets, Blowing in the Wind: Third Sector Groups, Cross Border Partnerships, and the EU Peace Programs in Ireland," *Nationalism and Ethnic Politics* 14 (1) (2008): 29–54, and Stephen Ryan, *The Transformation of Violent Intercommunal Conflict* (Aldershot: Ashgate, 2007).

19. Lederach, *Building Peace*, 32.

20. Ibid., 82.

21. Ho-Won Jeong, *Peace and Conflict Studies: An Introduction* (Aldershot: Ashgate, 2000).

22. John Coakley, "Has the Northern Ireland Problem Been Solved?," *Journal of Democracy* 19 (3) (2008): 102.

23. The Agreement, 1998, p. 3, http://www.nio.gov.uk/agreement.pdf, accessed January 15, 2011.

24. Katy Hayward, *Irish Nationalism and European Integration: The Official Redefinition of the Island of Ireland* (Manchester: Manchester University Press, 2009).

25. The Agreement, 1998, 14.

26. Ibid., 18.

27. Ibid., 2.

28. Coakley, "Has the Northern Ireland Problem been Solved?," 103.

29. The Agreement, 1998, 22–23.

30. Ibid., 23.

31. Ibid., 16–17.

32. Special EU Programs Body, About Us, http://www.seupb.eu/AboutUs/about-us.aspx, accessed January 15, 2011.

33. International Fund for Ireland, Background, http://www.internationalfundforireland.com/about-the-fund, accessed January 15, 2011.

34. Linda Racioppi and Katherine O'Sullivan See, "Grassroots Peace-Building and Third-Party Intervention: The European Union's Special Support Programme for Peace and Reconciliation in Northern Ireland," *Peace & Change* 32 (2) (2007): 361–90; McCall and O'Dowd, "Hanging Flower Baskets, Blowing in the Wind"; Buchanan, "Transforming Conflict in Northern Ireland and the Border Counties"; and Sean Byrne, "The Politics of Peace and War in Northern Ireland," in *Regional and Ethnic Conflicts: Perspectives from the Front Lines*, ed. Judy Carter, George Irani, and Vamik Volkan (Upper Saddle River, NJ: Prentice Hall, 2009), 212–26.

35. European Union Court of Auditors, "Special Report No. 7 Concerning the International Fund for Ireland and the Special Support Program for Peace and Reconciliation in Northern Ireland and the Border Counties of Ireland, 1995 to 1999, Together with the Commission's Replies" (Brussels: European Union Court of Auditors, 2000); Brian Harvey, "Report on the Program for Peace and Reconciliation" (York: Joseph Rowntree Charitable Trust, 1997); and Brian Harvey, "Review of the Peace II Program" (York: Joseph Rowntree Charitable Trust, 2003).

36. Roberto Belloni, "Northern Ireland: Civil Society and the Slow Building of Peace," in *Civil Society and Peacebuilding: A Critical Assessment*, ed. Thania Paffenholz (Boulder, CO: Lynne Rienner, 2010), 105–29, and Jessica Senehi, "The Role of Constructive Transcultural Storytelling in Ethnopolitical Conflict Transformation in Northern Ireland," in Carter, Irani, and Volkan, *Regional and Ethnic Conflicts*, 227–38.

37. Etain Tannam, "Cross-Border Co-operation between Northern Ireland and the Republic of Ireland: Neo-Functionalism Revisited," *British Journal of Politics and International Relations* 8 (2) (2006): 275.

38. Liam O'Dowd and Cathal McCall, "Escaping the Cage of Ethno-National Conflict in Northern Ireland? The Importance of Transnational Networks," *Ethnopolitics* 7 (1) (2008): 88.

39. Sean Byrne, "Consociational and Civic Society Approaches to Peacebuilding in Northern Ireland," *Journal of Peace Research* 38 (3) (2001): 329.

40. John McGarry and Brendan O'Leary, *Explaining Northern Ireland: Broken Images* (Cambridge: Blackwell, 1995).

41. Christine Bell, "Human Rights, Peace Agreements, and Conflict Resolution: Negotiating Justice in Northern Ireland," in *Human Rights and Conflict: Exploring the Links between Rights, Law, and Peacebuilding*, ed. Julie Mertus and Jeffrey Helsing (Washington, DC: United States Institute of Peace Press, 2006), 367.

42. James Dingley, "The Road to Peace?," and Rupert Taylor, "The Belfast Agreement and the Politics of Consociationalism: A Critique," *Political Quarterly* 77 (2) (2006): 217–26.

43. Dingley, "The Road to Peace?," 265.

44. Ibid., 280.

45. Taylor, "The Belfast Agreement and the Politics of Consociationalism," 217–18.

46. Dixon, *Northern Ireland*, 21.

47. Arthur Aughey, *The Politics of Northern Ireland: Beyond the Belfast Agreement* (New York: Routledge, 2005), 148–54, and Paul Dixon, "Political Skills or Lying and Manipulation?," 736.

48. Coakley, "Has the Northern Ireland Problem Been Solved?," 103.

49. Ibid., 103.

50. Bew and Gillespie, *Northern Ireland*, 403.

51. Roger Mac Ginty, "The Liberal Peace at Home and Abroad: Northern Ireland and Liberal Internationalism," *British Journal of Politics and International Relations* 11 (4) (2009): 702.

52. Ibid., 705.

53. Jeong, *Peacebuilding in Postconflict Societies*.

54. Byrne et al., "Building Trust and Goodwill in Northern Ireland and the Border Counties."

55. Sean Byrne, Arnold Jobb, Eyob Fissuh, Katerina Standish, and Pauline Tennent, "The EU Peace II Fund and the International Fund for Ireland: Nurturing Cross-Community Contact and Reconciliation in Northern Ireland," *Geopolitics* 14 (4) (2009): 649.

56. Racioppi and O'Sullivan See, "Grassroots Peace-Building and Third-Party Intervention."

57. Byrne et al., "Building Trust and Goodwill in Northern Ireland and the Border Counties," and Byrne et al., "The EU Peace II Fund and the International Fund for Ireland."

58. Byrne et al., "Building Trust and Goodwill in Northern Ireland and the Border Counties."

59. See, for example, John Whyte, *Interpreting Northern Ireland* (London: Clarendon Press, 1990).

60. Sean Byrne, Katerina Standish, Jobb Arnold, Eyob Fissuh, and Cynthia Irvin, "Economic Aid: The End of Phase II and the Impact on Sustainable Peacebuilding in Northern Ireland," *Journal of Intervention and Statebuilding* 3 (3) (2009): 369–87.

61. James McAuley, "Unionism's Last Stand: Contemporary Unionist Politics and Identity in Northern Ireland," *Ethnopolitics* 3 (1) (2003): 60–74; Peter Shirlow, *The End of Ulster Loyalism* (Manchester: Manchester University Press, 2012); and Lee Smithey, *Unionists, Loyalists and Conflict Transformation in Northern Ireland* (Oxford: Oxford University Press, 2011).

62. For further evidence, see Colin Coulter and Michael Murray, *Northern Ireland after the Troubles: A Society in Transition* (Manchester: Manchester University Press, 2008), and Peter Shirlow and Kieran McEvoy, *Beyond the Wire: Former Prisoners and Conflict Transformation in Northern Ireland* (London: Pluto, 2008).

63. Sean Byrne, Katerina Standish, Eyob Fissuh, Jobb Arnold, and Pauline Tennent, "Building the Peace Dividend in Northern Ireland: People's Perceptions of Self and Country," *Nationalism and Ethnic Politics* 15 (2) (2009): 160–88.

64. Kate Fearon, *Women's Work: The Story of the Northern Ireland Women's Coalition* (Belfast: Blackstaff Press, 1999).

65. Cynthia Irvin and Sean Byrne, "The Perception of Economic Aid in Northern Ireland and Its Role in the Peace Process," in *Peace At Last? The Impact of the Good Friday Agreement on Northern Ireland*, ed. Jorg Neuheiser and Stefan Wolff (Oxford: Berghahn, 2002), 167–91.

66. Brian Girvin, "Continuity, Change and Crisis in Ireland: An Introduction and Discussion," *Irish Political Studies* 23 (4) (2008): 457.

67. Diamond and McDonald, *Multi-Track Diplomacy*; Lederach, *Building Peace*; and Roger Mac Ginty and Andrew Williams, *Conflict and Development* (New York: Routledge, 2009).

68. O'Dowd and McCall, "Escaping the Cage of Ethno-National Conflict in Northern Ireland?," 97.

69. Byrne, "Consociational and Civic Society Approaches to Peacebuilding in Northern Ireland," 328.

70. Ibid., 342.

71. Lederach, *Building Peace*.

72. Ryan, *The Transformation of Violent Intercommunal Conflict*.

73. Thomas Edward Flores and Irfan Nooruddin, "Democracy under the Gun: Understanding Postconflict Economic Recovery," *Journal of Conflict Resolution* 53 (1) (2009): 3–29.

74. Joanne Hughes, Andrea Campbell, Miles Hewstone, and Ed Cairns, "'What's

There to Fear?'—A Comparative Study of Responses to the Out-Group in Mixed and Segregated Areas of Belfast," *Peace & Change* 33 (4) (2008): 542 and 540.

75. Racioppi and O'Sullivan See, "Grassroots Peace-Building and Third-Party Intervention," 384.

76. Dixon, *Northern Ireland*, 282.

77. McGarry and O'Leary, *Explaining Northern Ireland*.

78. Buchanan, "Transforming Conflict in Northern Ireland and the Border Counties."

79. Aughey, *The Politics of Northern Ireland*, 161–72.

80. Mari Fitzduff, "A View from Northern Ireland," in *Handbook of International Peacebuilding: Into an Eye of the Storm*, ed. John Paul Lederach and Janice Moomaw Jenner (San Francisco: Jossey-Bass, 2002), 139.

81. Ryan, *The Transformation of Violent Intercommunal Conflict*; Roger Mac Ginty, *No War, No Peace: The Rejuvenation of Stalled Peace Processes and Peace Accords* (London: Palgrave Macmillan, 2008); Mac Ginty and Williams, *Conflict and Development*; and Roger Mac Ginty and John Darby, *Guns and Government: The Management of the Northern Ireland Peace Process* (New York: Palgrave, 2002).

82. Mislav Matic, Sean Byrne, and Eyob Fissuh, "Awareness and Process: The Role of the European Union Peace II Fund and the International Fund for Ireland in Building the Peace Dividend in Northern Ireland," *Journal of Conflict Studies* 27 (1) (2007): 105–205.

83. Sean Byrne, Chuck Thiessen, and Eyob Fissuh, "Economic Aid and Peacebuilding in Northern Ireland," *Peace Research: Canadian Journal of Peace and Conflict Studies* 39 (1) (2007): 1–14. For more on the need for reconciliation, see chapter 9.

84. Sean Byrne, Mislav Matic, Eyob Fissuh Ghebretsadik, and Chris Cunningham, "The International Fund for Ireland and the Northern Ireland Peace Process," *The Sri Lankan Journal of International Law* 19 (2) (2007): 1–23; Sean Byrne, Mislav Matic, and Eyob Fissuh Ghebretsadik, "The European Union's Peace and Reconciliation Fund's Impact on Economic Development, Peacebuilding and Reconciliation in Northern Ireland and the Border Counties," *International Journal of World Peace* 27 (2) (2007): 85–109; and Sean Byrne, Cynthia Irvin, and Eyob Fissuh, "The Perception of Economic Assistance in Northern Ireland and Its Role in the Peace Process," in *Handbook in Conflict Analysis and Resolution*, ed. Dennis Sandole, Sean Byrne, Ingrid Sandole, and Jessica Senehi (Routledge, 2009), 473–92.

85. Sean Byrne and Michael Ayulo, "External Economic Aid in Ethnopolitical Conflict: A View from Northern Ireland," *Security Dialogue* 29 (4) (1998): 421–34, and Sean Byrne and Cynthia Irvin, "Economic Aid and Policy Making: Building the Peace Dividend in Northern Ireland," *Policy and Politics* 29 (4) (2001): 413–29.

86. Chuck Thiessen, Sean Byrne, Olga Skarlato, and Pauline Tennent, "Civil Society Leaders and Northern Ireland's Peace Process: Hopes and Wishes for the Future," *Humanity and Society* 34 (1) (2010): 39–63; Sean Byrne, Chuck Thiessen, Eyob Fissuh, and Cynthia Irvin, "The IFI and EU Peace II Fund: Respondents' Perceptions of Funded Projects' Success in Promoting Peacebuilding and Community Development in Northern Ireland,"

Peace and Conflict Studies 16 (1) (2009): 44–57; and Olga Skarlato, Sean Byrne, and Chuck Thiessen, "The EU Peace II Fund and the International Fund for Ireland: Transforming Conflict and Building Peace in Northern Ireland and the Border Counties," *Treatises and Documents: Journal of Ethnic Studies* 62 (1) (2010): 92–124.

87. Sean Byrne, Eyob Fissuh, Chuck Thiessen, Cynthia Irvin, and Pauline Tennent, "The Role of the International Fund for Ireland and the European Union Peace II Fund in Reducing Violence and Sectarianism in Northern Ireland," *International Politics* 47 (2) (2010): 229–50; Robin Wilson, *The Northern Ireland Experience of Conflict and Agreement: A Model for Export?* (Manchester: Manchester University Press, 2010); and Brian Harvey, "Review of the Peace II Program."

88. Sean Byrne, Jobb Arnold, Katerina Standish, Olga Skarlato, and Pauline Tennent, "The Impact of International Funding on Reconciliation and Human Security in Northern Ireland: Identity, Affinity, and Aversion in the Political Domain," *Journal of Human Security* 6 (3) (2010): 16–35; Sean Byrne, Chuck Thiessen, Eyob Fissuh, Cynthia Irvin, and Marcie Hawranik, "Economic Assistance, Development, and Peacebuilding: The Role of the IFI and EU Peace II Fund in Northern Ireland," *Civil Wars* 10 (2) (2008): 108–26; and Eyob Fissuh, Olga Skarlato, Sean Byrne, Peter Karari, and Kawser Ahmed, "Building Future Co-existence or Keeping People Apart: The Role of Economic Assistance in Northern Ireland," *International Journal of Conflict Management* 23 (3) (2012): 248–65.

89. Joseph Ruane and Jennifer Todd, *The Dynamics of Conflict in Northern Ireland: Power, Conflict and Emancipation* (Cambridge: Cambridge University Press, 1996); John McGarry and Brendan O'Leary, *Explaining Northern Ireland: Broken Images* (London: Blackwell, 1995); and Portland Trust, *Economics in Peacemaking: Lessons from Northern Ireland* (London: Portland Trust, 2007).

90. Ahmed Kawser, Sean Byrne, Peter Karari, and Olga Skarlato, "The Perceptions of Hope and Fears of Civil Society NGO Leaders in Northern Ireland: The Impact of the International Fund for Ireland and the European Union Peace III Funding," *Humanity and Society* 37 (1) (2013): 5–34; Kawser Ahmed, Sean Byrne, Peter Karari, and Olga Skarlato, "Meeting Rising Expectations of Hopes for Post Peace Accord Northern Ireland: The Role of the Good Friday Agreement and the Implications for External Economic Aid," *Treatises and Documents: Journal of Ethnic Studies* 69 (2) (2013): 8–35; and Peter Karari, Sean Byrne, Olga Skarlato, Kawser Ahmed, and Julie Hyde, "The Role of External Economic Assistance in Nurturing Cross Community Contact and Reconciliation in Northern Ireland and the Border Counties," *Community Development Journal* (forthcoming).

91. Byrne et al., "Economic Aid: The End of Phase II," 385.

92. Connie O'Brien, "Integrated Community Development/Conflict Resolution Strategies as Peace Building Potential in South Africa and Northern Ireland," *Community Development Journal* 42 (1) (2007): 114–30; Eamonn O'Kane, "Re-evaluating the Anglo Irish Agreement: Central or Incidental to the Northern Ireland Peace Process?," *International Politics* 44 (1) (2007): 711–31; Buchanan, "Transforming Conflict in Northern Ireland and the Border Counties"; McAuley, "Unionism's Last Stand"; and O'Dowd and McCall, "Escaping the Cage of Ethno-National Conflict in Northern Ireland?"

93. Mac Ginty and Williams, *Conflict and Development*; Oliver Richmond, *Palgrave Advances in Peacebuilding: Critical Developments and Approaches* (London: Palgrave Macmillan, 2010); Oliver Richmond, *A Post Liberal Peace* (London: Routledge, 2011); and Roger Mac Ginty, *International Peacebuilding and Local Resistance: Hybrid Forms of Peace* (Basingstoke: Palgrave Macmillan, 2011).

94. Michael Cox, "The War That Came In from the Cold: Clinton and the Irish Question," *World Policy Journal* 16 (1) (1999): 41–68.

95. Byrne et al., "The EU Peace II Fund and the International Fund for Ireland," 648.

96. Brendan O'Leary, "Academic Viewpoint: The Nature of the Agreement," *Fordham International Law Journal* 22 (1) (1999): 643.

97. Sean Byrne, "Toward Tractability: The 1993 South African Record of Understanding and the 1998 Northern Ireland Good Friday Agreement," *Irish Studies in International Affairs* 13 (1) (2002): 135–49.

98. Sean Byrne, "Mired in Intractability: The Roles of External Ethno-Guarantors and Primary Mediators in Cyprus and Northern Ireland," *Conflict Resolution Quarterly* 24 (2) (2007): 149–72.

99. Dixon, *Northern Ireland*, 345.

9 Extending Peace to the Grassroots

The Need for Reconciliation in Northern Ireland after the Agreement

TIMOTHY J. WHITE, ANDREW P. OWSIAK, and MEGHAN E. CLARKE

The dramatic reduction of violence since the signing of the Belfast Agreement suggests that the peace process in Northern Ireland has been generally successful. Nonetheless, this need not imply that the parties have resolved the conflict with finality. Indeed, as Maoz notes, conflict management and conflict resolution are two distinct concepts.[1] Conflict management involves limiting the escalation or expansion of violence (a negative peace). According to this measure, the Agreement succeeded, largely through the creation of inclusive processes and institutions. Nevertheless, inclusion only accomplishes so much after protracted conflict, and more must therefore be done to *resolve* the conflict fully. More specifically, conflict resolution aims to resolve the issues under dispute, transform relations between former combatants, and institute nonviolent conflict engagement systems within the society that can handle future disputes (a positive peace). The Agreement arguably accomplished some of these tasks, but it also failed to transform the relationship between opposing communities. It did not resolve fully the issues under dispute, as each side continues to interpret the conflict through its own lens (i.e., history) and remains distrustful of its former enemies. Northern Ireland has a way to go before achieving a truly durable peace.

In this chapter, we identify challenges to (continued) successful conflict management and the pursuit of conflict resolution in the wake of the Agreement. The peace process in Northern Ireland overcame significant hurdles—including those associated with interstate territorial disagreements, inclusive institutions, spoilers, and the implementation of peace agreements. Northern Ireland must be vigilant against the reemergence of such obstacles and address two remaining hurdles to positive peace: the creation of a civil society that integrates both sides of the conflict and the construction of a shared historical truth about the conflict itself. Absent such work, reconciliation—and therefore, conflict resolution—will elude those in Northern Ireland who waited and worked so long for peace.[2]

Successes of—and Challenges to—Conflict Management

Northern Ireland qualifies as an ethnic conflict—in the sense that it contains two social categories (Catholic and Protestant) that are largely hereditary and immutable, and conflict occurs between these groups.[3] Such a classification uncovers two characteristics about the Northern Ireland conflict. First, the ethnic (bifurcated sectarian) divide in Northern Ireland helps to explain the long duration of the Troubles.[4] Second, viewing Northern Ireland as an ethnic conflict points toward the source of the conflict. When groups believe that the state cannot effectively represent their interests, arbitrate intergroup disputes, or protect them, Lake and Rothchild argue that groups begin to fear their uncertain future and prepare to defend themselves against violence.[5] As the opposing group(s) witnesses these preparations, they fear their future more, expect that future violence is more likely, and therefore prepare for that violence as well. In other words, ethnically divided societies suffer from a domestic form of the security dilemma, in which each ethnic group perceives that greater security for the other group implies decreased security for itself.[6] The insecurity fuels conflict between the groups in a cyclical fashion. The fact that groups remain relatively immutable ensures that the conflict persists. Overcoming the security dilemma is therefore the key to the long-term resolution of the conflict.

Unfortunately, this dilemma cannot easily be surmounted. Some scholars (for example, Mearsheimer) believe that the security dilemma is endemic to anarchic relationships, which implies that very little can be done to alleviate the fear it causes when government does not function as it should.[7] Others, however, offer a more optimistic view. Vasquez, for example, argues that humans possess a tendency toward territoriality—that is, a predilection to divide the world into political units and defend those units with force. His theory maintains that territorial disputes will be more violent than nonterritorial disputes, that states will fight most about the placement of international borders, and that relations between actors will become substantially less violent once they agree upon the placement of their mutual borders (even if they still disagree about other issues).[8] The empirical evidence seems to confirm each of these predictions, thereby confirming that a clear boundary between former combatants may increase the prospects of peace.[9]

Northern Ireland can be seen as a case in which the communities involved could not agree upon the placement of the Irish-British international border.[10] Although it also contained ethnic components that greatly complicated its resolution, the conflict was based on determining whether Northern Ireland (or subcomponents of it) belonged properly within the Irish or British state. Indeed, the Irish Constitution claimed the whole of Northern Ireland until it was amended in accordance with the Agreement. Viewed from this—admittedly simple—perspective, the conflict in Northern Ireland was a territorial disagreement, the ideal solution to which seemingly involves partition of some kind—that is, an arrangement in which the two communities are separated into distinct, sovereign territorial areas and the border between them resolved. Such a solution therefore echoes the work of Kaufmann, who argues that partition remains the *only* mechanism by which ethnic groups can overcome their security dilemma.[11]

Partition, however, remains an imperfect solution for three primary reasons. First, partition does not *necessarily* resolve the security dilemma. Separating two communities from one another creates physical distance, but a security dilemma can theoretically persist between physically distinct communities. Diehl and Goertz demonstrate that the vast majority of conflict is centered on rivalries—that is, particularly hostile, competitive relationships between states.[12] Such rivalries form when states (defined as physically distinct units) contend over issues that they perceive as zero sum through the repeated use of military force. This may be viewed as a particularly intense form of the security dilemma in which actors expect military force to be the dominant foreign policy tool with their rival for the foreseeable future.

Although Diehl and Goertz speak to interstate relations, research suggests that their insight extends to interethnic relations as well. Sambanis, for example, finds that civil wars that end in partition are no more or less likely to recur than those that do not.[13] Furthermore, Sambanis also posits that while partition could make conflict less likely within states, it may increase the prevalence of conflict across states—a prediction consistent with research on rivalries. Even on this last point, Sambanis hedges slightly; there are conditions under which intracommunal violence may *increase* after partition—most notably when more people are killed or displaced, when the war did not end with a negotiated treaty, and when the partitioned society contains greater ethnic diversity. These findings cumulatively imply that the security dilemma can remain even after partition occurs. It is, therefore, not at all theoretically or empirically clear that partition solves the ethnic security dilemma or stops violence within or across territorial units controlled by different ethnic groups.[14]

Second, *what* groups fight about (i.e., the issues) may matter more than the background condition under which they fight (i.e., a security dilemma or fear). Scholars have dedicated the last two decades to understanding how actors handle disputes over different issues.[15] Importantly, their main finding may also apply here; much as territorial disputes between states seem to be handled more violently than nonterritorial disputes, territorial disputes may fuel ethnic conflict as well. Horowitz and Weisiger maintain that ethnic conflicts are not only about fear but also about who should exercise sovereignty over particular parcels of land.[16] These disagreements cannot be solved by partition because they either fail to address the underlying, overlapping territorial claims of competing groups or require people to move from land they claim.

Finally, much depends on how leaders actually execute the partition. Ireland was partitioned in 1922 with the creation of the Irish Free State. This created a formal international border between the Irish and British states (although one that Ireland failed to fully recognize, thus making it extremely porous). This division also isolated the two communities in Northern Ireland, empowering one at the expense of the other. Although the institutionalization of inequality remains a common outcome of partition when ethnic groups are not completely separated from one another (e.g., Rwanda), this action sets a violent process in motion. The disempowered group eventually perceives that its rights cannot be protected under the existing institutional arrangement.[17] Violence then emerges when the disempowered group sees no nonviolent options available for the pursuit of its goals or the empowered group feels threatened enough by the disempowered group that it attempts repression to hold onto its advantaged position.

The type of inequality that resulted and continued between Catholics and Protestants after the 1922 partition has been identified as a significant source of civil conflict globally. Cederman, Wimmer, and Min, for example, find that when political inequality exists between large ethnic groups (i.e., exclusion from government), the likelihood of civil violence increases.[18] Furthermore, Cederman, Weidmann, and Gledistch conclude that civil wars occur more frequently between economically disparate groups (as opposed to economically similar ones).[19] Therefore, to the extent that certain states institutionalize political or economic inequality between ethnic groups after independence (a common occurrence, especially in postcolonial states, e.g., Rwanda), these states place themselves at greater risk of experiencing interethnic violence in the future. For this reason, Chapman and Roeder argue that partition will only succeed in preventing a recurrence of civil war when ethnic groups achieve independent statehood (e.g., Bosnia in 1995 or Kosovo in 1999).[20] This did not occur in Northern Ireland, undermining any successful reduction in violence that partition might have offered.

The violence associated with and advanced by each community in Northern Ireland also had an additional effect: it undermined the common conception of a state as a unit that monopolizes the use of violence within society. Many therefore viewed Northern Ireland as a failed "state" (or territory)—not just in the sense that groups within Northern Ireland used violence as a strategy to achieve their goals but also because, as Ó Dochartaigh details, the police within Northern Ireland often refused to contain that violence when it occurred in certain ethnic districts.[21] As violence occurred and the police sometimes seemed hesitant to address it, the security dilemma between groups increased, thereby encouraging and reinforcing the informal partition of ethnic communities *within* Northern Ireland. This separation certainly provided adequate protest space for disadvantaged communities, but it also made violence easier to organize and execute against the opposing community.[22] To manage the conflict effectively, the peace process therefore needed to accomplish two things. First, it had to garner Irish support for the formal international border with the United Kingdom and alter the basis upon which Ireland accepted that border—from a view that the border was a temporary, internal border with an enemy to the understanding that it was a finalized border between two nonhostile neighboring states.[23] According to both Kocs and Owsiak, acceptance of the interstate border should foster peace and better relations between Ireland and Britain.[24] It seems to have had such an effect; as an illustration, the British monarch visited Ireland in May 2011 for the first time in Ireland's independent history, suggesting that relations were beginning to normalize between the two states. Nevertheless, the Northern Ireland conflict contained not only an interstate component but an intrastate one as well. Therefore, the peace process also had to address borders between communities within Northern Ireland as well as the policing institutions that preserved order.[25] The Agreement addressed both the interstate and intrastate borders, and in this regard, it took an important step toward reducing violence.

Despite such successes, the preceding discussion suggests that partition holds limited promise for reducing violence between two ethnic communities in conflict. Thus, we must consider other ways of resolving ethnic security dilemmas to achieve effective conflict management. A review of scholarly work in this area yields alternative strategies that fall under two related suggestions: building inclusive institutions and reshaping ethnic identities and beliefs.

The (formal and informal) institutions created by the Agreement addressed three interrelated problems: inclusion, spoilers, and the implementation of peace agreements.[26] First, the new institutions of local government created by the Agreement are inclusive. Members of both the nationalist and unionist communities therefore feel that the system fairly represents their interests. This increases the likelihood that the institutions will succeed as each community recognizes the legitimacy of the institutions and participates freely in them. Furthermore, it allows the Agreement to escape the historic preoccupation with sovereignty (and by extension, partition as the only solution) by providing a system of institutions that encourage the two communities to govern together. This accomplishment is remarkable, especially considering how difficult it is for parties to ethnic conflict to trust one another with the levers of government.

Second, by building inclusive institutions, the peace process marginalized spoilers—that is, those who would undermine peace through violence because peace threatened them in some way. As Kydd and Walter argue, spoiler groups (usually extremists) succeed when they convince more moderate groups that a peace agreement cannot be self-enforced by the signing parties.[27] More specifically, parties to a peace agreement fear being exploited—that they will uphold the agreement while another party will violate it. Violence confirms these fears and serves as tangible evidence that at least one party to the agreement cannot credibly commit to peace. In this way, extremist violence exploits the mistrust that derives from the ethnic security dilemma and undermines the peace process.

Despite some similarities, not all spoiler groups are alike. Stedman reviews numerous conflicts and offers a typology of spoilers, along with the best policy for dealing with each type.[28] Two of his dimensions seem pertinent to our discussion of Northern Ireland: groups outside (versus inside) the peace process and those with total (versus limited) goals. Spoilers outside the process may be excluded as a result of their own or another's decision, but either way, these outsiders are more likely than insider spoilers to initiate violence. This makes negotiation with outside spoilers challenging because actors will be less willing to negotiate in the future with those committing violence. Similar negotiating difficulties arise with total spoilers, who adopt an all-or-nothing position that eschews compromise of any kind. Because the spoiler adopts an inflexible bargaining position, other actors may not perceive any bargaining space—that is, a (range of) possible agreement(s) that both sides might accept.[29] This may either prevent negotiations from beginning or, once started, from successfully achieving a negotiated settlement.

Northern Ireland arguably had both types of spoiler in the form of one party: Sinn Féin. Both historically and currently, Sinn Féin seeks a unified Ireland free of British rule. If there is no compromise to be had on this point, unionists see no room for negotiation. Furthermore, Sinn Féin remained outside mainstream politics. At first, this occurred by choice, as party members opposed participating in the Irish parliament. By 1994, Sinn Féin became more willing to participate in Irish institutions. Yet other parties (notably Britain) were excluding it from the peace process because many officials believed Sinn Féin to be connected to the Provisional Irish Republican Army (IRA), and the IRA had committed and continued to commit violence as a means of achieving a unified Ireland. Because some groups did not want to negotiate with those employing violence, Sinn Féin was often excluded from talks. In short, Sinn Féin could be labeled both a total and outside spoiler.[30]

Interestingly, the peace process handled Sinn Féin as Stedman recommends. The all-party talks proceeded without Sinn Féin, and officials made it clear both that violence would not stop negotiations and that Sinn Féin might be admitted to talks when the IRA violence ceased.[31] This policy accomplished three things. First, it pressured Sinn Féin to control the violence (or distance itself from it), lest an agreement be reached without their input. Second, it pulled Sinn Féin into the process, ending their status as "outsider" and making it more challenging for them to endorse violence to undermine negotiations, especially if they believed negotiations offered a better policy outcome than any alternative.[32] Finally, it forced Sinn Féin to accept a more moderate outcome than the total one it sought (e.g., on decommissioning of the IRA)—as long as no alternative appeared to advance them closer to their ideal policy outcome. The peace process therefore handled spoilers in a productive way by removing the belief that violence could halt or stall negotiations and allowing spoilers to pursue their policy outcomes within the confines of the process.

Finally, the peace process effectively leveraged the international (British-Irish) component of the conflict as a means of supporting institutions and achieving a successful outcome to the domestic, ethnic (unionist-nationalist) component. As noted above, groups plagued by ethnic conflict may have difficulty convincing adversaries that they are truly committed to peace. This "commitment problem" can hinder progress in negotiations. It can also, however, be overcome.

Walter argues that involving a strong, invested, third party to enforce the peace agreement offers the best mechanism for surmounting the commitment problem in the short term.[33] She finds that parties to civil war *always* failed to reach a negotiated agreement *unless* a third party stepped in to guarantee the safety of the adversaries while institutions formed and strengthened. This finding accords well with other research on peacebuilding. Krasner, for example, maintains that those embroiled in civil conflict worry extensively about sovereignty but often lack the resources to exercise it.[34] He argues that a third-party actor should share sovereignty with former belligerents until they can manage on their own. Similarly, Doyle and Sambanis propose that successful peacebuilding depends on the intersection of reduced hostility, local resources, and international resources. In this model, greater hostility demands greater resources, and local and international resources can substitute for one another (so that, for example, a society with greater local resources requires fewer international resources). The consensus therefore seems to be that third parties have a prominent role to play in achieving a durable peace.

To be sure, third parties played such a role in the Northern Ireland peace process. The United States, for example, mediated the conflict—at times both empowering certain leaders (e.g., Gerry Adams) and restraining others (e.g., the British).[35] Furthermore, on the issue of decommissioning paramilitary groups, the British and Irish established the Independent International Commission on Decommissioning in 1997.[36] This group, comprised of representatives from Canada, Finland, and the United States, served a critical purpose: removing violence as a possible policy tool of extremist groups by overseeing the confiscation of their weapons. Because of the ethnic security dilemma noted earlier, paramilitary groups hesitated to lay down their weapons without achieving security guarantees; other groups hesitated to negotiate with paramilitary groups (or their political counterparts) without decommissioning. Third parties (to the ethnic component of the conflict) provided a way to overcome this commitment problem, much as Walter and others would suggest. The strong capacity of the British state, for example, allowed it to help implement the negotiated settlement for Northern Ireland. Thus, British resources, in effect, substituted for local resources (much as Doyle and Sambanis suggest). Having a strong state capacity to implement a peace settlement is a necessary (but not always sufficient) condition for successful implementation of peace agreements.[37] The peace process would not have succeeded without a strong state capacity to support it, and the British provided this capacity.

Furthermore, the British made an important substantive concession, which allowed the peace process to proceed: they allowed Sinn Féin to participate in all-party talks. Sinn Féin's political goals include(d) removing all British rule from the Irish island. Toward that end, the IRA engaged the unionists and British in what might be called a war of attrition. Foreign support of the IRA and the perception that the British were an occupying power fueled this war of attrition and prevented Britain from ending it decisively.[38] This placed Britain in a difficult position; it wanted to end the violence but could not easily achieve that end militarily. Furthermore, it refused to negotiate with Sinn Féin in the midst of IRA violence.

To escape this policy dilemma, the British eventually conceded. They permitted Sinn Féin to enter the all-party talks provided that the IRA maintained a cease-fire. This allowed the British to use the peace process as a means of conciliating extremists—a policy recommended by Kydd and Walter for dealing with extremist actors in civil conflict—without conceding sovereignty or core beliefs like majority consent.[39] As noted earlier, it also undermined Sinn Féin's position as an outsider/total spoiler, thereby reducing the prospect for violence in the future.

As a cumulative result of the successes noted above, the Northern Irish case may appear to defy the general argument that weak states (rather than ethnic divisions) create the conditions for civil violence.[40] Institutions existed and functioned at various times in Northern Ireland's history, and the United Kingdom (a strong state) exerted sovereignty over the territory. This would suggest that Northern Ireland could not be a "weak state" in the traditional sense. Nonetheless, although Northern Ireland might be perceived as a long-standing part of the United Kingdom, the treaty that initially separated the North from the South in Ireland may not have been as stable as many had presumed. Nationalist and republican opposition to the Northern governing institutions increased in the 1960s, and the Stormont local government had increasing problems governing. After the collapse of Stormont, Britain ruled directly (in the period of the Troubles). All of these facts point toward failed institutions—a symptom of weak states.

Furthermore, since the signing of the Agreement in 1998, institutions seem to have strengthened. Almost everyone in Northern Ireland now believes that political differences can be resolved through the institutions that exist. This shifting societal belief fundamentally undermined the claims of legitimacy for paramilitary activities and altered the way violence is perceived by the public and political elites in Northern Ireland. The evidence therefore seems to suggest that the conflict resulted from weak institutions. To the extent that the Agreement addressed these institutions, it should have corrected this deficiency, thereby preventing a relapse into conflict.[41]

This review of Northern Ireland's institutional history, however, points toward a second problem that remains unaddressed: conflicting ethnic identities. The institutions created by the Agreement have had difficulty transcending the sectarian divide that is the underlying source of political conflict.[42] Of course, we might expect this to some degree. Ethnic (i.e., identity-based) conflicts are difficult to resolve.[43] Furthermore, the problems associated with conflicting identities in multiethnic states often endure—even in long-established democracies (and especially among minority populations).[44] This suggests that even if the power-sharing institutions at Stormont functioned effectively (that is, Northern Ireland surmounted the "weak state" problem), conflict—especially, ethnic conflict—might still persist.[45]

Not only does ethnic conflict persist in the wake of the Agreement but it has been *institutionalized* as well. Such a position is supported by Wilson, who argues that the existing power-sharing arrangement in Northern Ireland created institutions that are not flexible enough to allow the sectarian divide to diminish.[46] By compelling those elected to identify with a sectarian group and by requiring all parties to be part of a grand coalition government, the political process ensures that differing identities persist. If these identities conflict on fundamental issues, then the more normal or typical processes of political negotiation and compromise are prevented. Furthermore, the underlying source of conflict—incompatible ethnic identities—remains unaddressed, leaving the conflict unresolved.

Because the institutions envisaged by the Agreement are up and working, politicians may become complacent regarding the much slower pace of change and the hardening of sectarian differences in Northern Ireland.[47] A failure to address these differences represents an enormous obstacle to the long-term goal of resolving the underlying conflict. So long as these differences exist, the ethnic security dilemma lurks below the surface of society, preventing a complete normalization of everyday life. What is needed to overcome this dilemma in Northern Ireland is therefore a transformation of identities.

Ethnic identities and beliefs are social constructions; as such, they are subject to change. Fearon and Laitin, for example, claim that identities (including their rules for membership and content—i.e., beliefs, values, and obligations) rely on construction by either societal discourse or individual-led social movements.[48] To the extent that individuals or discourse created identity, individuals or discourse can change it. Yet this does not imply that reshaping identities and their content happens easily. Chandra argues that ethnic identities resist change in the short term— although other attributes (e.g., obligations or lower-level beliefs) may not display such "stickiness."[49] To be sure, Chandra takes a much more restrictive view of ethnicity than Fearon and Laitin; she argues that ethnicity includes only descent-based attributes. This conceptualization of ethnic identities, and its insights into changing identities over time, yields two conclusions. First, it would be difficult to change the *descent-based* attributes of conflicting communities—in this case, religion itself—at least in the immediate future. Fearon and Laitin may agree with this statement, as descent-based characteristics (i.e., race, religion, or gender) should be more difficult to alter than cultural scripts that describe appropriate actions, obligations, and relationships with others in society. Second, we may be able to change non-descent-based characteristics, particularly those that would link Catholic identity in Ireland with the occupation of the entire island.

Consistent with the works noted above, Goddard claims that the conception that the territory of Ireland is indivisible is a social construction malleable to change.[50] In fact, the historical record supports her claim. Envisioning the island as a political whole, for example, did not rest on a single governing set of institutions that predated British rule but rather on a *postcolonial* conceptualization of Ireland as a whole unit previously conquered by Britain. Similarly, Lerner argues that the Irish constitution contains "symbolic ambivalence"—or a number of contradictions regarding how to cope with competing nationalist and unionist demands.[51] From Lerner's perspective, Ireland balanced these competing demands by placing both within the constitution, thereby postponing final decisions and allowing the contradictory positions to evolve (to perhaps make a final decision easier at a future date). This allowed Irish government to live with the partition of the island while also preserving historic territorial claims to sovereignty over the counties in Northern Ireland. It also, however, allowed those claims to decline in salience over time. By the time those in the Irish Republic had their independence from Britain for ninety years, the concern in Ireland over the partition of the island had faded as many had become more worried about the potential problem of violence spilling over into their territory than the plight of their nationalist brethren in the North.

In addition to reduced salience, a second mechanism that worked to mitigate Irish claims to the whole of Ireland involved the increasingly institutionalized norm of territorial integrity—the idea that force could not be used to alter international boundaries. Zacher traces the evolution of this norm between the seventeenth and twentieth centuries, noting that it has become widely accepted since World War II.[52] In the process, he demonstrates that the norm affected interstate conflict behavior throughout the world, and Northern Ireland serves as no exception. The territorial integrity norm reinforced the perception that violence will not and should not alter the political division of Ireland. The parties therefore eventually understood that negotiations offered the only acceptable mechanism by which the territorial conflict might be addressed.

The territorial integrity norm has become increasingly relevant in Northern Ireland since the signing of the Agreement, and the lack of mass support for violence has strengthened the capacity of political elites in Northern Ireland to govern. Nonetheless, a number of ethnic identity issues remain as obstacles to conflict management. The Agreement devised a governing system based on sectarian self-identification of elites, which therefore reinforced historic communal differences as opposed to providing an incentive to transcend them. As a result, these communal differences persist, causing prolonged delays in implementing the Agreement, difficulty in establishing trust across the communities, and too little peace at the grassroots. Although a failure to build trust most directly affects conflict resolution (as we have defined it earlier), it necessarily undermines conflict management efforts as well. According to Gormley-Heenan, a lack of trust creates immediate challenges for securing a durable peace—such as an inability to decommission paramilitary weapons completely, to reform police organizations and policies, and to institutionalize the governing arrangements of the Agreement fully.[53] Without a secure, nonviolent environment, the ethnic security dilemma outlined earlier persists, thereby lowering the likelihood that all sides will participate whole-heartedly in democratic institutions. And if, as Zürcher argues, elites remain skeptical of democratic institutions (let alone the general population), the prospect declines that a stable democracy will emerge from a society transitioning out of conflict.[54] In other words, a lack of trust prevents the creation of a secure environment, which can then cause actors to question the value of democratic institutions, even if actors previously agreed to these institutions and have the resources necessary for them to succeed.

The preceding discussion suggests that trust-building lies at the heart of effective conflict management and resolution. We contend that this is best done through strengthening civil society and working toward reconciliation.[55] Although we detail these propositions in the section that follows, we hasten to note three points here. First, both propositions require the people of Northern Ireland to redefine their identity—as Hancock (in chapter 3) and Wiedenhoft Murphy and Peden (in chapter 4) argue.[56] Spurk, for example, builds an integrated definition of civil society that is composed of seven functions, which include socialization (i.e., fostering tolerance, trust, and compromise), building community (i.e., bridging societal divides), and protecting individuals.[57] Identities that hinder groups within society from living peacefully or interacting easily and openly with one another cannot accomplish these tasks. Similarly, reconciliation often involves facing past behaviors and attitudes and writing a mutual history for the conflict. Identities that prevent a group from admitting the possibility of a shared interpretation of history or transcending the view that the group exclusively played the role of victim in the conflict (and, therefore, is "less responsible" for atrocities) will make reconciliation nearly impossible.

Second, it is only through strengthening civil society and achieving reconciliation that identities can slowly evolve over time.[58] Although paramilitaries and militias need to be disarmed after conflict, civilians are also often both perpetrators and victims of violence, and civilians therefore need to reconcile with their civilian adversaries.[59] Failure to do so carries grave consequences for positive peace, for it causes social tension, anxiety, fear, and unremitted grief—and as a result, the ethnic security dilemma— to persist. And when this dilemma persists, reconciliation eludes society. Therefore, although reconceptualizing sovereignty and creating innovative means of incorporating minorities have helped to promote solutions in ethnonational conflicts like the one in Northern Ireland, the solution for a *durable* peace must include efforts at bolstering civil society and reconciliation between the divided communities.

Finally, although civil society and reconciliation can be aided by external economic assistance as is suggested in chapter 8, ultimately the ethnic (or communal) groups in the conflict-torn society must come to their *own* internal settlement. This settlement, however, cannot be imposed from the leadership of an ethnic group upon its constituency; a just and lasting peace requires not just pacts or secret agreements by political elites but rather a true reconciliation between the formerly adversarial communities. Peace, in other words, requires a redress of the fundamental conflict that exists among groups (and individuals) within society.[60] One can therefore best explain the frustration and difficulty with implementing the Agreement by noting the failure of the peace process to focus on reconciliation at the grassroots level and the resultant lack of a vibrant civil society that minimizes or overcomes historic sectarian divisions. Thus, we believe that it is only by addressing civil society and reconciliation at the grassroots level that the Agreement can deliver what it promised: a durable peace.

The Need for Civil Society to Bridge the Sectarian Divide

Divided societies (like Northern Ireland) often encounter extreme difficulty when trying to overcome historic sectarianism. This results from two interrelated processes. On the one hand, ethnic groups feel threatened by one another. We referred to this earlier as the ethnic security dilemma. Faced with such a dilemma, Fearon and Laitin explain how interethnic cooperation can emerge by giving self-interested, rational individuals an incentive to cooperate.[61] They argue that either individuals need to believe that cooperation offers more benefits than conflict *or* that groups must be willing to hold their own members accountable for not cooperating across ethnic lines. Both strategies depend on the need for interethnic trust when a society transitions out of conflict. For individuals to believe that cooperation offers more benefits than conflict, they must trust that the other side will cooperate and that this cooperation will continue into the future.[62] Similarly, when a group agrees to self-regulate its members and hold them accountable for noncooperative behaviors, the other group must trust that this policing takes place, especially if it has less information about the other group's intracommunal proceedings. Cooperation therefore demands interethnic trust.

On the other hand, ethnic identities often contain narratives that reinforce negative stereotypes, thereby preventing trust from forming.[63] As Fearon and Laitin argue, an ethnic group's definition requires an understanding of both the rules of membership (i.e., who is or is not a member) and what it means to be a member (i.e., beliefs, values, physical attributes, etc.).[64] Hale maintains that groups then use such definitions as a heuristic to make sense of social interactions quickly within a complex, uncertain world.[65] This, however, creates two problems for societies plagued by sectarianism. First, ethnic groups often define themselves (at least partially) in contrast to another group (e.g., race, religion, gender), perpetuating an "us" and a "them." This may not be dangerous in and of itself, provided that ethnic violence does not break out; when it does, a second problem emerges. If threats coincide with ethnic identities, then the identities incorporate narratives that perceive the other group(s) as a threat and therefore marginalize the other group(s). Such a move allows ethnic identity to continue serving as a heuristic device for making sense of social interactions.

At first glance, these narratives might seem benign. One might argue that the narratives, or at least their poignancy, will change when conflict ends. Although we agree with this position, it need not imply that the adjustment will be quick or easy. Chandra, for example, notes that ethnic identities strongly resist amendment in the short term.[66] Furthermore, such changes require social coordination. Individual citizens, therefore, cannot change these narratives alone; they also cannot escape classification within certain ethnic categories. For example, even if an individual chooses not to identify with the group into which they were born, they may continue to be labeled or identified as such by members of the other community. This leads to perpetuating identities that contain conflict-enhancing narratives, which then create a continuing dynamic of conflict that is difficult to escape.

Such a process describes events in Northern Ireland well. Historically, nationalists saw efforts at improving community relations as an attempt to force them into a majority unionist culture. Meanwhile, unionists perceived these same efforts as a waste of resources that should be spent on finding and prosecuting terrorists.[67] In other words, each community viewed the betterment of intercommunal relations as a mechanism by which the opposing group sought to take advantage of it (either politically or violently).

The Agreement attempted to break this historical narrative by re-envisioning a Northern Ireland that belonged to both communities through the context of a devolved local government. As Nimmi maintains, encouraging various ethnic groups to participate jointly in governing a contested territory can overcome the historic problem that sovereignty poses for territories like Northern Ireland; it ensures that each group assumes that its beliefs, values, and security are protected by the state.[68] The effective implementation of complex and multilevel agreements (such as the Agreement) cannot be achieved by political elites in a democratic setting without mass-based support.[69] As an illustration, the Northern Ireland government published *A Shared Future* in 2005—a policy document that envisions a more inclusive, fair, and equitable society and proposes a number of strategies to reach that objective. Unfortunately, as Hughes notes, this document—created by political elites—did not offer an effective means of operationalizing or implementing this vision and may have failed to fully confront the role inequality plays in undermining the creation of a shared society.[70] A disconnect therefore existed within the document between elite policy making and the relevance and implementation of that policy within society.

In the end, a just and lasting peace in Northern Ireland requires not just agreements by political leaders but active involvement within and between the communities. This, in turn, requires two things. First, policies must convince the populace that better intercommunal relations offer them greater promise than the status quo. Although simple, this point often seems missed. For example, elites, not groups in civil society, drove the peace process and the implementation of the Agreement.[71] This is not necessarily bad, but the implementation of the Agreement seemed to offer little benefit to citizens' daily lives. For example, the Agreement did not alter or dramatically mitigate the underlying dynamics inherent in the conflict; interactions within civil society remained sectarian and potentially violent.[72] Moreover, the Agreement failed to fundamentally redefine the relationship between civil society and political institutions. Citizens did not have the opportunity to envision a future based on intercommunal cooperation—let alone discuss how a different way of being together could provide more benefits to them than the status quo.

Second, encouraging intercommunal cooperation requires trust, a characteristic lacking in societies emerging from ethnic conflict. Walter best explains why: she argues that civil wars often continue because opponents cannot credibly commit to fulfilling the agreements they sign.[73] More specifically, disputants are often asked to disarm, demobilize, and reintegrate themselves into society. Once they do this, however, they lose bargaining leverage and protection. If they are a minority group, they also fear retaliation by the majority through the legitimate political structures that exist. The only way to escape this commitment problem is through creating mechanisms for ongoing engagement, fostering legitimacy for minority groups (power sharing), and supporting reintegration efforts.

The persistence of ethnic cleavages undermines the development and functioning of civil society, but the meaning of this concept remains somewhat amorphous. Spurk, for example, claims that no generally accepted definition of civil society exists.[74] Nonetheless, he offers us hints of its characteristics and activities. Civil society lies at the intersection of the political, economic, and private spheres—though it is none of these things. It works with political parties and economic associations, but is itself equated with neither. Rather, civil society entails voluntary, public action among autonomously organized groups that act on behalf of the public (as opposed to private) interest. They seek the betterment of society through protecting individuals, minorities, and property; developing tolerance and trust; dissolving sectarianism; serving as an intermediary between individuals and the state; and ensuring accountability of government. Such characteristics and actions place civil society close to the grassroots level of society (despite the fact that it is a social, organized entity that permeates society).

To the extent that civil society attempts, *inter alia*, to overcome sectarian divisions, the endurance of these divisions demonstrates either a failure or weakness of civil society. If civil society remains weakened by ethnic division, we should also expect it to be less capable of performing its other tasks. Importantly, many of these tasks support the development of democratic institutions, so a weak civil society can undermine democracy directly. This connection between civil society and democracy can be inferred from many of the aforementioned tasks of civil society—for example, protecting rights and property or ensuring government accountability. Newton, however, offers a more direct link, arguing that effective civil society helps produce and support democratic states. In fact, he maintains that "poorly developed civil societies are unlikely to sustain developed democracies."[75] For this reason, even those that study democratic deficits in global governance institutions (such as Scholte) recommend developing (global) civil society (among other things) to reduce those deficits.[76] Theoretical arguments therefore confirm the insight derived from an examination of civil society's definition: democracy requires the development of civil society.

Thus, ethnic and sectarian divisions like those found in Northern Ireland are a long-term threat to liberal democracy.[77] They prevent trust from forming between different groups in society, which, in turn, impedes the consolidation of democracy (especially through the mechanism of civil society). In divided societies like Northern Ireland, trust means not only that individuals are willing to interact with members of the other community but that they are also willing to allow the other community to share in governance and societal institutions without fear of being harmed. As Freitag and Traunmüller demonstrate, this requires a pattern of positive interactions among the groups that confirms each side is committed to continued cooperation.[78] It is this pattern and expectation of reciprocal cooperation that then contributes to the social capital envisioned by Herreros and, by definition, moves groups out of the social trap described by Rothstein.[79] In short, societal trust exists when individuals expect that individuals of differing groups (many of which they have never met before) will cooperate with them even if they may never interact again in the future. Effective communication and empowerment also depend on trust, especially in states with long histories of identity-based conflict.[80] To the extent that society lacks trust, communication within institutions may therefore be incomplete or absent, and groups may feel that institutions do not afford them the opportunity to realize their goals. In mistrustful societies, democratic institutions may exist but do not function as they should.

The legacy of sectarianism in Northern Ireland makes the development of trust very difficult. Historic expectations of fear, suspicion, revenge, and recrimination are real for all sides of the conflict. Both republicans and loyalists feel victimized by the Troubles and their legacy.[81] Nevertheless, leaders built the Agreement on the expectation that enough cooperation across communities could develop the necessary trust to alter expectations about future cooperation. They hoped both that the Agreement might "unfreeze" long-held beliefs and attitudes (thereby stimulating a new culture of peace) and that emerging cooperation might create the expectation of future, reciprocal, cooperative interactions.[82]

Those who negotiated the Agreement recognized the importance of building trust as a means of consolidating and implementing the Agreement,[83] yet those who sold the agreement to the public in Northern Ireland, especially to the Protestant community, emphasized the *risk* of failure more than the *promise* of success.[84] Blair's effort to gain the support of Protestants to ratify (and thereby legitimize) the Agreement therefore led many Protestants to lose faith in the Agreement's ability to provide a framework for governing Northern Ireland effectively. Furthermore, Blair's failures to deliver on immediate decommissioning, to exclude Sinn Féin from the new governing institutions unless decommissioning had taken place, and not to allow prisoner releases without prior decommissioning created a sense of distrust regarding the implementation of the Agreement in the unionist community.

Thus, we have not witnessed the flowering of a civil society that transcends communal divisions; consequently, a greater sense of social trust across the communal divide remains lacking and undermines peace. While some individuals may have formed trusting relationships with those they both know and interact with frequently from the other community, this particularized trust does not translate into an overarching sense of trust for those of the other community—particularly those whom one has not met or interacts with rarely. It is this latter, generalized trust that the creation of social capital demands, as it creates the obligations of reciprocity that help bridge the communal divide and provide a sustainable peace.[85]

At this juncture, we have demonstrated three points. First, democratic institutions require a functioning civil society, which in turn depends upon societal trust. Second, Northern Ireland lacks this trust. Finally, absent such trust, it is difficult for Northern Ireland to surmount the ethnic security dilemma and commitment problems associated with ethnic conflicts. After such a glum assessment, one might ask: what is to be done?

First, those in Northern Ireland should refocus attention from institutions to civil society, from elites to the grassroots level. Although the Agreement creatively provided political institutions that allowed elites to share power, these institutions cannot promote peace at the grassroots level or at that of the level of a fully functional democracy while societal trust remains low. To fix societal trust, Northern Ireland must look outside of formal institutions. Peace processes need to create democratic political dynamics to implement agreements effectively. At a minimum, Reilly argues that peace agreements require the mass public to endorse them—if for no other reason than to give the new government, institutions, or arrangements legitimacy in the eyes of society and the world.[86] Beyond this requirement, peacebuilding researchers propose that local populations must be involved in the peace process and the subsequent new political institutions to make the peace process self-sustaining.[87] Successful peace processes promote grassroots efforts, and we propose that one of the most important of these efforts involves building and strengthening civil society.[88]

Second, Northern Ireland might foster civil society by finding and encouraging ways for the divided communities to interact, so as to create a united, ethnically mixed society. The public of Northern Ireland recognizes this need; in the 2010 Northern Ireland Life and Times Survey, for example, 88 percent of the public expressed the belief that mixing the two ethnic communities more would improve intercommunal relations.[89] Unfortunately, such mixing remains far from the norm. In Northern Ireland, associational life tends to reinforce existing community identities (i.e., bonding social capital) rather than link individuals from disparate religious communities (i.e., bridging social capital).[90] A strong and vibrant civil society of this type—built on sectarian divisions—thereby multiplies inequalities and tension within society by cementing or exacerbating differences.[91] These differences are then manifested politically, socially, and economically, which thereby often produces oppressive practices that go beyond physical violence to more insidious forms of emotional, cultural, spiritual, and economic harm. Such harms, in turn, spawn grievances that either remain unaddressed (creating latent conflict) or serve as a source of overt conflict.

Despite the potential for sectarian societies to reproduce and reinforce social cleavages, academic studies and survey data give us hope about the long-term prospects of Northern Ireland's overcoming this obstacle. First, academic researchers note moderation in many organizations' positions. Mac Ginty reviews the Orange Order—a grassroots, Protestant organization frequently involved in controversy and sectarian violence—and finds evidence that it has adjusted its position since the Agreement.[92] Some members of the Orange Order might even be said to have moderated their position on sectarianism, though this is not universally true of all members. Further evidence comes from the behavior of Northern Irish political parties. Tonge, for example, argues that there has been some moderation on the part of Sinn Féin; they have had to learn to work together with the

Democratic Unionist Party (DUP) and govern jointly in the Northern Ireland executive.[93] Similarly, we have witnessed a transformation of Ian Paisley and the DUP—from refusing to participate in the negotiations that produced the Agreement to agreeing to jointly rule in the Northern Ireland executive in May 2007.[94]

Furthermore, the most recent survey evidence indicates that relations between Catholics and Protestants have improved in the last five years even though important identity differences remain in Northern Ireland.[95] Significant minorities in both the Catholic and Protestant communities identify as Northern Irish, as opposed to either British or Irish. A larger percentage of these responses come from younger citizens (aged 18–24), which suggests a potential generational change on the horizon in the years to come. While 62 percent of survey respondents thought relations between Catholics and Protestants improved over the period 2005–10, only 3 percent said they worsened.[96] The majority of respondents (52 percent) thought intercommunal relations would continue improving over the period 2010–15; only 5 percent thought they would worsen.[97] Such statistics reveal a sense of optimism among residents of Northern Ireland.

Moreover, Northern Irish citizens also express a *desire* for mixed-ethnic communities. Although 83 percent said they would prefer to live in a mixed-religion neighborhood, only 12 percent wanted a religiously homogenous community.[98] Similarly, 94 percent of respondents preferred a mixed-religion workplace, and 70 percent preferred mixed-religion schools (compared with 3 percent and 24 percent that wanted religiously homogenous workplaces and schools, respectively).[99] Such responses are impressive given the ethnic violence of the past. They suggest that both communities would be *willing* to bridge the ethnic divisions within society if they knew how to do it.

Despite the preceding optimistic survey responses, we hasten to note that there is much work to be done. For example, 33 percent of survey respondents thought that intercommunal relations remained stagnant (neither improving nor worsening) during the period 2005–10; 41 percent expected such stagnation to persist for the period 2010–15.[100] These numbers reveal a sizable segment of the population that does not yet share in the optimistic belief that intercommunal relations are improving. Furthermore, a significant minority (24 percent) prefers religiously homogenous schools.[101] This position is more common among Catholics than Protestants (35 percent versus 21 percent). Finally, 61 percent of respondents said that all or most of their friends belong to the same religious group as they do, and most do not believe Northern Ireland has become a civic society where "all individuals are equal, where differences are resolved through dialogue, and where all people are treated impartially."[102] Thus, although Northern Ireland shows promise for overcoming sectarian divisions, it also demonstrates that much greater attention must be paid to the process of overcoming these divisions to achieve a strong, interethnic civil society.

Nonetheless, we do not wish to imply that Northern Ireland's civil society has been ignored entirely. Many organizations have been created over the past few decades to encourage peace and societal transformation at the grassroots level. Their level of effectiveness, however, remains negligible given the history of hostility and conflict between the Catholic and Protestant communities. Even church leaders and church-based groups, which we might expect to succeed at overcoming religious sectarianism, have been relatively ineffective at building bridges between the communities. Ganiel and Dixon suggest that this failure stems, in part, from an inability of religious groups to fully appreciate how religious identity reinforces sectarianism within the community.[103]

Some have claimed that the peace process has succeeded despite the lack of a civil society and social capital.[104] The peace process and the Agreement have reduced the level of violence in Northern Ireland and created an opening for civil society to develop. Nevertheless, dissident republicans still threaten the peace, if only with a minor (but continuing) presence. The decommissioning process and political mainstreaming of Sinn Féin has left a political vacuum through which fringe republican groups can potentially wreak havoc with the peace process. This is why it is so important that groups and organizations bridge the sectarian divide to help foster a civil society in Northern Ireland. Only a strong civil society— expectations of reciprocal cooperation—can prevent a return to violence in the face of dissident attempts to undermine the Agreement.

Moreover, only a strong civil society can ensure that the institutions created by the Agreement succeed in the long term, for it would have an emancipative effect on the role of the citizen in the political process. Liberal theorists suggest that the public comes to see their role as challenging existing elites rather than following the elites' lead.[105] In the Northern Irish context, this means that a strong civil society would give politicians an incentive to bargain and compromise with leaders from the other community rather than refuse concessions because of expectations that such concessions would convey a message of weakness or "selling out" their constituent community. Such political cooperation helps young institutions survive democratic transitions and fosters public trust in those institutions. Thus, without a strong, interethnic civil society, the long-term prospects for democracy in Northern Ireland remain bleak as commitment problems and security dilemmas persist.

Uncovering Truth as a Means of Reconciliation

Given the importance of trust, one might reasonably ask: how can trust be built? One critical avenue by which interethnic trust might emerge involves reconciliation. The complex goal of reconciliation lies, according to Lederach, at the intersection of truth, justice, mercy, and peace.[106] It seeks to manage the relational component of conflict—how members of society interacted with each other previously and how they expect to interact in the future. It also aims to address the emotional component of conflict by dealing with the experiences of citizens as both perpetrators and victims of violence. As Kaufmann notes, "violent conflict is a relationship between societies, not just leaders or armies, and that conflict resolution means remaking that relationship into a peaceful and constructive (though certainly not conflict-free) one."[107] Thus, reconciliation must involve a grassroots, societal effort to confront the events of conflict so that society might move past them. This, in turn, requires identity change, as victims and perpetrators of violence recast their future roles in society anew.[108]

Proponents of societal reconciliation regularly point to the South African Truth and Reconciliation Commission as evidence of their potential merits. In their perfect form, such tribunals investigate human rights abuses during a particular period of time (often within a given conflict).[109] These investigations frequently entail public hearings that bring together victims and perpetrators of violence. Balancing amnesty with accountability, the hearings attempt to uncover the truth of what happened during the conflict.[110] In the case of South Africa, for example, the commission possessed the power to grant amnesty for crimes committed during the conflict, and perpetrators often received this amnesty in exchange for disclosing the full details of their crimes. The hope was that perpetrators would provide victims with details that the latter needed to experience grief and closure (e.g., what happened to loved ones) while victims would offer forgiveness to those that participated in the violence. In other words, reconciliation helps both to empower victims and to restore the moral image of the perpetrators, thereby transforming society into a place where those of different backgrounds work cooperatively together.[111]

As the preceding discussion highlights, truth plays a critical function in reconciliation processes. It is therefore concerned with questions like: Who (i.e., which individuals) participated (i.e., overtly or covertly, intentionally or unintentionally) in violence and oppression? What actually happened (i.e., facts) during the conflict? How did events during the conflict cause harm to people within each community? In what way were they harmed? Should perpetrators be brought to justice, and if so, which ones?

Answering such questions is not an easy task for two reasons. First, the process can be lengthy. As is the reality in many long-standing conflicts, both sides played the roles of victim and perpetrator. Each side involved in the conflict therefore naturally needs an opportunity to share the myriad ways that they have been victimized as well as listen to the ways that the other side feels victimized. Collecting these histories and perspectives requires an investment of time. Second, accounts will certainly conflict. Each person involved will have his or her own story about what actually occurred. Furthermore, each person may feel strongly that they are telling the truth, even when accounts conflict. These accounts, though crucial for finding the truth, may need to be delicately reconciled—so that victims feel heard and the process generates a collective truth rather than a series of disparate perspectives about what happened.

Nonetheless, personal healing and truth alone cannot restore society. Reconciliation also requires fundamental political and economic reforms. Such a position can be derived from our earlier discussion of how sectarian divides can be reinforced within society and how these divides can, in turn, seep into political, economic, and social structures to promulgate inequality. These inequalities cause grievances to fester. When such inequalities also fall along identity cleavages, the identity conflict continues, as groups associate their political, economic, and social conflicts with ethnic divisions. Therefore, to change the interethnic relationships in society, all forms of oppression must be acknowledged (along with the effects that this oppression has had on continually dividing society) and corrected. Only then can those within formerly divided societies see that injustices will not carry forward, thereby creating the promise of interacting differently with one another in the future.

Armed with this conceptualization of reconciliation, what can be said of reconciliation in Northern Ireland? At a basic level, we can say that reconciliation in Northern Ireland is difficult to achieve (and has sometimes deliberately been postponed) for three reasons. First, as occurs after any ethnic conflict, it can be challenging to identify "victims." Both communities played victim and perpetrator at one point or another, which creates confusion about who the true victims might be. This definitional challenge can get more difficult when victims demand justice.[112] As Cochrane notes, postwar justice can fall into two camps: retributive (punishing perpetrators of crimes) and restorative (repairing relationships). Many believe that restorative justice first requires retributive justice—that forgiveness only comes when society holds perpetrators accountable for their actions. Yet, when many individuals played the role of perpetrator, it may not be possible to achieve retributive justice. It may take time to convince victims to forego it.

Second, no leader in Northern Ireland championed a reconciliation process like that found in South Africa. Based on the perceived success of the South African Truth and Reconciliation Commission, many expected a similar truth and fact-finding commission to be part of the peace process in Northern Ireland.[113] Guelke argues that comparing Northern Ireland to South Africa is inappropriate because South Africa achieved a great deal of reconciliation prior to the Truth Commission. No one in Northern Ireland played a conciliatory role similar to Mandela, making Northern Ireland unready for a Truth Commission.[114]

Third, Northern Ireland prioritized the Agreement (and its negotiations) over reconciliation. For example, Northern Ireland decided to include organizations previously involved in (or associated with) sectarian violence in the peace process. This created an inclusive agreement, but it also implicitly rewarded violence. Furthermore, leaders established a one-person Victims Commission in 1997–98, but this person, Kenneth Bloomfield, operated within the context of the Agreement. Some unionists therefore did not believe in or participate in the commission, just as they did not participate in the negotiations that produced the Agreement.[115] Without full societal participation, the commission in no way replicated the more thorough and systematic reconciliation efforts found in other conflicts. It is therefore no surprise that Wilson, for example, notes that the peace process may have produced an Agreement at the expense of reconciliation.[116]

Despite such a negative interpretation, rational reasons to postpone reconciliation may exist. McGrattan, for example, argues that the pursuit of truth in Northern Ireland may prompt ethnic competitions for the truth rather than healing. In other words, trying to discover the identity of perpetrators associated with the Troubles may lead to further interethnic resentment.[117] Whether this counterfactual would play out were reconciliation to be attempted remains uncertain. We *do* know that postponing reconciliation has had effects on the development of civil society. The fact that those responsible for the violence and deaths committed during the Troubles have never been identified and brought to justice means that many remain suspicious of leaders and members of the other community who they associate with those events. Moreover, many (especially in the unionist community) also believe either that they are *only* victims or that the claim that they are blameless cannot be challenged in the absence of a truth recovery process.[118] Fear and mistrust therefore persist and may continue to do so, for it seems highly unlikely that perpetrators will easily acquiesce to a truth and reconciliation process that threatens their claims as pure victims.

Evidence of this mistrust can be found in a second attempt at a truth commission, which occurred in the summer of 2010. The Saville Report, released at that time, provided a lengthy and exhaustive review of the British government's and military's actions on Bloody Sunday. The report condemned the excessive use of force and unjustified killings on the part of the British Army. Nonetheless, some loyalists claimed that the Saville Report amounted to a one-sided Truth Commission, and they demanded further investigation into killings by republicans. In other words, continued mistrust prevented various actors from acknowledging the confessed wrongs of other parties, thereby beginning the process of forgiveness. Thus, although there seems to be a general recognition of the need for those guilty of crimes during the Troubles to be identified and brought to justice, many clearly remain skeptical that "all" of the truth would ever be gained.[119] Such doubts, symptomatic of failed reconciliation, thereby undermine future reconciliation efforts.

Besides perpetuating mistrust, a lack of reconciliation threatens the implementation of the Agreement as well.[120] The Agreement recognized the rights of victims as well as the need for all to be included in the political process. It also built institutions that demand acknowledging (if not addressing) the history of wrongs and injustices. The people of Northern Ireland have failed to confront the fullness of their history—the good and the bad. Absent such a confrontation of history, the Agreement creates a truce that contains the historical antagonism without transforming the communal divide.[121] It also gives fuel to spoiler groups who seek to undermine the process, as well as efforts at reconciliation, and can use mistrust and division to achieve this goal.[122] It is therefore crucial for all citizens of Northern Ireland to reconcile and to define and create a shared vision for the future.

Such a prescription is easy to make, but it begs the question: how does Northern Ireland reconcile to create a shared vision? Lederach's integrated framework for building sustainable peace offers a clue.[123] This framework contains two dimensions: a level of response and a time frame of activity. The level of response varies along a continuum from the issue to the system—that is, a range from addressing the specific issue that produced conflict to addressing the structures that make conflict (over any issue) more likely. Similarly, the time frame varies along a continuum from crisis intervention (i.e., the immediate conflict or violence) to the desired future. To get to a shared vision of the future, Lederach's framework proposes that disputants must shift their attention. Rather than focus on immediate issues and violence (i.e., conflict management), they must expand their time horizon as well as where they look for the causes of conflict. By examining relationships (i.e., questions of equality, oppression, and social justice) and the structures that enforce those relationships, disputants will begin to address the root causes of conflict, not just the symptoms (such as violence). Furthermore, by expanding their time horizon, they can begin to confront questions regarding how to design social change and build a desired, shared future. These dual shifts—from issues to relationships/structure and the short term to the mid and long term—allow societies to pursue true conflict resolution.

Lederach's framework produces two recommendations for Northern Ireland. First, a truth commission of some kind is needed. As Barash and Webel mention, truth commissions offer a unique benefit. As a result of constructing a shared, societal truth during their proceedings, these commissions may prevent historical revisionism.[124] They therefore take fuel away from spoilers who would undermine the peace process by interpreting history through an ethnic lens.

Of course, this recommendation comes with two caveats. First, any Northern Ireland commission need not follow the exact model used in South Africa, or anywhere else for that matter. After all, Northern Ireland has a unique context, and much of the criticism of using truth commissions in Northern Ireland stems from the belief that the South African model may not work there. The truth commissions in Peru, Rwanda, Argentina, El Salvador, and other states were designed to engage appropriately with the issues unique to those states' respective conflicts. In Northern Ireland the failure to confront the truth of the Troubles contributes to fear and mistrust, thus feeding the cycle of the ethnic security dilemma. A societal truth-seeking process must therefore be created.

Second, truth commissions are not a panacea. It would therefore be a mistake to place too much emphasis on the lack of a truth commission in Northern Ireland. Even were an effective one to exist, a quick and easy transformation of long-held beliefs and attitudes does not follow. Reconciliation is a long, incremental, arduous process; in Northern Ireland, it must uncover the harms that precipitated the Troubles and escalated the violence. Such a process demands encounters between unionists and nationalists in which each side can talk honestly and openly. Creating that environment will take time, and conducting the hearings will demand even more. Regardless, we believe the commitment might be beneficial to those who desire a more secure Northern Ireland.

The second recommendation derived from Lederach's model is to build on those efforts that are moving in the right direction. Earlier, we presented survey data that suggested the majority in Northern Ireland desired mixed-religion communities, schools, and work places. Survey respondents also remained hopeful that relations would improve in the future. These survey data might offer clues about where to focus further efforts. For example, 61 percent of Catholics think that intercommunal relations will improve over the period 2010–15.[125] In contrast, only 44 percent of Protestants think this, with more Protestants (49 percent) asserting that relations will remain "about the same." Efforts might therefore focus on this skepticism. Similarly, optimism varies by age group, with the young (18–34) and the old (55+) showing slightly less optimism than the middle-aged groups (35–54). Such surveys therefore reveal both who the most optimistic proponents of reconciliation might be as well as who might need more convincing before reconciliation can proceed.

A second illustration of how to do this comes from existing reintegration efforts. McEvoy and Shirlow detail how former political prisoners, many of whom were released as part of the Agreement, have played constructive roles in their communities.[126] These ex-prisoners encourage decommissioning and demobilization and dissuade younger generations from using violence. Furthermore, McEvoy and Shirlow show these ex-prisoners have engaged in a type of "truth commission" through the Ex-POW Consortium, in which members of both communities meet to foster understanding about ethnic positions and beliefs as well as to share interpretations of past events. Through such efforts, we can see that reconciliation has already begun in some areas of society. Future efforts might expand on those that are already shifting attention to relationships, structures, and the future.

We do not suggest that reconciliation will be easy. The legacy of the Troubles in Northern Ireland clearly traumatized both communities. The collective memories and interpretations of the Troubles make it difficult for members of both communities to make peace.[127] Nonetheless, peace requires reconciliation. For people at the grassroots level to move beyond past wrongs requires those guilty of past injustices to either admit to them or (at least) to be identified as guilty. Such accountability brings peace to victims and hope to perpetrators, as an attempt at making "whole" what was broken apart as a result of the violence. Of course, reconciliation may not eliminate all the tension that exists between members of society (especially those who have been victims of violence), but it offers the possibility that people can learn to live with what occurred.[128] It is for this reason that many believe sustained peace requires reconciliation.[129]

As we look to the future in Northern Ireland, reconciliation between the communities would clearly make the building of civil society a much easier task. It alleviates fear and mistrust, thereby opening possibilities for and raising expectations of future interethnic cooperation. Of course, this process, if it is to happen, will take a long time and will need to be experienced as broadly as possible to have the desired effect of providing a mechanism for healing the rift between the communities in Northern Ireland.[130] Nonetheless, it holds the greatest promise for helping long-term conflict resolution in Northern Ireland. By constructing a shared history, the two communities can delink identity from the events of the past, and by changing these identities, they set the foundation for healing the deep rifts that reinforce sectarianism, undermine civil society, and fuel the ethnic security dilemma.

Conclusion

We believe that sustainable peace in Northern Ireland cannot rely solely upon elite accommodation and power sharing but, rather, needs to be built from the ground up. Such an approach stresses building better relationships between the communities at the grassroots level.[131] We argue that the betterment of these relationships requires that identities change to resolve the ethnic security dilemma that remains in the wake of the Agreement. This can best be accomplished through reconciliation and the strengthening of civil society, each of which reduces fear and mistrust and raises expectations of future cooperation. Of course, evidence exists to suggest that Northern Ireland has begun working on both civil society and reconciliation. This evidence, however, also indicates that much more work remains to be done. Such a conclusion comes as no surprise, for peace processes have often been characterized by their ambiguity, gradualism, and cumulative effect.[132] Northern Ireland is no different in this respect, and we anticipate that both building civil society and reconciling the two communities will involve a slow and difficult process—though one that warrants greater attention and investment.

Importantly, civil society and reconciliation promise to support the Agreement and the progress it has made in conflict management. The Agreement works best when constituents expect cooperation from their representatives, permitting the type of negotiations and compromise commonly found in successful democracies. In this way, societal trust can generate trust in the political process.[133] These institutions, in turn, can then reinforce social trust. States or political institutions like those at Stormont may build societal trust (and, ultimately, social capital) by acting as enforcers of agreements between the communities and by facilitating power sharing—that is, by supporting and demonstrating cooperation. All of this suggests that peace and the consolidation of democratic institutions are not suddenly achieved but, rather, are processes characterized by break-throughs, setbacks, and a long-term attempt to ameliorate the legacy of violence in society.

Peace processes often aspire to conflict resolution—that is, to ensure that a preceding conflict cannot be repeated through similar conditions. Although Northern Ireland made great headway on containing violence, conflict resolution will not be realized without an improved associational life that successfully integrates Catholics and Protestants in social networks that create the interpersonal trust, social capital, and civil society necessary for a fully functioning democracy. This will require groups to address their past and construct a shared vision of the future, thereby reducing sectarian identities and providing room for other identities to develop and assert themselves.[134] Such actions require a long-term perspective, in which the initial difficulties of implementation comprise part of a protracted transition to a more peaceful Northern Ireland.

NOTES

1. Zeev Maoz, "Conflict Management and Conflict Resolution: A Conceptual and Methodological Introduction," in *Multiple Paths to Knowledge in International Relations:*

Methodology in the Study of Conflict Management and Conflict Resolution, ed. Zeev Maoz, Alex Mintz, T. Clifton Morgan, Glenn Palmer, and Richard J. Stoll (Lanham, MD: Lexington Books, 2004), 1–32.

2. This chapter builds on the conception of emancipatory peacebuilding. See Charles Thiessen, "Emancipatory Peacebuilding: Critical Responses to (Neo)Liberal Trends," in *Critical Issues in Peace and Conflict Studies*, ed. Thomas Matyók, Jessica Senehi, and Sean Byrne (Boulder, CO: Lexington Books, 2011), 115–40.

3. Kanchan Chandra, "What Is Ethnic Identity and Does It Matter?" *Annual Review of Political Science* 9 (2006): 397–424.

4. Collier, Hoeffler, and Söderbom find that states possessing moderate levels of ethnic difference (meaning that there are only two or three major contending groups—as in Northern Ireland) experience longer civil wars. See Paul Collier, Anke Hoeffler, and Måns Söderbom, "On the Duration of Civil War," *Journal of Peace Research* 41 (3) (2004): 253–73.

5. David A. Lake and Donald Rothchild, "Containing Fear: The Origins and Management of Ethnic Conflict," *International Security* 21 (2) (1996): 41–75.

6. See Barry R. Posen, "The Security Dilemma and Ethnic Conflict," *Survival* 35 (1) (1993): 27–47.

7. John J. Mearsheimer, *The Tragedy of Great Power Politics* (New York: W.W. Norton, 2001).

8. John A. Vasquez, *The War Puzzle Revisited* (Cambridge: Cambridge University Press, 2009).

9. On the conflict-prone nature of territorial disputes, see John A. Vasquez and Marie T. Henehan, "Territorial Disputes and the Probability of War, 1816–1992," *Journal of Peace Research* 38 (2) (2001): 123–38. On territorial disagreements (and the role of borders within them), see Paul K. Huth, *Standing Your Ground* (Ann Arbor: University of Michigan, 1996). On less violent interstate relations after border settlement, see Andrew P. Owsiak, "Signing Up for Peace: International Boundary Agreements, Democracy, and Militarized Interstate Conflict," *International Studies Quarterly* 56 (1) (2012): 51–66.

10. Paul K. Huth and Todd L. Allee, *The Democratic Peace and Territorial Conflict in the Twentieth Century* (Cambridge: Cambridge University Press, 2002).

11. Chaim Kaufmann, "Possible and Impossible Solutions to Ethnic Civil Wars," *International Security* 20 (4) (1996): 136–75.

12. Paul F. Diehl and Gary Goertz, *War and Peace in International Rivalry* (Ann Arbor: University of Michigan Press, 2000). See also Michael P. Colaresi, Karen Rasler, and William R. Thompson, *Strategic Rivalries in World Politics* (Cambridge: Cambridge University Press, 2007).

13. Nicholas Sambanis, "Partition as a Solution to Ethnic War: An Empirical Critique of the Theoretical Literature," *World Politics* 52 (4) (2000): 437–83.

14. See also Brendan O'Leary, "Debating Partition: Evaluating the Standard Justifications," in *Routledge Handbook of Ethnic Conflict*, ed. Karll Cordell and Stefan Wolff (New York: Routledge, 2011), 140–57.

15. For an overview, see Vasquez, *War Puzzle Revisited*.

16. Michael C. Horowitz, Alex Weisiger, and Carter Johnson, "The Limits to Partition," *International Security* 33 (4) (2009): 203–10.

17. See Kristin Henrard, "Relating Human Rights, Minority Rights and Self-Determination to Minority Protection," in *Managing and Settling Ethnic Conflicts: Perspectives on Successes and Failures in Europe, Africa and Asia*, ed. Ulrich Schneckener and Stefan Wolff (New York: Palgrave Macmillan, 2004), 40–56.

18. Lars-Erik Cederman, Andreas Wimmer, and Brian Min, "Why Do Ethnic Groups Rebel? New Data and Analysis," *World Politics* 62 (1) (2010): 87–119.

19. Lars-Erik Cederman, Nils B. Weidmann, and Kristian Skrede Gleditsch, "Horizontal Inequalities and Ethnonationalist Civil War: A Global Comparison," *American Political Science Review* 105 (3) (2011): 478–95.

20. Thomas Chapman and Philip G. Roeder, "Partition as a Solution to Wars of Nationalism: The Importance of Institutions," *American Political Science Review* 101 (4) (2007): 677–91.

21. Niall Ó Dochartaigh, "Territoriality and Order in the North of Ireland," *Irish Political Studies* 26 (3) (2011): 313–28.

22. Diarmuid Maguire, "Local Space and Protest in Divided Societies," in *The Challenges of Ethno-Nationalism: Case Studies in Identity Politics*, ed. Adrian Guelke (New York: Palgrave Macmillan, 2010), 211–31.

23. Martin Mansergh, "Counterterrorism and Conflict Resolution in Northern Ireland," in *The Lessons of Northern Ireland*, ed. Michael Cox (London: LSE IDEAS Special Report 008, November 2011), 14. The importance of settling or resolving border disputes in fostering peace is stressed in Owsiak, "Signing Up for Peace."

24. Stephen Kocs, "Territorial Dispute and Interstate War, 1945–1987," *Journal of Politics* 57 (1) (1995): 159–75, and Owsiak, "Signing Up for Peace."

25. Niall Ó Dochartaigh, "Territoriality and Order in the North of Ireland."

26. On the characteristics and designs of international institutions, see Barbara Koremenos, Charles Lipson, and Duncan Snidal, "The Rational Design of International Institutions," *International Organization* 55 (4) (2001): 761–99. Similar characteristics apply to domestic institutions as well.

27. Andrew Kydd and Barbara F. Walter, "Sabotaging the Peace: The Politics of Extremist Violence," *International Organization* 56 (2) (2002): 263–96.

28. Stephen John Stedman, "Spoiler Problems in Peace Processes," *International Security* 22 (2) (1997): 5–53.

29. On bargaining ranges, see P. Terrence Hopmann, "Bargaining and Problem Solving: Two Perspectives on International Negotiation," in *Turbulent Peace: The Challenges of Managing International Conflict*, ed. Chester A. Crocker, Fen Osler Hampson, and Pamela Aall (Washington, DC: United States Institute of Peace Press, 2001), 450–56.

30. On the history of Sinn Féin, see Brian Feeney, *Sinn Féin: A Hundred Turbulent Years* (Madison: University of Wisconsin Press, 2003). The IRA may also have been using violence as a means of communicating with Sinn Féin; for a similar argument with respect

to Palestinian groups, see Wendy Pearlman, "Spoiling Inside and Out," *International Security* 33 (3) (2008/9): 79–109.

31. On the debate regarding Sinn Féin's admission to the negotiations, see George Mitchell, *Making Peace* (New York: Alfred Knopf, 1999), chapter 12. Negotiations between the British and Irish governments (separately) and Sinn Féin did occur, but Sinn Féin was omitted from the all-party talks until IRA violence ceased. On this history, see Feeney, *Sinn Féin*.

32. On converting rational actors using violence to those using peaceful means through conciliation, see Peter C. Sederberg, "Conciliation as Counter-terrorist Strategy," *Journal of Peace Research* 32 (3) (1995): 295–312.

33. Barbara F. Walter, "The Critical Barrier to Civil War Settlement," *International Organization* 51 (3) (1997): 335–64. See also Robert Powell, "War as a Commitment Problem," *International Organization* 60 (1) (2006): 169–203.

34. Stephen D. Krasner, "Sharing Sovereignty: New Institutions for Collapsed and Failing States," *International Security* 29 (2) (2004): 85–120.

35. Feeney, *Sinn Féin*, chapter 11.

36. Final Report of the Independent International Commission on Decommissioning, July 4, 2011, http://cain.ulst.ac.uk/events/peace/decommission/iicd040711.pdf, accessed February 25, 2013.

37. Karl DeRouen, Mark J. Ferguson, Samuel Norton, Young Hwan Park, Jenna Lea, and Ashley Streat-Bartlett, "Civil War Peace Agreement Implementation and State Capacity," *Journal of Peace Research* 47 (3) (2010): 333–46 (especially 340).

38. See Jason Lyall and Isaiah Wilson III, "Rage Against the Machines: Explaining Outcomes in Counterinsurgency Wars," *International Organization* 63 (1) (2009): 90–91.

39. Andrew H. Kydd and Barbara F. Walter, "The Strategies of Terrorism," *International Security* 31 (1) (2006): 64. See also Sederberg, "Conciliation as Counter-terrorist Strategy."

40. See James D. Fearon and David D. Laitin, "Ethnicity, Insurgency, and Civil War," *American Political Science Review* 97 (1) (2003): 75–90.

41. Well-crafted peace agreements enhance the durability of peace. See Virginia Page Fortna, "Scraps of Paper? Agreements and the Durability of Peace," *International Organization* 57 (2) (2003): 337–72.

42. See, for example, Paul Dixon, "In Defence of Politics: Interpreting the Peace Process and the Future of Northern Ireland," *Political Quarterly* 83 (2) (2012): 265–76.

43. They may, however, be no more difficult to resolve than non-identity-based ones. See Caroline Hartzell, Matthew Hoddie, and Donald Rothchild, "Stabilizing the Peace After Civil War: An Investigation of Some Key Variables," *International Organization* 55 (1) (2001): 183–208 (especially 198–99).

44. Zachary Elkins and John Sides, "Can Institutions Build Unity in Multiethnic States?" *American Political Science Review* 101 (4) (2007): 706.

45. These power-sharing arrangements, however, may minimize the long-term likelihood of a renewed *secessionist* movement. See Ian S. Lustick, Dan Miodownik, and Roy J.

Eidelson, "Secessionism in Multicultural States: Does Sharing Power Prevent or Encourage It?," *American Political Science Review* 98 (2) (2004): 223.

46. Robin Wilson, "Autonomy and Power-Sharing in Northern Ireland: A Model for Global Export?," *Dynamics of Asymmetric Conflict* 4 (3) (2011): 242–58.

47. This argument is made in Aoibhín de Búrca, "The Republic, Northern Ireland and the UK: A Little Less Conversation, a Little More Action Please," in *Next Generation Ireland*, ed. Ed Burke and Ronan Lyons (Dublin: Blackhall, 2011), 139–59.

48. James D. Fearon and David D. Laitin, "Violence and the Social Construction of Ethnic Identity," *International Organization* 54 (4) (2000): 845–77.

49. Chandra, "What Is Ethnic Identity and Does It Matter?," 414–16.

50. Stacie E. Goddard, "Uncommon Ground: Indivisible Territory and the Politics of Legitimacy," *International Organization* 60 (1) (2006): 35–68.

51. Hanna Lerner, *Making Constitutions in Deeply Divided Societies* (Cambridge: Cambridge University Press, 2011), 152–90.

52. Mark W. Zacher, "The Territorial Integrity Norm: International Boundaries and the Use of Force," *International Organization* 55 (2) (2001): 215–50.

53. Cathy Gormley-Heenan, "Northern Ireland: Securing the Peace," in *Beyond Settlement: Making Peace Last after Civil Conflict*, ed. Vanessa E. Shields and Nicholas D. J. Baldwin (Madison, NJ: Fairleigh Dickinson University Press, 2008), 224–36.

54. For this general argument, see Christoph Zürcher, "Building Democracy While Building Peace," *Journal of Democracy* 22 (1) (2011): 81–95.

55. See Rob Aitken, "Consociational Peace Processes and Ethnicity: The Implications of the Dayton and Good Friday Agreements for Ethnic Identities and Politics in Bosnia-Herzegovina and Northern Ireland," in *The Challenges of Ethno-Nationalism: Case Studies in Identity Politics*, ed. Adrian Guelke (New York: Palgrave Macmillan, 2010), 232–53; Sean Byrne, "Consociational and Civic Society Approaches to Peacebuilding in Northern Ireland," *Journal of Peace Research* 38 (3) (2001): 327–52; and Stefan Wolff, "Conclusion: The Peace Process Since 1998," in *Peace at Last? The Impact of the Good Friday Agreement on Northern Ireland*, ed. Jörg Neuheiser and Stefan Wolff (New York: Berghahn Books, 2002), 225.

56. This point was stressed in John Morison, "Constitutionalism, Civil Society and Democratic Renewal in Northern Ireland," in *A Farewell to Arms? Beyond the Good Friday Agreement*, 2nd ed., ed. Michael Cox, Adrian Guelke, and Fiona Stephen (Manchester: Manchester University Press, 2006), 238–52.

57. Christoph Spurk, "Understanding Civil Society," in *Civil Society & Peacebuilding: A Critical Assessment*, ed. Thania Paffenholz (Boulder, CO: Lynne Rienner, 2010), 3–27.

58. On the connection between peacebuilding and civil society, see Thania Paffenholz, "Civil Society and Peacebuilding," in Paffenholz, *Civil Society & Peacebuilding*, 43–64. For how identities can change and be redefined over time, see chapters 3 and 4 of this volume.

59. Feargal Cochrane, *Ending Wars* (Cambridge: Polity, 2008), 6–7.

60. John Paul Lederach, *Building Peace: Sustainable Reconciliation in Divided Societies* (Washington, DC: United States Institute of Peace, 1997). See also Jennifer Todd, "Equality

as Steady State or Equality as a Threshold? Northern Ireland after the Good Friday (Belfast) Agreement, 1998," in Guelke, *The Challenges of Ethno-Nationalism*, 145.

61. James D. Fearon and David D. Laitin, "Explaining Interethnic Cooperation," *American Political Science Review* 90 (4) (1996): 715–35.

62. Robert Axelrod, *The Evolution of Cooperation* (New York: Basic Books, 1984).

63. See Katy Hayward, "Introduction: Political Discourse and Conflict Resolution," in *Political Discourse and Conflict Resolution: Debating Peace in Northern Ireland*, ed. Katy Hayward and Catherine O'Donnell (London: Routledge, 2011), 1–15; Roberto Belloni, "Northern Ireland: Civil Society and the Slow Building of Peace," in Paffenholz, *Civil Society & Peacebuilding*, 109; and Rebecca Graff-McRae, *Remembering and Forgetting 1916: Commemoration and Conflict in Post-Peace Process Ireland* (Dublin: Irish Academic Press, 2010).

64. Fearon and Laitin, "Violence and the Social Construction of Ethnic Identity," 848.

65. Henry E. Hale, "Explaining Ethnicity," *Comparative Political Studies* 37 (4) (2004): 458–85.

66. Chandra, "What Is Ethnic Identity and Does It Matter?," 414–18.

67. Joanne Hughes, "Peace, Reconciliation and a Shared Future: A Policy Shift or More of the Future?," *Community Development Journal* 44 (1) (2009): 24.

68. See Ephraim Nimmi, "Nationalism, Ethnicity and Self-Determination: A Paradigm Shift?," *Studies in Ethnicity and Nationalism* 9 (2) (2009): 319–32.

69. Jennifer Todd, "Northern Ireland: From Multiphased Conflict to Multilevelled Settlement," in *Pathways from Ethnic Conflict: Institutional Redesign in Divided Societies*, ed. John Coakley (London: Routledge, 2010), 87–88, and Jan Teorell, *Determinants of Democratization: Explaining Regime Change in the World, 1972–2006* (Cambridge: Cambridge University Press, 2010), 12. Farrington contends that the new institutions and arrangements created by the Agreement ironically undermined the role of civil society. See Christopher Farrington, "Models of Civil Society and Their Implications for the Northern Peace Process," in *Global Change, Civil Society and the Northern Ireland Peace Process: Implementing the Political Settlement*, ed. Christopher Farrington (New York: Palgrave Macmillan, 2008), 113–41.

70. Hughes, "Peace, Reconciliation, and a Shared Future," 22–37.

71. Kevin Bean, "Civil Society, the State and Conflict Transformation in the Nationalist Community," in *Building Peace in Northern Ireland*, ed. Maria Power (Liverpool: Liverpool University Press, 2011), 154–71.

72. Belloni, "Northern Ireland," 105.

73. Walter, "The Critical Barrier to Civil War Settlement," 338–40.

74. The discussion of civil society and its activities comes largely from Spurk, "Understanding Civil Society."

75. Kenneth Newton, "Trust, Social Capital, Civil Society, and Democracy," *International Political Science Review* 22 (2) (2001): 212.

76. Jan Aart Scholte, "Civil Society and Democracy in Global Governance," *Global Governance* 8 (3) (2002): 281–304.

77. See, for example, Nathan Glazer, "Democracy and Deep Divides," *Journal of Democracy* 21 (2) (2010): 5–19.

78. Markus Freitag and Richard Traunmüller, "Spheres of Trust: An Empirical Analysis of the Foundations of Particularized and Generalized Trust," *European Journal of Political Research* 48 (6) (2009): 782–803. See also Roy J. Lewicki, "Trust, Trust Development, and Trust Repair," in *The Handbook of Conflict Resolution: Theory and Practice*, 2nd ed., ed. Morton Deutsch, Peter T. Coleman, and Eric C. Marcus (San Francisco: Jossey-Bass, 2006), 92–119. The importance of trust is increasingly recognized both in international relations and comparative politics; see Michael P. Jasinski, *Social Trust, Anarchy, and International Conflict* (New York: Palgrave Macmillan, 2011).

79. Francesco Herreros, *The Problem of Forming Social Capital: Why Trust?* (New York: Palgrave Macmillan, 2004), chapter 2, and Bo Rothstein, *Social Traps and the Problem of Trust* (New York: Cambridge University Press, 2005).

80. Gregory M. Maney, Ibtisam Ibrahim, Gareth I. Higgins, and Hanna Herzog, "The Past's Promise: Lessons from Peace Processes in Northern Ireland and the Middle East," *Journal of Peace Research* 43 (2) (2006): 182–85.

81. Paul Arthur, "Memory, Forgiveness, and Conflict: Trust-Building in Northern Ireland," in *Commemorating Ireland: History, Politics, Culture*, ed. Eberhard Bort (Dublin: Irish Academic Press, 2004), 68, and Marie Smyth, "Putting the Past in Its Place: Issues of Victimhood and Reconciliation in Northern Ireland's Peace Process," in *Burying the Past: Making Peace and Doing Justice after Civil Conflict*, ed. Nigel Biggar (Washington, DC: Georgetown University Press, 2001), 108.

82. For this model of conflict resolution, see Daniel Bar-Tal and Eran Halperin, "Overcoming Psychological Barriers to Peacemaking: The Influence of Beliefs about Losses," in *Prosocial Motives, Emotions, and Behavior: The Better Angels of Our Nature*, ed. Mario Mikulincer and Phillip R. Shaver (Washington, DC: American Psychological Association, 2010), 434.

83. Jonathan Powell, *Great Hatred, Little Room: Making Peace in Northern Ireland* (London: The Bodley Head, 2008), 312.

84. Landon E. Hancock, "There Is No Alternative: Prospect Theory, the Yes Campaign and Selling the Good Friday Agreement," *Irish Political Studies* 26 (1) (2011): 95–116.

85. Herreros, *The Problem of Forming Social Capital*, 17; Bo Rothstein, *Social Traps and the Problem of Trust*; and Eric M. Uslaner, "Producing and Consuming Trust," *Political Science Quarterly* 115 (4) (2000–2001): 573.

86. Ben Reilly, "Democratic Validation," in *Contemporary Peacemaking: Conflict, Peace Processes and Post-War Reconstruction*, ed. John Darby and Roger Mac Ginty (New York: Palgrave Macmillan, 2008), 230–41. See also Richard English, *Terrorism: How to Respond* (Oxford: Oxford University Press, 2009), 84.

87. Jacob Bercovitch and Richard Jackson, *Conflict Resolution in the Twenty-First Century: Principles, Methods, and Approaches* (Ann Arbor: University of Michigan Press, 2009), 173; Michael W. Doyle and Nicholas Sambanis, *Making War and Building Peace: United Nations Peace Operations* (Princeton, NJ: Princeton University Press, 2006).

88. Ian O'Flynn and David Russell, "Deepening Democracy: The Role of Civil Society," in *Routledge Handbook of Ethnic Conflict*, ed. Karl Cordell and Stefan Wolff (New York: Routledge, 2011), 225–35, and Harold H. Saunders, *A Public Peace Process: Sustained Dialogue to Transform Racial and Ethnic Conflicts* (New York: St. Martin's, 1999), xxiii.

89. See http://www.ark.ac.uk/nilt/2010/Community_Relations/PROTRCMX.html, accessed December 21, 2011.

90. See Nicholas Acheson, Carl Milofsky, and Maurice Stringer, "Understanding the Role of Non-aligned Civil Society in Peacebuilding in Northern Ireland: Towards a Fresh Approach," in Power, *Building Peace in Northern Ireland*, 31–57, and Linda Racioppi and Katherine O'Sullivan See, "Engendering Democratic Transition from Conflict: Women's Inclusion in Northern Ireland's Peace Process," *Comparative Politics* 38 (2) (2006): 195. For the theoretical differentiation of bridging and bonding social capital, see David Halpern, *Social Capital* (Cambridge: Polity, 2005), 19–22, and Robert Putnam, *Bowling Alone: The Collapse and Revival of American Community* (New York: Simon & Schuster, 2000), 22–23. Ross A. Hammond and Robert Axelrod demonstrate, in "The Evolution of Ethnocentrism," *Journal of Conflict Resolution* 50 (6) (2006): 926–36, that ethnocentrism (like that found in Northern Ireland) creates bonding social capital and undermines the prospect of bridging social capital between groups.

91. This danger is highlighted in Ayhan Akman, "Beyond the Objectivist Conception of Civil Society: Social Actors, Civility and Self-Limitation," *Political Studies* 60 (2) (2012): 321–40. In Northern Ireland the entrenchment of the sectarian divide means that relationships have polarized or "pillarized" society. See Manlio Cinalli, "Below and Beyond Power Sharing: Relational Structures across Institutions and Civil Society," in *Power Sharing: New Challenges for Divided Society*, ed. Ian O'Flynn and David Russell (London: Pluto Press, 2005), 172–87.

92. Roger Mac Ginty, *International Peacebuilding and Local Resistance: Hybrid Forms of Peace* (New York: Palgrave Macmillan, 2011), 183–206. Wiedenhoft Murphy and Peden similarly argue that unionists can redefine their identity in the wake of the Agreement. See chapter 4.

93. Jonathan Tonge, "Nationalist Convergence? The Evolution of Sinn Féin and SDLP Politics," in *Transforming the Peace Process in Northern Ireland: From Terrorism to Democratic Politics*, ed. Aaron Edwards and Stephen Bloomer (Dublin: Irish Academic Press, 2008), 59–76.

94. James Greer, "Paisley and His Heartland: A Case Study of Political Change," in *From Parnell to Paisley: Constitutional and Revolutionary Politics in Modern Ireland*, ed. Coimhe Nic Dháibhéid and Colin Reid (Dublin: Irish Academic Press, 2010), 224–49.

95. The following statistics are taken from the 2010 Northern Ireland Life and Times Survey. Of the survey respondents, 61 percent of Protestants identify as British, and 58 percent of Catholics identify as Irish. See http://www.ark.ac.uk/nilt/2010/Community_Relations/NINATID.html, accessed December 21, 2011.

96. See http://www.ark.ac.uk/nilt/2010/Community_Relations/RLRELAGO.html, accessed December 21, 2011.

97. See http://www.ark.ac.uk/nilt/2010/Community_Relations/RLRELFUT.html, accessed July 16, 2012.

98. See http://www.ark.ac.uk/nilt/2010/Community_Relations/MXRLGNGH.html, accessed July 16, 2012.

99. See http://www.ark.ac.uk/nilt/2010/Community_Relations/MXRLGWRK .html and http://www.ark.ac.uk/nilt/2010/Community_Relations/OWNMXSCH.html, accessed July 16, 2012.

100. See http://www.ark.ac.uk/nilt/2010/Community_Relations/RLRELAGO.html and http://www.ark.ac.uk/nilt/2010/Community_Relations/RLRELFUT.html, accessed July 16, 2012.

101. See http://www.ark.ac.uk/nilt/2010/Community_Relations/OWNMXSH.html, accessed July 16, 2012.

102. See http://www.ark.ac.uk/nilt/2010/Community_Relations/SRELFRND.html and http://www.ark.ac.uk/nilt/2010/Community_Relations/TARGET1A.html, accessed December 21, 2011. On the latter, 70 percent rank Northern Ireland in the bottom half of a 10-point scale, where 1 means civil society has not been achieved and 10 indicates the achievement of a civil society.

103. Gladys Ganiel and Paul Dixon, "Religion, Pragmatic Fundamentalism and the Transformation of the Northern Ireland Conflict," *Journal of Peace Research* 45 (3) (2008): 419–36.

104. Nicholas Acheson and Carl Milofsky, "Peace Building and Participation in Northern Ireland: Local Social Movements and the Policy Process since the 'Good Friday' Agreement," *Ethnopolitics* 7 (1) (2008): 63–80.

105. Marlies Glasius, David Lewis, and Hakan Seckinelgin, "Exploring Civil Society Internationally," in *Exploring Civil Society: Political and Cultural Contexts*, ed. Marlies Glasius, David Lewis, and Hakan Seckinelgin (New York: Routledge, 2004), 6, and Christian Welzel, Ronald Inglehart, and Franziska Deutsch, "Social Capital, Voluntary Associations and Collective Action: Which Aspects of Social Capital Have the Greatest 'Civic' Payoff," *Journal of Civil Society* 1 (2) (2005): 121–46.

106. John Paul Lederach, *Building Peace: Sustainable Reconciliation in Divided Societies* (Washington, DC: United States Institute of Peace Press, 1997), chapter 3. See also Daniel Bar-Tel and Gemma H. Bennink, "The Nature of Reconciliation as an Outcome and as a Process," in *From Conflict Resolution to Reconciliation*, ed. Yaacov Bar-Simon-Tov (New York: Oxford University Press, 2004), 11–38, and John Paul Lederach, *The Journey toward Reconciliation* (Scottsdale, PA: Herald Press, 1999).

107. Stuart J. Kaufman, "Escaping the Symbolic Politics Trap: Reconciliation Initiatives and Conflict Resolution in Ethnic Wars," *Journal of Peace Research* 43 (2) (2006): 201–18, especially 212. For a further development of the role of symbolic politics in ethnic conflict, see Stuart J. Kaufman, *Modern Hatreds: The Symbolic Politics of Ethnic War* (Ithaca, NY: Cornell University Press, 2001).

108. See Herbert C. Kelman, "Reconciliation as Identity Change: A Social-Psychological Perspective," in Bar-Simon-Tov, *From Conflict Resolution to Reconciliation*, 111–24.

109. Bercovitch and Jackson, *Conflict Resolution in the Twenty-First Century*, chapter 11.

110. For the debate between amnesty and accountability, see David P. Barash and Charles P. Webel, *Peace and Conflict Studies*, 2nd ed. (Los Angeles: SAGE, 2009), chapter 20.

111. Nurit Shnabel and Arie Nadler, "A Needs-Based Model of Reconciliation: Perpetrators Need Acceptance and Victims Need Empowerment to Reconcile," in *Prosocial Motives, Emotions, and Behavior: The Better Angels of Our Nature*, ed. Mario Mukilincer and Phillip R. Shaver (Washington, DC: American Psychological Association, 2010), 409–29; Erin Daly and Jeremy Sarkin, *Reconciliation in Divided Societies: Finding Common Ground* (Philadelphia: University of Pennsylvania Press, 2007); and Mike Morrissey and Marie Smyth, *Northern Ireland after the Good Friday Agreement: Victims, Grievance and Blame* (London: Pluto, 2002), 13.

112. Cochrane, *Ending Wars*, 6–7. See also Marie Smyth, "Lost Lives: Victims and the Construction of 'Victimhood' in Northern Ireland," in Cox, Guelke, and Stephen, *A Farewell to Arms?*, 20–21. The problem of defining victimhood in the Northern Ireland context is further explored in Morrissey and Smyth, *Northern Ireland after the Good Friday Agreement*, 4–9 and 24–25.

113. James L. Gibson, in "The Contributions of Truth to Reconciliation: Lessons from South Africa," *Journal of Conflict Resolution* 50 (3) (2006): 409–32, highlights how this truth commission led to reconciliation in South Africa. For further analysis of how the South African Truth and Reconciliation Commission worked with the purpose of not only discovering the truth but having this truth lead to reconciliation, see Audrey R. Chapman, "Truth Commissions as Instruments of Forgiveness and Reconciliation," in *Forgiveness and Reconciliation: Religion, Public Policy, and Conflict Transformation*, ed. Raymond G. Helmick, S.J., and Rodney L. Petersen (Philadelphia: Templeton Foundation Press, 2001), 247–67.

114. Adrian Guelke, "The Lure of the Miracle? The South African Connection and the Northern Ireland Peace Process," in *Global Change, Civil Society and the Northern Ireland Peace Process: Implementing the Political Settlement*, ed. Christopher Farrington (New York: Palgrave Macmillan, 2008), 73–90.

115. See Smyth, "Lost Lives," 16–17.

116. Robin Wilson, *The Northern Ireland Experience of Conflict and Agreement: A Model for Export?* (Manchester: Manchester University Press, 2010).

117. Cillian McGrattan, "Spectres of History: Nationalist Party Politics and Truth Recovery in Northern Ireland," *Political Studies* 60 (2) (2012): 455–73; Mitchell B. Reiss and Eric Green, "Lessons of the Northern Ireland Peace Process," *American Foreign Policy Interests* 27 (2005): 475; Cochrane, *Ending Wars*, 151; Daly and Sarkin, *Reconciliation in Divided Societies*; Ryan Gawn, "Truth Cohabitation: A Truth Commission for Northern Ireland?," *Irish Political Studies* 22 (3) (2007): 339–61; Patricia Lundy and Mark McGovern, "Telling Stories, Facing Truths: Memory, Justice and Post-Conflict Transition," in *Northern Ireland: After the Troubles*, ed. Colin Coulter and Michael Murray (Manchester: Manchester University Press, 2008), 33; McCaughey, "Northern Ireland," 261–65; Norman Porter, *The Elusive Quest: Reconciliation in Northern Ireland* (Belfast: Blackstaff Press, 2003); and Ronald A. Wells, "Northern Ireland: A Study of Friendship, Forgiveness, and Reconciliation," in

The Politics of Past Evil: Religion, Reconciliation, and the Dilemmas of Transitional Justice, ed. Daniel Philpott (Notre Dame, IN: University of Notre Dame Press, 2006), 189–222.

118. Cheryl Lawther, "Unionism, Truth Recovery and the Fearful Past," *Irish Political Studies* 26 (3) (2011): 361–62.

119. Patricia Lundy and Mark McGovern, "Attitudes towards a Truth Commission for Northern Ireland in Relation to Party Political Affiliation," *Irish Political Studies* 22 (3) (2007): 321–38, and Smyth, "Putting the Past in Its Place," 123–25.

120. Bertie Ahern, *Bertie Ahern: The Autobiography* (London: Arrow Books, 2009), 231–33.

121. Duncan Morrow, "After Antagonism? The British-Irish Ethnic Frontier after the Agreement," *Irish Political Studies* 26 (3) (2011): 301–12.

122. Joanna Etchart, "Loyalism and Peacebuilding in the 2000s," in Power, *Building Peace in Northern Ireland*, 148.

123. The following framework comes from Lederach, *Building Peace*.

124. Barash and Webel, *Peace and Conflict Studies*, 446–47.

125. See http://www.ark.ac.uk/nilt/2010/Community_Relations/RLRELFUT.html, accessed July 16, 2012.

126. See Kieran McEvoy and Peter Shirlow, "Encumbered by Data: Understanding Politically Motivated Prisoners and the Transition to Peace in Northern Ireland," in Power, *Building Peace in Northern Ireland*, 111–30. Religious organizations might also help build reconciliation; see Daniel Philpott, *Religion, Reconciliation, and Transitional Justice: The State of the Field* (New York: Social Science Research Council, 2007).

127. Brewer, *Peace Processes*, 141–93, and Graham Dawson, *Making Peace with the Past? Memory, Trauma and the Irish Troubles* (Manchester: Manchester University Press, 2007). On the role of memory in forging political culture and shaping international relations, see Eric Langebacher, "Collective Memory as a Factor in Political Culture and International Relations," in *Power and the Past: Collective Memory and International Relations*, ed. Eric Langebacher and Yossi Shain (Washington, DC: Georgetown University Press, 2010), 13–49.

128. Susan Dwyer, "Reconciliation for Realists," *Ethics and International Affairs* 13 (1999): 87.

129. Paul Arthur, "Memory Retrieval and Truth Recovery," in *Handbook of Conflict Resolution and Analysis*, ed. Dennis J. D. Sandhole, Sean Byrne, Ingride Sandole-Staroste, and Jessica Senehi (London: Routledge, 2009), 369–82; Bercovitch and Jackson, *Conflict Resolution in the Twenty-First Century*, 166; Tristan Anne Borer, *Telling the Truths: Truth Telling and Peace Building in Post-Conflict Societies* (Notre Dame, IN: University of Notre Dame Press, 2006); Paul F. Diehl and Daniel Druckman, *Evaluating Peace Operations* (Boulder, CO: Lynne Rienner, 2010), 111; Brandon Hamber and Gráinne Kelly, "The Challenge of Reconciliation in Post-Conflict Societies: Definitions, Problems and Proposals," in O'Flynn and Russell, *Power Sharing: New Challenges for Divided Societies*, 188–203; Priscilla B. Hayner, *Unspeakable Truths: Facing the Challenge of Truth Commissions* (New York: Routledge, 2002); Lederach, *Building Peace*; and William J. Long and Peter Brecke,

War and Reconciliation: Reason and Emotion in Conflict Resolution (Cambridge, MA: MIT Press, 2003). For the difficulty of achieving public forgiveness in a political context, see Jean Bethke Elshtain, "Politics and Forgiveness," in *Burying the Past: Making Peace and Doing Justice after Civil Conflict*, ed. Nigel Biggar (Washington, DC: Georgetown University Press, 2001), 40–56 and especially 46–47. John Darby suggests that reconciliation falsely assumes that a prior conciliation previously existed among the parties and fails to recognize the continuing conflict of interests that is at the heart of the conflict. See John Darby, "Reconciliation (Reflections from Northern Ireland and South Africa)," in *Palgrave Advances in Peacebuilding: Critical Developments and Approaches*, ed. Oliver P. Richmond (New York: Palgrave Macmillan, 2010), 294–306.

130. David Bloomfield, Teresa Barnes, and Luc Huyse, *Reconciliation after Violent Conflict: A Handbook* (Stockholm: International Institute for Democracy and Electoral Assistance, 2003), 13.

131. This different approach is also highlighted in Landon E. Hancock, "The Northern Irish Peace Process: From Top to Bottom," *International Studies Review* 10 (2) (2008): 225–31.

132. Recent analysis of the outcomes of civil wars suggest that while negotiated settlements like the Agreement may initially be fragile they become more durable over time. See T. David Mason, Mehmet Gurses, Patrick T. Brandt, and Jason Michael Quinn, "When Civil Wars Recur: Conditions for Durable Peace after Civil Wars," *International Studies Perspectives* 12 (2011): 171–89. From the Irish experience, Fitzduff argues that the effect of the peace process is cumulative. See Mari Fitzduff, *Beyond Violence: Conflict Resolution Process in Northern Ireland* (New York: United Nations University Press, 2002), 181.

133. See Newton, "Trust, Social Capital, Civil Society, and Democracy."

134. See chapter 3 of this volume and Mícheál D. Roe, William Pegg, Kim Hodges, and Rebecca A. Trimm, "Forgiving the Other Side: Social Identity and Ethnic Memories in Northern Ireland," in *Politics and Performance in Contemporary Northern Ireland*, ed. John P. Harrington and Elizabeth J. Mitchell (Amherst: University of Massachusetts Press, 1999), 122–56.

10   Sources of Peace

The Decline of Revolutionary Nationalism and the Beginning of the Peace Processes in Northern Ireland and the Middle East

ROBERT S. SNYDER

Until the negotiations that led to the Agreement in 1998, the conflict in Northern Ireland seemed intractable. It appeared as if it would continue well into the future, perpetuating the centuries-old violent struggles between the Protestants and Catholics. Like the dramatic turns in the conflicts between the Palestinians and Israelis and the blacks and whites in South Africa in the early 1990s, however, the negotiations that brought together Sinn Féin, the Protestants in Northern Ireland, the British government, and the Irish government offered surprising hope to resolve the conflict. What explains this shift from such long-standing hostility to pursuing a path of cooperation and reconciliation?

A major explanation for the process that led to the Agreement is based on the changes that occurred in international politics with the end of the Cold War. Michael Cox maintains that the Agreement needs to be understood within the context of the end of the Cold War, and that the decline of radicalism worldwide, the new cooperation that brought Ireland and Great Britain together in the European Union (EU), and the contributions of the United States in the 1990s—now the lone superpower—significantly contributed to this new path of cooperation in Northern Ireland.[1] Nevertheless, critics contest Cox's thesis that international factors played a significant role in bringing about the peace process.[2] How important a role did the changes associated with the end of the Cold War play in leading to the Agreement?

In attempting to address these questions, this chapter argues that the Irish Republican Army's (IRA's) gradual renunciation of revolutionary nationalism was a primary factor that contributed to this dramatic shift in Northern Ireland, and the collapse of this ideology at the global level was a major factor in getting the IRA to shed its own ideological identity. In repudiating revolutionary nationalism, Sinn Féin and the IRA came to renounce violence, to embark on negotiations with the British government, to embrace the idea of a pluralistic community with the Protestants in Northern Ireland, and to renounce the goal of a radical transformation of a unified Ireland itself. Moreover, it led the British government to negotiate with Sinn Féin.

In highlighting how the decline of revolutionary nationalism largely related to global events has facilitated a peace process, this chapter compares the case of Northern Ireland to ones in the Middle East. These seminal cases, along with the South African one, illustrate the importance of ideology and how ideological change at the global level had powerful demonstration effects in making the ideas of revolutionary nationalism obsolete.[3] The chapter expands and defends Cox's thesis about the importance of the international dimension by relating it to a theory of international politics, by connecting the international to the domestic level, and by answering critics of the thesis. The first part of the chapter offers a theory about international politics based on revolutionary nationalism. The next two parts highlight the theory with respect to Northern Ireland and the Middle East, demonstrating their similarities while recognizing important differences in the local context and agents involved in the peace processes in both regions.

Revolutionary Nationalism

Cox's thesis that the peace process in Northern Ireland cannot be understood without the context of the international environment has two problems.[4] First, Cox needs to clarify the relationship between the domestic and international so as to avoid the implication that these international changes would necessarily have caused the shift in Northern Ireland regardless of the domestic situation. Second, Cox should connect his thesis to a theory about international politics. The changes at the global level had a particularly poignant effect because of distinct features of international politics that have not been fully appreciated, even by many international relations scholars. The claim that the peace process in Northern

Ireland primarily resulted from a decline in revolutionary nationalism assumes that revolutionary nationalism played an unusually strong role in international politics.

Indeed, international politics since World War II should largely be seen as a series of struggles between a core of liberal states and different revolutionary actors largely motivated by their opposition to liberalism.[5] This ideological theory of international politics stands in contrast to the realist view that emphasizes conflicts between great powers that are largely unaffected by ideas as well as the liberal perspective that stresses the pacific nature of democratic states in interaction among themselves and international institutions.[6] Owen argues that the history of international politics has seen three waves when the "clash of ideas," or what Haas calls the "clash of ideologies," defined international politics:[7] the religious wars of the sixteenth and seventeenth centuries, the conflicts between monarchism and republicanism in the eighteenth and nineteenth centuries, and the struggles between the fascists, communists, and liberals that dominated international politics during the twentieth century. Haas claims that the degree to which there was ideological polarity largely determined the severity of conflicts. Owen asserts that the distinguishing feature during these waves was the large number of attempts by major powers to promote regime change in other states. These waves came to an end when one ideology proved superior and the alternatives collapsed. In short, international demonstration effects had tremendous impact on local movements highly motivated by ideology.

The Cold War was mainly an ideological struggle between the liberal West, led by the United States, and the Soviet Union, as the leading revolutionary state. The new historiography of the Cold War has largely come to see it in ideological terms.[8] In writing on Soviet foreign policy, Vladislav Zubok characterizes it as having been based on what he calls the "revolutionary-imperial paradigm." "The combination of traditional Russian messianism and Marxist ideology produced something larger (though more fragile) than its parts taken separately. The two phenomena became completely blurred in the USSR by the 1920s and remained that way until the collapse of the Soviet regime in 1991. Together they provide a theoretical explanation of Soviet foreign policy behavior—the revolutionary-imperial paradigm."[9] The struggle between the two superpowers largely involved other revolutionary states, such as China, Cuba, Vietnam, Iran, and Nicaragua. If international conflict during this time was largely driven by this ideological clash involving revolutionary actors, it stands to reason that as revolutionary radicalism declined, the prospects for peace would increase significantly.

As distinct from liberal revolutions, revolutionary nationalism produced "social revolutions."[10] They entailed the violent overthrow of the government, were led by a dictatorial vanguard party, and were committed to promoting a radical transformation of state and society. Social revolutions placed communitarian values over individual ones, favored the socialist economy over the market, and promoted the dictatorship of the party over the people. Most importantly, they sought to vanquish their foes, repudiating the concept of pluralism. If social revolutions borrowed heavily from Marxism-Leninism, many saw political conflict in nationalistic terms. Revolutionary nationalism pitted the virtuous, but dominated, colonized nation against the imperialist one and sought to reverse the power relationship. It embraced policies that turned the heroic postcolonial nation inward after independence, favoring import substitution as opposed to export-oriented growth. As has been shown, an inward, nationalistic orientation fosters international conflict.[11] Thus, the end of decolonization, which predates the end of the Cold War, also helped to undermine revolutionary nationalism and its tendency to cause international conflict.

In comparing the peace processes in Northern Ireland and the Middle East, Maney and his colleagues assert that the best theoretical framework utilizes concepts based on power and identity.[12] They argue that these peace processes began because the two opposing sides became more equal in power, implying that when the status quo parties recognized the revolutionary actors as their equals, the peace process commenced: "A skewed distribution of group power results in unequal life chances that create latent if not open conflict. . . . A sustainable reduction in violence, therefore, requires increasing the power of less powerful groups."[13] Contrary to the authors, however, the process developed when the revolutionary actors demonstrated a willingness to curtail their violent tactics and radicalism. Likewise, these authors maintain that these negotiations depended on both sides' willingness to recognize their common identity as shared. But before this common identity could develop, the revolutionaries had to shed their revolutionary identity, and the status quo actors had to forgive the revolutionaries for their past violence.

A major issue is what type of international factors led the revolutionary actor to change its approach and embark on negotiations. One approach to conflict resolution emphasizes the idea that peace arises when one actor or its ally loses or is defeated.[14] (A balance of power may prevent further conflict but does not necessarily reduce tensions.) An example is Qaddafi's Libya after the United States ousted Saddam Hussein in Iraq in 2003, perhaps compelling Tripoli to give up its nuclear weapons program or face a similar fate. An alternative perspective to peace suggests that actors change their identities and interests as a result of some institutionalized interactions with others, often involving third parties.[15] Accordingly, Qaddafi might have turned over his nuclear program because he had already embarked on some reconciliation with the West before the 2003 Iraq War.[16]

Both approaches are relevant with respect to the cases at hand, but the first one offers more explanatory power. Although engaging in certain interactions with third parties might have been necessary for a peace process to emerge, the revolutionary actors would not likely have done so if they did not believe that their prospects had declined as a result of international setbacks. Nevertheless, these revolutionary actors did not feel as if they had experienced a defeat that left them no alternative other than to engage in a peace process.

The Road to the Agreement in Northern Ireland

The decline of revolutionary nationalism in Northern Ireland largely led to the Agreement, and this was largely brought about because of events at the global level. While Cox identifies the "international dimensions" of the peace process, they are best understood as related to the global decline of revolutionary nationalism that came at the end of the Cold War. By not sufficiently highlighting the revolutionary aspect of Irish republicanism, Cox's explanation of the peace process in Northern Ireland may imply that the British had to make the most concessions in order to reach an agreement.[17] However, this was not the case. Given the global decline of revolutionary nationalism, Sinn Féin and the IRA had to give up their defining ambition, a radically transformed united Ireland, and instead focus on more immediate improvements in the lives of the republicans and nationalists they sought to represent.[18] In criticizing Cox, Dixon argues that it is not clear if the decline in republican nationalism came about for domestic reasons or as a result of international changes, and he favors the former interpretation.[19] Even if domestic factors contributed to the decline of republicanism, such that international factors tipped Sinn Féin and the IRA into changing course, that does not diminish the importance of the international. Dixon characterizes the situation in the mid-1980s as a stalemate between the British and IRA.[20] Thus, the international factors related to the decline of revolutionary nationalism and the end of the Cold War indeed made a huge difference in convincing the IRA to take a different path. These international changes would not necessarily have led the IRA to take a new course if the stalemate that had developed did not already have a certain level of ripeness.[21] Hence, it is difficult to disentangle the relative weight of domestic and international factors, and some of the domestic factors could be seen as having been part of the global trend in the decline of revolutionary nationalism.

Originally inspired by the French Revolution,[22] republicanism emerged in the nineteenth century but became the idea of an incomplete Irish national revolution after 1921. Patterson writes: "The pervasiveness and strength of this notion derive from its fusion of two crucial aspirations within Irish nationalism—for a 'sovereign' 32-country state and also for a state that would be socially, economically and culturally different from Britain."[23] The republican movement continuously fractured after the Treaty, but it consistently embraced the principles of militant nationalism and a socialist transformation. In addition to believing that the British could only be removed through force, republicans rejected both the parliaments at Stormont and the Dáil as illegitimate. Although Sinn Féin stood for election at times, it practiced abstentionism. Thus, revolutionary politics through violence and the vanguard actions of the IRA took precedence over electoral politics and a commitment to pluralist compromise. As republicanism ebbed and flowed, it had to change and accommodate itself to shifts in the political environment. Patterson claims that there was an inherent tension between militant nationalism and social radicalism, but the bigger problem was that each would become outdated as the late twentieth century passed.[24]

Although there is a tendency to believe that revolutionary actors come from either the old communist world or the Third World, the IRA fits the model of a social revolutionary actor committed to extreme nationalism. Breaking from the old IRA headed by Cathal Goulding, the Provisional IRA came to represent the main part of the movement following the Troubles that erupted in 1969.[25] The Troubles rejuvenated the (Provisional) IRA, as numerous new recruits signed on to battle the British through terrorist tactics during the violent 1970s.[26] The IRA honed its revolutionary agenda by the late 1970s as Gerry Adams, jailed from 1973 to 1977, emerged as the principal leader of the group. Adams denounced the negotiated cease-fire of 1974–75 with the British, repudiated older leaders' support of elections, and proposed that the doctrine of what a new Irish state would represent be cast in more radical terms.

The IRA threw in its lot with Qaddafi's Libya, which portrayed itself as the global anti-imperialist revolutionary model, and which from 1972 onward supported the IRA through arms and money.[27] Inspired by radical ideas, Qaddafi's revolution was based on the Green Book, which called for the government to be run by "peoples' committees." Likewise, the IRA developed its own "Green Book" and Adams reorganized the IRA. In keeping with Leninist principles, the Army Council was the primary organ of decision making for the IRA, but Adams added a Revolutionary Council. The Green Book said: "The IRA, as the legal representatives of the Irish people, are morally justified in carrying out a campaign of resistance against foreign occupation forces and domestic collaborators."[28] Traditionally, the IRA supported a rural socialism based on cooperatives and a federal state. Adams replaced the idea of a federal state and called for a "democratic socialist republic," and he supported Marxism and an aggressive trade unionism that would topple the capitalist elite. In 1977 Gerry Adams and Danny Morrison wrote: "Hatred and resentment of this Army cannot sustain the war, and the isolation of socialist republicans around the armed struggle is dangerous and has provided, at least in some circles, the reformist notion that 'Ulster' is the issue, which can be somehow resolved without the mobilization of the working class in the twenty-six counties."[29] Indeed, in 1977 the IRA began assassinating capitalist leaders in Northern Ireland, and "many doing the fighting in the North identified fully with other revolutionary movements elsewhere in the world and saw the IRA's struggle as fully consistent with them."[30]

A stalemate emerged between the IRA and the British by the late 1970s and early 1980s. Adams recognized this as he devised a new strategy of attrition based on the idea of a "long war." The level of violence had dropped by the late 1970s, and the British became more adept in containing the IRA's violence. Adams also contemplated reversing course and supporting elections. A turning point occurred when IRA hunger strikers in jail in 1980 and 1981 gained support in Northern Ireland and worldwide attention.[31] Most prominent among them was Bobby Sands. His name was placed on the ballot in the spring of 1981, and he won. Despite his victory, Sands was the first of the hunger strikers to die, on May 5, 1981. Sands's victory and the sympathy that came with his death inspired further support and candidacies for Sinn Féin candidates. Gerry Adams stood for election in 1983, and he also gained a seat. "The hunger strikes transformed the political character of the Northern Ireland problem. Now republican prisoners appeared in the role of men prepared to accept suffering for their cause rather than simply inflicting suffering on others."[32] The IRA's commitment to armed struggle and its willingness to contest elections created a dilemma, pushing it to take one path or the other. Support grew for the republican cause, but new recruits sought to join Sinn Féin over the IRA.[33]

Third parties have often been important, if not critical, in helping to lessen the radicalism of revolutionaries. The Catholic Church and particularly the intermediation work of Father Alec Reid opened up channels of communication to the IRA.[34] After Charles Haughey became the taoiseach in 1982, Reid established contacts between the leader of Fianna Fáil and Adams. In order to attempt to get Adams to renounce his revolutionary nationalism, Haughey instead suggested a pan-nationalism with respect to Northern Ireland.[35] Haughey denounced Northern Ireland as a failure, called for Great Britain to recognize the idea of a united Ireland, and proposed an all-Irish conference. Most important, he suggested that the Irish accept the principle of consent with respect to unionists and nationalists in Northern Ireland, but the consent could not be transferred to or include British wishes. Although Haughey refused to meet with Adams, who in private communications renounced socialism, he worked through John Hume of the Social and Democratic Labour Party (SDLP) as Adams and Hume sought to find common ground in secret talks.

The basis for the Agreement was developed in secret communications between Adams and Tom King, the Northern Ireland secretary in 1987.[36] King maintained that the British would support the will of the nationalists and unionists in Northern Ireland regarding its final status and would not stay if the two communities did not wish so. This was asserted in a public statement by Peter Brooke, the Northern Ireland secretary, in 1990. Sinn Féin could become part of the negotiations if, as Haughey had insisted, the IRA renounced its violence. London's claim that it did not seek to stay in Northern Ireland went against IRA dogma. Nevertheless, Adams was not prepared to take this peaceful path, which few in the IRA knew he was pursuing, as the IRA was preparing for a "Tet Offensive" of attacks against the British in 1987. Patrick Magee of the IRA believes that it was the IRA's bombing of the Conservative Conference at Brighton in 1984 that began the peace process by getting the British to deal with the IRA.[37] But as Eamonn O'Kane states: "The issue of the conditions that republicans had to fulfill before they were to be allowed to enter into direct dialogue with the British government is what is too often glossed over in the accounts of those who stress the importance of dialogue. . . . The record shows that republicans were pushing for 'substantive' negotiations with the British, which the government consistently refused until the IRA ended violence."[38]

Given this stalemate at the domestic level, changes at the global level in the mid to late 1980s strongly encouraged the IRA to alter its course and, in effect, slowly renounce its revolutionary ways. The end of the Cold War had a major impact on the IRA because of its strong similarity and identity with other revolutionary actors and the larger revolutionary agenda at the global level. Not only did the Cold War define international politics as a struggle between radical and status quo forces, but the Soviet Union itself was a revolutionary state. Thus, its demise struck a huge blow to the very idea of a social revolution. It had become customary during the Cold War to believe that there were a variety of left-wing revolutionary states and movements that had little ideological connection to one another. This included the assumption that these groups were increasingly alienated from the original revolutionary state, the Soviet Union, since it had become regarded by many as a status quo power.[39] Nevertheless, Yugoslavia, for example, violently disintegrated following Moscow's fall, even though it had no formal alliance with the Soviet Union and defined itself in distinct ideological terms. Moreover, the fact that the British, a core player during the Cold War, emerged a huge victor has not been fully appreciated. The British victory dealt a blow to the IRA, which had emphasized the string of losses that the British had long suffered from anticolonial movements. The fact that the republicans defined themselves in opposition to the British and were geographically close helps to explain the greater poignancy for them than for other revolutionary movements, such as, for example, the FARC in Columbia and the Tamil Tigers in Sri Lanka, who were relatively far removed from the Cold War. Of course, the end of the Cold War did not lead to the end of Castro's Cuba, but unlike Havana, Sinn Féin had to worry more about gaining and holding onto supporters than about holding onto power in an established autocratic regime.

Just as global radicalism associated with social revolutions has faded, so too has extreme nationalism. Its death knell came with globalization. The winding down of the Cold War, to be sure, resulted in the fragmentation of states based on nationalist sentiments, but this has been different from the previous long era of integrative nationalism that the IRA represented in seeking the unification of Ireland. Likewise, the extreme ethnic nationalism that the IRA embraced supported exclusionary politics, but the global ascendancy of civic nationalism encouraged Sinn Féin to respect the principle of consent and to consider the interests of the unionists. Europe was the birthplace of integrative nationalism, which led to huge wars and international conflict. This integrative sense of nationalism later led to the creation of supranationalism as embodied in the EU. Moreover, the EU has been based on the elimination of import substitution policies of its member states in favor of export-oriented growth. In short, the rise of supranationalism, international cooperation, and export-oriented policies— particularly within the European theater—made the IRA's core nationalist agenda obsolete.

Another critical international development that led to a changed nego- tiating posture for the republicans was the changed economic and social conditions in the Irish Republic itself. Republicans in Northern Ireland historically looked to the southern Free State and later Republic and high- lighted its economic and social shortcomings. In fact, the policies that were in place through the 1950s in the south of Ireland kept this state's population poor and agrarian.[40] The southern state did not provide economic and social conditions that Northern Irish nationalists and republicans sought to emulate. The radical critique of capitalism that was at the heart of the republican agenda in the North was viable when capitalism was seen as a failure. As economic conditions began to improve in the 1960s, and improve dramatically in the 1990s during what has been called the Celtic Tiger period,[41] the allure of Marxist solutions to Ireland's economic problems faded rapidly. Instead, the success of the south made many nationalists in Northern Ireland seek to replicate the Republic of Ireland's polices of low corporate taxes and an emphasis on export-oriented growth as the basis for increasing prosperity. As these developments rapidly emerged in Northern Ireland, Sinn Féin knew it had to forego its advocacy of revolutionary economic policies that were increasingly seen as antiquated in the Ireland of the 1990s.

The British also had to change for the peace process to commence, and international factors contributed to this as well. Dixon claims that the British actually had to concede little during the peace process of the 1990s, for the Agreement reached in 1998 was not much different in its terms from Sunningdale in 1973.[42] However, this contention misses the fact that the greatest challenge for Britain was accepting the IRA as a negotiating partner, since London had historically regarded the IRA as a terrorist organization. Britain needed to be convinced that it could deal with the IRA, and other international actors played a role in persuading London to negotiate with Sinn Féin. Dixon discounts the improvement in Anglo-Irish relations in advancing the peace process, for he asserts these relations had changed little since the early 1970s. However, the Irish government's own secret negotiations with Sinn Féin convinced the Irish government of its sincerity and desire to move beyond the Troubles, which Dublin effectively communicated to the British government. The ability of the Irish to influence British policy in Northern Ireland had developed in the 1980s as Prime Minister Margaret Thatcher and Taoiseach Garret Fitzgerald negotiated the Anglo-Irish Agreement of 1985. English maintains that it "formally changed the dynamic between the two governments, with Dublin now having a structural role within the running of the north of Ireland."[43] It also was built on a British assumption that the Irish government was a constructive partner that also sought an end to the Troubles. Improved relations between the British and Irish governments continued as the British no longer considered the Irish government as seeking eventual unification at the expense of short-term cooperative relations over Northern Ireland. The Irish government came to accept the British government, as London proclaimed in the Downing Street Declaration that it had no selfish or strategic interest in Northern Ireland. This allowed both states to engage in intense cooperative diplomatic efforts and develop trust in this process. Not only did these improved relations allow for the signing of the Agreement, but they were also critical in overcoming the obstacles to implementing the Agreement.

As the Cold War ended the United States became increasingly able and willing to pressure the British government to include Sinn Féin in the negotiations and to encourage the British to make the necessary concessions to reach an agreement.[44] Against the wishes of the Major government, President Clinton approved a visa for Adams to come to the United States in 1994. As a consequence, the IRA announced a cease-fire. Cox correctly attributes this move to the idea that, with the end of the Cold War, the United States could be more flexible and relax its "special relationship" with Britain. He also cites US domestic considerations for Clinton's actions, but an important factor was also the rise of Ireland as a strong player. In sum, the international developments at the end of the Cold War provided many changes in the structural conditions of the conflict in Northern Ireland and allowed the governments in Britain, Ireland, and the United States as well as republicans in Northern Ireland to recalculate their interests and revise their policies accordingly. These had the effect of promoting the peace process in Northern Ireland.

From Revolutionary to Pragmatic Nationalism:
The Camp David and Oslo Accords

As in Northern Ireland, the key development that led to breakthroughs in the Middle East peace process was the abandonment of revolutionary nationalist goals for a more pragmatic nationalist agenda, which was largely affected by events at the international level. The decline of revolutionary nationalism was the primary factor that led to the Camp David Accords (CDA) in 1978 and the Oslo Accords in 1993. Signed by Egypt and Israel, the CDA committed Israel to return the Sinai Desert to Egypt in exchange for a peace treaty between the two states, signed on the lawn of the White House in 1979. Egypt regained the territory it had lost in the 1967 War, and Israel gained diplomatic recognition and peace with the largest and most important Arab state. Following a history of four wars in a short period, the CDA represented a dramatic shift in the Arab-Israeli conflict. It came about because Anwar Sadat of Egypt reversed Gamal Abdel Nasser's policies based on revolutionary nationalism.

Nasser became the embodiment of Arab nationalism, and it was fundamentally revolutionary at the time.[45] Arab nationalism was distinctive in that it encouraged pan-Arabism, the unity of all Arabs separated by multiple states. Nevertheless, a main purpose of this Arab unity was to come together to confront Israel. Arab nationalism was revolutionary in that it called for Israel's violent destruction, offering no compromise or reconciliation. For Arab nationalists, Israel epitomized imperialism, representing a Western colonial state in the Arab heartland. Nasser's populist movement was spearheaded by a Leninist party, the Arab Socialist Union. He created a highly authoritarian and centralized state committed to transforming Egypt in a radical way, nationalizing the economy in the name of Arab socialism. As Egypt increasingly turned inward, it became ever more hostile to Israel.

Sadat's peace with Israel came about because of his desire to regain the Sinai for Egypt and because of his rejection of Arab nationalism.[46] Indeed, his goal of reclaiming the Sinai required the repudiation of Arab nationalism. Thus, Sadat rejected revolutionary Arab nationalism in favor of a traditional Egyptian nationalism. The idea of Arab unity was replaced with a respect for the nation-state system, which entailed acceptance of Israel as a legitimate state. Economic changes undermined Arab nationalism, making reconciliation with Israel easier. As the Egyptian economy stalled before Nasser's death, Sadat sought to reverse the socialist course. Dubbed "infitah," his policies attempted to encourage private business and attract international capital.[47] In keeping with a more open economy, Sadat abolished the Arab Socialist Union as a party and allowed other parties that had been outlawed by Nasser to reemerge. Revolutionary nationalism was weakened by the rise of the oil-rich states of the Gulf, which had opposed Nasser and pan-Arabism, and which contributed to private investment in the Egyptian economy. As Egypt changed its domestic policies in the mid-1970s, it moved to improve its relations with Israel.

The big shifts that Egypt made that led up to the peace process were not matched by comparable concessions by, or changes in, Israel. In fact, the election of Menachem Begin in 1977 signaled Israel's unwillingness to make concessions short of dramatic shifts on the Arabs' part. After making peace with Egypt, Israel became even more hard-line toward the Palestinians. The big blow to revolutionary nationalism was international in character: the Arabs' loss of the 1967 War.[48] Nevertheless, Egypt was not so defeated that it needed to make peace with Israel, and Sadat believed that Egypt could only engage in a peace process if it felt a sense of confidence. Thus, he embarked on the 1973 War in order to remove the cloud of humiliation that had hung over Egypt's head since the 1967 War and to get the superpowers, particularly the United States, to foster a peace process. It is difficult to imagine that Sadat would have made his stunning trip to Jerusalem in November 1977 if there had not been some peace process, though indirect or rudimentary, in place. Henry Kissinger's "shuttle diplomacy," leading to two disengagement agreements after the 1973 War between the two states that did not talk to one another, paved the way for Sadat's trip and demonstrated the importance of earlier cooperative interactions with third parties. Ten months later Sadat signed the CDA, putting the final nail in the coffin of revolutionary Arab nationalism.

The groundbreaking Oslo Accords between Israel and the Palestinian Liberation Organization (PLO) in 1993 seemed to begin the process of resolving the Israel-Palestine conflict, the core one in the larger Arab-Israeli conflict. The Israelis and the Palestinians mutually recognized one another. Israel agreed to turn over two areas of the Occupied Territories to the PLO and begin negotiations that would in the future determine the final status of the West Bank and Gaza Strip. Far more complicated than the CDA, the Oslo Accords came about in large measure because of the decline of revolutionary Palestinian nationalism brought about by international setbacks. Another important factor was the pressure that the Palestinian uprising, the intifada, begun in late 1987, put on Israel.

Founded in 1964 by the Arab states, the PLO by the late 1960s became not only the embodiment of revolutionary Palestinian nationalism but the international symbol of revolutionary nationalism itself under the leadership of Yasser Arafat.[49] In calling for the "liberation of Palestine," the Palestinian National Charter of 1968 implied that Israel would have to be destroyed. The PLO took the Arab lead in engaging in violent attacks against Israel. Like other Arab nationalists, the PLO was committed to the radical transformation of Palestinian society along socialist lines. The Palestinians began what Hoffman calls the "internationalization of terrorism," with airplane hijackings in 1968 and the killing of Israeli athletes at the Munich Olympics in 1972.[50]

Over the course of two decades, the PLO moderated its revolutionary agenda, and during the 1980s this was decidedly because of international setbacks.[51] The Jordanian military dealt a big blow to radical factions in 1970. At the Twelfth Palestine National Council (PNC) in 1974, the PLO seemed to embrace the idea of a revolution in stages, implying that it might accept a Palestinian state in the West Bank and Gaza Strip as opposed to all of Palestine.[52] That year the PLO was recognized by several organizations and states as the legitimate representative of the Palestinian people, and Arafat was invited to address the United Nations (UN) General Assembly. At the PNC meeting in 1977, the moderates eclipsed the radicals in encouraging diplomatic actions over military ones.[53] Nevertheless, after the CDA the Israelis accelerated their building of settlements on the West Bank. In 1982 Israel attacked the PLO in Lebanon, leaving Arafat to shift his headquarters from Beirut to Tunis. After twenty years under Israeli occupation, frustrated Palestinians on the West Bank and Gaza Strip rebelled by demonstrating, throwing stones, and disrupting Israeli operations. These actions, known as the intifada, continued for years in spite of harsh Israeli retaliation. Israel and the United States had long insisted that they could not recognize the PLO until it renounced violence and accepted UN Resolution 242, which called for recognition of Israel as a state. In 1988 the PNC formally did so, leading the very pro-Israel Reagan administration to begin a dialogue with the PLO. The PLO suffered a huge setback, however, following the Gulf War of 1991 for having supported Saddam Hussein. Following the war, the United States sponsored a peace conference in Madrid, but upon Israel's insistence the Palestinian representatives could not come from the PLO. The Palestinian representatives insisted that no meaningful deal could be struck without the PLO, and Israel and the PLO began secret talks that resulted in the Oslo Accords.

One might argue against the idea that a decline in revolutionary nationalism led to Oslo and that it was instead the intifada that caused Israel to cut a deal with the PLO. It is difficult to imagine, however, that Israel would have entered into negotiations with the PLO without Arafat's prior acceptance of Resolution 242, and Israel could have repressed the Palestinians even more forcefully, as shown after the eruption of the second intifada in 2000. Writing about Israel's reaction to the PLO, Susan Hattis Rolef says: "In fact, it was after the PNL [Palestinian National Liberation] meeting in Algiers in November 1988, at which the Palestinian state was proclaimed and an implied recognition of Israel was issued, that a growing number of academic observers and political figures became convinced that a real change was taking place within the PLO with regard to the organization's willingness to give up its maximalist goals, and accept a compromise implying coexistence with the State of Israel."[54] The intifada itself did not represent revolutionary nationalism, for instead of seeking the destruction of Israel the protesting Palestinians mainly wanted respect for their rights and an end to Israeli occupation.[55] After flirting with the idea of renouncing violence in the 1970s, the PLO took nearly a decade to do so because its situation had sharply deteriorated in the late 1980s: "Its position in the post–Cold War and post–Gulf War era was much weakened, and it had consciously come to terms with Israel and secured a foothold on Palestinian soil before its regional and international standing declined still further."[56] This highlights that a failure to achieve the PLO's revolutionary objectives was more important than moderating its views as a result of contacts with third parties, which mainly occurred in the 1970s. Writing at the time, Hisham Sharabi adds: "Progressive thinking in the Arab world has shifted from the revolutionary model to the model of democracy. As in many post-colonial countries, the goal of revolution is no longer viable, for wherever revolution has occurred it has led not to freedom but to authoritarianism and neopatriarchy."[57] Arafat's international patron, the Soviet Union, the leading revolutionary state, was collapsing, leaving him with a lone superpower in the United States, which had done little in the 1980s to pressure Israel on behalf of the Palestinian cause. Moreover, the intifada threatened to move beyond the PLO's control because of Arafat's long distance (being in Tunis) from the event. Just as the IRA had done with its planned "Tet Offensive" in the late 1980s, the PLO made one last gasp in support of revolutionary nationalism when it threw its support behind Iraq's efforts to dominate the Gulf region following

Saddam Hussein's invasion of Kuwait in 1990. After Iraq's defeat, the PLO found its coffers virtually empty when the oil-rich monarchies of the Gulf withdrew their financing of the organization. Nevertheless, would Israel, which had built settlements on Palestinian land, co-opted a number of Palestinian notables, and resisted recognizing the idea of a Palestinian nation, have entered into negotiations with a PLO that had accepted Resolution 242 absent Palestinian pressure as seen during the intifada? One cannot confidently answer in the affirmative, for the situation probably required a hurting stalemate similar to that in Northern Ireland in the 1980s.

Why did the same decline in revolutionary nationalism related to changes at the global level not sustain the Oslo Accords as they did the Agreement? In many respects, the situations in Northern Ireland and Israel/Palestine were not comparable, for the Catholics in Northern Ireland had far more rights and equality with the Protestants than the Palestinians had vis-à-vis the Israelis. Israel bears considerable blame for the failure of Oslo in refusing to stop the settlements. In contrast with its successful role in Northern Ireland, the United States also failed to get the Israelis to halt settlements. Nevertheless, Arafat never renounced his revolutionary style in being autocratic and corrupt and in failing to build institutions. In seeking the right of return, the Palestinians failed to reconcile themselves with Zionist principles.[58] But the biggest immediate factor, feared by Prime Minister Yitzak Rabin a few years earlier, was the rise of a new and even larger revolutionary nationalist movement in Hamas, which was based on militant Islamism. Thus, the Israeli willingness to engage in negotiations with the PLO at Oslo was based on the perception that one could negotiate with a more pragmatic national representative of the Palestinians than the more radical and revolutionary group, Hamas, which was sponsored by revolutionary Iran.

One of the big lessons of the Northern Ireland peace process is that "spoilers" need to be marginalized.[59] In contrast with fringe elements among republicans, Hamas represented a sizeable alternative to Arafat's PLO. Moreover, as White notes, spoilers can thrive if they have support among their publics.[60] Unlike fringe republicans who were rejected by Catholics for their violence, Hamas gained considerable backing among Palestinians. White contends that it is important to sustain the momentum of the peace process in order to marginalize spoilers, and this was not accomplished after Oslo between the Israelis and Palestinians.

Conclusion

This chapter has argued that the peace processes in Northern Ireland and the Middle East emerged largely because of the decline of revolutionary nationalism in these respective places, and that a big factor was the collapse of revolutionary nationalism at the global level. Similarly, the peace process in South Africa in the early 1990s came about in large measure because of the moderation of the new revolutionary government in neighboring Zimbabwe and the fact that the African National Congress had shed its revolutionary agenda. These developments convinced F. W. de Klerk to seek negotiations for a new constitution with Mandela.[61] The decline of the IRA's revolutionary nationalism was affected by the collapse of communism, the economic transformation of Ireland, improved British-Irish intergovernmental relations, and increased pressure from the United States on Britain to negotiate and come to an agreement. At the global level, both revolutionary radicalism and militant nationalism were becoming antiquated. The apparent success of the Agreement, however, should not obscure the fact that progress needs to be made at the grassroots level to mend the rifts between Protestants and Catholics in Northern Ireland. Nevertheless, in contrast with the failure of Oslo and the reincarnation of revolutionary nationalism in Hamas, one of the critical lessons from Northern Ireland is the need for revolutionary nationalism to give way to a more pragmatic political agenda.

NOTES

I have benefited from the comments of Albadr Abubakr, two anonymous reviewers, and especially Timothy White.

1. Michael Cox, "Rethinking the International: A Defense," in *A Farewell to Arms? Beyond the Good Friday Agreement*, 2nd ed., ed. Michael Cox, Adrian Guelke, and Fiona Stephen (Manchester: Manchester University Press, 2006), 427–42, and Michael Cox, "Cinderella at the Ball: Explaining the End of the War in Northern Ireland," *Millennium* 27 (2) (1998): 325–42.

2. Paul Dixon, "Rethinking the International and Northern Ireland: A Critique," in Cox, Guelke, and Stephen, *A Farewell to Arms?*, 409–26.

3. This chapter focuses more on how the changes at the global level undermined the logic of revolutionary nationalism than on the perceptions of the IRA.

4. Cox, "Rethinking the International."

5. Fred Halliday, *Revolution and World Politics: The Rise and Fall of the Sixth Great Power* (Durham, NC: Duke University Press, 1999); Mark N. Katz, *Revolution: The*

International Dimension (Washington, DC: Congressional Quarterly Press, 2001); Robert S. Snyder, "The U.S. and Third World Revolutionary States: Understanding the Breakdown in Relations," *International Studies Quarterly* 43 (2) (1999): 265–90.

6. On ideology and international politics, see Mark L. Haas, *The Clash of Ideologies* (New York: Oxford University Press, 2012); Mark L. Haas, *The Ideological Origins of Great Power Politics, 1789–1989* (Ithaca, NY: Cornell University Press, 2005); and John Owen IV, *Clash of Ideas in World Politics: Transnational Networks, States, and Regime Change, 1510–2010* (Princeton, NJ: Princeton University Press, 2010). For the realist view of world politics, see Kenneth N. Waltz, *Theory of International Politics* (Reading, MA: Addison-Wesley, 1979); Robert Gilpin, *War and Change in World Politics* (New York: Cambridge University Press, 1981); and John J. Mearsheimer, *The Tragedy of Great Power Politics* (New York: Norton, 2001). For liberalism, see Bruce Russett, *Grasping the Democratic Peace* (Princeton, NJ: Princeton University Press, 1993); Robert O. Keohane, *After Hegemony: Cooperation and Discord in the World Economy* (Princeton, NJ: Princeton University Press, 1984); and G. John Ikenberry, *Liberal Leviathan: The Origins, Crisis, and Transformation of the American Order* (Princeton, NJ: Princeton University Press, 2011).

7. Owen, *Clash of Ideas in World Politics*; Haas, *The Clash of Ideologies*.

8. For example, see Nigel Gould-Davies, "Rethinking the Role of Ideology in International Politics during the Cold War," *Journal of Cold War Studies* 1 (1999): 90–109; John Lewis Gaddis, *We Now Know: Rethinking Cold War History* (Oxford: Clarendon Press, 1997); Odd Arne Westard, *The Global Cold War* (Cambridge: Cambridge University Press, 2007); V. M. Zubok and Constantine Pleshakov, *Inside the Kremlin's Cold War: From Stalin to Gorbachev* (Cambridge, MA: Harvard University Press, 1996); and V. M. Zubok, *A Failed Empire: The Soviet Union in the Cold War from Stalin to Gorbachev* (Chapel Hill: University of North Carolina Press, 2007).

9. Zubok, *A Failed Empire*, 4.

10. Although Marxism-Leninism repudiated nationalism, one can look at it as a form of nationalism since most movements were at the national level. Likewise some see social revolutions as having been relatively rare, yet most anticolonial movements sought to promote some type of social transformation. On social revolutions, see Theda Skocpol, *States and Social Revolutions* (New York: Cambridge University Press, 1979).

11. Etel Solingen, "Pax Asiatica versus Bella Levantina: The Foundations of War and Peace in East Asia and the Middle East," *American Political Science Review* 101 (4) (2007): 757–80.

12. Gregory M. Maney, Ibtisam Ibrahim, Gareth I. Higgins, and Hanna Herzog, "The Past's Promise: Lessons from the Peace Processes in Northern Ireland and the Middle East," *Journal of Peace Research* 43 (2) (2006): 181–200. This conception of power and identity is similar to a recent conceptualization of political culture that stresses how identities and cultures can be reinvented and changed based on power considerations. See Jeffrey C. Goldfarb, *Reinventing Political Culture: The Power of Culture versus the Culture of Power* (Cambridge: Polity, 2012).

13. Maney et al., "The Past's Promise," 182–83.

14. Monica Duffy Toft, *Securing the Peace: The Durable Settlement of Civil Wars* (Princeton, NJ: Princeton University Press, 2010), chapters 1–2.

15. On how institutions can change identities, see Alexander Wendt, *Social Theory of International Politics* (New York: Cambridge University Press, 1999).

16. Bruce W. Jentleson and Christopher A. Whytock, "Who Won Libya? The Force-Diplomacy Debate and Its Implications for Theory and Policy," *International Security* 30 (3) (2006): 47–86.

17. Dixon, "Rethinking the International and Northern Ireland."

18. This point is stressed in the discussion of the lessons learned by nationalists and republicans in chapter 1.

19. Dixon, "Rethinking the International and Northern Ireland."

20. Ibid.

21. For a review of ripeness or readiness theory, especially in the Northern Ireland context, see Navin A. Bapat, "Insurgency and the Opening of Peace Processes," *Journal of Peace Research* 42 (6) (2005): 699–717; Jonathan Powell, "Security Is Not Enough: Ten Lessons for Conflict Resolution from Northern Ireland," in *The Lessons of Northern Ireland*, ed. Michael Cox (London: LSE IDEAS Special Report 008, November 2011), 23–24; Joseph Ruane and Jennifer Todd, "Path Dependence in Settlement Processes: Explaining Settlement in Northern Ireland," *Political Studies* 55 (2) (2007): 442–58; Kirsten E. Schulze, "The Northern Ireland Political Process: A Viable Approach to Conflict Resolution," *Irish Political Studies* 12 (1997): 92–110; I. William Zartman, "Ripeness: The Hurting Stalemate and Beyond," in *International Conflict Resolution after the Cold War*, ed. Paul C. Stern and Daniel Druckman (Washington, DC: National Research Council Press, 2000), 225–50; and I. William Zartman, "The Timing of Peace Initiatives: Hurting Stalemates and Ripe Moments," in *Contemporary Peacemaking: Conflict, Violence and Peace Processes*, ed. John Darby and Roger Mac Ginty (New York: Palgrave Macmillan, 2003), 19–29.

22. Paul Bew, *Ireland: The Politics of Enmity, 1789–2006* (Oxford: Oxford University Press, 2007), 1–48.

23. Henry Patterson, *The Politics of Illusion: A Political History of the IRA* (London: Serif, 1997), 13.

24. Although Patterson sees the linkage of militant nationalism and social radicalism as problematic, it occurred in many other places as well. See Patterson, *The Politics of Illusion.*

25. On the history of the IRA, see Ed Moloney, *A Secret History of the IRA* (New York: Norton, 2002), and Richard English, *Armed Struggle: The History of the IRA* (New York: Oxford University Press, 2003).

26. On the Troubles, see J. Bower Bell, *The Irish Troubles: A Generation of Violence, 1967–1992* (New York: St. Martin's Press, 1993).

27. Moloney, *A Secret History of the IRA*, 152–56.

28. Quoted in Tim Pat Coogan, *The IRA* (London: HarperCollins, 1987), 679.

29. Quoted in English, *Armed Struggle*, 217.

30. Moloney, *A Secret History of the IRA*, 184.

31. Ibid., 196–216; English, *Armed Struggle*, 198–206.

32. Bew, *Ireland*, 528.

33. English, *Armed Struggle*, 207–8.

34. Moloney, *A Secret History of the IRA*, 219–45.

35. Ibid., 275–76.

36. Ibid., 250–54.

37. English, *Armed Struggle*, 248.

38. Eamonn O'Kane, "Learning from Northern Ireland? The Uses and Abuses of the Irish 'Model,'" *British Journal of Politics and International Relations* 12 (2) (2010): 249.

39. Some even argue that the demise of the Soviet Union was caused by the counterrevolutionary efforts of Mikhail Gorbachev. See Robert Snyder and Timothy J. White, "The Fall of the Berlin Wall: The Counterrevolution in Soviet Foreign Policy and the End of Communism," in *After the Berlin Wall: Germany and Beyond*, ed. Jana Braziel and Katharina Gerstenberger (New York: Palgrave Macmillan, 2011), 127–48.

40. For a good review of the policies of this period, see Tom Garvin, *Preventing the Future: Why Was Ireland So Poor for So Long?* (Dublin: Gill and Macmillan, 2004).

41. For the best explanations of the Celtic Tiger phenomenon, see Dan Breznitz, *Innovation and the State: Political Choice and Strategies for Growth in Israel, Taiwan, and Ireland* (New Haven, CT: Yale University Press, 2007), 146–89; Seán Ó Riain, *The Politics of High-Tech Growth: Developmental Network States in the Global Economy* (Cambridge: Cambridge University Press, 2004), 39–65; Kenneth P. Thomas, *Investment Incentives and the Global Competition for Capital* (New York: Palgrave Macmillan, 2011), 67–95; and Timothy J. White, "Unleashing the Celtic Tiger: Globalization, Economic Growth, and Cultural Consequences," *Internationalist Review of Irish Culture* (2009): 78–99.

42. Dixon, "Rethinking the International and Northern Ireland."

43. English, *Armed Struggle*, 243; see also Thomas Hennessey, *The Northern Ireland Peace Process* (New York: Palgrave, 2001).

44. See Mary Alice Clancy's chapter 7 in this volume for a complete review of the US role in Northern Ireland.

45. On the Nasser years, see Raymond William Baker, *Egypt's Uncertain Revolution under Nasser and Sadat* (Cambridge: Cambridge University Press, 1978), and Kirk J. Beattie, *Egypt during the Nasser Years: Politics, Ideology, and Civil Society* (Boulder, CO: Westview Press, 1994).

46. On Sadat, see Raymond William Baker, *Sadat and After: Struggles for Egypt's Political Soul* (Cambridge, MA: Harvard University Press, 1990).

47. John J. Waterbury, *The Egypt of Nasser and Sadat: The Political Economy of Two Regimes* (Princeton, NJ: Princeton University Press, 1983).

48. Fouad Ajami, *The Arab Predicament* (New York: Cambridge University Press, 1981).

49. On the PLO, see Helena Cobban, *The PLO: People, Power and Politics* (New York: Cambridge University Press, 1984).

50. Bruce Hoffman, *Inside Terrorism*, rev. ed. (New York: Columbia University Press, 2006), chapter 3. Hoffman also acknowledges that Zionists promoted terrorism in the Middle East in seeking to establish Israel (see chapter 2).

51. Mark Tessler, *A History of the Israeli-Palestinian Conflict*, 2nd ed. (Bloomington: University of Indiana Press, 2009).

52. Mark Tessler, "The Israeli-Palestinian Conflict," in *The Middle East*, ed. Ellen Lust (Washington, DC: Congressional Quarterly Press, 2011), 271.

53. Ibid., 272.

54. Susan Hattis Rolef, "Israel's Policy Toward the PLO: From Rejection to Recognition," in *The PLO and Israel*, ed. Avraham Sela and Moshe Ma'oz (New York: St. Martin's Press, 1997), 257.

55. Mary Elizabeth King, *A Quiet Revolution: The First Palestinian Intifada and Nonviolent Resistance* (New York: Nation Books, 2007).

56. Yezid Sayigh, *Armed Struggle and the Search for State: The Palestinian National Movement, 1949–1993* (New York: Oxford University Press, 1997), 660.

57. Hisham Sharabi, "A Look Ahead: The Future State of Palestine," in *The Palestinians: New Directions*, ed. Michael C. Hudson (Washington, DC: Center for Contemporary Arab Studies, Georgetown University, 1990), 163.

58. In 2000 the Camp David Accords between the Israelis and Palestinians fell apart when Arafat refused to accept it on the grounds that Palestinians should have the right to return to Israel. As Jonathan Rynhold argues, having a majority of Palestinians living in Israel would be a repudiation of Zionism. See Jonathan Rynhold, "Realism, Liberalism, and Collapse of the Oslo Process: Inherently Flawed or Flawed Interpretation?," in *The Failure of the Middle East Peace Process*, ed. Guy Ben-Porat (New York: Palgrave MacMillian, 2008), 111–34.

59. See Timothy White's chapter 1 in this volume.

60. Ibid.

61. For a discussion of South Africa, see Adrian Guelke, "Political Comparisons: From Johannesburg to Jerusalem," in Cox, Guelke, and Stephen, *A Farewell to Arms?*, 366–76.

11   Conclusion

TIMOTHY J. WHITE

While the peace process has been successful in reducing sectarian violence in Northern Ireland, this volume has highlighted the challenges that lay ahead. Even though this peace process is far from perfect, its successes are worth noting. Seeing how they apply to other ethnic and religious conflicts in the world provides an opportunity to improve our capacity to confront regions of the world torn by conflict. As Jack S. Levy has argued, learning in foreign policy can best be examined in the context of a specific crisis.[1] Understanding both the context and conditions that led to the peace process as well as the design and implementation of the peace agreement are critical in understanding the success and limitations of what has been achieved in Northern Ireland.[2] The authors in this collection have analyzed the peace process in Northern Ireland from many different perspectives, and in doing so they have attempted to identify the appropriate lessons.

The first lesson stressed by William A. Hazleton in chapter 2 is that the different parties to the conflict learned very different lessons. They approached both the negotiations culminating in the Agreement of 1998 and the efforts to implement this Agreement afterward from their own particular perspective. These differences represented not only the various communities and states involved in the negotiations but even the different political interests of the political parties in Northern Ireland. Ironically, the two leaders who won the Nobel Peace Prize for their efforts in negotiating the Agreement in 1998 subsequently saw their political parties lose favor to the more extreme parties in what has been identified as an ethnic outbidding process. The peace process has not therefore ultimately benefited the political interests of those who led the process even if it has minimized the violence and provided for new governing arrangements that appear to be stable.

Another lesson this volume stresses is that negotiations leading to peace agreements and the agreements themselves need to be inclusive. The peace process must incorporate most if not all of those who have seen violence as an appropriate and perhaps the only means of pursuing their political objective. This does not mean that those who continue to use violence are allowed to simultaneously use ballots and bullets. However, there must be a path created so that those who have advocated violence in the past perceive it to be in their interest to enter negotiations and live up to the terms of the peace agreement. Thus, preconditions for negotiations need to be mini-mized so as to encourage all to participate in the peace process.

Providing security for all the different social groups involved in the negotiations and the peace process is critical. Insecurity undermines peace and inspires violence.[3] If any group feels threatened or believes policing and the use of force is not being carried out in their interest, they are likely to abandon the peace process. In many cases, as in Northern Ireland, this may require a fundamental reordering of the police function and creation of new institutions to ensure that those who serve as police in society are not seen as biased for or against any group in society. Providing security also means that paramilitary groups must disarm and no longer threaten society with violence. Decommissioning and police reform proved to be two of the most difficult challenges in Northern Ireland, but having an inter-national body that is respected by the different groups in society responsible for reforming security builds credibility for this process.

The role of third parties or outside actors can be constructive and helpful both in terms of promoting diplomatic options and in providing economic assistance to promote peace once an agreement has been reached. The actions of these third parties are invariably quite complex and are based on the interest of these parties. While well intentioned, external parties often fail to understand the complexity and nuances of local conflicts. Thus, it is difficult to generalize too much about their role as mediators and aid providers except to say that they may be useful but insufficient in the peacebuilding process.[4]

Negotiations and peace processes often occur between political elites, and these leaders make the peace agreement, but it is important to recognize the need for grassroots reconciliation as part of conflict resolution and peacebuilding in what are, in the end, ethnic or sectarian conflicts. In Northern Ireland, the peace process and Agreement was first made by leaders of the British and Irish governments and most of the leaders of the political parties in Northern Ireland. Because the Agreement was built on power-sharing arrangements if not consociational institutions, it did not directly attempt to overcome the historic sectarian conflict that was at the heart of the Troubles. The fact that the Agreement has dramatically minimized violence across the communities has provided an opportunity for civil society to begin to develop. The pace of this change has been much slower than the more dramatic institutional success that has taken place since Sinn Féin and the DUP agreed to lead the Stormont-based government. The future success of the peace process greatly depends on the ability of this positive peace to emerge and complement the negative peace that has been achieved thus far in Northern Ireland.

The peace process in Northern Ireland did not happen by accident but by the consistent and skillful effort of a number of political leaders as well as other subordinates and interested citizens who served key roles in promoting the peace process. Because of the historic differences between the parties, leaders had to be creative and relentless in pursuing an agreement and then implementing it afterward. Various leaders demonstrated their determination to overcome those who opposed the peace process (spoilers) and those who, while supportive of the peace process, were pursuing policies that offered little chance of overcoming historic positions. Moderates or those who agreed to support the peace process had to be supported, and those who were intent on preventing an agreement or its implementation had to be marginalized. The diplomatic skill and personal commitment of many involved in the peace process in Northern Ireland need to be both recognized and commended.

While fatigue with the violence clearly played a role in informing the actors that they could not achieve their goals through violence, we also experienced a string of perceived failed negotiations. Paul F. Diehl and Gary Goertz have argued that rivalries and conflicting dyads deescalate when political shocks provide foreign policy entrepreneurs and statesmen the opportunity to take advantage of what they have learned from past conflict to build and identify a way forward that goes beyond the historic conflict.[5] Circumstances changed, which placed pressure on actors to make concessions in negotiations. Not only did the Cold War end, making revolutionary nationalism seem unlikely to achieve its end through force, but 9/11 and the need to defeat terrorists made those who continued to harbor weapons as paramilitaries increasingly marginalized. It was not events alone or the structure of the system that promoted the peace process in Northern Ireland—it is also important to recognize the significant role played by individuals who took risks for peace. The Northern Ireland peace process thus provides a rich set of lessons that focus on structural changes that promoted the possibility of peace, but these changes required various actors to recognize opportunities and the advantage that peace offered in comparison with continued violence.

Recently, scholars have looked to complexity theory to explain the complex nature of peacemaking and conflict resolution.[6] These theories hold the promise of integrating the diverse lessons that various actors to a conflict have. They take into account the accumulated effect of a continuing dynamic that reinforces conflict from the past and that reproduces it in the present. Complexity theory also emphasizes contingency and the unknowability of outcomes that leaders and policy makers must confront when they make decisions.[7] The solution or means of addressing intractable conflicts is to alter the process of interaction between groups. In the context of Northern Ireland, the Agreement the parties made in 1998 and operationalized in 2007 reflects a change in relationships as much as it does a change in institutional governance. This is the key to the peace process in Northern Ireland. It undermined a historical narrative of the "other" and replaced it with one that recognizes continuing conflict but one that need not require a violent response.

Scholars have also increasingly turned to chaos theory to explain the nonlinear patterns of conflict and intractable conflict.[8] This theoretical approach emphasizes the sensitivity of different actors to events. Chaos theory allows us to understand how one seemingly unimportant event can lead to conflict spiraling out of control. Not only can chaos theory explain the dynamic of conflict and the negative unintended consequences of leaders' decisions but it can also be reversed to explain how a positive process of mutual interest can emerge in a peace process. The Northern Ireland peace process allows us to understand how different actors grew to appreciate the circumstances and limitations of other actors. This made them increasingly aware of how their own actions and decisions would likely reverberate in the context of the conflict. As the peace process gained momentum in the 1990s, actors increasingly took into consideration not only what they thought their opponents would do but how their own actions would impact the interests of others involved in the negotiations. Whether it was a desire to "save Dave" and preserve David Trimble as leader of the UUP as a means to keep unionists on board with the peace process or the sensitivity the British government showed to the safety and security of the Sinn Féin leadership in the context of decommissioning, most, if not all, actors took into consideration the likely responses of other actors in making their decisions. The desire to not be blamed for stalling or thwarting the peace process became an important means of keeping the process moving forward despite delays and obstacles.

The success of the peace process has made some argue that social healing has begun. This healing is best understood not as a linear or sequential process. Circular images of relationships and connectedness allow one to understand how historic communal conflict and rivalries can be transformed without following a linear formulaic peace process. These circular relationships allow identities to be redefined, and the salience of exclusive and hostile images of identity can be transformed to more encompassing and inclusive senses of identity. For reconciliation and social healing, individuals must reorient their identities to connect with the larger community or social unit that provides individuals validation, meaning, and purpose, not alienation, frustration, or fear, which characterizes the era of conflict.[9]

For republicans the peace process means that Ireland is on its way toward inescapable unification.[10] There is much to be achieved before this nationalist aspiration could be realized. As Martin Mansergh has indicated, what Ireland needs in the near term is a more constructive process of interaction among the different communities based on improved mutual understanding and an assumption that no one can impose their will on another community. While physical force republicanism could not achieve the ultimate goal of a united Ireland, constitutional republicanism will only be successful in attaining this goal if it accepts and partners with the Protestant tradition on the island.[11] However, as this volume has stressed, this lesson, which reflects nationalist sentiment, is not shared by unionists. Many unionists contend that the Agreement has solidified their claim that Northern Ireland is and will remain part of the United Kingdom. Perhaps the ambiguity of the future of Northern Ireland allows the two communities to concentrate on what can be achieved in the present and the near term. The Agreement has succeeded not because it fulfilled either side's aspirations but because it did not deny these aspirations.[12] Indeed, by not concentrating on ultimate ends or goals but focusing on what can be achieved in the near term, the Northern Ireland peace process has successfully marginalized violence amidst the continuing communal conflict and differences that are likely to remain the basis of Northern Ireland's politics for the foreseeable future.

NOTES

1. Jack S. Levy, "Learning and Foreign Policy: Sweeping a Conceptual Minefield," *International Organization* 48 (2) (1994): 279–312.

2. See Ulrich Schneckener, "Managing and Settling Ethnic Conflicts: The Context-Design Nexus," in *Managing and Settling Ethnic Conflicts: Perspectives on Successes and Failures in Europe, Africa and Asia*, ed. Ulrich Schneckener and Stefan Wolff (New York: Palgrave Macmillan, 2004), 271–85.

3. Gavan Duffy, "Insecurity and Opportunity in Conflict Settings," in *Conflict Transformation and Peacebuilding: Moving from Violence to Sustainable Peace*, ed. Bruce W. Dayton and Louis Kriesberg (New York: Routledge, 2009), 107–22. For the importance of providing order in postconflict situations to create a sustainable peace, see Eric D. Patterson, *Ending Wars Well: Order, Justice, and Conciliation in Contemporary Post-Conflict* (New Haven, CT: Yale University Press, 2012), 38–66.

4. See Bruce W. Dayton, "Useful but Insufficient: Intermediaries in Peacebuilding," in Dayton and Kriesberg, *Conflict Transformation and Peacebuilding*, 61–73.

5. Paul F. Diehl and Gary Goertz, *War and Peace in International Rivalry* (Ann Arbor: University of Michigan Press, 2000), 218–39.

6. For one such effort that combines complexity theory with social identity theory, see Peter T. Coleman, *The Five Percent: Finding Solutions to Seemingly Impossible Conflicts* (New York: Public Affairs, 2011). For more on complexity theory and how it applies to conflict resolution, see Lynn Davies, *Education and Conflict: Complexity and Chaos* (London: Routledge Falmer, 2004), 19–37; Dennis J. D. Sandole, *Capturing the Complexity of Conflict: Dealing with Violent Ethnic Conflicts in the Post–Cold War Era* (London: Pinter, 1999); L. Deborah Sword, "A Complexity Science View of Conflict," *Emergence: Complexity & Organization* 10 (4) (2008): 10–16; and Robin R. Vallacher, Peter T. Coleman, Andrzej Nowak, and Lan Bui-Wrzosinska, "Rethinking Intractable Conflict: The Perspective of Dynamical Systems," *American Psychologist* 65 (4) (2010): 262–78. For an attempt to use complexity theory to explain the Northern Ireland peace process, see Adrian Little, "Sunningdale for Slow Learners? Towards a Complexity Paradigm," in *Consociational Theory: McGarry and O'Leary and the Northern Ireland Conflict*, ed. Rupert Taylor (London: Routledge, 2009), 252–63. For a less formal argument that complexity needs to be added to the conventional analysis of the Northern Ireland peace process, see Paul Bew, "Collective Amnesia and the Northern Ireland Model of Conflict Resolution," in *The Lessons of Northern Ireland*, ed. Michael Cox (London: LSE IDEAS Special Report 008, November 2011), 17–21.

7. Adrian Little, "Political Action, Error and Failure: The Epistemological Limits of Complexity," *Political Studies* 60 (1) (2012): 3–19.

8. Alexander J. Argyos, *A Blessed Rage for Order: Deconstruction, Evolution, and Chaos* (Ann Arbor: University of Michigan Press, 1991); Stephen H. Kellert, *Borrowed Knowledge: Chaos Theory and the Challenge of Learning Across Disciplines* (Chicago: University of Chicago Press, 2008); L. Douglas Kiel and Euel Elliot, *Chaos Theory in the Social Sciences:*

Foundations and Applications (Ann Arbor: University of Michigan Press, 1996); John Law, *After Method: Mess in Social Science Research* (New York: Routledge, 2004); Mark S. Mosko and Frederick H. Damon, *On the Order of Chaos: Social Anthropology and the Science of Chaos* (New York: Berghahn Books, 2005); and Suda M. Perera, "The Congo, Conflict and Chaos: Non-Linearity and Self-Similar Patterning in Conflict Analysis" (unpublished paper, University of Kent, 2011).

9. For this conception of reconciliation as social healing, see John Paul Lederach and Angela Jill Lederach, *When Blood and Bones Cry Out: Journeys through the Soundscape of Healing and Reconciliation* (New York: Oxford University Press, 2010).

10. This argument is made in Deaglán de Bréadún, *The Far Side of Revenge: Making Peace in Northern Ireland*, updated ed. (Cork: Collins Press, 2008), 387–406.

11. Martin Mansergh, *The Legacy of History for Making Peace in Ireland* (Cork: Mercier Press, 2003), 11.

12. Gregory M. Maney, Ibtisam Ibrahim, Gareth I. Higgins, and Hanna Herzog, "The Past's Promise: Lessons from Peace Processes in Northern Ireland and the Middle East," *Journal of Peace Research* 43 (2) (2006): 196.

Contributors

KAWSER AHMED is a Ph.D. candidate in peace and conflict studies, Arthur Mauro Centre for Peace and Justice at St. Paul's College, the University of Manitoba. He is a retired Lt. Colonel in the Bangladeshi army who spent time as a peacekeeper in Cyprus and the Western Sahara.

SEAN BYRNE is a professor of peace and conflict studies and director of the Peace and Conflict Studies Ph.D. and Joint Master's programs, and director of the Arthur V. Mauro Center for Peace and Justice at St. Paul's College at the University of Manitoba. He is a former vice president of the International Sector of the Society for Professionals in Dispute Resolution and was also co-chair and board member of the Network in Community Peacemaking and Conflict Resolution. From 2004 to 2006 he served as chair of the peace studies section of the International Studies Association. Dr. Byrne also served as editor in chief of *Peace and Conflict Studies*. His publications include numerous articles and books.

MARY-ALICE C. CLANCY is a visiting research fellow at the University of Aberdeen. She has previously held research fellowships at the universities of Exeter and Ulster. Her research has focused on the United States' role in Northern Ireland, and has been featured in the BBC, the *Guardian*, and the *Observer*. Her most recent publications include (with John Nagle) *Shared Society or Benign Apartheid? Understanding Peacebuilding in Divided Societies* (New York: Palgrave Macmillan, 2010) and *Peace without Consensus: Power Sharing Politics in Northern Ireland* (Burlington, VT: Ashgate, 2010).

MEGHAN E. CLARKE is a principal of M E Clarke Consulting, LLC, in Cincinnati, Ohio, where she specializes in facilitation, mediation, organizational development, and conflict engagement. Clarke received her bachelor's degree from Xavier University and a master's degree in peace and conflict resolution at the School of International Service at American University. Previously, she worked for the ARIA Group and the Search for Common Ground. She has designed, facilitated, and partnered on dozens of small- and large-scale community reconciliation initiatives. These projects include environmental harms, police-community relations, educational inequities, and religious-based conflicts. Her publications include "Polarization: The Role of Emotions in Reconciliation Efforts," *Law & Contemporary Problems* 72 (2) (2009): 27–31.

PAUL DIXON is a reader in politics and international studies in the Faculty of Arts and Social Sciences at Kingston University. He has published extensively on Northern Ireland and the peace process. His books include *Northern Ireland: The Politics of War and Peace*, 2nd ed. (New York: Palgrave Macmillan, 2008) and *Northern Ireland Since 1969* with Eamonn O'Kane (New York: Longman, 2011). His research on the Northern Ireland conflict has been published in *Political Studies, Review of International Studies, Political Science Quarterly, Terrorism and Political Violence,* and *Political Quarterly.* Dr. Dixon has recently edited *The British Approach to Counterinsurgency: From Malaya and Northern Ireland to Iraq and Afghanistan* (New York: Palgrave Macmillan, 2012). He is currently completing his long-awaited book, *The Northern Ireland Peace Process: Choreography and Theatrical Politics.*

JOHN DOYLE is Director of the Institute for International Conflict Resolution and Reconstruction and Executive Dean of the Faculty of Humanities and Social Sciences at Dublin City University (DCU), Ireland. John has taken part in a number of studies of comparative peace processes, including two EU-funded projects with colleagues in South Asia, which brought academics from India, Pakistan, Sri Lanka, Bangladesh, and Afghanistan together for a series of workshops, in New Delhi, Brussels, and at DCU, examining both European examples such as Northern Ireland and the Balkans and South Asian cases including Kashmir, Sri Lanka, Nepal, the Indian North East, and Afghanistan. He has been a visiting professor in conflict resolution in India, at the Nelson Mandela Centre in Jamia Millia Islamia, New Delhi, and in Pakistan, in the School of Social Sciences in Lahore University of Management Sciences (LUMS). He also serves as the editor of *Irish Studies in International Affairs.* He has numerous publications on Northern Ireland and the peace process and edited *Policing the Narrow Ground: Lessons from the Transformation of Policing in Northern Ireland* (Dublin: Royal Irish Academy, 2010).

EYOB FISSUH is a research advisor with Human Resources and Skills Development Canada, and a recent Ph.D. graduate from the Department of Economics at the University of Manitoba. He earned a B.A. in economics at the University of Asmara in Eritrea and an M.Comm in economics from the University of Cape Town in South Africa. He has coauthored articles in the journals *Review of Income and Wealth, Peace and Conflict Studies, Peace and Justice Studies, Global Business, Peace Research, Civil Wars, Nationalism and Ethnic Politics, Geopolitics, Irish Political Studies,* and *Economics Anthropology.*

LANDON E. HANCOCK is an associate professor of conflict management and political science at Kent State University. His publications include articles in *Ethnopolitics,*

Peace & Change, Irish Political Studies, Peace and Conflict Studies, Conflict Resolution Quarterly, and *Journal of Peace Education*. He is coeditor (with Christopher Mitchell) of two volumes, *Zones of Peace* (2007) and *Local Peacebuilding and National Peace* (2012). His research is focused on identity-driven conflict, from the reasons for its inception and outbreak to its resolution and to periods of postconflict peacebuilding and transitional justice.

WILLIAM A. HAZLETON is a professor emeritus of political science at Miami University in Oxford, Ohio. He has previously served as Distinguished Fellow in Politics, University of Adelaide, South Australia, 2003–4, Senior Research Fellow, Institute of Irish Studies, Queen's University Belfast, 1999–2000, and Visiting Professor in the School of English and American Studies, University of East Anglia, Norwich, England, 1992–93. His numerous publications on Northern Ireland include "Devolution and the Diffusion of Power: The Internal and Transnational Dimensions of the Belfast Agreement," in *Irish Political Studies Reader: Key Contributions*, ed. Conor McGrath and Eoin O'Malley (London: Routledge, 2007), 334–50.

PETER KARARI is a Ph.D. candidate in peace and conflict studies, Arthur Mauro Centre for Peace and Justice at St. Paul's College, the University of Manitoba. He earned an M.A. in peace and conflict studies from the University of Magdeburg in Germany and a B.Sc. in social work from the University of Nairobi. He has coauthored two articles in *Peace and Conflict Studies*.

ANDREW P. OWSIAK is an assistant professor in the Department of International Affairs at the University of Georgia. His research focuses on the bilateral processes or characteristics that promote peaceful relations between disputing countries and the role of third parties in peacefully (or diplomatically) ending or transforming conflicts. His most recent publications include "Signing Up for Peace: International Boundary Agreements, Democracy, and Militarized Interstate Conflict," *International Studies Quarterly* 56 (1) (2012): 51–66; "Democratization and International Border Agreements," *Journal of Politics* (2013): forthcoming; "Clearing the Hurdle: Border Settlement and Rivalry Termination," with Toby J. Rider, *Journal of Politics* (2013): forthcoming; "The Conflict Management Efforts of Allies in Interstate Disputes," with Derrick V. Frazier, *Foreign Policy Analysis* (2013): forthcoming; and "Demanding Peace: The Impact of Prevailing Conflict on the Shift from Peacekeeping to Peacebuilding," with Alexandru Balas and Paul F. Diehl, *Peace & Change* 37 (2) (2012): 195–226.

MINDY PEDEN is an associate professor of political science and a former associate dean in the College of Arts and Sciences at John Carroll University. She has published work in *Contemporary Political Theory, Studies in Political Economy, Politics and Policy*, and elsewhere. While teaching the Belfast Summer Institute on Peacebuilding and Conflict Transformation under Wendy Wiedenhoft Murphy's leadership, she came to a consciousness of her identity as not only Irish and culturally Catholic, as she had previously thought, but also Scottish and Scotch-Irish.

OLGA SKARLATO is a Ph.D. candidate in peace and conflict studies, Arthur Mauro Centre for Peace and Justice at St. Paul's College, the University of Manitoba. She earned a B.A. and an M.A. degree in North American studies from the School of International Relations, St. Petersburg State University, Russia. She also studied and worked in Germany, the United States, and Canada doing research on the topics of environmental conflict prevention and resolution, human security, and international economic development. She has coauthored articles in *Geopolitics*, *Irish Political Studies*, and *Journal of Human Security*.

ROBERT S. SNYDER is a professor of political science at Southwestern University in Georgetown, Texas. Dr. Snyder has won numerous awards and grants from various foundations, including the Emirates Center for Strategic Studies and Research in Abu Dhabi, the Earhart Foundation, the Joseph Malone Fellowship at the National Council on US-Arab Relations, the Foundation for the Defense of Democracies, and the Center for Strategic Education Fellowship at Johns Hopkins University. His research has focused on the study of revolutions, revolutionary movements, and relations between the United States and revolutionary actors. His publications have appeared in *International Studies Quarterly*, *Review of Politics*, *Foreign Policy Analysis*, *Orbis*, and *International Studies Perspectives*.

TIMOTHY J. WHITE is a professor of political science at Xavier University. He was a visiting research fellow at the Moore Institute, National University of Ireland, Galway, for the fall of 2011 when this volume was edited. In the summer of 2010 he organized the seminar "Lessons Learned from the Northern Ireland Peace Process" at Bansha Castle in County Tipperary for Xavier University. This seminar inspired the contributions to this volume. His publications on Northern Ireland politics have focused on the role of civil society in promoting peace in Northern Ireland. They include: "The Role of Civil Society in Promoting Peace in Northern Ireland," in *Building Peace in Northern Ireland*, ed. Maria Power (Liverpool: Liverpool University Press, 2011), 37–52, and "Consolidating Peace and Democracy in Northern Ireland: The Role of Civil Society and the Need for Reconciliation," *Dynamics of Asymmetric Conflict* 4 (3) (2011): 259–71.

WENDY ANN WIEDENHOFT MURPHY is an associate professor of sociology at John Carroll University. She was the 2006 director and 2005 lead faculty member of the Belfast Summer Institute on Peacebuilding and Conflict Transformation. Her latest work, "Touring the Troubles in West Belfast," was published in *Peace & Change: A Journal of Peace Research* 35 (4) (2010): 537–60. Her other interests include consumer culture and environmental justice.

Index